THE
COMPLETE GUIDE TO
PAINTBALL

D1033671

THE
COMPLETE
PAINT

Written by Steve Davidson, Pete "Robbo" Robinson, Rob "Tyger" Rubin, and Stewart Smith

Special Contributions by Jerry Braun, Durty Dan, and Sarah Stevenson

Photographed by Peter Field Peck

Illustrations by Mark Smith

GUIDE TO
BALL

CONCEIVED BY: Andrew Flach

EDITED BY: Adam W. Cohen

RESEARCHED BY: Tracy Tumminello

Adaptations of "Getting Started," "Rules to Play By,"
and "Common Mistakes," courtesy of splatterzone.com

Before beginning any strenuous exercise program consult your physician. The
author and publisher of this book and workout disclaim any liability, personal or
professional, resulting from the misapplication of any of the procedures
described in this publication.

The Complete Guide to Paintball
A GETFITNOW.com Book

Copyright ©1999 GETFITNOW.com
All rights reserved. No part of this book may be reproduced in any form or
by any means, electronic or mechanical, including photocopying, recording,
or by any information storage and retrieval system, without permission in
writing from the publisher.

Hatherleigh Press/GETFITNOW.com Books
An Affiliate of W.W. Norton & Company, Inc.
500 Fifth Ave
New York, NY 10110
1-800-367-2550

Visit our web site: www.getfitnow.com

All GETFITNOW.com titles are available for bulk purchase, special
promotions, and premiums. For more information, please contact the manager
of our Special Sales Department at 1-800-367-2550.

Library of Congress Cataloging-in-Publication Data
TO COME

Illustrations by Mark Smith
Photographed by Peter Field Peck with Canon® cameras
     and lenses on Fuji® and Kodak® print and slide film
Text design and composition by edn Design
The text is set in Agenda
Designed on Apple® G3 Macintosh computers and Hitachi® 7515 monitors

Printed on acid-free paper
10 9 8 7 6 5 4 3 2 1
Printed in Canada

"A friend of ours found this gun in an agricultural catalogue that was used by cattlemen to mark cows. It wasn't long afterwards that we bought two of these things and had ourselves a little duel. After it was over, we just knew we had stumbled upon something great."

- Hayes Noel

Acknowledgments

The editors and publisher are grateful to the following individuals for their assistance and encouragement in the publication of this book.

Jerry Braun and Paintball Sports International, for their endless help and support.

Cousins Paintball, for the use of their field in Medford, NY for our photo shoots. Paul Sattler, Fred Dorski, and Elio Napolitano, for giving so generously of their time and knowledge.

Jay Tavitian, and everyone at Oceanside Paintball, for showing us the time of our lives.

Sarah Stevenson, Karen Barber, and the entire 2 Die 4 team for their knowledge, enthusiasm and determination.

Cleo and Paul Fogal, for sharing their home, their field, and their story with us.

Mike Henry, Jim Lively, and Colin Thompson, for always leading us in the right direction.

NY Dogs, a great bunch of guys and a terrific team of paintball players. It was an honor playing with them.

Glenn Palmer, for always lending his assistance and equipment so willingly to this project.

Graham Easton, for helping outfit us for this paintball adventure.

Dawn and Bill Mills, of warpig.com for all their guidance and assistance.

Guy Cooper of Pro Star Sports, for his informative "Paintball Field Operator's Guide."

Steve Dunn and Extreme Adventures Canada, for the use of their Flak Jacket. It helped make Peter's job a little less painful.

National Paintball Supply, for the use of Squeegee Man.

The entire Wild Geese team, and especially Ralph Torrell, for sharing with us his extensive paintball gun collection.

Jim Della Constanza, for making Skyball such an enjoyable tournament.

Matthew Howard, for all his assistance with our Australian paintball directory.

We would also like to thank the following companies for generously loaning us equipment.

ADCO, Brass Eagle, Diablo, Diggers, JT, Kingman International, Lapco, Palmer's Pursuit Shop, Pro-Team Products, R. P. Scherer, Sheridan, Smart Parts, Soft Boards & Barriers Co., Tippmann Pneumatics, WDP, and Zap.

To everyone in the paintball industry — the players, manufacturers, field owners, distributors, and fans. We couldn't have written this book without your help and support. Thank you!

Contents

WHO IS THIS BOOK FOR?

This book is for everyone who plays or is interested in playing paintball. Everyone will appreciate the scope of this first edition; it is as much a tribute to the diversity within the game and its players as it is a guide. Regardless of your skill level, this book holds something for you.

We cover the fascinating history of the game (with firsthand accounts from its originators!), and the basic rules of the game (and descriptions of exciting variations on the paintball theme!). We offer in-depth equipment and gun information, and include essential tactical insights, as well as a thorough glossary and resource guide. Beginners and novices take note: Insights from the best players in the world make this book an ideal starting point for those of you serious about adding new dimensions of fun and excitement to your hobby and becoming great at this game.

For those of you who have played for a few years or are seasoned veterans, check out this book's authoritative analysis of guns and air systems, articles on advanced strategy, exclusive input on injury prevention stretches from former Navy SEAL, Stewart Smith, discussion of accessories, and comprehensive listing of international resources for both playing and purchasing equipment.

Our authoritative sections on the physics of paintball and guidelines for cleaning your gun correctly are among many gems in this book. We're sure that you'll find our interviews with great players both enlightening and useful in your search for competitive advantages. Motivated to elevate your game to the next level and beyond? Read on!

And then, of course, there are the pictures—visually arresting, dynamic shots taken by Peter Peck, who was himself "shot" innumerable times garnering these photographs. If you just love the game and want a book that captures the action, look no further.

Although we have attempted to be comprehensive, we realize that this volume is not the last word on the sport. For example, such luminaries as Jerry Braun, Bob Long, Jim Lively, and Dawn and Bill Mills of warpig.com gave of their time and shared insights that made this book possible. We would have loved to include more from them. We did not cover scenario games, a paintball format that we learned early on truly merits its own book. That said, we believe that we're off to a strong start. In the interest of ensuring that future editions raise the bar, we encourage you to contact us with your feedback about aspects of the game we ought to cover for the first time or in greater depth.

WHO IS PAINTBALL FOR?

For those of us who play paintball and love it, the question is what are you looking for in a game?

The answers that lead directly to paintball are listed below

If these are your answers, welcome home! This game is for you. Otherwise, you should read on. You just may want to change your mind.

I want fast-paced, totally immersive action.

There isn't a single, true standstill in paintball play, nor is there a moment where you don't feel like something is at stake. You are on offense and defense constantly, and your objectives require you to be alert and decisive—not hyper, mind you, just in the flow of the game. Opponents lurk around every corner and paintballs travel at up to 300 feet per second. You need to survive, but be willing to make a coordinated sacrifice to win the game for your team. Your teammates count on you to act with caution and precisely controlled aggression from one moment to the next. You can hear your competition moving toward you. You see paintballs flying and hear them splat against trees or barriers. You slide forward on your knees, dive behind a tree, cover your teammates' advance, celebrate victory after a hard-fought contest. Guaranteed to render "first-person, shoot'em-up, networkable computer simulations" a permanent second choice, paintball is the premiere action game.

I want a vigorous mental challenge as well as a rigorous physical one.

This is a thinking person's game. A lapse in concentration leads to elimination. If you're indoors, you may choose tactics based on speedy deployment with constant movement and firing in support of advances. If you're outdoors on a wide open field, you may want to split your force in two and converge on the enemy from opposite directions. To win at this game consistently, you and your team must use appropriate tactics while communicating (that means speaking and listening) coherently, and thinking quickly to adapt to the unexpected. It takes maturity to act as an individual without losing sight of your role in a team effort. It takes intelligence and quick decision making to prevail in the hair-raising scenarios that paintball presents.

I want a game I can play.

Except for the newborn, paintball is for everyone! The rules are straightforward, there are games and formats for every skill level, and the costs of playing are affordable. You can play the game with family and friends, with your church group, with corporate colleagues, or even go on your own simply to meet people who share your passion for intense, team-oriented sports. Whether things go well or not during your game, you will form a unique bond with whomever you play. And you can't make friends of strangers any faster than by playing paintball with them. It's safe to say that paintball is an unparalleled social experience, and open to all comers.

I want to be the best at whatever game I play.

If you put in the time and energy, form a great team, train together regularly, and have a little luck, you can become a professional paintball player, experience a tempo of game play that is unsurpassed, and vie for national and international championships against the best players in the world. For some, being a weekend warrior is enough. Others play for the thrill of victory, and seek out ever higher levels of competition. Paintball serves up plenty of opportunities for everyone. How far you go in this sport is largely up to you.

Whether you played tag or hide-and-seek when you were younger or yesterday, this game, in any of its manifestations, represents the most thrilling experience of competition you are likely ever to experience. Add to that the extraordinary comraderie you invariably develop with teammates, and you have one of the best games ever invented!

PAINTBALL IS FOR YOU!

Everybody wants to experience adventure—a highly intensified, dramatic realization of acting heroically and skillfully to attain a goal. We seek a sense of mission, of honoring our values, of taking advantage of opportunities that present themselves in our professional and romantic lives. Paintball is a microcosm of the adventure we experience each day. It crystallizes the sense of drama we seek to lend meaning to our choices and actions. Paintball taps into your imagination—*what if my life hinges on what I choose to do in the next moment?* Paintball provides a rapid succession of such moments that lead to an unparalleled gaming experience that is both universal and highly personal for every player. For those of you looking for a game that is more than the sum of its parts, here it is. Seize it!

WHO ARE WE?

The authors and interviewees are among the finest and most influential men and women ever involved with the game of paintball. For them, paintball is a passion of one sort or another. They share in common a singular devotion to the widespread enjoyment of this game, and that is why we sought their involvement with this endeavor. We think you'll be thrilled with the results.

The publisher of this book is a multifaceted multimedia company that perceived a unique opportunity to present an authoritative text on the subject of paintball to the game's growing base of enthusiastic participants, among whom we count ourselves.

GETFITNOW.com is an imprint of The Hatherleigh Company, Ltd. committed to developing multimedia health and fitness products for consumers of all ages. We believe that leading a healthy life-style can and should be a source of enjoyment and fulfillment. Paintball combines vigorous physical activity and tactical thinking in a way that we find irresistably fun.

You should go play this game as soon as possible.

—AWC

PART 1

WELCOME to the Game of PAINTBALL

Genesis of the Game

WHAT IS PAINTBALL REALLY ABOUT?

Paintball is an extraordinarily simple game in its basic form. A couple of people alternately hunt and evade one another, until one person or a team emerges triumphant over another. The victor is the first to achieve an objective or the last left standing. Yes, the game uses sophisticated technology, which is constantly evolving as people come up with new paintball accessories and gun mechanisms, and the specific objectives vary according to game designers' imaginations. But the basic game remains the same.

No matter what version of the game you find yourself most attracted to, its essence is constant. What is paintball's essence? The answer is two-fold.

Paintball is a Game

Paintball is, in the final analysis, one of many games people play with balls. In what is basically an advanced version of tag, the balls—gel-encased, water soluble goo—are propelled at up to 300 feet per second by a special, gas-powered gun. You *eliminate* (tag) opponents when paintballs you or your teammates shoot hit and break on them. Simple, right? And, as with any game, the whole point of it is to have a good time in a competitive context. Like football, basketball, and baseball, elements of paintball require players to acquire and practice certain skills. Like these other games, it has rules, some hard and fast and others that are subject to interpretation. It shares in common with more free form activities, like skateboarding and surfing, built-in enthusiasm for innovation, personal style, fast-thinking, and highly individualistic approaches. As the people who played the first game did, anyone can come up with their own version of the game. Once

Smart-thinking, alert and precise action, and good fortune lead to victory

with other people—family, friends, coworkers who are our team members. There is no escaping the fact that however well we may do on our own, we lead more fulfilling lives when we spend time in meaningful pursuits with others who share our values and goals.

Especially in America, with our culture of "manifest destiny," and the "American Dream," we are hard-wired with an optimistic and moral sense that people should put forth their best effort, go for it, "just do it," when it comes to just about everything in life. We attach importance not only to our goals, but how we achieve them.

**Be honest. Don't lie.
Be considerate. Don't be violent.
Follow the rules. Don't cheat.
Be creative. Don't be predictable.
Have fun. Don't have a negative outlook.
Be a team player. Don't be egotistical.
Be resilient. Don't ever give up.**

you're equipped with the essential safety equipment, there is enormous room for having your own kind of fun with this game.

Paintball is About Survival

Paintball is also more than just a game. At its most exhilarating moments, it is an intensified version of what people do everyday. With varying degrees of success, we're all avoiding and confronting obstacles on our way to reaching goals. This is the case whether you're in school or pursuing a career, a man or a woman, regardless of your beliefs or ethnicity.

We're all survivors. We all have goals that we're in different stages of reaching. We take risks. We learn from our mistakes and get back into the fray. We improve at the skills necessary to meet daily objectives and lifelong dreams. We do all of this

Of course, these are things all people value, not just Americans. They work for everybody in all situations. But it is no accident that paintball was created in America.

Paintball captures the essence of the basic struggle of every living being. Staying in the game is the most obvious metaphor for staying alive. And winning is about being great at surviving while vanquishing foes in fair play.

The game of paintball creates a situation in which the only way to survive is to act in manner that balances precise aggression with caution. You attain objectives by taking risks that you have a good chance of handling.

Being great at paintball requires you to learn how to take great risks and succeed.

It is also a very physical game, and to play it well means executing moves quickly and dynamically. The height of game play is achieved by mastering basic techniques and tactics, improvising effectively, working well with a team, and being fit.

The notion of paintball as a test of survival skills is what inspired its progenitors, Hayes Noel and Charles Gaines.

BIG QUESTIONS

A little less than 20 years ago, these two very close friends discovered a way to test ideas they had debated extensively during their relationship. *Are we born with all the resources we need to survive, or do we learn how to survive in response to our environment? Are survival skills learned in one context portable to other contexts? How does a person's tolerance for risk affect his ability to prevail in adverse conditions? What is the relationship between honesty and survival?* To address these tremendous questions, Noel and Gaines devised a game they called, simply, "survival." Today, we know that game as paintball. When you play, give a moment's thought to the questions this game was first invented and played to resolve. What are your answers? You can learn more about what the founders were thinking in their interviews in this book.

FROM "THE NATIONAL SURVIVAL GAME" TO TODAY

Seizing a unique opportunity to turn the game into a profitable business model, Noel and Gaines teamed up with a friend, Bob Gurnsey, and started selling marking guns and paint, and access to fields where people could get together to play the survival game. The first guns—"Splatmasters"—were made by the Nelson Paint Company, which actually had the guns manufactured under contract by the Daisy Manufacturing Company Incorporated. They made up rules for simple games like Capture the Flag and Total Elimination. This was the birth of the first paintball franchise, The National Survival Game, and what would grow to a 800 million dollar industry.

Soon other franchises emerged that started to experiment with new kinds of team games. New technologies and the development of unique paintball products dramatically accelerated the evolution of multiple paintball formats, from recreational play to scenario games, from amateur tournaments to professional, international championships.

The game has undergone dramatic changes over the years. If you look closely, however, you'll see that its essence has survived.

—AWC

Walking through the woods one day...

The actual genesis of the game really started in my mind on a walk through the woods of Virginia with a friend of mine who lives in Charlottesville and has a farm there. We were walking through the farm and he was talking about hunting wild buffalo. I'm not a hunter myself, but I was enthralled by his story. He was talking about hunting buffalo in Africa and how he was in these bulrushes and couldn't see the beasts but could hear them, about having to be aware of wind direction, about the feelings he had experienced in this extreme scenario.

I was really caught up in the thrill and the excitement and the high that he clearly had felt doing that kind of thing. The severity of the situation he was describing, the notion of survival being boiled down to a few decisive moments, just blew me away. This was 1976 and I was 35 years old. I said, "Why don't we just stalk and hunt each other on the way back to the house?" I'd done this as a kid, playing cowboys and Indians and things. But somehow the context of his story made me feel like more was at stake, and I had this remarkable adrenaline rush. I didn't forget it when I returned to New York City where I lived for 15 years making my living trading the markets on the American Stock Exchange.

I used to go to New Hampshire about once every two months to see Charles Gaines, who's one of my best friends, as well as a big outdoorsman, hunter, writer... a guy just totally at home in the wilderness.

Charles said something like, "You know, if I ever got you in the woods you'd be dead meat in a second." So we began a conversation and then sort of a debate over almost a year and half about surviving in the wilderness and what qualities it would take.

I told him that if I could survive in the Wall Street jungle, I would survive in any jungle. Charles thought this was nonsense, but I was convinced that survival skills were transportable across environments. For example, to my way of thinking tolerance for risk-taking, aggressive and defensive tendencies, a tempo of decision making and action are things that one masters in order to excel in any context. Charles believed that survival skills were inextricably linked to context, and could be learned or acquired in one environment without the benefits accruing to experiences in others. So I could be great on Wall Street, but would be devoured in the forest. Needless to say, this was a great debate.

We'd read Richard Connell's "The Most Dangerous Game" in high school and stuff like that always really turned us on. And then we were in the midst of this debate for over a year and half, and gradually over the course of our conversations we tried to devise good survival tests. And maybe with that story kicking around subconsciously somewhere in there, we developed a sense that we needed a hunting game to test our theories.

But we really never could come up with anything, until a friend of ours, George Butler, found this paintball gun in an agricultural catalogue that was used by cattlemen to mark cows. It wasn't long afterwards that we bought two of these things and had ourselves a little duel. After it was over, we just knew that we had stumbled upon something great. Almost right away we were talking about the potential for games based on survival using this kind of gun.

—Excerpt from interview with Adam W. Cohen

Hayes Noel currently trades the markets in Santa Cruz, CA, where he lives with his wife and two children.

PAINTBALL AT GROUND ZERO

Hayes Noel

ADAM COHEN: So who won that first duel?

HAYES NOEL: [Laughs] Charles did. He's a much better shot than I am. In fact, he shot me directly in the ass. [Laughs] I was wearing a bathing suit. We didn't have goggles or any protective gear, but what did we know. We were just thrilled to be doing this finally. I shot at him first and missed. Then he got me in the butt. His shot raised a little welt, which stung for a while. As far as I was concerned, that just made it more realistic.

We could see right then that we had the tool we needed to play this kind of hunting game that we wanted, because it wasn't like these tomato wars that they have in New Hampshire or Vermont. These guns were fairly accurate and could really tag you from quite a distance away. So they were sort of like guns without the danger of guns.

Not long after the duel, we played a little stalking game out in one of the wooded fields around his house. I was ecstatic because I knew that now we could play these awesome games whenever we wanted.

So then Bob Gurnsey got involved in it when we started to formulate the rules and an idea of the game. The three of us spent another six months arguing about the rules, and how a large-scale competitive version of the game would be structured.

We had decided to invite 9 different people that we knew to join us and play this game. The participants were from all over the country, people who were successful in whatever they had undertaken to accomplish. For example, we invited a guy from Alabama, who was one of the best wild turkey guides and hunters in the sport. We had two guys who had been long-range reconnaissance patrol leaders in Vietnam. Among the others were a lawyer or two, a doctor from Chicago, a movie producer from Los Angeles, and the outdoor writer for Sports Illustrated who had been cleared to do an article on the game.

The mix of people was exciting. Some were local New Hampshire friends of Charles. The man who eventually won, Richard White, was a local lumber man and deer hunter.

Anyway, we took this 80 acre cross-country ski area, filled with second growth woods. You could see through it. There were trails and it was clear enough that you could move pretty well through these woods. We marked off the boundaries of the space and appointed a responsible friend of ours to be head judge.

So we had these four flag stations. In each flag station there were 12 flags of the same color, one for each player. So there was one flag station with 12 blue flags just hanging out in the open and others with 12 green flags, 12 yellow flags, and 12 red flags. Each flag station had a judge with a whistle.

At 10 o'clock in the morning, we positioned people at equal distances apart along the circumference of the area. Some guy fired a shotgun and it started.

The first person to go in and get one flag of each color and get back out without being shot won the game as soon as he reached the home base where the head judge was waiting. We didn't know how long it would take. Everybody had a different color paint, so you could tell who shot you by color. And if you got any paint on you at all, even splatter from a hit on a tree, you were out. That's not the way it's done now, but that was the way that we did it then. Everybody was cammoed up and looked really intense. I'm certain that observers would be simultaneously a little bothered and titillated by the militant look. We weren't striving for that. We were just wearing what made sense to wear when you're running around in the woods trying not to be seen.

Photo courtesy of Hayes Noel

At the beginning of the game, everybody had maps. And as I said, we had a judge with a whistle at each flag station. These judges blew their whistles every 15 minutes so that the non-woodsmen who couldn't read the map that well had a way of gauging their progress toward a given flag.

ADAM: What are some examples of strategies that you saw?

HAYES: One obvious strategy involved running full speed to the station you were closest to at the outset of the game, and then shooting every person who approached it. The idea was that once you shot 11 people you knew there was nobody else and you could just walk through the woods and get the other flags. This would be rational, but very risky.

Another strategy was just to wait. Remember, we didn't know how long it would take for everything to work out, and nobody wanted to get eliminated early. After waiting, you could move and feel relatively confident that your opponents weren't behind you. This was less risky.

Another strategy was to hunt everybody down, play aggressive until there was nobody left—definitely the riskiest approach. There were a lot of different ways to play it.

ADAM: What was your strategy?

HAYES: Well, I was in really good shape. I knew that I would not get tired, no matter how long the game took. My strategy was to walk the perimeter, basically run around our field of 80 acres.

Since I was running along the boundary, I only had to worry about one side of me. When I got close to where a flag station was, I followed a straight line to it, and then returned along the same path. I knew I was unlikely to encounter someone where I had just been.

And it turns out there was not a lot of activity around the flag stations; the bottom line is that 80 acres was probably way too big for the game.

But we didn't know that. I was doing well. I actually got three flags before anybody did. But then I couldn't find the fourth flag station [*laughs*], and as I wandered around looking for it, I ended up getting in a fire fight with a doctor, Bob Carlson, who was this intensely aggressive guy. He was having fun trying to shoot everybody. I don't think he even got a single flag. In general, the more shooting fights you go into, the greater your chance of elimination. He eliminated me. Anyway, that was my strategy. And it was just totally exciting.

As it turned out, the illusion of danger was so real, it was the most exciting thing I had ever done. Every cell in my body was turned on. After the first 15 minutes, every breeze that blew something was like an alarm bell; you didn't know if it was somebody behind you, around you, above you. I mean it was a whole new level of excitement.

And it ended up that the game was over after about two and a half hours and I'd say at least nine or ten of the people were out of it at that point, or had been shot. The guy who ended up winning it had been in the woods all his life. Richard White never fired a shot at anybody, and he was never shot at the whole time. He just walked through the woods and kept himself out of trouble.

ADAM: How did this outcome inform your debate?

HAYES: The conclusion you can draw from the first game is essentially that the less aggressive you are, the better off you are. But that needs to be qualified. The guy who won was not taking a riskless strategy. He went for the flags. He just avoided firefights.

ADAM: He was on offense, but cautious.

HAYES: Yeah, he was invisible. I don't think we really settled the debate. But we did know that this game was amazing. Bob and Charles and I knew that this was fun. Bob pushed this more than anybody, but we all knew that we were onto something that many people were going to want to do.

I mean, it would just turn people on when they read this Sports Illustrated article. We decided to start some type of operation, a company, to try and promote this game and make a business out of it, basically.

ADAM: So that's really how the first game went, and led directly to the formation of your company.

HAYES: That's pretty much the idea and origin of the first game and the experience playing it. It was unique for everybody, you know. Charles and everybody there had a different experience. For some people, like myself, I took it pretty seriously and I was really into it.

We played in June of 1980, and in November of '80, the Sports Illustrated article came out.

ADAM: Not soon after this experience, you started a paintball company.

HAYES: That's right.

ADAM: Tell us about how you made that happen.

HAYES: Sure. Bob and I flew out to the Nelson Paint Company that made the paintball gun and sought an exclusive contract with them to sell the guns to us and nobody else except cattlemen.

We knew there were people who wanted to play the National Survival Game. It wasn't called "paintball" back then. We named the company after the game as we'd named it, and we called the various scenarios we promoted survival games. Paintball is probably a better name, but that came later.

We flew out to their Michigan headquarters, and we asked them, "How many markers [paintball guns] did you sell last year?" Bob and I didn't have any idea of what their business was like. The paintballs were made by a company called R.P. Scherer that makes vitamins and gelatin capsules. They sold the paintballs to Nelson. Nelson just made the guns to try and sell paint. It was just a product they had.

So anyway, they responded, "Oh, we sold about 700 last year." And we said, "If you give us this price, we can guarantee sales of 2000." I literally just picked a number. It turned out in the first year we sold about seven or eight thousand. Nelson couldn't keep up with our orders. We didn't know whether we'd be a mail order firm or how it would work out. We ended up authorizing people to set up deals for fields and resell our merchandise.

Guys from Atlanta would call and say, "I'd like to start a paintball company. I'll buy 30 guns." So instead of selling guns to individuals, we'd sell 25 to a guy who was going to rent them out to people to play.

Eventually, areas around the country were covered by people who owned franchises, and we wouldn't sell guns to anybody else within their area. For the first two or three years, we were the only show in town.

Then, people found out about Nelson. Nelson began selling to them at the original retail price. We couldn't control that after a while.

ADAM: How was business?

HAYES: Incredible. Sales skyrocketed. We turned a profit after about six months. Most startup companies take two or three years to show a profit. These days you've got Internet companies that don't make anything but vaporware but are worth millions and billions. We were legitimately successful from the start.

We were never as confident as we probably should have been. We were preoccupied with the image thing, how the game was perceived.

ADAM: I've heard that the game's militant look was a publicity problem from the start.

HAYES: Unfortunately, yes. For instance, during the early going, I went to Chicago. The Donahue Show had called and wanted us to talk about what we were doing. Local news shows, anybody who had heard about it, they all wanted to come cover us, because it was kind of controversial and looked really violent. Of course, it really wasn't, but they were selling their story, and it made good copy and dramatic pictures.

I went out to Chicago for the Donahue Show, and then did a segment of Nightline with Ted Koppel in New York.

So, I talked a little bit to the Donahue producer about the game, and we sent them a gun. I really wanted Donahue to shoot me on the set, inside the studio, at point blank range. I figured that it would take something that dramatic, that looks cool and would make clear to people that paintball wasn't really dangerous, to soften people's impression of the game. Donahue wouldn't do it. Instead, he invited me and an "anti-violence" psychologist for a debate format. The psychologist thought any G.I. Joe toys and stuff like that were problematic. They also had a woman and her son who had played the game. There were four of us on the show.

Donahue came in and said, "Now listen, this is not like school, you don't have to raise your hands, it's going to be over in 15 minutes. If you guys have anything to say, you'd better say it." Then he said, "When I open the show, I'm going to shoot a police target." He didn't want to shoot me, so he planned to use a police target instead.

So we go into the studio and there's the live audience ready to go. I know there's a psychologist who's going to try and do me in, so I'm kind of nervous. Donahue's ready to fire away at this silhouette type target that you might see that police shoot at. It was a white, paper silhouette hanging on the back stage curtain.

I said, "Wait a minute. Hey! You can't do that. The paintball will go right through that paper target." And he said, "Oh yeah, you're right." So he got somebody behind the curtain to hold a blackboard up behind the thing. But then he said [Laughs], "Tonight we have the survival game. Is it a game or is it more than a game?"

Then he turned and shot this thing and it sounded like a cannon going off. [Laughs] And it went right through the paper target. [Laughs] It looked as though he could have shot it with a .38 caliber handgun. I mean, the hole looked just like what a bullet would make.

Then the paintball broke when it hit the curtain, and it was red paintball exploding on that white backdrop.

ADAM: So that was kind of bad. [Laughs]

HAYES: [Laughing] I said, "I know this looks really bad," to myself, and I got pretty uptight. Donahue went and rubbed his finger around the hole like it was a wound or something. He looked at me right in the face and said, "This scares the shit out of me." Just like that.

Well, I knew I was in trouble right there. At the opening of the show, Donahue said, "Well, we just shot the paintball, and I think I'd rather play this game in armor, than with goggles." The woman ended up shooting me on the show, and that was fine. But still, at the end of the show, the audience gets to ask questions, and some woman said, "I just don't even understand what this is all about."

ADAM: How did Nightline go?

HAYES: You wouldn't believe it. They had Ted Koppel doing a live interview with a guy named Frank Camper, who ran a mercenary school in Alabama. About four months earlier, a Pakistani airline flying into England had blown up and people had gotten killed. They had traced some of the terrorists back to this Frank Camper guy. So they presented this information, and then Koppel asked Camper if he ever killed anybody. Frank Camper looks right at the camera and says, "Yeah. Yeah, I have."

So they were saying, "Hey, look, this is what's going on in America. We've got terrorist training bases and now look what people are starting to do for recreation. Look at the games they're playing."

They showed pictures of people playing the paintball game out in the woods, and they really tried to do a number on us. Anyway, that was on a Saturday night. Well, Monday morning in the office we got about 200 calls. [*Laughs*] "Where can I play this game. It looks great! It looks like fun."

After that we started to relax a little bit about the image. But we were always concerned about it. So anyway, the acceptance of it, it just really grew and it started evolving. And then other companies started making paintball guns and just like any business, rival manufacturers and stuff crept up and the industry took off.

ADAM: We've heard that the industry is up to 800 million dollars in total revenue.

HAYES: Yeah. So it's a really big business. And whether it's going to continue to grow and so forth will be interesting to see.

ADAM: To hear you talk about it sounds like it was a game that on some basic level everybody was playing. All kids play one form of tag or another, and hide-and-seek.

HAYES: Right.

ADAM: You guys sort of tapped into this whole idea of using the paintball gun instead of make-believe or fruit. You formalized the game, gave it a new instrument and more mature format. But it's still a game that human beings just play, because they are naturally excited by the chase and the hunt.

HAYES: Yeah, I mean, you can ask any kid why he plays cops and robbers or cowboys and Indians. It's a raw, primal thing that never goes away.

In order to become a business, the game had to evolve from the individual game, which is far and away the most interesting in my opinion. The game we played where every individual was against every other individual was the ultimate. It became a game where teams played against other teams. When you play it that way in smaller fields, you shoot more paint.

So the name of the game is selling guns and selling paintballs. We were always against that. Let me clarify. We weren't against the idea of the team game, because from a business respect, that made more sense. But we opposed the virtual extinction of the individual game. Unfortunately, it just doesn't work as well from a business standpoint.

ADAM: What do you think about the game as it is played today?

HAYES: I was at this convention recently, they were debating whether they should have a rate of fire where the gun can't shoot more than 20 balls a second. Twenty balls per second? I think it's crazy, but if that's what the market demands.... It's still the same game underneath. It's just become something totally different on the surface.

The more you start to make it look like war, the more worried I get about the game's image.

I talked to Charles at length and we both agree. The industry needs to make the game visually pleasing. To make it viewer friendly for TV.

My opinion is that the flight of the ball is what's pleasing to see in any sport. If you watch people watching a tennis match, they don't watch the players, they watch the ball. And in football, you know you love to watch a pass spiraling through the air and the receiver running under it. You would never watch a guy drive or putt a golf ball, if you couldn't see the ball.

So the challenge for paintball is to make the ball visible in a way that pleases the senses of the person watching it. I mean, it's totally uninteresting otherwise. Charles and I sort of both worked up this idea about how to make paintball visually pleasing. But it would involve slowing the game down, slowing the paintball down, making it bigger, playing an individual game rather than a team game.

And it wouldn't affect the game at the field level, they could still play the tournaments and have the 20 balls a second and these things that they do. They'd sell a lot of paintballs at the field level.

However, in order to get sponsorship and TV revenue and live gate revenue, in order to put asses in the seats, so to speak, you have to make it viewer friendly. Right now, it's not a viewer friendly sport. And so you look at the magazines that come out and this and that, and all the advertisers are basically people who are producing products that people who play the game use and I think the only people that buy the magazines are people who play the game.

Whoever gets paintball on TV will make as much money as all the people selling all the paint and guns that exist today.

But, you know, that's not where they're at right now. They want to sit around and debate about whether to shoot 23 balls or ten balls. And to a certain extent they're not wrong to do so. 14-year-old boys want the best paintball gun money can buy for Christmas, and that's the market they're serving.

ADAM: Any final thoughts on the game, your sense of its essence, what you love about it?

HAYES: Have you seen "Life is Beautiful?"

ADAM: Yes, I have.

HAYES: That character was a survivor. I thought it was a great movie, that it dealt with the holocaust from the standpoint of a survivor. I felt the movie was about the perseverance of an individual in the face of this total horror. His humor, his resilience, his creativity, his courage-he was a total survivor. And I'm not saying that people who didn't survive somehow didn't measure up. Obviously, not. It's just that here was this guy doing everything he could to save his family. And at any moment, his luck could have run out, but he made sure that as far as he had anything to do with it, could have any control over what might happen, his son would live. And even though he

dies, he wins. That guy would have won our first game.

ADAM: Interesting.

HAYES: I don't even know why I'm bringing this up, except to say, that really, to me, this survival game is about whoever does well in the individual game. I'm not trying to be too heavy about it, but you know, a guy from the hills of Tennessee or a guy on Madison Avenue in New York is just as likely to have the qualities of a survivor as not.

This was an extraordinary man who, however he did it, faced this horror, dealt with it, and saved his genes. I don't know, I just thought it was very moving, a great movie.

So I wouldn't say a country or city boy is a better survivor than the other.

ADAM: It's the individual.

HAYES: Absolutely.

ADAM: Got it. Do you ever actually get together with these guys and just play the survival game, because just listening to you talk, it's hard to picture you enjoying the team approach much.

HAYES: No, I never did it in a recreational way. And honestly, to be on the floor of the American Stock exchange...

The thing is I used to love to play poker, and once I started trading the market by myself, I never played poker anymore. I know better than anybody who I know of what risk is. I get to take 50 risks a day if I want to. Or 20 risks or 10 or five. I get to practice what it feels like all the time. This is an important thing about survival games.

This wasn't initially why I wanted to start paintball, but it was very clear to me that because of the illusion of danger that you create in the game, it allows people to feel what it feels like to take risks.

ADAM: People don't usually like that feeling,

but they're enticed by it.

HAYES: No, they don't like it at all. It's the same feeling whether you're falling in love or whether you're making a commitment, a real commitment to something or whether you're taking a financial risk. People don't really like that feeling.

At some point, you have to learn that on the other side of risk is growth and not death. It's one of T.S. Elliot's points in "The Wasteland." Between the thought and the action falls the shadow—between the conception and realization falls the shadow. The shadow is the personal fear that people feel, the anxiety they feel, and it's a physical feeling, in all of these things. I think it's an actual physical anxiety that people feel. You need to practice getting through that.

So I don't really play paintball anymore. Except for that first game, the survival game, which was so new. But I do "play" every day.

ADAM: Understood. Thank you for your time, Hayes.

HAYES: You bet.

The Attraction of Paintball

Jerry Braun

A Game for Children of All Ages

Stop and think about the very first games you ever played. There are two games most of us played as children. One of them was Follow the Leader. The other one was a primal hunt and chase game, such as tag or hide-and-seek. You can be Chinese, you can be Venezuelan, you can be American, you can be Aleutian, you can be anyone from anywhere in the world. These are games you have played, the ones you started with, the ones you associate with being a child bursting with energy.

Remember when you were a kid playing hide-and-seek? Your heart would be in your mouth because your friend was three feet away from you and was just about to find you out. You felt that the world was going to come to an end if you were discovered. Remember playing tag? There was always a safe spot, but you'd leave it and run as hard as you could in order not to get tagged. Sometimes you'd run behind an obstacle to gain time. The exhilaration of not being found or tagging another player is what you experience playing paintball. That is why it is so appealing.

Now, some of us pretend it isn't so, but human beings, like most animals, have predatory instincts. Look at the very first games played by kittens and puppies, they are primal hunt-and-chase games. They stalk each other, bat at and chew on each other. Basically, they playfully attack one another. Pure play is nature's way of teaching survival. Playing paintball triggers the same kinds of responses in humans, except that we don't have to learn how to "go for the jugular" to survive the way animals do. So our enjoyment of games like paintball is a little different than theirs.

Jerry Braun, 4th from left in back row, at Skyball 1999, Toronto, Canada.

People talk about the game being violent. No doubt the images of adults brandishing guns looks intimidating and suggests violence. The basic characteristics of violence—the use of force to destroy or hurt others and a chaotic lack of structure that promotes reckless and dangerous behavior—are simply nowhere to be found in paintball. The objectives never involve hurting people, and the rules are clear and enforced. Nothing like the bench-clearing brawls that occur in professional baseball or hockey ever occurs in amateur or professional paintball.

When you first play the game, it elicits emotions in you that you may not have experienced since you were 3 years old. It's a sophisticated game of tag, except that it doesn't involve physical contact, incorporates teamwork, and frequently involves objectives beyond eliminating your opponent . And the pure joy you see on the faces of kids playing tag, that's what paintball provides. That's why people who play it once usually come back for more.

PAINTBALL'S PIERCING TRUTHS

Charles Gaines

ADAM COHEN: Do you think the skills that you acquire and develop by playing paintball are applicable to everyday real-life experiences?

CHARLES GAINES: Absolutely! More to the point, I think the survival game, as it was played back when Hayes [Noel] and I played it, is illuminating for anyone who plays it. Unlike Hayes who held that people are born with certain survival skills, I think that for the most part, we learn them based on our will to immerse ourselves in an environment and discover it. And so the game is a way of finding out about yourself...if you want it to be. I can't say too much about the game as it's played today, because I haven't played it recently and it's definitely changed. But I imagine from what I read about it and hear about it, that at the very least, the game's essential experience still heightens your awareness of yourself as a survivor in a specific context. Your ability to win is related to your receptiveness to the details and the nuances of your surroundings and your response to the scenario you're in. So I do believe that it's true that you can take lessons learned in the midst of playing any version of paintball, and apply those to improving your everyday life.

ADAM: Knowledge is power, and what you learn in paintball is often very personal knowledge. In terms of risk-taking, in terms of learning about how you function under pressure, in terms of making quick decisions, in terms of communicating with others effectively. You agree?

CHARLES: It's true. The survival game is like a little paradigm for real life. You know, it's more this way with the original game. After all, we play life as individuals, not as a team, regardless of our social experience. I mean, you can be part of a team in a business or family, but we're all individuals and we play life that way. Each of us has to make decisions and live with the consequences of acting on them.

I believe that the initial game, the every-man-for-himself format, was more paradigmatic of life than the team game. But, of course, both of them are nice paradigms. The point is always to succeed at what you're trying to do. And either alone or as part of a team, you have to act.

ADAM: The responsibility is still on each individual in the team game. Especially at the pace that the team game is played today, "teamwork" is really driven by individual actions that are more implicitly than explicitly coordinated.

CHARLES: That's how the initial paradigm plays out in today's game. Of course, in life, you're trying to make something of yourself. You're trying to succeed at making money or becoming happy or famous or all of these things. And accomplishing these things means taking steps. In the survival game, you're trying to succeed at a very limited task. You know, in the case of the team game, you go in and grab the other team's flag. In the case of the individual game, the way we played it, you grab all four flags and get out without being put out of the game. These are great metaphors for staying alive that are impossible to ignore, especially for first time players.

If you're smart about it, you bring to both the game and your life who you really are. You don't try to fake it. In other words, the people who got put out the quickest and the easiest in the game when I played it were people who were trying to be something other than what they were, the one who pretended to have talents and skills that they didn't actually own. Being good at this game means being willing to play within yourself.

ADAM: Like a baseball pitcher in a clutch situation, you shouldn't throw a pitch you can't handle.

CHARLES: Exactly. But then you learn new

Photo courtesy of Charles Gaines

pitches and start working them in as you get better at them. I think that may be the deepest and most piercing truth that overlaps playing paintball and playing at real life. All we know after a certain age in life is that the only way to achieve success is to be who we are, to rely on our real strengths, not our perceived or dreamed about strengths. And to play honestly. That was one of the things that we learned very early on about the game.

Now, I don't know if any of these things relate as profoundly anymore to the current game. I just literally don't know. I haven't played it and I don't even know how it's played. I hope it's the case. But the original game, the reason it was so resonant and the reason it was so much fun for us, was that it was so clear from the very beginning that we were doing something that really was alive with these metaphorical implications we're talking about now. You really teach yourself something about who you are, where you are, and something about the condition of life.

ADAM: Awesome. I completely understand what you mean. It's basically the kind of experience you have when you're faced with an extreme challenge and you have to rely on yourself to succeed.

CHARLES: That's it.

ADAM: And you know in that moment that whether or not you succeed is going to require you to keep your cool, keep focused, and simultaneously go for it. I mean it's a higher level of alertness. For me it comes in situations where I've been in sports competitions, or acting on stage, or speaking in public. Anytime I'm pushing myself.

CHARLES: Right. And so much of it has to do with timing, which is another thing that you learn in life. You can make the same choice at two different times and one time you'll be successful and the other time it'll cost you big time.

ADAM: Right. Having spoken with a number of people who are in the game now, I can say, that it has lost this sort of philosophical edge. I wouldn't say the game itself isn't enjoyable as it's being presented now. It's just not what it was for you guys, an experiment, playing with ideas of survival. It's a business now, a diversion, recreation, entertainment. You have any comments on that.

CHARLES: Yeah. That's the way I perceive it to be. And it's one of the reasons for my sort of inattention to the game in its present version. But I bet that the idea of surviving is still a factor, still part of the attraction of the game.

I mean, as far as I'm concerned, we who founded it had it at its very best. After we invented it, we started playing on a regular basis, both the individual game and more and more the team game. We had a field that we rented out, or borrowed. My kids played it, and my wife played it once and [Bob] Gurnsey's kids played it and we had our children out there acting as field judges. We'd make whole weekends out of this thing. And it was just joyous and wonderful. Good, simple fun with friends and family.

We'd have people come up from New York and out from Los Angeles to play the game. They would play it for the first time and immediately "grok" it and see how cool it was. I had my friend P.J. O'Rourke up to play it and he loved it.

It was great because it started as our little secret game. And then we introduced it to the world, which was like telling a very witty joke or some marvelously resonant parable for the first time. People could really see what we were talking about, especially after they played it. They'd say, "Ah, yes. Exactly. I get it. This is so cool!"

But then, we and the game were attacked by people who never played it but assumed that the presence of paintball guns somehow supported violence. Of course, in football and hockey, where they show highlights of people knocking each other's heads off, this criticism is virtually nonexistent. We had to fight this bad reputation that we really didn't deserve. And the business became somewhat difficult for me. The commercialization of the game, which literally turned it into what I perceive to be little more than shooting each other in the woods, cost me my entire interest in it.

ADAM: It turned into a team game when you started to turn it into a business, basically.

CHARLES: Yeah. That's right. But initially, we wanted it to be both a team and an individual game. But the individual game just sort of died out, out of lack of interest.

ADAM: That's mystifying.

CHARLES: Yeah, I thought so. I mean, to me it's a much more interesting version of the game. And would continue to be, I think. Maybe nobody even knows about it anymore. I don't know. But to me it would still be a more interesting version even given the high powered guns and the maga-

zines that hold hundreds of paintballs. Given all of that it seems to me it would be more interesting than the team version.

ADAM: Well, you know, maybe it'll come back.

CHARLES: Maybe it will. That would be great.

Charles Gaines is an extraordinarily prolific and accomplished writer, published in magazines ranging from American Sportsman *and* Forbes F.Y.I. *to* Architectural Digest *and* Men's Journal. *He has also written various books, most recently,* Survival Games (1997). *He was also author of the international bestseller,* Pumping Iron (1974), *and Associate Producer of the film based on the book,* starring Arnold Schwarzenegger. He and his wife of 37 years currently live in Nova Scotia.

PAINTBALL EVOLUTION

ADAM COHEN: Steve, it's great to have a chance to sit down with someone who has been around the sport for as long as you have.

STEVE DAVIDSON: Thank you for having me.

ADAM: Let's jump right into the thick of things.

STEVE: Sure. Where would you like to begin?

ADAM: Everyone has their own take on the initial game. What do you make of it?

STEVE: Yeah, the story's kind of become the game's creation myth. A couple of guys had a debate about survival skills, and agreed on a way of settling it by playing a free-for-all version of capture the flag. The fact that a forester won without ever firing a shot is significant. It's a true story, and it's a simple one that tells you what the game is all about.

ADAM: The fact that being the last one standing isn't just about shooting loads of paint.

STEVE: Yes.

ADAM: Let's discuss how the game became widespread. That's what we're really interested in learning more about from you.

STEVE: Okay. Well, after that first game, these three guys, Hayes Noel, Charles Gaines, and Bob Gurnsey knew that this could become something more than a free-for-all recreational activity. They saw an entrepreneurial opportunity. They went to a couple of different companies and attempted to have a gun made specifically for playing the game. They eventually had "Splatmaster" manufactured and they went to the company that had made the original gun that they'd used, which was the "Nelspot Marker" made by Nelson Paint Company, to get the paint, which was oil-based. This was within months of that first game.

I did play a couple of games when the oil-based paint was still around, and boy are we all glad that was short-lived.

ADAM: Pretty disgusting, I take it?

STEVE: We're talking turpentine parties after every game, or just burning your clothes. But it was

STEVE DAVIDSON'S PAINTBALL BIOGRAPHY

When Steve Davidson began playing paintball in 1983, he fell in love with the game.

1983	Began playing paintball
1984	Formed Muthers of Destruction team
1986	IPPA representative for NJ & Coordinator of Team Registration program
	First article printed in APG magazine—*10 Ways to Becoming a Better Team Captain*
1989	Columnist for Paintball Sports International, PaintCheck & Paintball News; Forms Were-wolves competition team
1990	Introduces team rankings & seedings; ranking & seeding services for World Cup, Lively Masters, ASO series, Paintcheck 5 Player & other events; Forms World Paintball Federation
1991	Authors, *MAXING: A Guide to Winning in Tournament Play*
1992	Organizes National Professional Paintball League
1996	Secretary, NPPL
1997	Forms GTO tournament series
1999	Introduces United States Paintball League patented game format (visit getfitnow.com for more details!)

fun. I wouldn't change the way it was then, but I'm glad we're using water-soluble food dyes now.

Anyway, they started franchising the game across the country. Jerry Braun in upstate New York was one of the first franchises, as was Deborah Dion out in Pittsburgh.

Around that same time it didn't take more than maybe about nine months there were at least two other franchise corporations on the scene. One was based in Florida called the "Ultimate Game" and the other was Pursuit Marketing Incorporated (PMI), which remains one of the biggest and best

distributors in the industry today.

National Survival Game (NSG) had a turnkey type of an operation: "We will supply you with the paint, with the guns, with the goggles, the rules of play, the insurance, and show you how to set a game up."

You had to buy everything from them. Until some far-thinking individuals said, "I ought to be able to find something similar elsewhere for less." People approached Nelson directly, and they had no hard core exclusivity agreement with NSG. Before you knew it, Skirmish USA, Paul Fogal's company, entered the scene. Fogal had approached NSG, but they couldn't work things out. He basically said, "No way," to their rates and went and started searching for other suppliers. He hooked up with Jeff Perlmutter from PMI.

Ultimate Game didn't last. They got crushed in what I call the Franchise Wars. NSG eventually went away because they remained, I guess the word would be "hidebound." They had a vision of what they thought the game should be and how it should be played and what you should use and how it should be organized. They weren't really interested in adjusting themselves to changes in the industry.

ADAM: Are we still in 1981?

STEVE: We're still in 1981, but we're kind of talking about stuff that happened between then and 1983. Specific dates on these things, I can't give you.

ADAM: NSG goes south within the first three years?

STEVE: They were still around and doing well, but they didn't have an adaptive long-term strategy. All of these independent fields were popping up all over the place. Then, Perlmutter introduced the water-soluble paintball. That opened things up for a large number of people. Abolishing the need for turpentine parties was progress.

NSG also had a tournament series and you could only qualify for this tournament series by finishing first or maybe second-place at a regional tournament that was held at an affiliated NSG field. So, for the first couple of years, the only tournaments were being played by NSG teams or maybe local stuff, but not on a national basis.

In 1986, Fogal had his first major national tournament with Perlmutter, and Jerry Braun had the Air Pistol Open. The word "Open" is what's significant there because any team, whether they were coming from an NSG field or not, could enter this event. That was a major step toward opening up the game across the board.

ADAM: And technologically?

STEVE: Tech-wise, the mid-eighties were explosive. During 1981, 1982, and the first half of 1983, people were playing with paintball guns that were hand-cocked, single-shot, twelve gram deals. Nelson's Nelspot 007, NSG's Splatmaster, and Benjamin Sheridan's PGP were the three that you had available to you. They were all tilt-feed/gravity-feed types of things.

At the end of 1983, people started putting pumps on the Nelspots and PGPs. The plastic Spotmarker from NSG became basically a low-cost, field rental piece of equipment and the "Tech Wars" started to pick up steam. Very shortly after the pump was first introduced, and this is still 1983/1984, Constant Air (CA) came out. Some ingenious people figured that there had to be a way to hook a larger canister of air up to their gun. They found a way to do it and, bang, they were immediately banned from tournament play. which slowed things down tremendously for a good couple of years.

ADAM: Were they welcome at Jerry's Opens, or not even those?

STEVE: No, absolutely not. People, including me, fought it viciously. To us, the whole game, the nature of the competition, was about to change radically. If we allowed those guns in tournament play, everything would be different. The simple necessity of having to change those twelve grams after twenty or thirty shots maximum, the necessity of having to carry that stuff, of not being able to stand there for fifteen minutes, made the game a certain, special kind of experience.

ADAM: So you weren't opposed to the CA technology *per se*. You just wanted the competition to be driven by tactics rather than guns.

STEVE: That was the issue. There were people out in California in particular who had gone the Constant Air route. Interestingly enough, the Iron Men, who are one of the top teams now, were originally a CA team. They beat everybody, left right and center in California, but they didn't do any of the tournaments because they didn't want to give up their CA. They were the best team in the country at the time, but they couldn't prove it because they weren't willing to compete on the level that all the competition teams were.

Gravity Feeds came in right after the pump—again, the end of 1983, beginning of 1984—PVC pipe and a forty-five degree elbow. Then, around the middle of 1984 Gramps and Grizzly's started producing guns that came with those features standard.

ADAM: So the technology was driven by recreational play? It seems that way because the tournaments resisted these new tech features, but they were selling well to the rec players who were in the game for the fun of it.

STEVE: Sort of. It's interesting because you'd go to the tournament and you'd sit there and talk about all the nifty things that you could do to your gun, or that you were planning on doing to your gun, or that somebody else was thinking about doing to their gun.

We all recognized that there had to be some kind of a leveler at the tournaments. A bunch of people who were more into military simulation than they were

The guns on the next few pages are identified by manufacturer, type and description, in this order.

Carter; Buzzard; Top Level custom made tournament pump gun. Includes Smart Parts barrel. *Courtesy of Ralph Torrell*

Gotcha; Deuce; Double barrel stock gun with two-step trigger. *Courtesy of Ralph Torrell*

Palmer's Pursuit Shop; Nasty Typhoon; Customized double barrel semi with muzzle brake, double finger trigger, cosmetic trigger guard, bottleline with mounting brackets, and iodized blue. *Courtesy of Ralph Torrell*

Airgun Designs; Sydearm; *Courtesy of Ralph Torrell*

Nelson Paintball Company; Nelspot 007; 12 gram pump gun. *Courtesy of Rob Rubin*

Nelspot 007 with grip removed showing 12 gram CO_2 cartridge.

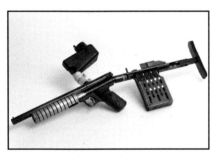

Sheridan; Piranha; Pump gun with 12 gram six pack from AirGun Designs, Inc. *Courtesy of Rob Rubin*

Detail of six pack.

paintball were trying to get things like smoke grenades and hand grenades and walkie-talkies and heavier weaponry introduced into tournament play. In response to this, Fogal was the one who put it the best: "We can count on the fact that every paintball player is going to have a gun, but if we start asking everybody to have to bring forty smoke grenades and radios and all this other kind of stuff, we're just going to price ourselves right out of the market. So we have to make a conscious effort to cut it off somewhere. Where should that cutoff be?"

Things went back and forth for a while. Jerry limited the barrels to ten inches; you couldn't have a barrel more than ten inches long.

ADAM: That doesn't make too much of a difference, does it?

STEVE: No, it doesn't make a difference. But we were trying everything. People were trying to sneak that kind of stuff in all the time.

There was a huge fuss over back check valves, these things that keep the pressure in the gun even when you remove the twelve gram or the bottle from it. It made it so you could remove your gas source and still have five or six or seven shots left in the gun. That was a big deal because we trained ourselves to listen for low air levels. You'd think to yourself: "He's about to change twelve grams, so we're going to rush him and take

him out." Well, if I'm that guy running low and I've got a back check valve, baby am I ever waiting for you to come at me. I'm going to make the biggest, most obvious twelve gram change that I possibly can. Some cocky guy's going to charge me, hopefully with all of his friends, and I'm going to take'm out. "Boink, boink, boink! See you all later. Thank you for listening!"

ADAM: Back checks sound very cool. Did they survive?

STEVE: No, those were banned. That little extra ability seemed to us like tinkering with the game, and we wanted to keep things very balanced and clear in terms of the mental and physical requirements.

ADAM: So the back check valve came along in 1984. 1984 seems like a big year for the game.

STEVE: It was a huge year for paintball technology. Absolutely. A lot of stuff was introduced in 1984. The back check valve came along with the CA.

Another big thing was a barrel extender. You take a piece of aluminum, stick it on the end of your barrel, and you have a longer barrel. Now, what that did for anybody? To this day, we still don't know. But somebody brought out the first barrel extender and they sold like hot cakes. So somebody else said, "Well, I'm going to come out with a field strip screw set for the gun," and people were begin-

Werewolves, 1989. Steve Davidson sits third from left, front row.
Courtesy of Steve Davidson

ning to realize that they could make serious money selling paintball equipment.

ADAM: Cleaning kits and harnesses emerge circa 1984?

STEVE: Everything, all kinds of stuff.

ADAM: Flak jackets and shin guards?

STEVE: You name it and it probably had its origins back somewhere between 1984 and 1985, right around in that period of time.

ADAM: Was there anyone keeping track of how many people were playing?

STEVE: No, it was really a very garage-type business. Somebody would order twenty guns from NSG and post business cards to resell the stuff at the local restaurant. Stuff like that.

Fogal was actually marketing himself. He went on to teach a lot of people how to play, how to do that. Jerry [Braun] also, and Deborah [Dion], too. Sat Cong Village out in California, Three Rivers Survival Game out in Pittsburgh, NSG, Skirmish USA, National Survival Game-New York, and then a little bit later on, Challenge Park in the Chicago area. Around Chicago you come upon the really big fields that pioneered how to market the game to people, how to set up the game for people, how to get folks to come in, what to

charge, how to organize, how to train referees— all those kinds of things. Those five fields are really the major contributors to all that kind of stuff.

ADAM: And virtually all of these fields were playing the basic Total Elimination and Capture the Flag types of games.

STEVE: Yes, exclusively. The first scenario game was, I think, 1985.

ADAM: Actually the first game sounds like a scenario game.

STEVE: I guess you could probably put it like that.

ADAM: But it soon thereafter became a team-based game.

STEVE: That that was probably the way NSG decided to package it. Somebody somewhere recognized that twelve individuals running around in the woods was not economically viable. So they probably figured, "We'll play 'Capture the Flag.'" I'm sure that those were the words used by somebody somewhere.

ADAM: And the other major game would have been just total elimination.

STEVE: The total elimination games were pretty funny. You have to understand, the games were initially two hours long, on hundreds of acres in the woods. I played a couple of games where neither team saw anybody from the other team, and it lasted the full hour and a half. Of course, it was fun. You were crawling around in the dirt and leaves. You were scanning for opponents. But after a couple of games where you literally couldn't find the people you were supposed to be shooting at, it just seemed silly. And the field-owners were losing money, because they weren't selling paint.

Then again, the objectives were totally different then. Your goal was to get somebody to surrender to you, to psyche out the other team. Today, it's more about actually getting in their

Line SI; Bushmaster; Sliding stock. *Courtesy of Rob Rubin*

Line SI with stock extended.

Worr Games Products; '95 Autococker; ACI expansion chamber, hardline bottom line, copperhead sight, Lapco barrel. *Courtesy of Rob Rubin*

Pro-Team Products; Retro-Valve Micromag with double trigger in Red Nights, with Millenium Series nitrogen system (gas-through foregrip). *Courtesy of Steve Davidson*

face and pumping them full of paintballs. The technology supported that kind of play because you could only get so many rounds out of the gun in a minute.

I loved it. If you could convince somebody that you could shoot, or if you could get somebody to fire and blow their wad before you had fired, then you could get them to surrender. There was a lot of sneaking around, a lot of finding the perfect ambush site. It was beautiful when they couldn't see you, had no idea you were going to be there, and you just know that plenty of them are going to come walking past that one particular spot. Knowing was as much fun as springing the trap.

ADAM: But then, somewhere along the line, they started to make the fields smaller.

STEVE: It started when some genius, somewhere, recognized that the more paint they got their customers to shoot, the more money they would make.

ADAM: The field owners made this happen?

STEVE: I would assume so. It kind of went hand in hand. The field-owners want to sell paint. That's their job, to sell paint. The players like to pull the trigger. And boy, do they. If you go to any field and you take a look at how much money they're spending at the target range just goofing off. It's incredible. But they're having a great time, and that's the bottom line.

ADAM: As the game has become more about splattering opponents with paint, are people spending more on paint now than they used to?

STEVE: Interestingly enough, the average usage per player has not changed significantly, in terms of the amount of money they're spending on their paint. For instance, back in 1983, 1984, 1985, if you were spending twenty cents a ball and carrying a hundred rounds onto the field, you were spending X for a day's worth of play. Now, the price has come way down, so you're carrying a case, case and a half out onto the field, literally thousands of balls. You're still spending the same amount of money, but you're shooting more paint.

ADAM: The player's perception is that they're getting more bang for their buck.

STEVE: Right. On top of that, some unsung hero recognized that when the games lasted more than fifteen minutes, customers end up sitting around while two or three people are running around in the woods trying to find each other. So fields started to get smaller. Smaller fields require fewer referees. Faster games, field owners gave people the feeling that they had played more frequently. I don't think anybody could tell you exactly who brought that concept into being.

ADAM: Sounds like a smart business move.

STEVE: Yeah. I don't think a lot of people realize that the concept of smaller tournament fields came from England. They were the ones that introduced the postage stamp size and everybody said, "Ding, ding, ding, it's a lot easier for four referees to cover two hundred feet by a hundred feet, than it is forty acres in the woods."

ADAM: Let's talk about the tournaments.

STEVE: The first tournament was in 1983—an NSG National Survival Game Championship. I believe it was the Taxidrivers from Hell, a Canadian team, that won. I think NSG held a national tournament through 1990. NSG's structure of only allowing teams that came from the regional championships was cutting down on their attendance because there were fewer and fewer NSG fields. Fields realized they could thrive by going independent.

ADAM: So suddenly you have all these independent groups. How do they get together? How do they form a tournament? Spontaneously?

STEVE: Yes, pretty much. Jerry decided that he wanted to do his Air Pistol Open and Fogal got together the same year with PMI and started the North American Championship. That lasted five years and then faded.

Lively came along in 1989 and showed everybody how to do a trade show. He's definitely great at that. There's always been this disparity. The people who put on these major events know how to do one thing really well—put on a great trade show and lots of parties, or run the game on the field so that it's fair and quick. But they've never put the two together. That's the nut that still has to be cracked.

So NSG faded out. Jerry had his two Air Pistol Opens. But that was it for him for a couple of years.

ADAM: And up to this point, it's virtually all been outdoors?

STEVE: All outdoors.

ADAM: Let's back up from tournament play for a second. When did recreational indoors paintball start?

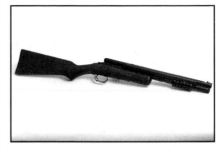

Sheridan; KP2; Stock gun with horizontal side mounted ammo tube. *Courtesy of Ralph Torrell*

Palmer's Pursuit Shop; Hurricane (serial #47); Originally a pellet gun, converted in 1992 to a constant air semiautomatic. *Courtesy of Ralph Torrell*

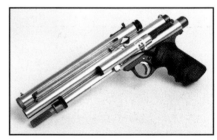

Palmer's Pursuit Shop; Squall (3rd one ever made); Semiautomatic spring feed, quicksilver, insta-pierce. *Courtesy of Ralph Torrell*

Member of the team, Lords of Discipline, at the 15-Man North American Championships at Skirmish, USA. That series ran from 1985–1990. *Courtesy of Cleo Fogal*

Crossman 3357 Spotmarker; 50 caliber paintball gun. *Courtesy of Ralph Torrell*

Crossman 3357 open to show removable cylinder.

Pro-Team Products; Car 68; Police and military training semi-automatic. Can also come with 35 mm grenade launcher attachment. *Courtesy of Pro-Team Products*

Car 68 with stock extended.

STEVE: The first person to open an indoor field was Caleb Strong up in Buffalo, New York. That was in November, 1984. That was pretty cool. I went up there with Paul Fogal to check it out, because he was thinking of opening up an indoor location in Philadelphia. They had this maze built, it was totally alien. Like no paintball we had ever seen before. Going through a door became an entirely new experience for me, let me tell you, because you had no idea what was happening on the other side. They played freaky music. There were places covered with black plastic so it was pitch black. You could not see anything in those areas. You were thinking somebody was in there. And if there was, they'd be able to see you well before you could see them. So I almost died a couple of times just because I was preoccupied with the dark sections. Then Paul and I would approach a door and we'd talk about who was going to go through it first. "Well, you're smaller, Steve." "Okay, Paul." [*Laughs*] That was just great fun.

ADAM: Let's get back to the tournaments.

STEVE: Okay. So Lively became the big thing on the tournament scene in 1989. We had Jerry with the Air Pistol Open, we had North American Championships and NSG still kind of all running simultaneously.

ADAM: Throughout the mid- to late-eighties.

STEVE: 1987, 1988, yes. Lively introduced his event in 1989. He got everybody in the industry to support it and that became the big thing. North American Championships went away quickly. Jerry was still there for another year or so and then he introduced the World Cup, which was supposed to be the first tournament that was going to have a hundred thousand dollar prize. Didn't quite make it, I think he gave away about eighty-two thousand dollars, which was still significant at the time. Nobody could compete with what Lively was able to do.

Eventually, Lively held five events a year, across the country in Tennessee, Texas, Chicago and San Francisco.

ADAM: No professional teams yet, right?

STEVE: Right. Everybody who played in tournaments was a professional team, literally. There were maybe five hundred people across the country who you could call professional tournament players, and everybody knew who everybody else was. We saw the same faces at every single tournament. The same rivalries were carried from one event to the next.

ADAM: Was there any emphasis on drawing people in to watch these things happen?

STEVE: No, none whatsoever. It was a very closed, tight-knit, insular community. We knew what we were doing and everybody else sucked. No offense, but you know how it goes. We were into our own cool thing.

I was big into science fiction before I got into paintball and I was putting on science fiction conventions and stuff like that. Paintball was built on the same kind of insulated special kind of a community. We were more than happy to see each other in the city and then next month in another city.

ADAM: So nobody was in a rush to promote this game to the masses?

STEVE: The field owners were into getting new people to come out and play, but the person who made the transition from a recreational player to a regular member of a team had to be tough-skinned and talented. You had to be very motivated and to get noticed and invited onto a team.

On the other hand, these teams throughout the '80s and early '90s were fifteen player teams. Organizing fifteen solid players who had the time to practice, the time to travel, and the money to afford everything... it wasn't easy. We wanted players who could think on the run, and there were so few. Every fifteen man team from those days could have used another two

or three or four players, but they just couldn't find bodies. It's amazing to me, looking back now, that I played with such a tremendous team.

ADAM: Today's tournaments mostly have 10-man and 5-man teams. What happened to the 15-man team?

STEVE: It's definitely history. A combination of factors just made it untenable. First of all, it wasn't easy to get 15 man teams together, so there really weren't that many of them. And as fewer of them were able to make the tournaments, the promoters started to raise their prices. The total effect of this was lower attendance at the tournaments. Around 1992, Jim Lively had the idea that making the teams smaller and reducing the entry fees slightly would get far more people to attend. Boy was he right. The team size requirement was reduced from 15 to 10. So if it cost $100 for a 15 member team, they dropped the price to $70 for a 10 player team. Attendance blasted off, so the promoters were making good money off of this move. But the game play suffered. It was far easier for teams to get into tournaments, but the level of competition really started to drop. Then the promoters wanted to move to 5 player teams. Well, it doesn't take much to realize where this was headed-the pro-

Tippmann Pneumatics; SMG 60; Bulldog version, first full automatic, requires 62 caliber paintballs, first paintball gun banned. *Courtesy of Cousins Paintball*

Components Concepts Inc. (CCI); Phantom; Stock class with 45 grip frame and vertical 12 gram adapter. *Courtesy of Cousins Paintball*

Kingman; Spyder S.E.; Double trigger with expansion chamber, locking external velocity adjuster, and 45 grip. *Courtesy of Cousins Paintball*

These are two players at Skirmish, USA, 1984. They're using the Mark-4 guns, which were the first guns produced specifically for paintball and marketed by someone other than the National Survival Game. Note the shop goggles and lack of facial protection. *Courtesy of Cleo Fogal*

ingenious about this first year was that all of the teams competed against one another in the first round. The idea was that amateurs should experience the difference so that they could see what it takes to take their play to the next level. It was humbling for a lot of teams that thought they were good because they'd played several weekends together and done well against lame competition. For other teams it was eye-opening, because they were quite good, held their own, and saw possibilities for their team play that hadn't occurred to them. Based on their records in preliminary rounds, the top 8 pro teams went forward into exclusively professional play to determine the professional champions, and the top 8 amateur teams moved on to compete among themselves for the amateur title.

If an amateur team placed ahead of a pro team in the preliminary round, they had the choice of going pro, literally in the midst of the event! In fact, in that first year, Dallas 1993, a team did this and ended up taking 4th place!

In 1993 and 1994, there was a balance in the number of amateur and pro players. In 1995, however, there were almost 3 times as many amateur teams. Depending on their draw, some amateur teams had to play against pro teams whereas other amateur teams didn't. So this had awful consequences, and it still does today, because

moters were getting richer and the players were getting worse.

NPPL was formed at the end of 1992. It was made up of 24 team captains. I was the coordinator for the first year, and I pretty much gave up playing so that everyone would view me as neutral. From the start, one of our central concerns was that diminishing team size requirements were diluting skills. Just about everybody could put a team together, and just about everybody did.

NPPL wanted to preserve the highest possible level of competition, to set competitive standards that average paintball enthusiasts couldn't meet unless they put significant time and energy into training as a team. We were really pushing for the division that eventually arose at tournaments between professional and amateur game play. The NPPL tournaments in 1993 made this distinction for the first time. People registered themselves as pro or amateur according to their own sense of their level of play. What was really

ADAM: You sound like you want to get back into the fray. Any chance that we'll see you in any tournaments.

STEVE: Truth be told, there's simply nothing like playing with people whose minds you can practically read.

Given the chance to play at that level again, and I mean with a truly fantastic team that could compete for a title, [*grins*] I would have to go for it.

you get good amateur teams taken out of the running and ill feelings. They simply haven't reset the rules to reflect the reality that there are so many amateur teams.

Anyway, all of the tournaments pretty much adopted this pro/amateur distinction by the mid-1990s, or simply banned pro teams from certain tournaments.

ADAM: How do you feel about 15-man versus 5-man teams?

STEVE: 15 man teams are harder to put together, but you can do more with them. More is possible in terms of tactics. People don't account for the substantial role chance and dumb luck play in a 5-on-5 game. I mean really, you lose 1 guy and you've lost 20% of your force! On 15 player teams, you can adapt after losing 8 guys and go on to win the game. There's very little opportunity for true team play in today's 5-on-5 game. It was more rewarding and more competitive with 15-man teams. More about skills and training than it's become. That, at least, is my perspective on it.

The British had 12-on-12 for a while, but that became 10-on-10. It's strictly 10- and 5- man teams now.

Flag in hand, Steve Davidson sprints to victory.
Courtesy of Steve Davidson

The Paintball Necessities of Life

• **Goggles** • **Guns** • **Hoppers** • **Compressed Air** • **Paintballs**

GOGGLES

It's all fun and games until someone loses an eye

Without a doubt, protective eyewear is the most essential piece of paintball equipment you will ever purchase. A paintball travelling at 300 feet per second fired from 20 feet away can easily obliterate an eyeball, so safety must be your primary concern. As Rob Rubin is fond of saying to beginners before he takes them out for a game, "Your goggles must remain on at all times when you're on the field. If I see you even start to lift them, I'm going to tackle you, which may be unpleasant, but is infinitely better than losing an eye. Do yourselves a favor and follow this rule." Whether you are playing at a field or in your backyard, be sure to wear a paintball certified goggle system. Reliable goggle systems can be purchased for $30–$40, but the better ones cost $80–$90.

Most come with face armor and ear protection, which is required at every reputable field. The lens must be American Society for Testing and Materials (ASTM) tested, and approved for paintball. Other goggles are not acceptable, because they simply can't withstand the impact of a paintball.

Superior goggles come with features that maximize your field of vision, minimize glare, are well ventilated to prevent fogging, and have lenses that are easily and quickly replaced. They also use materials that increase the likelihood that paintballs will bounce rather than break.

There are many different kinds of goggles, and some are bound to fit you better than others, both physically and monetarily. We recommend trying on different kinds before making a purchasing decision.

Is that a gun in your pocket or...

Firepower

The second most important piece of equipment is your paintball gun, sometimes referred to as a marker because it literally marks other players. For the purposes of this book, guns are used only to shoot paintballs (and wouldn't it be a better world if that were the case). As you'll see, guns come in all shapes and sizes, but employ very similar firing mechanisms.

Main Body

The main body or frame of the gun is the handle, trigger, and the chamber, which contains the cocking mechanism and the bolt.

Some guns give you the option of attaching your own barrels and different sized hoppers and compressed air. The chamber or breech is where the ball awaits the rush of air that fires it when you pull the trigger. Near the chamber is something called a *ball detent*. This mechanism holds the paintball in place so it doesn't roll out. It also stops more than one ball from feeding into the chamber. The paint-

ball is fired out of the chamber and through the barrel. The barrel is a long tube that guides the paintball in a straight path as it leaves the gun. There are many styles available and they screw into the main body. Many say that brass barrels are the best because they have the least friction on the paintball (they are the cheapest). Others swear by heavier stainless steel barrels. Some only play with aluminum. A lot of designs have holes (called porting)drilled into them in different patterns.

Keep the ammo coming!

Hopper or Loader

Basically a hopper is a plastic inverted bottle that holds your paintballs and allows them to feed into the chamber. Most hoppers rely on a gravity feed approach. Some however, are motorized and ensure that another paintball will fall into place after one is shot. If rapid firing is key to your game, make sure you have one of these.

Hoppers come in all sorts of sizes, some hold only 40 balls, while others can hold up to 300. The range of sizes is as follows (60, 80, 100, 130, 150, 200, 230, 300). Of course, by the time you read this, larger sizes may be available. Smaller hoppers are lighter, but carry fewer balls, creating that possibility of being caught short at the worst possible moment. The larger the hopper, the more balls you can fire before having to reload. Of course, this also makes the gun itself heavier. Most experienced players gravitate toward the large hoppers.

Bringing on the air!

Air Power

The air tank is crucial. On most guns, it attaches horizontally off the back of the gun, and literally screws on. Some players prefer a vertical mount to keep liquid CO_2, which is an inevitable and potentially very annoying byproduct of firing, on the bottom of the tank away from the gun. The most common propellant used in paintball is CO_2. Almost all fields supply a tank with their rental guns. Other propellants include nitrogen and high pressure air (HPA). HPA is just regular air. The great thing about it is that it won't freeze or turn to liquid in the cold like CO_2 and nitrogen. HPA containers have very high pressures (as high as 4500 psi).

Most of the tanks are currently made of aluminum, which is preferred to steel because it is lighter. More expensive air tanks enable you to check the status of your air reserves. Some of the more elaborate models can even be worn on your back. This changes your experience of the game entirely; the gun no longer has weight, and you're not going to run out of air as quickly, but you're running around with air tanks strapped to your back, which some players find annoying.

STEVE DAVIDSON BEING CAUGHT SHORT

"When I started playing in the early 1980s, fields were charging twenty to thirty cents a ball and fifty cents a twelve gram. You were considered a nut if you carried more than about fifty rounds onto the field. Well, I was a nut. I carried a hundred rounds. You see, I got caught short one time. But never again. I'm never going to be stuck out there without ammunition again."

Paintballs

By now it's probably clear that a big part of this game is about splattering paintballs on your opponents. Paintballs come in a variety of sizes: .50, .62 (which is often called, .60), .63, .68, and .72 caliber. .68 caliber paintballs are spherical and dominate the market. The paint substance is composed of washable, nonflammable, food grade dye. In the early days it was oil based, and players held *de facto* turpentine parties at the end of the day. Not so anymore. Today, regular laundry detergents will do the trick!

Accessories

In most cases, you play a couple of 15 minute paintball games using 1 air tank and topping off your hopper in between sessions. But there will come a time when you'll be playing a significantly longer game, and will need to replenish your supplies on the field. Or, a ball may break in your gun, and you'll need to clean it with a squeegee on the fly. In those moments, you'll be glad you brought the following accessories.

Harness—Usually something worn around the waist that holds extra supplies—extra air, extra paint, maybe even smoke bombs. Typically they are called 4-1 or 8-1 or 6-1. The "1" is usually a vertical receptacle for an air tank. The other numbers signifies spaces for horizontal guppies (tubes for holding paintballs).

Squeegee—An instrument you'll find enormous useful if a paintball explodes in your barrel. This is also useful for the maintenance and upkeep of your gun.

Enter a game with these add-ons and you'll never be caught short

Remote—An air supply separate from your gun carried on your harness. This tank is connected to your gun by a long, flexible hose. This is useful because it takes weight off your gun and makes it lighter and more maneuverable. It is a cheap addition. A good used one runs about $30–$40.

Now let's take a look at the game of paintball, from the perspective of a new player.

—AWC

You're not a paint magnet, you're a newbie!

Rules to Play By

DON'T GET SPLATTERSHOCKED!

Here's a shocker. When you play paintball for the first time, you're going to make mistakes. We all did and we all still do. Knowing this going in will help you avoid splatter-shock: the distinct feeling that you are a paintball magnet who is hopelessly awful at this game. Bottom line: Don't get bent out of shape if things don't go well during your first couple of games. Mistakes early on are to be expected and present you with great learning opportunities.

In this section, you'll find the not-so-secret secrets of top-notch paintball players. You could study every word of these insights, memorize and recite them 3 times each before going to bed every night for many months, and still not improve your game. That's because you have to play the game to get good at it.

But, these 'secrets' are useful as guides. Store them in the back of your mind. Visualize yourself doing these things. They're worth being aware of, no doubt about it. They're even more effective when you're so accustomed to them that they become practically instinctual. To make that happen, there's absolutely no substitute for playing experience.

The key to becoming a player whose name strikes fear in the hearts of your opponents and commands respect among the elite is quite simple. Play the game. And then play it again. And then play it some more. Play with and against people who are better than you are. Stand back from the game and see it as a whole. Experiment with being aggressive and defensive, with taking different positions. Be creative. Above all, play the game for the fun of it. That is, after all, the main point, and, it just so happens that having fun will make you demand more of yourself every time.

You have to spill much paint before the wisdom in the following tidbits will become second nature.

Being a great paintball player is a path, not a destination. Enjoy every second of your journey!

- **The very first rule is never EVER take off your goggles!** This can't be stressed enough. Taking off your mask can be very detrimental to your vision's health. A paintball travelling at 10 feet per second would easily pop your eye out of your head. **Don't ever take your facial protection off.** Even in designated areas, look around yourself to make sure there isn't some doofus waving an uncorked gun.

- Make sure you understand your gun and its limitations, whether it's a rental or your own.

- As soon as you get off the field of play, put a barrel plug in the end of your barrel and switch on the safety. This is essential paintball etiquette and is only meant to save you from experiencing or causing excruciating pain or injury to others. If you see somebody waving a gun around that doesn't have a plug in it, remind them to put one in immediately.

- **Paintballs do not hurt when they hit.** Well, sometimes they hurt a little bit, but usually they just sting for a moment. You won't really feel sore until the day. I have found that paintballs that hit you and don't break hurt a little more because they hit and bounce off. The time they are in contact with you is shorter and thus the force is greater (for all you wannabe nerds out there, the impulse equation from physics justifies this statement). When it does break, it is in contact with you longer and is cushioned by your skin, fat, etc.

- **Wear dark clothes; don't wear white.** White is just too bright, you will be too easy to spot and eliminate.

- **Wear some type of boots or comfortable hiking/running shoes.** Some people prefer football or soccer cleats. They are comfortable, light, quick, and provide excellent traction in grass and mud. A lot of paintball players are using cleats these days.

- **Always be honest.** If you get hit and see the splat on you, please raise your hand and exit the game. Redeem yourself in the next game; there's always a next game. People who try to wipe their paint off and think they can get away with it are simply lame. Ask yourself if being perceived as a loser is worth staying in the game. When everybody knows you're a cheater, you'll find it increasingly hard to find anyone who wants to

Welcome to the Game of Paintball

play with you. *If you cheat, you'll never truly win!*

- **Don't ever call an advanced paintball player a cheater.** They hate that and take their games really seriously. No matter what happens, don't do this. That is how seriously some people take their game. They are mostly very honest, down to earth people. But, sometimes they'll respond less than graciously. And you know what? It just isn't worth it. If an advanced player (or any player!) cheats on a regular basis, talk discreetly about it to the referee and your friends between games.

- **Don't be afraid to ask or learn.** Even with the amount of information technology available these days, broadband connections to the web sites like splatterzone.com or warpig.com are no substitute for asking questions on the field between games. There are certain basic things that more experienced players can clarify for the beginner (e.g., tactical stuff, tidbits of advice) that may make a difference in your play.

- **Always appoint a team captain and follow his orders no matter what.** The team captain does not have to be the most experienced or the wildest or the most intelligent person in your group. But there has to be one captain. Follow orders even if you think you have a better plan. Don't be a gloryhound. When a team commits to a plan, it's able to do things that individuals acting alone can't do. Obey your captain even if it does not conform to your method of play. If you think you have a great plan, ask to be captain for a game. You have nothing to lose.

- **Be alert and never focus too much on one thing.** Don't keep shooting at the same guy behind the same bunker over and over again. Move on and surprise him from the side or another angle.

- **Don't stay in the same spot too long.** If you are in a fort, don't keep shooting from the same side forever. It's not productive. Go to the other end; go to the second level. Move away from the bunker, walk out unprotected and hold people down. *Don't stay put!*

- **Never give up.** Whether you run out of air, paint or energy, just don't ever stop or quit. You are still useful. No one has to know that you are on your last leg.

- **Never call yourself dead if you are unsure.** If you question whether a shot hit you and splatted, call a paintcheck and the referee will find out if you've been eliminated. Don't just call yourself out because you felt a hit. Wait for the referee to confirm.

  —AWC

That's just for starters!

Mistakes New Players Make

WHERE THE HECK AM I?

Beginners are so pumped up with adrenaline that they aren't able to focus on the game as a whole. They tend to lose track of their position in relation to their teammates and foes. Because they feel like they're all alone in the game, they tend to be overly concerned with protecting themselves. Rather than engaging their opponents aggressively, they crouch behind the thickest bush or in the deepest hole available. Effectively, they take themselves out of the action: they can't see anything, are unable to provide information or cover fire, and are basically squatting on the spot where they'll be eliminated. They may tell themselves that they're in a great ambush position. The problem is that most beginners who think this way end up getting themselves ambushed. Take a few deep breaths and look from side to side every once in a while. Stretching your neck out before playing is a helpful way of reminding yourself to look from side to side.

CHARGE!

Some beginners are so pumped up that they run headlong into the fray only to find themselves pinned down by copious hostile paint without support or a good escape option. Their initial eliminations can be fantastic to watch as they squirm under a barrage of paint, but they probably don't feel so great. So listen up! It's always a good idea to choose your first

shelter before the game starts. A good shelter is one that will provide you with reasonable cover, while allowing you good opportunities to see the field, shoot, and advance. You must be within range of your opponents, but not so close that you can't use trees or barricades for cover. If the shelter you're behind is so small that you can't stick your head out, make sure you'll have a teammate behind you and call for him to keep your opponents busy while you reach a better position.

ARE YOU MY MOTHER?

It's going to sound simplistic, but you should really take a moment to meet the people on your team. You don't have to swear blood oaths, but it's definitely in your interests to talk to them a little and briefly study their appearance. The last thing you want to do is shoot your own teammates, and they'll be more likely to respond to your pleas for help if you call them by name.

HEY, THAT HURT...WHOA, THAT ONE REALLY...OUCH!!!

To watch the way they go out, you'd think newbies are masochists. When hit, they'll wait for the incoming paint to stop pouring before they stand up and walk away. This means they'll get out wearing two or three layers of bright colors. The best policy is to get out of the way of incoming paint and stand up right away. Remember, if you surrender and your opponents keep pumping you full of paint, referees will take *them* out of the game! So if you're shot, and know it, get up and out of the way quickly.

EYES WIDE SHUT!

Usually, if you see your opponent before he spots you, you've won. Of course, although this fact is probably self-evident to most beginners, they tend to be averse to sticking their heads out for a look-see at the action. So they never look around. Then, the newbies who do use their eyes tend to get tunnel vision, focusing so intensely on one single direction that they they close their ears to all noises, especially those coming from their sides. Don't be afraid to look around. You need as much information as you can get. Of course, your head will be a target, so look by the side of your barricade rather than above the top of it. If you decide to look above the top, don't do it for more than one or two seconds. It'll take that long for your opponents to spot you, take aim, shoot, and hit you.

FOR OUR MAIN COURSE, WE'LL BE SERVING A SITTING DUCK...

Newbies don't move enough. If you're not useful where you are, don't stay there.

The game is about moving, sighting, and shooting. It is dynamic. There may be situations in which you will be playing defense or setting up an ambush, and staying put is appropriate for a set amount of time. But for the most part, responding to the game as it evolves requires you to stay in motion. If the rest of your team breaks through the enemy's defenses, it means they would have done better with you among them; additionally, there

are no opponents left to protect your station against. If the rest of your team is beaten, they may have done better with you among them, and when your opponents arrive at your base, boy will you feel alone! Another example: Look at a newbie under fire. He's trying to make himself as flat as possible. As flat and useless as a flat tire. When you're in a position where you are easily pinned down, with no close help at hand, there are only three things you should think of doing:

1. Get away as fast as possible
2. Shoot back
3. Yell for help and indicate your opponent's location. If they're shooting at you, it means they've spotted you, so don't be afraid to give your position away.

Finally, when you are spotted (when you shoot at someone, you almost always are), be prepared to move to a new location so your opponent won't know where you are or from where your next shot will come.

HELP ME ... HELP YOU

Beginners very seldom communicate well. A beginner keeps his problems to himself (he doesn't ask for help when needed) and doesn't brag about his knowledge (he doesn't tell you about the opponents he's spotted).

The only good reason to be quiet is to remain stealthy. Once you're spotted, there's no reason not to yell, scream, and shout if you have something useful to say. You'll get the help you need, and give your teammates the information they need to kick in.

I LOVE THE SMELL OF PAINTBALLS IN THE MORNING...

Usually, beginners are very accurate and seldom miss a player who's 10 feet away, especially if he is on the same team. They imagine that their gun has the power to nail targets over a hundred yards away. They also shoot too soon, and at everything that moves. Of course, all this does is give away their position and waste paint. If you haven't been spotted, your first shot must take your target out. Wait until the flight path is clear, or until the opponent sees you. Be patient, especially when you're on defense. The price of paint being what it is, they think that a ball that doesn't end on an opponent's camouflage is lost, so they never provide cover or intimidating fire. Sometimes, you have to shoot at opponents you can't see.

- **To help a teammate out of a dire situation!**
- **To make an opponent nervous behind his tree!**
- **To keep his head down while one of your teammates is closing in on him.**
- **To make noise to distract opponents' attention.**

—AWC

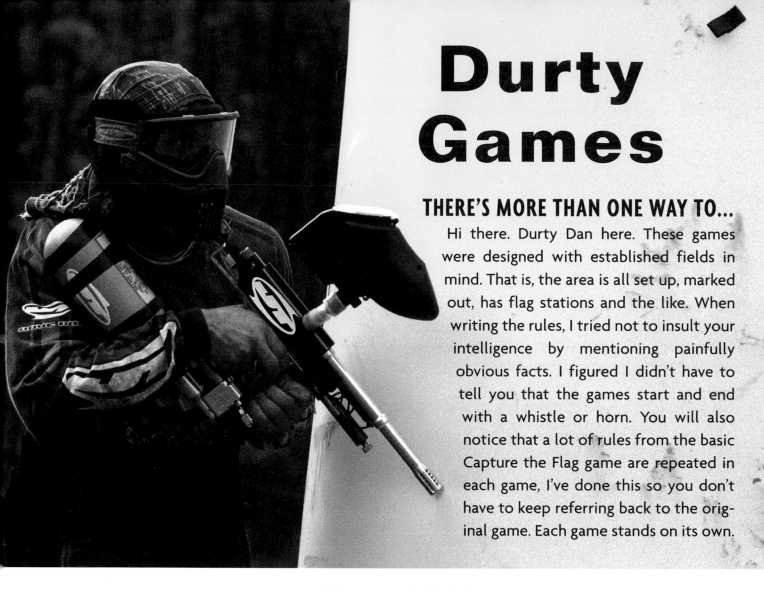

Durty Games

THERE'S MORE THAN ONE WAY TO...

Hi there. Durty Dan here. These games were designed with established fields in mind. That is, the area is all set up, marked out, has flag stations and the like. When writing the rules, I tried not to insult your intelligence by mentioning painfully obvious facts. I figured I didn't have to tell you that the games start and end with a whistle or horn. You will also notice that a lot of rules from the basic Capture the Flag game are repeated in each game, I've done this so you don't have to keep referring back to the original game. Each game stands on its own.

Field owners will find these games an interesting addition to the games they may already run on their field. You may need to adapt the rules to your own particular needs, but remember that safety is always your number one concern.

I purposely did not include games like speedball. (These games and other games requiring structures will already exist where the structures exist on the field.) Not every field will have a speedball course, a village or a fort. The reason for not including these types of games is an attempt on my part to make these games universal. With a little preparation you should be able to play these games on any field in the world.

Speaking of fields, do not confuse "established" fields, with "commercial" fields. Established fields have a playing area already set up to play at least Capture the Flag. Whether it's a "legitimate/commercial" field or a "bootleg/outlaw" field is beside the point.

I have been to some "legitimate/commercial" fields where I was afraid to take off my goggles at any time, unless I was in my car with the windows rolled up. I have also heard of a "bootleg/outlaw" field who sent a guy home for having a hot gun!

Unless otherwise stated, these five rules apply to all the games in this chapter. These are referred to as…

GENERAL RULES

1. All players must begin the game at their flag station (or assigned starting point) and cannot leave that area until the game begins.

2. Players who are hit are out of the game.

3. Players who are eliminated may not, by word or gesture, indicate any intentions or locations of the opposing team members.

4. If a player is eliminated while he is carrying the flag, he must drop the flag where he was hit, or hang it on the nearest available object (not another player).

5. When a player is carrying the flag, it must remain visible at all times and be carried in the hand, over the arm, or around the neck.

—DD

Known as the "World's Most Famous Recreational Player," Durty Dan started his writing career in 1992 when Randy Kamiya (then Editor for *Action Pursuit Games Magazine*) published his first article in the February issue. Since then he has written for *Action Pursuit Games*, *Paintball Sports International* (in his column Rec-Ball), *Paintball Industry Magazine* (no longer in publication), *Paintball News*, *Paintball RAGazine* (no longer in publication), and *Paintball Magazine*.
He has been playing since 1984 and has just recently celebrated his 15th anniversary of playing paintball. Since 1992, he has had an amazing two hundred and fifty articles published, and is in the process of writing a paintball book.

CAPTURE THE FLAG

Requirements

Two flag stations

Two even teams

Two flags, hung in opponents' flag stations.

Duration

30 minutes

Rules

All players must begin the game at their flag station (or assigned starting point) and cannot leave that area until the game begins.

Players who are hit are out of the game.

If a player is eliminated while he is carrying the flag, he must drop the flag where he was hit, or hang it on the nearest available object. (Never another player).

Players who are eliminated may not indicate any intentions or locations of the opposing team members.

When a player is carrying the flag, it must remain visible at all times and must be carried in the hand, over the arm, or around the neck.

Objective

Capture the opposing team's flag and return it to your base!

CHARGE OF THE LIGHT BRIGADE

Requirements
Two flag stations.
Two even teams.
Two flags hung in opponents' stations.

Duration
20 minutes.

Rules
All General Rules apply.

Objective
Hang your flag in the opposition's flag station.

SHOOT THE CAPTAIN

Requirements
Two flag stations.

Two even teams.

The teams are brought to their respective flag stations.

The Captain is tied to one end of a 20 foot rope, the other end of which is tied to an immobile object like a tree or fence post.

To spice up the action, tether the Captain's gun rather than him.

Another variation is to limit all offensive players to 20 paintballs and give the Captains unlimited amounts of paint.

Duration
30 minutes

Rules
The Captain cannot undo his tether.

If playing the tethered paintgun variation, the Captain can abandon his paintgun, but cannot use another paintgun.

If you use the limited paint option, players cannot share paintballs.

General Rules 1,2, and 3 apply.

Objective
Eliminate the opposing team's captain.

DUEL

Requirements
Two players are the duelists with the same type of pistol.
A third person to play the Warder.
A clear area.

Duration
As long as it takes, usually no more than 12 seconds.

Rules
Two players stand back to back.
The Warder is standing about ten feet to the side.
Both players are armed with pistols. The pistols each have one paintball in them ready to fire.

The paintguns can have no other paintballs in them. This is a one shot deal.
The warder then says, "This, Gentlemen, is an affair of honor. You will take ten paces on my command, then turn and fire. If either of you turn before the count of ten, it will be my unfortunate duty to shoot you down." (Or something to this effect.)
The duelists then pace off in time to the Warder's cadence. At the count of ten they turn and fire.
The paintball has to break for the elimination to count.
Players cannot side step or lie down, but they may kneel if they wish.
No other rules apply.

Objective
The person who is not eliminated wins.

ATTACK AND DEFEND

Requirements

Two teams of equal strength:One team, the Attackers; the other, the Defenders.

Choose a defensible area to serve as a flag station.

Defenders should be restricted to the confines of the flag station.

Set boundaries that limit the movement of the defenders out of the flag station.

Duration

10 minutes.

Rules

Defenders cannot leave the flag station area, or the areas of the flag station they are charged with defending.

The Attackers can attack from any place on the field.

General Rules 1, 2, 3 apply.

Objective

Attackers: Pull the flag off its support (a string, branch, cone, etc.)

Defenders: Stop the Attackers from pulling the flag.

ANNIHILATOR

Requirements

Set up multiple five man teams.

The maximum limit is four teams for every acre of playing area.

Place teams in the area so that they are not in line of sight of each other.

To make score-keeping easier, the teams may be accompanied by a referee and each team may should their own distinct color of paint.

Duration

30–45 minutes

Rules

Teams will stay in their starting stations until the start of the game signal.

Teams get points for each elimination they inflict on other teams.

There are no points for surviving members of the team.

General Rules 1, 2, 3 apply.

Objective

Survive and be the team with the highest score at the end of the game.

BLACKJACK

Requirements
Two flag stations
Two even teams
Two flags, hung in opponents' flag stations.
Each player is only allowed 21 paintballs.

Duration
30 minutes

Rules
Players are not allowed to share paintballs.
Players who shoot all of their paintballs must
    leave the game immediately.
All General Rules apply.

Objective
Capture the opposing team's flag and return it to
    your base!

BUNNY HUNT

Requirements
A "Bunny" (one person) and Hunters (everybody
    else).
One player volunteers to be the Bunny. To give the
    Bunny some kind of advantage, choose one of
    these options.
OPTION 1-Give the Bunny a semiautomatic
    paintgun plus a garbage can lid or other device
    to use as a shield.
OPTION 2-Give the Bunny as much paint as he's
    comfortable with, and restrict the Hunters to 20
    paintballs each.

Duration
20 minutes.

Rules
If the Bunny chooses OPTION 1, hits on the shield
    do not count as an elimination.
The Bunny has a 5 minute head start into the
    playing area.
A signal will be given so that the Bunny knows
    when the game is started.
All hunters must start at the same time and from
    the same place.
When using the limited paint option, if a hunter
    runs out of paint, he is out of the game.
General Rules 1, 2, and 3 apply.

Objective
If you're the Bunny, SURVIVAL IS THE GOAL!
If you're a Hunter, eliminate the BUNNY!

RECON

Requirements

Multiple Five-Man Teams.

Checkpoints (one for every team on the field) are spaced throughout the field. Each is clearly marked with a flag or similar ornament.

Each checkpoint also has a gun hanging from a string. Each checkpoint has a different colored gun.

Each player has a card attached to his wrist (a playing card will do!) by a string, rubber band, or elastic band.

Each team starts near a checkpoint.

Duration

20 minutes.

Rules

Players must mark their card with the guns provided at the checkpoint.

Every team member must attempt to mark his card, although this is not mandatory.

Players who are eliminated are not allowed to count the points they collected with their final team score.

General Rules 1, 2, and 3 apply.

Scoring

- 1 point for each different-colored mark on a card.

- 5 bonus points if all team cards are marked by at least two checkpoints.

- 5 bonus points for each additional checkpoint where all team cards are marked.

- 2 bonus points for every team member with card marks from every checkpoint.

Objective

The team with the highest score wins.

GETTYSBURG

Requirements
No bulk loaders, loading tubes or any solid
  apparatus used to hold or feed paintballs.
Two flag stations.
Two evenly numbered teams.
Two flags, hung in their respective flag stations.

Duration
30 minutes.

Rules
Players can carry as many paintballs as they
  wish.
Paintballs must be loose or in a plastic bag.
They cannot be in tubes, hoppers, or any kind of
  bulk loading system.
Players can only load paintballs by hand, one at
  a time into their paintguns and cannot load
  another paintball until they shoot the one in
  the paintgun.
General Rules apply.

Objective
Capture the opposing team's flag and return it to
  your base.

DOWN BUT NOT OUT

Basic Requirements
Two flag stations.
Two even teams.
Two flags, hung in their respective flag stations.
One white sock per player to be provided.

Duration
30 minutes.

Rules

1. When a player is hit, he calls himself out and lays or sits on the ground (using common sense). The player then places a sock over the barrel of his paintgun to indicate that he has been hit. He cannot move from this location until tagged. This is referred to as Waiting.

2. If a waiting player is tagged by a teammate he is back in the game. (The player, of course, removes the sock.)

3. Players who are waiting cannot shoot or disclose the positions or intentions of opposing players.

4. If a waiting player is tagged by an opposing player, he is out of the game.

5. If a waiting player feels that no one will find him, or he is tired of waiting, he can take himself out of the game. In this case the player cannot be tagged back into the game.

6. There is no limit to how many times a player can be tagged back into the game.

7. Players waiting to be tagged cannot shoot or be shot at.

8. All General Rules 1, 3, 4, and 5 apply.

Objective
Capture the opposing team's flag and return it to your base.

PAINTBURNER

Requirements

Create, depending on group size, as many three man teams as you can.

Odd players out will wait in the Designated Holding Area for enough eliminated players to return and will make up the next in-going team.

Teams start the game in different areas of the field.

Duration

30 Minutes.

Rules

1. Once a player is hit, he proceeds to the Designated Holding Area.

2. Once there are three players in the Designated Holding Area, they rejoin the game as a new team.

3. A referee will escort a newly formed team out into the field, away from the action and any other teams, if possible and signal their entry with a short whistle blast.

4. Players cannot shoot or be shot at while being escorted by the referee.

5. Only General Rules 1, 2, and 3 apply.

Objective

Fun! In which case, everybody wins!

REINFORCEMENTS

Requirements
Two flag stations.
Two even teams.
Two flags, hung in their respective flag stations.
Flag stations double as Reinforcement Rally points.

Duration
30 minutes.

Rules
1. Eliminated players go back to their flag station.

2. One player wears a special armband. This is the only player that can go back to the flag station to get reinforcements.

3. If the player wearing the armband is eliminated, he proceeds back to the flag station. He then collects those players who wish to rejoin the game and he himself rejoins the game. In this case the eliminated players have not choice but to be reinforcements. They cannot stay behind and defend the flag station.

4. Players can elect to stay behind and defend the flag station, with the exception of REINFORCEMENTS Rule 3. When they return to the flag station they are automatically active defenders.

5. Players returning to the flag station must physically tag the flag to become active defenders. If the flag is not at the flag stations the players are considered out of the game as they enter the flag station.

6. Players who are hit are out of the game but the player is only out until he reaches his flag station. Players eliminated at the flag station are out of the game.

7. Only General Rules 1, 3, 4 and 5 apply.

Objective
Capture the opposing team's flag and return it to your base.

KICK THE BUCKET

Requirements
Two flag stations.
Two even teams.
Instead of flags, a bucket is placed on the ground under where the flag usually hangs. This bucket must be made of a light plastic (remember, someone is going to kick this thing).

Duration
15 minutes.

Rules
1. The bucket cannot be moved by the team which owns it.

2. If a player is hit before he kicks the bucket, the kick (if completed) does not count as a win, the referee then resets the bucket as quickly as possible.

3. Only General Rules 1, 2, and 3 apply.

Objective
Kick the opposing team's bucket over.

TROPHY HUNTER

Requirements

Players act individually to gather trophies on the field. No teams.

Each player wears three armbands on one arm (these are referred to as trophies).

Players are interspersed in the playing field.

A signal will sound every five minutes (referred to as the five minute signal) and will be different than the start and end of game signal.

(The period between these signals will be referred to as the waiting period.)

Duration

30 Minutes.

Rules

1. Players who are hit must drop to the ground (using common sense) and remain motionless and quiet until the next five minute signal.

2. Another player (not necessarily the one who hit him) has the waiting period to collect one trophy. Once the trophy is taken no more trophies can be taken from the player during that Waiting Period.

3. When the five minute signal sounds the player is immediately in the game.

4. Only general rules 1, 2, and 3 apply.

Objective

The player with the most trophies wins.

HOSTAGE RESCUE

Requirements
Two teams:
1. Rescuers
2. Terrorists

Terrorists pick one Rescuer to act as the Hostage.

Two hostage holding areas are designated. The location of one of the hostage holding areas is disclosed to the Rescuers. Terrorists do not know which location was disclosed.

Establish an area the Rescuers will have to take the Hostage in order to win the game.

This is known as sanctuary.

Terrorists know where sanctuary is.

Duration
30 minutes.

Rules
1. Terrorists are given a five minute head start to take the hostage to one of the hostage holding areas.

2. A start of game signal is given to let terrorists know when the game has begun.

3. Terrorists cannot move the hostage out of the hostage holding area.

4. The Hostage cannot attempt escape.

5. If the Hostage is hit, the team that hit him looses.

6. The Hostage must have at least one Rescuer with him when he reaches sanctuary for the Rescuers to win.

7. If the Hostage finds himself alone for some reason, after being rescued, he must stay where he is and wait for the Rescuers to find him again. He may call out for help if he wishes.

8. Only General Rules 1, 2, and 3 apply.

Objectives
Terrorists: Stop the Rescuers from bringing Hostage to sanctuary.

Rescuers: Bring Hostage to sanctuary.

TAG

Rules

1. No teams-this is a free-for-all!
2. Select a person to be "It."
3. Disperse players in the playing area.
4. The player who is "It" starts the game by sounding the start game signal.
5. The player who is "It" must wear an armband,which must be clearly visible.
6. When a player is hit by "It" he must stand where he is. The player then receives the armband from "It" becomes the new "It."
7. The player who is "It" and the player who is receiving the armband cannot shoot or be shot at.
8. The new "It" puts the armband on and cannot shoot or be shot at until the player calls out "ready."
9. The new "It" cannot shoot at the old "It," and vice versa.
10. When "It" has been eliminated, the game is over.
11. Only General Rules 1, 2, and 3 apply.

Objective

Everybody wins by just having fun.

TRAITOR

Requirements

Two Teams

Two flag stations required but only as starting points.

A deck of cards is taken two kings and two jacks are removed, then a number of normal (nonface) cards are taken from the deck.

The number is the total amount of players MINUS 4. (It's minus four because two people will be drawing jack and two will be drawing kings.)

Then two piles are made, a king and a jack goes into each pile and then the remainder of the cards that were drawn will be separated evenly between the two piles.

The two piles are shuffled separately and one team will draw from one pile and the other team will draw from the other.

Duration

30–45 minutes.

Rules

1. Only those players who drew the kings are to reveal their cards. The players who drew the kings are the leaders for each team.

2. The players who drew the jacks are the TRAITORS. They do not reveal their identity.

3. Leaders will wear two armbands on EACH arm to designate themselves as leaders.

4. Traitors may turn on their teams at any time they see fit, once the game starts.

5. Only General Rules 1, 2, and 3 apply.

Objective

Eliminate the other team's leader.

(If the TRAITOR eliminates the leader the opposite team wins. e.g. Red team TRAITOR nukes Red team Leader, Blue team wins.

HITTING HOME ON THE RANGE

I often harp on about marksmanship and accuracy. I advocate shooting hundreds of balls at the range. But, for most people, this is not very entertaining.

Just because I love you guys and gals so much, I've invented seven fun games for you to play on the range. All games can involve any number of players, taking turns, unless otherwise noted. Also, the games are more or less designed to allow a mix of technology, semis can go up against pump and stock classes.

So now, not only will you be having fun, you'll also be learning a valuable skill. (Whether you want to, or not!)

HIDE 'N' SEEK

Requirements
No teams-everyone for themselves.

Rules
1. Select one player to be "It."
2. Establish a "home" area and within It, an object players have to tag to be "home free."
3. Establish two different signals, one as the start/end game signal and one as "home" signal.
4. All players gather at one entrance to the playing field.
5. The player who is "It" begins a slow count to one hundred, during this count the players race into the playing area and hide.
6. At the end of the count the player who is "It" sounds the start game signal and enters the playing field.
7. Players must try to make it back to "home" before getting caught by"It."
8. The player who is "It" does not have to hit the players to eliminated them. He simply calls to them and points them out ("It" has to actually see them at the time) and the player must go back to "home."
9. Players who are hit by other players or the player who is "It" are out of the game and must return to "home."
10. Each player returning home, no matter what the reason, must sound the player "home" signal.
11. The game is ended when the player who is "It" is hit.
12. Only General Rules 1 and 3 apply.

Objective
Long Version—The player, when he or she was "It" who caught the most players. (Players hit by "It" are not included in this number.)
Short Version—(One game) the player who eliminates "It."

How to Settle a Tie
Replay the game from beginning between tied players. Repeat if necessary. With Reach for the Top, replay the last round, players must get 10 for 10. For One Player Dual replay one round for the best time.

RAPID FIRE

Requirements
More than one shooter.
5-10 targets

Rules
Select a number of targets (between 5 and 10)

Shooters fire at the targets as fast as they can, but are restricted to shooting at a target only once.
An official measures the time with a stop watch.
Penalties: add one second to the time for every miss.
To win: Shortest time.

RANDOM RAPID FIRE

Requirements
Ten targets, each has its own number

The official calls out the numbers in random order (the order is determined for each player by a random drawing of ten numbered cards, prior to the player's arrival on the range.)

Shooter can only shoot at the target whose number was called.

Official calls the number (after the first target is called) as the player shoots the previous target.

Penalties
Add one second for every miss

Add two seconds for shooting at the wrong target (hit or miss)

Objective
Shortest time

SNAP SHOT

Requirements
Players and targets, as many of each as you want.

Rules
1. The paintgun cannot be put to shoulder or brought to eye level.
2. Several targets at several different ranges, number and position are up to the players.

3. Players are restricted to as many paintballs as there are targets, and can only shoot at each target once.

Scoring
Add 1 point for each hit; and

Subtract 1 point for each miss.

Objective
Person with the highest score wins.

LONG SHOT

Requirements
One target—a small can placed on an object at least 3 feet off the ground.

The can must placed so that it will fall over when hit.

Rules
Players shoot at can until they hit it and knock it to the ground.

Official counts the number of shots it took them to knock the can over (including the shot that knocked it over.)

Objective
Hit the can in the least number of shots.

REACH FOR THE TOP

Requirements
10 targets
-3 at short range (15–20 feet)
-4 at medium range (35–50 feet)
-3 at long range (80–100 feet)

Rules
1. Three rounds of shooting
2. To pass the round

First round—minimum 6 out of 10

Second round—minimum 7 out of 10

Third round—10 out of 10 (at this point the player has completed the game).

3. If the minimum is not met, the player cannot proceed to the next round and is eliminated for competition. Players can score higher than the minimum.

4. Players are limited to 10 paintballs per round.

5. Players can only shoot at target once per round.

Scoring
One point per hit.

Objective
Have the highest score.

FOLLOW ME

Requirements
Two shooters.

Rules
The two players flip a coin to see who will be the first shooter.
The first shooter calls a target and shoots at it.
If the first shooter hits the target: the second shooter must hit the target as well;

If the second shooter misses the target, the first shooter gets one point; and the first shooter calls a target and shoots again.
If the first shooter misses the target: the roles are reversed. (e.g., Billy is the first shooter, Joey is the second shooter. Billy misses, Joey takes the first shot until he misses)

Objective
The first shooter to reach 20 points.wins.

ONE PLAYER DUEL

Requirements
One player and one target

Rules
1. Player stands with his/her back to the target.
2. On command from official, the player begins to pace off, according to official's count.
3. Player turns and fires when official says "Fire".
4. Player is only allowed one shot.
5. Official starts timer at the start signal and stops if target is hit.
6. If the target is not hit, the round is not counted.
7. Players have three chances (rounds)
8. The players must be at the following distances, order is random, as chosen by the official (one distance for each round). Official draws only three distances out of the five.
   - 10 paces;
   - 5 paces;
   - 3 paces;
   - 8 paces; and
   - 12 paces.
9. Players take the best time out of the three rounds. If the player missed in all three rounds, the player is disqualified.

Objective
Hit all targets in fewest turns.

Photo courtesy of Jerry Braun

"When it comes to paintball, I live for the Big Game!"

For some players, the tournament is the highest level of play available. For others, like me, the pinnacle of paintball is **the big game.** An army of players, cheap paint prices, freaky people in hilarious costumes, big-name celebrities, massive confrontations, a sense of comraderie—the big game is where you'll find all of these things and more.

SO WHAT IS THIS BIG GAME THING?

In my neck of the woods when ten people show up to play, we say it's a good sized crowd. If forty people come, we praise the paintball deities for smiling upon us. I've heard some players talk about 200 players just arriving on a single day; if I ever experience anything like that, I'd be temporarily paralyzed with happiness.

But the Big Game blows all of these experiences out of the water.

Technically, the 'Big Game' is one that has a large number of players on the field at any given moment. Regionally, a game with 70 players at an unknown field is certainly awesome, but it pales in comparison to games with well over 500 players. These are the numbers you'll find at the Skirmish World Record Games.

Scenario Game or Big Game?

You may have heard of 'Scenario' games. It's true that those games attract large numbers of players, but they aren't what I mean by big games.

Scenario games either reenact an event of real combat, or invent a plausible chain of events for players to act out in a sort of large-scale, live-action, role-playing game. Role-playing games are not new. The concept has been around in paper formats before 1975 with such staples as Advanced Dungeons & Dragons (TSR). Players are even given a new identity to assume during the course of the game. It's pure fantasy play, and it definitely appeals to many paintball players, but it doesn't have anything to do with the Big Game.

Big Games are still paintball games, only on a larger scale. They have flag objectives and eliminations. Of course, players can assume any identity they wish to, but they are not playing out a 'story' as they would in a scenario game. No matter what or whom they look like, the game they're playing is still "Capture the Flag" or "Total Elimination."

Well run scenario games have point values for achieving special missions. Such as holding a 'bridge,' capturing a specific target, achieving specific operations and so on. This is meant to bring the scenario somewhat close to the actual event that occurred (or, at the very least, to what the organizers want to accomplish). Teams get points for achieving specific objectives, and a winner is tabulated at the end of the game.

The distinctions between scenario games and some big games may blur. Some big games have 'objective flag stations' to be held for points. And some are worth more than others. It helps to be 'in the know'.

Scenario games and Big games do share a bit in common, and, with a little tweaking, you can use the following information in both contexts.

Recon!

The first step is to find a big game. Where should you look? They're advertised in many mainstream publications, and by word of mouth. Ask the guys who run the fields you frequent; they should know (they're probably as eager to go as you are). You may wish to find somewhere close to home, although traveling can be half the fun if you're with friends!

It's very important to *know what you're getting yourself into before you play a big game.* Once you've discovered one, call for information. You want as much time as possible to plan properly for this kind of event. I recommend at least a month, but three months is better. You want to know the cost of the event and what it covers (e.g., does it include CO_2 and nitrogen refills?), how much paint will cost (or, even better, if you can bring your own?), will food be provided or available. You get the idea.

If you're not familiar with the area, ask about where you can stay in the area (e.g., local hotels, motels, or campgrounds). Most big game flyers will include most of this information, but it's still a good idea to verify everything , just in case something has changed.

Another good idea is to ask about the field. Knowing a bit about the terrain can be a good thing. My feet were sore for weeks after playing on the rocks of Pennsylvania. I could have protected them better if I'd learned about the field in advance.

The newest venue for information about big games is on the internet. You may already know about 'rec.sport.paintball' and 'alt.sport.paintball.' Through these two usenet newsgroups you can gain access to what I call the 'paintball hive-mind.' If you have a question about a specific field or a place that you've never played before, you can probably get an answer in a few days from someone who has been there. Some events have web pages about them as well.

The more informed you are, the better time you will have.

GEAR, GARB, AND GOODIES

What Do I Bring to the Big Game?

Bring what you bring to any paintball game! Yourself, goggles, harnesses, gun, gloves, squeegee, and all that stuff you probably play with all the other times you play. If you wear contact lenses, bring your eyedrops. Always bring multiple pairs of underwear and socks and backup sneakers or boots. Just make sure you've packed everything you need. When you're a few states away from home, realizing you forgot your goggles is pretty demoralizing.

Then there are the things you'd never think of bringing, but they don't hurt.

Bring extra money. Whoever thinks you can bring too much money is silly. Some big games have a vendors tent with more goodies to bring home with you. Not to mention how quickly eating out drains your cash no matter how affordable. Bring a tent, or some kind of portable shade; parking lots never have trees in them! Lawn chairs are great (trust me, car bumpers get uncomfortable after a few minutes!), and a cooler filled with ice, water, and Gatorade will make you the envy of many dehydrated participants. Packing a small first aid kit is invaluable as well. You get the idea.

Preparation is the key to playing the big games.

Photo courtesy of Jerry Braun

Arrival

As with any major event, showing up early has it's advantages. Better parking is worth it, believe me! If the event starts at 9 AM, you want to try and get there by 7:30 AM. I've had to walk a half a mile to the staging area with all my gear in tow. Avoid this if you can.

Once there you want to sign in right away. The sooner you do, the easier it is to get all your gear together, chronograph in (all guns must fire under 300 fps!), and just get comfortable. It's also pure joy to sit back and watch the people arrive in a panic as they try to prepare for mass orientation in under 10 minutes.

I'm Here, Now What?

First, relax. It's just another game of capture the flag. It's just that this time you've got company. You may have as many as 500 people on your team-way more people than you're accustomed to. But that's still not a problem.

Just like a normal walk-on day, you go through an orientation speech. Pay attention to it! You may have played a billion times before, but it's important that you listen to this orientation!) They will go over the rules of the game, as well as special rule variations specific to the big game. And it's important to be at least acquainted with those rules.

Paintball Sam's in Racine, Wisconsin runs a few big games every year. One of the rule modifications there always involves medics. If you are hit below the knee or below the elbow you are 'wounded.' You can be 'healed' by a designated 'medic' player three times before you are eliminated from that particular game.

For some time, the rule stated that a hit below

the knee, elbow, and above the chin line counted as a 'wound.' The year they switched to head shots counting as eliminations was confusing to a lot of the players who weren't paying attention to the orientation speech and frustrating to those of us who lit them up.

Listen to the rules at the beginning of the game!

Motor Easy

One of the things I cherish about the big game format is how laid back players are, in general. Sure, you get your hyper players out there who make down-the-middle rushes. But, for the most part, everyone is in a casual frame of mind. Sometimes players hang up the camouflage for a day. Among the things to expect people will be wearing, I've seen jeans and t-shirts, tuxedos, three-piece business suits, a Fred Flintstone outfit, a Moose hat (I mean antlers and all!), Viking helmets and costumes, even a Waldo sweater (as in "Where's Waldo?"). Me? I wear a deer costume. It's a midwestern thing.

Meanwhile, other players dust off their stock guns to play amongst the other semi-autos. (In the midwest, it's rare to see one on the field at all. Big Games bring them out of hiding.) When there are a few hundred opponents, you know you're going to meet at least a few of them. So some players generally take it easy on firepower for the day.

Before I forget, let me mention that you should leave your temper at home. A big game is not for proving how many people you can eliminate. Angry, overly intense players ruin this kind of experience for everyone else. Your priority at this game is to relax, have fun, meet people, and make friends! This is another major difference between the Big Game and Scenario Games, which tend to be intense because people are making believe that a great deal is at stake (e.g., the future of human civilization, the outcome of WWII).

Tactics aren't as important in the Big Game as they are in normal play. Having a few tricks up your collective sleeves isn't a bad idea, but any more organization than that and you're going to end up in pretty lame arguments with people who have thought way too long and hard about the game to be enjoying it.

As you'd expect, most players will play offense. This is natural. People generally feel safer when they're flanked by hundreds of players. On the offensive side, there's a lot you can do.

As much as I hate to say it, grandiose military tactics can work on big game fields. This is due to the size of the field, and the game's typically longer time frame. Checking with the rules is important here. Do you have enough time for wide flanking maneuvers? Do you have time to make an ambush happen? These are things you need to know to avoid expending tons of energy only to discover that the game is over before you've engaged anyone.

The Big O

Grab as many people as you can for your flanking moves. Sometimes it's a good idea to make a 'sacrifice' maneuver to spring ambushes, or to determine numbers. Also, keep in mind the overall objective. Fifty people chasing five guys for an hour is a waste of time that you could be using to build momentum.

Players have a tendency to group in a circle formation, and you should use this to your advantage. The front-most players should be watching forward, the rear-most players should be watching the back (literally facing backwards and walking backwards!), and players on the sides should be covering your group's flanks. You have to think as a very large pack of wolves on the prowl. You have to trust everyone else in the pack to do their part. **Trust works if everyone is equally committed to it.**

Having a 'team' mentality helps, but knowing

how to get your fellow teammates to share it is important as well. You can do this by rallying everyone in earshot to move forward, or go through the bunkers. Or by adding yourself to the push so you can gain some more feet of real estate.

Shouting has its time and place. Once you and another person pushes forward whoopin' and hollerin,' people will be more apt to follow you. This is a 'herding' effect that I touch on in detail a bit later on. By the same token, there's something to be said for people who hang back and observe the whoopin' and hollerin' advance, especially if it's ambushed. Then it's their turn to shout out the position of the other team, direct people to regroup and engage, pursue, or retreat.

Transmitting information from one side of the playing field to the other is vital. Send more than one person as a messenger. The faster you can tell the "center" crowd that the "left" crowd is punching through the left side, the more people you can slam through it, and the more likely it is that you'll win the game. If you hear something about a push, or that the opponents are making a move, pass it along as fast as possible, and make sure you get a few more to pass it as well.

Information is power. Spread the word.

Individual Offense

Big games get chaotic. So, despite their size, what you do as an individual can make a difference. The first thing you should realize is that, outside of your friends, you are surrounded by individuals.

Paintball is a team sport, and remains so even if both teams consist of 300 people a side. Stuff happens, however. Your entire team gets shot, or they all abandon a situation and you find yourself alone. What can you do? Switch gears.

Lone Hunter Mode

Now you are the lone hunter. You are individually outnumbered, but that's not really important. As an individual, you have strengths against big numbers of opponents.

Sink into your camouflage and start to crawl around. It's nerve-wracking to let a team of guys walk past you, but let them go. Sneak up on your opponents and take out a few of them from behind. Then, run for the hills. You may be able to draw them away from your teammates or your flag, weakening their offense. Or, you can go for the other team's flag! You may be able to fake them out, saying you're on their team (if the rules allow it).

As a loner, you'll experience the game at a higher level of alertness. You have to watch your own back. Your movements must be quick, subtle, and quiet. You will only fire your gun if you have a clear shot.

Even if you get eliminated, you can still do a lot for your team. If you think in ratios, if you eliminate 5 players, and tie up 20 more in the process, that's 25 guys on you that aren't on your team's flag station. And if you can tie them up for a length of time, you'll really be doing a favor to your team.

Or, perhaps you'll become a spy. As a spy, your challenge is to gather intelligence behind enemy lines about their allocation of resources, sheer numbers of people in certain places and the direction their moving in, and then to get it back to your forces in time for it to be useful. The cool thing is, you can always switch into 'Lone Hunter' mode if it looks like there isn't enough time to get your information back to your people. Let out a shout that gives away an enemy position (this works better if you have a friends in your main group who will know what you mean when you holler!), take a few of them out, and start running. Of course, doing this kind of thing is dependent on the length of the game.

Which brings me to defense.

"Are we leaving any defenders?"

I actually heard this on a big-game field once.

A Big Game defense is fully dependent on the

Photo courtesy of Jerry Braun

scenario objective. A game of "Capture the Flag" will have more defense than, say, capture and hold a point bunker. I'll talk about both types.

First, let's look at Capture the Flag defense. A good defense can hold off an opposing offense. But what is the best defense?

A common 'big game' mistake is to make the offense the defense by not letting anyone through the cracks. This isn't a good idea, because then only a few players can slip through to capture your flag. Leaving a few people behind, or at least near the back of the field is always a good idea.

A good defense is layered. Meaning that you have players 200, 100, and 50 yards out, then the final flag station. (This can be modified, but you get the idea.)

However, the defense should be aware that if they can not stop and rout the offense by 70 yards out, the game is pretty much over (Again, this distance changes from field to field, but if they can longball you *en-masse*, you're history.) I call this the 'Final Approach' zone. In this zone, the offense gets motivated to win, and your defense has nowhere to go.

Bottom-line
If you run out of real estate, you're a sitting duck.

Other big games have specific point bunkers. These work differently. Your team gets points by holding such bunkers for allotted periods of time (20 minutes), or on specific time marks (every half hour) Defending this type of bunker is different.

For starters, you probably have to defend against 360 degrees of terrain. So having a lot of defenders is a good idea if you have the power. You are probably going to want to organize the same kind of layered defense as I had mentioned earlier, for many of the same reasons. Your 'final approach' distance will be shorter, but it may be worse. Always try to leave an avenue of escape if you can. That way you can always do an end run and flank behind the

other team. If they totally surround you, it's over.

Still, if the other team surrounds you or reaches the "Final Approach," your chances are not totally gone. You can get reinforcements from some angle if the game allows for reinsertions or if your teammates find you. Hold your position as long as you can. If you get eliminated after the points are allotted, you've done your job for your team.

Either way, stopping a rampaging offense is no easy task. You do it through sheer will, determination, and discipline. Shooting a lot of paint doesn't hurt either, but it's not necessary. As a defensive group, you don't want to all concentrate on one 'zone'. You want to take a line of approach, and cover it. Communicate with your teammates, and have overlapping lanes of fire. The idea is to stop their forward movement and rout them.

By halting their approaching push, they have nowhere to drive but backwards. This breaks their attack momentum, and they lose the 'will' to keep driving at you. It's hard to recover from a rout. The hard part is figuring out when to change gears from defense to offense, or even if you need to go at them. That becomes a 'feel' thing, best determined by experience and what's happening on the field.

When the offense gets into the "Final Approach" zone, they tend to get a little blood-thirsty. Meaning that they start to 'smell' the flag, taste the victory. If you get caught as a defender in this situation, you will get pounded unless you can rout them.

If you do get tagged, the best thing to do is scream, "I'm out! I'm hit!" repeatedly and just vacate the hot zone as fast as you can. Keep your paintgun high (Don't worry about your barrel plug, you'll have time to put it in when you're out of the hot zone), Then, put your barrel plug in. It'll save you from getting more welts than you deserve.

The Human Herd

When a few hundred people are milling about, they usually act like a mob. If you have mediocre leadership skills you can guide them. Heck, even if you have none it's really easy. You just may need to shout (or a megaphone will substitute nicely.)

There's always times when you see from your side that another side of the field needs reinforcements. That's when, classically, you start shouting "SHIFT RIGHT! SHIFT RIGHT!" When the shift begins, just guide players to the appropriate area.

Unfortunately, there's usually at least 20 people trying to do this. All you can really do from the rear ranks is become a 'caller'. This is the player who announces to the pack where opponents are. "THREE BEHIND THE SPOOL! TWO BEHIND THAT TREE! TEN ON THE LEFT TAPE!" The caller is the first player to go hoarse, by the way. The caller can also do the same thing from the front line as well.

SOUNDING SCARIER THAN YOU ARE

Once one player starts to scream like a maniac, other players will join in and follow him. I'm not sure why it works, but it does. (I think it's a psychology thing, I'm not sure.) You don't have to scream. But sometimes that really does the trick!

A good example of this happened in Racine Wisconsin's Big Game a long time ago. While sneaking around on the tapeline, I heard someone playing a bugle, it was the classic "Charge" tune. Soon followed by the loudest screaming match I've ever heard, and what sounded like a stampede. Thankfully, the player was on my team. We used that momentum to carry us to the flag and victory.

"Rebel Yells" "Kamikaze Screams" "Whoops & Hollers"

Primal screams do two things. They provide an adrenaline rush to your teammates who will rush into positions without fear. Moreover, it scares the living daylights out of your opponents. This intimidation is infectious on both sides, and can get a lot of results quickly. It burns your team out quickly, however, so use it only when things stagnate or when you need to make the push.

Part two of the process is getting your teammates to go with you. Some people have the charisma to do it, some don't. Sometimes all you need to do is get into a great position and coax your players to join you. Other times you need to make an impression.

Making a bold—read: *stupid*—charge to take a bunker will do this. People will be impressed you made it and either join you or shake their heads in disbelief. Either way, you'll have their attention. Use the opportunity to yell to them to move up. Keep reassuring your teammates that you're going to win, you've got the opponents on the run, and so on.

The idea here is to get your players to move up as one group rather than piecemeal. See, the more people moving forward, the better your odds are in getting things to go your way. So a lot of people moving together is a good thing. And convincing a bunch of walk-on players to all do this is part diplomacy, part intimidation, part luck.

But when they all go at once, you've got something good happening, and then it's up to you and the two or three other guys who are interested in taking the lead to maintain it!

Radio Communications

The ability to communicate is always important in paintball, especially in the big game format. Knowing what is happening on the other end of your skirmish line becomes more difficult when you can't see the length of it.

Many big games allow the use of radios as long as you do not cross-talk onto the referee channels. Radios put a whole new dimension on the game.

Remember, you're not going to be alone, so some common courtesy is a good thing. Use a 'push to talk' radio system if you can. I've experienced hard breathing sounds and shooting pain in my right ear. That's not fun, by any stretch of the imagination.

Keep your radio chatter as short as possible if you're in a firefight. Too much information can be confusing and useless to your other teammates. Assume that nobody cares what your teammates think of your paintgun or the referees. Save that for after the game.

Be courteous to your fellow players, and let them have some air-time as well. If you need to talk that much, switch stations.

Radios also have a dual-edged purpose as well. Whatever you broadcast can (and usually will) be intercepted by your opponents, and be used against you. I've personally used this phenomenon myself to try to convince opposing players to surrender the flag. (I bribed them with a six-pack of soda! They respectfully declined.) Another use is to run a campaign of false information on the assumption that you'll keep your opponents off-guard if they think you're moving in one direction, but then end up doing the opposite.

Several models of radios are available, I prefer a hands-free model with a remote push-to-talk button. This way, I can control what I broadcast. I place the button in my off hand, and run the wire down the sleeve and under my pullover. This way I don't have to reach over to broadcast anything, and the electronics are protected under my pullover.

For scenario games some players go as far as to use portable CB radios. I've also heard of a few people who used a cellular phone when the situation got desperate. I think that's a bit extreme myself, but go for it if it works for you (and it's allowed by the rules).

Photo courtesy of Jerry Braun

GO GET'EM!

With these small bits of information, you're set to go.

All in all, the 'big game' is tremendously fun, no matter where you go to do it. The key to this kind of event is forethought. To quote a song by Rush "An ounce of perception, a pound of obscure." Being prepared is the best way to enjoy the 'big game' and to avoid unpleasant 'surprises' along the way. And remember: Never say 'follow me' and trip into the creek. You'll have a lot of soggy compatriots.

—RR

THESE LADIES ARE 2DIE4

Meet Karen Barber and Sarah Stevenson, two of the top professional paintball players in the world.

ANDREW FLACH: We were just at Skyball (Toronto, 1999), and your team, 2 Die 4, was there, and The Iron Maidens were there. As far as I know, those are the only two all-women teams playing at a semi-professional tournament level.

There are some co-ed teams, but the vast majority of the paintball teams that regularly compete are all male teams. Tell me about your experience as women in such a male dominated sport? Are you treated with equal consideration? Are you considered an equal competitor?

SARAH STEVENSON: It's getting there. The first time that I played with Maidens, the guys had the attitude, "Oh, we're just playing a bunch of girls. Big deal! We'll smoke 'em." And they were pretty much right. They did, but not because we were women.

We stayed with it. We plugged away, trained ourselves, and now we're kind of a wild card. They don't know what to do with us. They don't know how to predict what we're going to do. Most teams are very predictable. You can read the field and know generally where they're going to go. As you saw at Skyball 1999, our team pulled off things that the other players never expected.

It's been nice to see that we register on the men's respect meter. All it took was a year and a half, hard work, practice, and execution, and now the other teams can't take us for granted. Attitudes changed pretty quickly once we started to win.

ANDREW: So the two of you first played together on The Iron Maidens?

From Left: Karen Barber and Sarah Stevenson

all that testosterone. I did become accustomed to that style of play. The guys I played with are all like brothers to me. They always took care of me and made sure I was okay.

The men didn't treat me any differently, which I respected, and they knew that's what I wanted. I always worried that they were just keeping me around because my husband was on the team. We had this talk many a time, and that wasn't the case.

In fact, for a couple of years, my husband stayed with the All Americans and I went to the All Americans 2. I decided to see what it was like to step down a level and play the amateur league. We eventually went pro because we kept working at it.

KAREN BARBER: We met each other at World Cup '96.

SARAH: We had known each other before, and then I went and talked with the team and the team captain, Tracy Roberts. Tracy was just absolutely crazy about Karen and for good reason. Tracy had been in the sport for a long time and knew about Karen and had watched her career as a paintball player evolve. We discussed things and decided to let Karen and a few other All Americans play with us at a tournament in San Antonio.

We contacted Karen and a couple of the other All Americans and they agreed to come down and play with us. This was a big coup. Our team was legitimized overnight.

ANDREW: When did you start playing with The Iron Maidens.

SARAH: Around the middle of 1995.

ANDREW: Having played on co-ed teams, and having played on all-women teams, have you noticed any difference in the way the team works.

SARAH: Completely. Yeah, you're looking at two polar ends.

KAREN: The men are definitely more competitive and more aggressive than the women. Probably

I definitely think that women, individually and as a team, are more level headed, more patient. And some of them are better shots. Women are few and far between in this sport, but if you find the right ones and put them together, I believe women's teams would be very dangerous.

SARAH: I agree with Karen. Women are a notch

more level-headed than men on the field. They have their mind set on where they want to go as a team, and they're a little more deliberate and less erratic than their male counterparts.

The men's teams that I've played on—probably the most serious being a team called Texas Shock Force—were tremendous. But they couldn't quite set their egos aside and play the game as an entire team with one unifying goal. They couldn't knit it together.

Whereas, when 2 Die 4 went to Skyball, I had no problems with egos on the team. No particular team member felt a need to be the star of the show. And I went up and told one of my players: "You're going to sit this game. I'm going to put so and so in." "Sure, no problem," was the response.

In my experience, men hear this kind of statement as, "You're just not good enough for this game, so I'm going to put somebody else in." So they can tend to get a little disenchanted, to put it mildly.

KAREN: Women tend to reason it out and deal with things. That's been very refreshing with this group. I haven't had to deal with any of that. Our team members are very supportive. Like a family.

ANDREW: What is your goal with 2 Die 4? As captain, where are you taking the team?

SARAH: Pro status. I've always wanted to go further, I've always wanted to go higher, but I don't want to get onto a team that's already pro, I want to build a team that can do well in any competition.

ANDREW: So you got on the telephone and

called Karen at some point. Karen, what did you think when the idea was broached?

KAREN: At first I didn't grasp the seriousness of her proposal. I knew she had asked me to play and that she was going to organize this team. And I said, "Okay, yeah. That'll be fine." And then I realized that all the girls involved were very serious and very talented. I saw right away that we had a good group of people that could probably go further.

ANDREW: Do you think we'll see separate women's paintball leagues, the way they have segregated basketball?

KAREN: Not for a long time, if ever. We're far from having enough players.

SARAH: I don't think the women would really want that. I like the competitive level we have now in a co-ed environment. We compete effectively as it is.

ANDREW: Paintball is a sport where skill, technique, and decision making take precedence. Just

the fact that you have testosterone coursing through your body, doesn't mean you will win more games, does it?

KAREN: Well, I've always thought the All Americans are where they are today because they're the most competitive group of people I've ever met in my life. For instance, we'll be waiting at the airport because a plane is delayed. They find something to do and make a game out of it until each person wins. Everyone has to win.

I've never met women like that before, that competitive. I think that's one thing that the men have that we don't. Innate competitiveness. Maybe professional women volleyball or softball players have it, but most women simply aren't like that.

ANDREW: How about in terms of strength issues. Would you say that paintball is a fairly accessible game for both men and women?

KAREN: Yes.

ANDREW: In terms of competition?

KAREN: Hmm. I don't know about that. In one way the sport's changing now, at least in the NPPL. You need to be fast and aggressive. Running quickly is becoming important. Unfortunately, speed is one thing I lack.

ANDREW: I'm sure if you had a couple of fast running players, sprinters, on the team...

SARAH: And a lot of teams do...

ANDREW: ...that might even things out, don't you think?

KAREN: Yes. You need key bunkers and they are always the front ones that you have to hit. You need to get people into those quickly. We used to play with three or four "backup" players. Now there's only one or two. The rest of the team is forward. You have to be aggressive, because the only way to get the other team out is to keep moving or just go "bunker" them. That's the trend in competitions today.

ANDREW: What words of encouragement would

you have for women interested in playing paintball?

SARAH: Stick with it. Don't let the things guys say get in your head. Somebody's always going to give you a hard time. I've found that in a lot of situations—being a Mom, I'm able to see this—men at the fields will test a woman the same way a kid would test a Mom. They see how far they can push her and see what they can do, maybe to get her to leave.

These guys think: "Paintball is our world, stay out of it." And, maybe four years ago, that would have been the case, for the most part. And so they would test and they'd push and they'd do the "Hey baby, hey honey," thing. That's gotten better, but they still will push on the women to see if they really want to stick around. Maybe they're a little intimidated by the presence of women, since there's a ton of baggage attached to being eliminated by a girl. I say stick it out.

ANDREW: Is paintball as a sport arriving at time when it can develop as its own unique co-ed activity? Is it poised for that?

KAREN: I think it's always going to be co-ed. I don't think there will ever be enough women interested in playing the sport continually. Women get married, or pregnant. And, today, if you ask a girl, "Would you rather run around in the woods, where you may break a nail or get paint in your hair, or go swimming or play volleyball?" ...

ANDREW: She'd choose the other sports?

KAREN: I think she would, without ever having tried paintball. You find very few women who absolutely love it and are willing to make a serious commitment to playing the game regularly.

Some women are also very intimidated by the fact that it hurts when you get hit. They don't like pain. I think women, even though they give birth, don't enjoy that kind of pain.

SARAH: And I just want to say—it's a different

Member of 2 Die 4 discusses a call with a referee at Skyball in Toronto, 1999.

breed of women that wants to do this.

ANDREW: So women are concerned about getting hit by a paintball?

KAREN: Oh, yeah. I mean, when I used to work in an office and wore a dress and nylons, people would see the bruises left from paintballs and say, "You are absolutely a mess."

SARAH: It's always a good idea to wear protection—cups for the men, padded bras for the women. They're available. Use them. You're a little silly if you don't.

ANDREW: It's been great meeting with you. Are there are any last thoughts you'd like to share with our readers.

SARAH: We appreciate the support that we do get from people. At Skyball, men and women came up to me, shook my hand, and said, "Your team is a good example of how teams should be at these events."

And that means a great deal to us. We don't want half compliments. Don't say, "Well, I've got to go back home with my tail between my legs because a girl shot me." Don't give me that. Give me, "You play well. You're a good player." Not as a woman. Just as a player. Period.

If more men in this game would adopt that way of thinking, that would be tremendous. In paintball, the men have all kinds of support. They have oodles of support. Verbal support from the crowds. Financial support in the form of sponsorships from the manufacturers. We're starting to get the sponsorship and we are starting to get the verbal support, too. We greatly appreciate that.

All we ask is to be treated like equals on the playing field. Give us your game, and we'll give you ours. May the best players win. It's as simple as that.

INDOOR PAINTBALL BY THE OCEANSIDE

Jay Tavitian

An Interview with Jay Tavitian, Manager, Oceanside Indoor Paintball, Long Island, NY.

Jay at Oceanside

Indoor paintball can be a wild experience; it's fast and furious, dark and dangerous, and has more bunkers than you can imagine. If you want to experience the wide range of paintball play, you must check out the indoor game!

For this interview we met with Jay Tavitian, Manager of Oceanside Indoor Paintball, at his 10,000 square foot facility on Long Island, New York.

ANDREW FLACH: Jay, what's the fundamental difference between the indoor and outdoor paintball experience?

JAY TAVITIAN: The difference between the two fields is like the difference between night and day. Outdoor fields present a slower game. They tend to be more strategic and tactical, whereas the indoor game is played at a much faster pace. Tactics have their place in the indoor games, but everything's done at a very quick pace. I mean, you take your eyes off the field for one second and someone's come right up on the side of you already. With the outdoor field you can close your eyes for a few minutes, and you probably won't miss much.

Also, you get a lot more distance on outdoor fields. The guns are set up differently. The velocities are higher out there.

ANDREW: What's the velocity of a paintball indoors versus outdoors?

JAY: It's 220 feet per second indoor. The outdoor field's are usually 290. When you're outdoors, you need more distance. I'll put it in perspective: if you get a player that's playing here constantly and they're real good at the indoor field, they go to the outdoor field they get a reality check out there.

They try to move fast and they wind up getting shot up because there's a lot more open space out there. If you get an outdoor player in the indoor field, they'll sit back and relax. And they'll get shot up.

ANDREW: Indoor is just a different flavor of the game. Some people like chocolate ice cream, other people like strawberry ice cream.

JAY: Exactly.

ANDREW: Hard core indoor players probably have little or no interest in going out in the woods and shooting guns. Other guys who are fanatical about the outdoor game just aren't into the indoors style. They want the big field.

JAY: I originally played on outdoors fields, and then I made the transition to an indoor field. So I know both sides. What you're saying is true. But then there are people who just love both.

For some people, when winter comes, that's it for playing. They can't play the outdoor field because it's too cold, and they don't want to freeze, so they put the equipment away until spring time. Other players think "it's getting too cold to play outside, so it's time to go indoors for a while." So they start coming down to the indoor field on the weekends just to keep themselves in shape and ready to go when spring returns.

ANDREW: It's really just a matter of the individual player finding what it is that they like to do.

The indoor game has it's own sort of unique flavor because you're covering less ground between bunkers. Then again, you've got to constantly move because the other team is covering ground quickly, too. So there's a different speed to the game, it's almost more like speedball?

JAY: Basically, yes. You can call it a hundred percent speedball.

ANDREW: How do you find playing without a flag? Does it make for a different kind of a game just from the mind set of the player?

JAY: Yes. We used to use a center flag. We just took the flag out. The game is basically total elimination, and because you're in close quarters here, we felt a flag would just be overkill.

Which isn't to say that we didn't try having a flag. But you have to understand that people's primary objective in a small space like this is not to get hit. So with the flag they were thinking: "If I keep going for the flag, I'm getting hit." Then everybody sits back and the flag just sits there and no one touches it. So we just took it out and went to an elimination game.

ANDREW: Do you have other variations of the elimination game you play?

JAY: We change corners, we switch sides. This totally changes the field. Everything's opposite, backwards, and upside down. When we do this, even our regulars stand around with their guns in their hands just shaking their heads. They have no clue about where to go or what to do, and they love it. All you've got to do is just start from different corners and it just totally throws the whole game off.

Another thing we do is take "the house" out of bounds. The house is a key objective on our field. You can control the game from that position. We declare it out of bounds and we square the field off. You take the house away from everybody and they say "okay, now where do I go?"

ANDREW: Explain your version of the elimination game.

JAY: Let's say you have 20 people. It's 10 on 10 with a ten minute maximum game. The object of the game is to eliminate the other team before time runs out.

ANDREW: Indoor fields are ideal for urban and suburban settings where there's not a lot of land to play in. You can play year round in fair or foul weather. I played at another indoor field. They turned all the lights off except for a black light. Do you play in the dark?

JAY: No. The problem with playing in a darkened environment is safety. Not only the safety of the players, but the safety of the referees. It gets dark enough in here, but you can always still see what's going on. We don't need to turn off the lights to make it fun or challenging.

Besides, the worst thing you can do to a person is take their eyesight away from them. Once you blind them, they lift the mask. If the lights are off they lift the mask thinking "I'll see better without the mask." Now the referee can't see the player lifting the mask, and a person takes a shot in the eye. Then you're out of business or in serious trouble.

Safety is our number one priority. We just don't take chances when it comes to safety.

FIELDS OF DREAMS

Paul Fogal

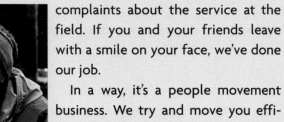

Achieving the ultimate recreational paintball experience drives Paul Fogal, Founder of Skirmish USA, located in Jim Thorpe, PA.

When it comes to recreational paintball, Skirmish USA is one of the best run facilities out there. It offers plenty of fields to choose from encompassing wide variety of playing experiences and environments-from deep woods to wide open spaces. Over 700 acres and 44 fields are devoted to the recreational paintball experience. Every other year, the World Record Game attracts over a thousand players from all over the world.

If you want to know what makes for a great paintball experience, there's one man to ask, Paul Fogal. He has set the standards for recreational play.

ANDREW FLACH: What are your standards for a successful day of paintball?

PAUL: You should have an exciting time running around with your friends in the woods, and no complaints about the service at the field. If you and your friends leave with a smile on your face, we've done our job.

In a way, it's a people movement business. We try and move you efficiently, so you're out there playing as soon as possible and can play the number of games you want. Then we try to change the games and the terrain around so you've got to think a little bit about what you're doing. You shouldn't be running to the same tree all day. You'll play one time and you're on one side of the field and then the other side of the field and sometimes you go to another field or sometimes you might play three games on a field if you really like it.

We try to give the players the field experience they want. One field might have more open terrain and another might be real thick. One might be dry, another wet. Then we have the Village Fields and the Scenario Fields where there are buildings, structures, and unique bunkers.

ANDREW: A field like The Alamo?

PAUL: Yes, there's a couple like The Alamo. People like to play those fields at the end of the day. They're bigger and they're paint-eaters. Near the end of the day, when players want to run out of paint, we hear them say "The hell with this hunting thing. Let's just shoot it out."

ANDREW: From what I observed from just a brief experience interacting with your staff, it strikes me that there are several keys to your success. And I think these are things all people should expect when they go to a paintball field. Number one is the emphasis on safety. Safety is paramount.

PAUL: The most critical safety issue is that you have to keep your goggles on your face at all times on the field of play. There are some people

who don't understand that and you have to keep pushing them and reminding them. Some people just blank out and start to lift their goggles after a game is over. You just can't do that, and we never let people forget it.

Beyond keeping their eyeballs in their heads, we like our players to feel like they're spending most of their time doing what they came to do. Players are there to get their money's worth. They expect to be moved efficiently through the entire process—get their release forms filled out, get their gun and equipment rentals in hand quickly, buy paint, get to the field. Players should be able to start playing very quickly and play as many games as possible during the course of the day. Sufficient logistics are of primary importance.

To accomplish this, we need a professional staff—motivated, helpful people, who know how to treat customers properly and handle situations

in an appropriate manner. People who enjoy delivering on customer service.

ANDREW: You're doing something right in terms of the way you're conducting your business. People speak very highly of their experience here. Word of mouth is priceless. People tell other people, "I had a great time at Skirmish. They were really nice people, I felt really comfortable, and their fields are awesome." These are all things that add up to a successful operation.

PAUL: You have to run your field in a professional, businesslike manner. That has been a problem in paintball, but it's improving. For years there were a lot of fields that weren't being run well, but as the sport matures, only the fields that have their act together will survive. Most of the poorly run fields are dropping by the wayside. Not long ago, an insurance guy told me he figured that about forty percent of the fields still didn't have any insurance. That's just ridiculous. Wake up, field-owners. You could lose everything and hurt paintball's reputation in the process!

ANDREW: It seems that to engineer a fun day of paintball, a certain plan is required. Are you guys following a program, whereby teams that start on field "A" will move on to field "B", whereas teams that start on field "Y" go on to field "Z"?

PAUL: No, it's not that scientific. There are large, open fields and small, wooded fields, and fields thick with 15-foot-high rhododendron bushes. We have a general manager, Karen, who evaluates the groups and she puts them on the field where she thinks it's appropriate for that group to start. For example, if it's forty people she puts you on a field that would handle forty people size-wise.

During the course of the day, the judges talk to the players, who are usually pretty forthcoming about what they want. They'll request fields, and we try to accommodate them.

There's one person whose job it is to keep track of who's playing where and they radio in about which fields are open. That person will look at the group and see how many people there are, see what fields they've played, which field is open. You just try and vary it a little bit. You're kind of throwing them a curve, keeping things exciting and new.

I really think the secret to our success is that the fields are a little bit bigger and there's a little bit more anticipation before the shooting starts than in most places. Most places really pack you in.

ON FIELD DESIGN

ANDREW: Who's job is it to design the field?

PAUL: Dewey Green and I are the chief designers. It's a constant tinkering and feed-back process. Various judges and players also make suggestions regarding their preferences and desires. Once or twice a year, a group of us will get together over beer and pizza. We brainstorm new field designs and game for-mats.

THE ROLE OF THE JUDGE

ANDREW: It seems important to have some-one on the field who is a representative of the paintball field's operator-the judge. What is a judge?

PAUL: On a recreational level, a judge is a combination of referee and guide. He or she helps the group with their equipment, leads them through the day, and then will make some calls on the field. By the very nature of the fact that you're playing on a number of acres in the woods, the referees cannot make all the calls. There always has to be an honor factor.

The best judges are people with extroverted personalities, who kind of enjoy the woods. A lot of the judges are there because they like to run around in the woods. I often hear them say things like, "I sit behind the computer terminal all week, so it's fun to get out here and get some exercise."

ON CLOTHING

ANDREW: How should I prepare myself for a day of play? What would you recommend as the proper clothing?

PAUL: Just wear old clothes. If you have a set of fatigues, wear them. Dark colors are a good idea—black, brown, green. Clothes that you will not mind getting wet, dirty, muddy, or splattered with paint.

As an option, most fields offer some sort of camouflage overalls, or "cammies," for rent. You just step into them; they fit over your clothes. At the end of the day, you turn them in and let someone else worry about cleaning them.

Shoes are probably the most important consideration. Go for something light with ankle support and avoid heavy boots.

ANDREW: What about food and water?

PAUL: A good field will provide that stuff for you. Of course, you can bring your own. A good field will have adequate food service and drink. You've got to stay hydrated to avoid cramps and overheating.

WHAT KIND OF GAMES ARE PLAYED

ANDREW: What are the different games you play at Skirmish?

PAUL: There are an infinite variety of games you can play. Center Hang is when you put one flag in the middle of the field and both teams try to get it and take it through to the other team's side of the field. It's like scoring a touchdown. That's a pretty popular game.

The top one is certainly Cap-

Your basic rental gear.

ture the Flag. The second most popular game is probably Center Hang. Number three would be Offense/Defense or Attack and Defend. One team defends their position and the other team just attacks it and they usually have to go in and get the flag or pull it down, or take it out beyond a boundary.

Frankly, the twenty-four hour scenario games are my favorite. They are as interesting as the people who come to play them. We're talking serious paintball hobbyists. In a twenty-four hour scenario game, you've got what seems like unlimited time. So you're not worried about it. And the field of play is huge.

You can go out on a mission and it might take you two hours to try and attain a certain objective. The guy that's directing it, the scenario director, he's just playing with you. He basically sends you out on this mission and then calls up the other coordinators on their radios and he gives them codes that tell them where you're going so that you can be ambushed.

Now, you as a player understand that he's doing this, so you know you have to be careful. Your opponents are going there for the same reason and maybe they've had a half an hour head start on you. Even though you know what's going on, there's still a great deal of suspense.

Sometimes a squad will go out and count how many tents are set up in the enemy's base camp. The players have to try and get that information and bring it back. You earn points if you complete that mission.

Another mission may involve a downed pilot in Sector Five on your map. One of the judges goes out and lays there and makes believe he's the downed pilot. Sometimes they've got to take a stretcher out there, put him on it, and bring him back on it. Very intense stuff.

Whatever the mission, scenario games are highly complex and some people are really into this role playing. Guys come out here with night vision goggles, radios, set up "booby traps" and ambushes. We even have homemade tanks.

We do run three or four scenario games a year, but we only do two twenty-four hour games. The other ones last about eight hours—we call them "mini-scenarios."

ANDREW: How does outdoor paintball differ from indoor paintball?

PAUL: When you play outdoors, the fields are larger and it takes time before "engaging" your opponents. From your position, you can see them coming and you can watch and you can hide and you don't have to move.

Whenever I've played indoors, there's no ambush factors really. You can hide against this wall, but your opponent is still right there . You cannot set an ambush and watch him moving towards you, waiting for the right moment to open fire. Everything happens at a much further distance in the woods, so it's not quite as scary. Indoors can be pretty scary. People are shooting at close range, surprising you from around corners and obstacles.

ANDREW: That's how I experienced it. Indoors does have a frantic intensity. This one place I went to played the Mission Impossible theme before the game. Everybody gets revved up. Add

that to the craziness that you're already experiencing. It was wild.

At the very end of the game, I had run out of paint, but I was still able to get these guys out because I was adrenalized. I just shouted, "You guys are out. Drop your guns right now." They didn't even question it. I love that energy rush. What is it about the game of paintball that you enjoy?

PAUL: I play paintball because I like the game itself. My son and I went out and played the other day. He's starting to play very well, so now I can play with him on an equal basis. It was fun for me—not just because he's my son, but because I'm engaged in this competitive experience that is so exciting.

Paintball is a great equalizer. Psychological make-up, not social status, really attracts certain people to the game. I played on a team that included a couple of guys that were engineers, a fellow who was working for AT&T, another who was a mason's helper, one was unemployed, another guy drove a forklift in a factory, yet another was a movie stuntman. All different walks of life come to have fun in the woods.

For me, male camaraderie and bonding are a large part of my enjoyment of the sport. I liken it to the way primitive hunters must have felt at the end of the day:

"We just had a successful hunt. We just killed a woolly mammoth." The sense of having survived is unique.

MISTAKES TO LEARN BY

"DOH! I'M OUT AGAIN!"

Every player who is new to the game makes the same basic mistakes. That's part of learning the game and a necessary step to becoming a skilled paintballer.

Reading about what not to do won't prevent you from making mistakes. Playing paintball is the only way to learn what you can and cannot do. To be more precise, playing paintball well is the inevitable result of learning not to force yourself to do things that simply can't be done.

Moving, shooting, and communicating are critical to successful play. Failure to use these skills consistently and creatively will almost always result in an early elimination.

GETTING FROM HERE TO THERE

You can't get an angle on your target if you don't move. You can't grab a flag if you don't move. Learning to move, especially while someone is shooting at you, is perhaps the hardest paintball skill to master.

You're going to get hit when you play. Even the best tournament player on the face of the planet has been hit thousands of times. Most of those hits occurred while they were moving. That's because they've learned that failing to move will get you eliminated every single time, while moving may offer you some chance of staying in the game.

The purpose of moving is to 'get an angle' on your opponents. If you or one of your teammates can see the side or rear of an opponent, you've gotten the angle, and usually an easy elimination.

SHOOTING

Face it. In order to take someone out of the game, you need to hit them with a paintball. In order to do this, it is necessary to pull the trigger of your gun.

Far too many players get taken out of the game because they fail to realize what a versatile tool their paintball gun can be. Not only can it be used to shoot an opponent, it can also be used to keep an opponent from shooting at you.

Your paintball gun can be used in a wide variety of offensive and defensive ways—from the 'one shot, one kill' of the sniper to the diversionary shooting of air while reloading. After your brain, your gun is your main tool on the field. Use it.

This doesn't mean that you should start the game pulling the trigger. It does mean that before you play it would be a good idea to step over to the target range and get used to the feel and operation of your gun. Shoot a few targets. See how accurate you are; how fast you can shoot, how far you can shoot. And, once you know what you can do with your paintball gun, remember to use it when on the field.

COMMUNICATING

In order to be able to move, to find targets, or maybe even just to find out how to get back to the flag station, you'll need to communicate with the other players on your team.

During your first few games this may be very difficult, especially if you are playing with a group of relative strangers. Nevertheless, talking can help you stay in the game longer, and may even help you get more eliminations.

The purpose of communicating is to coordinate your moves on the field with your teammates. At first it could be something as simple as asking a fellow player if they can see any opponents ahead of them. Or perhaps even if they know where the other team is!

The important thing to remember is that your unknown teammate will be very happy to have someone to talk to, and please remember that answering a teammate is just as important as asking your own questions.

As your knowledge of the game increases, communicating will become a very effective tool which you can use to flank opposing players, determine the number of remaining opponents, coordinate charges or 'pushes' and transmit some very sophisticated information about what is happening on the field.

MORE "LEARNING OPPORTUNITIES"

Once you get past the basics, you'll find yourself running into a whole host of other little lessons and tricks. Learning them will smooth out your game and keep you in the action longer. Although these aren't nearly as important as the three basic skills, learning them will increase your enjoyment of the game.

DEAD MEAT

NICE & TIGHT

LOOKING

In order to stay in the game, new players need to avoid tunnel vision, or the tendency to fixate on one object, one opponent or one activity, to the exclusion of all else.

To avoid tunnel vision, practice shifting your attention among all of the activities in the game in a regular order. Look to your left, look ahead of you, look to your right, check your gun's condition, the paint in your loader, check your rear and your front, and then repeat the procedure.

Eventually you will learn to split your attention properly. You will also learn what you need to pay attention to and what you can ignore. Your main goal during your first few games should be to get a pattern down and then remember to use it.

"WHY IS MY GUN SHOOTING SIDEWAYS?"

This is a simple, yet forgettable, skill. Before you go on the field, make sure that your gun is clean, your goggles are clear, "your tank has enough gas," and you're carrying enough paint for the game.

SELF-ELIMINATION

Too many players lose game-time, and valuable experience, by thinking that because they've run out of paint or air, or their gun goes down, the game is over for them.

You can leave the field if you want to, but why would you want to. Stay and concentrate on learning. Find ways to stay in the game longer. Learn to hide. Learn to crawl. Learn to bluff the other team.

Get as much playing time as you can, regardless of the condition of your equipment.

FAILURE TO REDUCE THE TARGET

Making yourself small is an important skill. The smaller you are, the harder you are to see and to eliminate. In order to 'tuck in' effectively, you have to be aware of exactly where your arms, legs, head, gun, and other equipment are at all times.

This is one of those skills that simply takes time to acquire. However, you can speed up the process by paying attention to where you get hit after the game and by looking at how you take and use cover during the game.

Once in cover, pull your elbows into your body. Tuck your legs in. Get your head down. When you come out of cover to view the field, only expose one eye. While you are shooting, keep your gun barrel as close to the edge of your cover as possible.

Don't use a classic shooter's hold on your gun. Twist the arm of your trigger hand down under the gun. Place the arm of your support hand under the gun as well. When done correctly, both of your elbows should be almost touching on or in front of your chest.

TELEGRAPHING YOUR MOVES

When you break cover, and if you really want to play you're going to have to, you don't want to meet up with a paintball just hanging in the air waiting for you.

Take the precaution of varying where, when, and how you break cover. If your head constantly pops up over the top of a bunker, in the exact same place every time, someone on the field is going to target that spot and keep on shooting at it until you are gone.

To avoid telegraphing, never pop out in the same place two times in a row. Change everything: pop out low on the left, high on the right, from close in on your cover to backed away from your cover. There are thousands of ways you can break cover, and you should be trying to use every one of them.

FAILURE TO USE ANGLES

If you are using cover properly, the last player on the field who is a threat to you is the one directly in front of you. Once you're down behind that bunker or tucked in behind a tree, you can't shoot at the players to your front, and they can't hit you.

This basic situation means that you must shoot to the sides, or at an angle from your cover. Forget about the players in front of you and look for the ones off to the left and the right. Look deep across the field if you are towards the center, or look out to the opposite boundary if you are near the tape. You'll be surprised at how many targets you can find.

LACK OF AGGRESSION

Being aggressive does not necessarily mean running straight down the field hollering your head off. And yet, you might be surprised to learn that this actually works once in a while.

Aggression is a finely balanced thing; too much and you end up in an over-exposed position with the inevitable result. Not enough and you end up making your moves too little, too late.

Pushing the envelope will help you learn just how far you can go. Next time you play, try to get to a piece of cover that is just a little closer to your opponents. And then the next, and the next. Try to get behind them. Try running further down the field at the opening of the game. Push it, and then keep on pushing it. If you see an opportunity to win the game, rally your teammates around you, and make it happen.

A MULTI-DIMENSIONAL GAME

Paintball is not just a stand-up game. It's a kneeling game. A crouching game. A lying game. A crawling game. A timing game.

Being in a particular location on the field at the beginning of the game may be very safe. Towards the end of the game, the same spot might be the last place you would want to be.

If you can't move up the field by running, try crawling. If you are lying behind cover and can't make the shot, try it from a sitting position. If you want to move to another position, wait until no one is looking at you.

Use the entire field, all of the time.

—SD

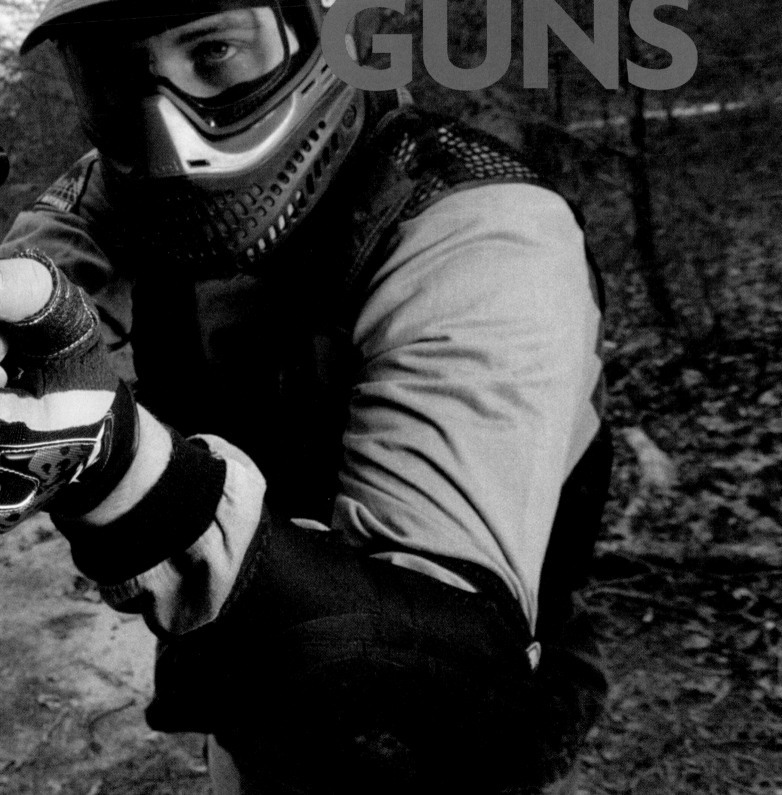

GUNS

The Science of Paintball

PAINTBALL 101

Required reading for hard core paintball enthusiasts!

At its inception, paintball borrowed its technology and science from other sources out of sheer necessity. There was no such thing as a 'paintball gun', a paintball designed to be shot at 300 feet per second, paintball specific goggles, or any other piece of specialized equipment, simply because the game did not yet exist. But there was precedent for the development and production of these things, so paintball really hit the ground running.

During paintball's formative years, enterprising individuals and companies developed products using a trial-and-error, cut-and-paste, tinkering-in-the-garage approach. In scientific circles this is known as an 'empirical' method. You come up with an idea, build something based on the idea, identify its flaws and errors by using it, make corrections, add refinements, and continue on to a finished product.

Science, in the form of highly educated and degreed individuals working out complex formulas on blackboards, was not necessary. That work had already been done. The art of creating paintball products and equipment was simple and straightforward. If you could understand how a paintball gun worked, if you could cut PVC tubing with a hacksaw, work a mill or a lathe, or sew a few pieces of material together, you were in business.

Things have changed dramatically over the past decade and, while it is not yet possible to earn a degree in paintball science (something which is not all that far from happening), *a firm grounding in such things as physics, ballistics, pneumatics and hydraulics, chemistry, materials science and related disciplines, will come in very handy when attempting to work with today's paintball technologies.* And paintball players may even find all of this interesting, too!

One of the most interesting aspects of paintball is the wide range of sciences, both hard and soft, that it touches upon. The fact that equipment designers use the laws of physics is no surprise, but the use of the 'soft' science of ergonomics (fitting tools to the human body) might be. The use of ballistics is another obvious match for paintball. Psychology's relationship to paintball, on the other hand, is less intuitive; nevertheless several well-respected psychologists have studied paintball in relation to risk-taking behavior, stress, and a variety of other aspects of human behavior.

Just as scientific disciplines underly the paintball industry's growth, unique technologies that have emerged from paintball have found applications beyond the game. At present, gas regulators developed for paintball guns are used by a major manufacturer of computer chips (for clean room regulation), a tire manufacturer is investigating the use of pressure gauges designed for paintball (for use with self-inflating tires for military vehicles) and aerospace technicians are investigating paintball gun electropneumatic systems as possible maneuver control systems for small spacecraft.

Paintballs in Space!

This is only a brief sampling of how far and wide paintball science has already spread.

For those who do want to delve into the science of paintball, a basic understanding of physical laws, calculus, physics, ballistics, aerodynamics, pneumatics, fluid dynamics and electronics will give you a good start.

HOW PAINTBALL WORKS

Integrating scientific disciplines in the name of paintball fun!

The art of designing a paintball gun (or a gun barrel, goggles, or propellant system), is an interdisciplinary one. You can't work with electronics to the exclusion of ballistics; paintball technology requires an understanding of how these and other scientific disciplines interact.

You also have to appreciate the fact that no one knows everything yet. There are still some very interesting puzzles to be solved.

Newtonian Basics
To understand the science of paintball, you need to start with Isaac Newton. Newton discovered the

law of gravity (he's the guy the apple fell on) and several related laws of motion and energy that affect everybody and everything.

Newton's laws can be found in any basic physics text. A summary is provided here.

- Two objects with mass attract each other; the force of attraction is proportional to their mass and depends upon how far apart they are. This is gravity.

- An stationary object will remain stationary unless something acts upon it. Likewise, an object in motion will remain in motion unless something acts on it. These are laws of motion.

- Energy is never lost, although, it may take different forms. Now you know the conservation of energy principle.

How do these laws affect paintball? It should be obvious to anyone that a paintball fired from a gun is not going to keep on going forever. Gravity will eventually pull it to the ground. You need something to get a stationary paintball started; how expanding gases propel a paintball down the barrel of a gun is partially a result of the effects of the laws of motion and conservation of energy.

These are fundamental laws of the natural universe. Only by taking them into account, can you truly understand how and why a paintball gun works the way that it does, or why a paintball behaves as it does after being fired.

Fluid Dynamics

An understanding of fluid dynamics also comes in handy; this is the study of how fluids (in this case,

gasses) operate in varying conditions, as well as how to manipulate them. This particular science is one that is still not completely understood, not even by NASA. However, the laws of fluid dynamics tell us certain essential things, such as the fact that the faster a fluid is moving, the lower the pressure will be (and consequently the temperature). These laws explain to some degree what happens when a stream of moving gas interacts with a stationary mass of gas, or why a golf ball with dimples travels farther than one without dimples—or, for that matter, why a paintball with dimples does not travel as far as a paintball without them.

Fluid dynamics can be used to understand and manipulate the way in which the gas propels the paintball, how it flows down the barrel, how to get faster or greater flow of gas through a regulator and related uses.

Ballistics

Ballistics is the science (and art) of the motion of projectiles. How and why do a rock shot from a catapult, a bullet from a gun, a man from a cannon or a paintball from a paintball gun behave the way they do? Ballistics attempts to answer these and other questions. It is also used to predict what might happen to a projectile given a particular set of circumstances (e.g., the shape and density of the projectile, its mass, the speed at which it is fired, the air density, gravity, the angle of the shot).

Some specialized equations, formulas, factors, and laws have been developed specifically for the understanding of ballistics. Among these are:

- The **ballistic coefficient**—a constant relating to the mass and shape of the projectile

- The **form factor**—another number which mathematically represents the shape or surface area of the projectile.

Because (1) the ballistic coefficient is essential to any equation which seeks to explain how a paintball in flight will act, (2) the form factor is critical to establishing a ballistic coefficient, and (3) developing an accurate form factor for the paintball has proven elusive (given its large size, small mass and inconsistencies of its surface features), the ballistic properties of the paintball have yet to be accurately modeled or understood.

So how does all of this relate to paintball?

Is a paintball a solid mass, at least for the purposes of resolving an equation? Does the fluid (paint) inside the shell move? If it moves, does it move enough to affect anything? Does the shell rotate around the fluid when the ball is in flight or does the fluid move?

Fluid dynamics quickly gives way to aerodynamics—the study of the forces acting upon an object which is moving through a gas. The most common application of aerodynamics is the airplane. The forces that aerodynamics studies are the same ones which make an airplane fly. A law of fluid dynamics, Bernoulli's Law, states that the faster a fluid (or gas) moves, the lower its pressure will be. An airplane's wing takes advantage of this *force* by causing the air which travels over the top to go faster than the air passing under the wing: since the pressure above the wing is lower, the air below the wing wants to move in that direction, creating lift and allowing airplanes to fly.

If a paintball were perfectly spherical in shape (which it isn't) the airflow around, over and under the paintball would be the same. Does the additional friction caused by the seam of the paintball create any lift? Does it cause the paintball to rotate so that it presents the surface area with the least resistance to the air? Would a spinning paintball behave differently from a stationary one? Would the direction of spin affect its flight?

These questions are being asked today by paintball researchers and designers. A huge debate currently centers on what effect (if any) *forward* and *back* spin has and if the 'Magnus Effect' is operating. The Magnus Effect says that a spinning object will have regions of higher and lower pressure around it, which will create lift. Theoretically, if a paintball is backspinning the air moving over the top of the ball is moving faster than the air below the ball, creating lift, while frontspin causes the air below the ball to move faster, which might actually cause the ball to drop towards the ground faster than if it weren't spinning. Musket balls are a pretty good analogy for paintballs (they even have seams from molding); perhaps the mass of the musketball has more influence.

If you could see the ball as it flew from your barrel, the ball would either be spinning towards you—backspin, or away from you—frontspin.

Might controlling this spin allow paintballs to travel further? Will a ball that is spinning rapidly be more stable than one which isn't? Bullets are spun by their barrels, so that they are spinning around their long axis. This gives them stability in flight. Do the same forces act in the same way on paintballs. Most of the evidence seems to say, "No," because paintballs are not spun anywhere near fast enough to gain any benefit from this effect. Furthermore, testing seems to indicate its spin will probably have negative effects on performance.

PRINCIPLES OF GAS PROPULSION

Chemistry and Paintball

Chemistry should not be overlooked either. Imagine the precision needed to create a gelatin shell that is elastic enough to withstand being accelerated to speeds in excess of 300 feet per second in a few milliseconds, yet also remains brittle enough to break against a relatively soft and yielding surface after it has given up most of its momentum.

However, there are several things which are much better understood than the flight characteristics of paintballs. The 'Gas Laws', for instance, were formulated in the 1700s and remain fairly predictable to this day. Among other things, the gas laws state:

- A gas will expand to equilibrium. In other words, gas in a closed volume will be at the same pressure everywhere in that volume.

- Gas pressure increases proportionally to temperature. This means that pressure in a given volume increases when it is heated and decreases when it is chilled.

- Gas pressure also increases proportionally with a decrease in volume. This means that if you compress gas in a volume to half its original size, the pressure of the gas in the volume will double. If you increase the available volume by doubling it, the pressure will decrease to half of its original pressure.

Taking advantage of the action of gasses according to these laws is what allows a paintball gun to fire a paintball. Gas (carbon dioxide, nitrogen, or air) is compressed into a tank, such that the pressure of the gas inside the tank is many hundreds of times greater than the surrounding air. This gas stored under pressure is an energy source, better known as 'potential' energy.

Potential energy is energy which is waiting to be used. Energy which is being used is referred to as Kinetic energy.

When you open the valve of the tank, the gas contained inside wants to achieve equilibrium with the surrounding volume, which in this case happens to be the Earth's atmosphere; 14.7 pounds per square inch is the generally accepted air pressure at sea level.

When we use compressed gasses in a paintball gun, we are turning potential energy into kinetic energy, or transferring the energy we get from the gas to the paintball. This occurs by briefly opening the valve to the propellant tank, which allows some high pressure gas to escape into the barrel of the gun. This gas enters a volume in the barrel which is behind a loaded paintball. The energy in the expanding gas is sufficient to overcome the balls' inertia (its tendency to remain motionless and its tight fit against the wall of the barrel), which pushes the ball down the barrel. Energy continues to be imparted to the paintball so long as the gas behind the ball, seeking equilibrium, continues to expand.

Understanding the gas laws allows us to 'regulate' (i.e., finely control the duration and volume of a gas flow) gases, to use gas as both a mechanism for firing the paintball and re-cocking a semi-automatic gun, and for a variety of other applications.

Electronics, and even computer science, have recently been rearing their heads in paintball as well. The latest technological buzzword in the sport is *electropneumatic*. This is simply another name for using electronics in place of mechanical systems in some semi-automatic paintball guns. Initial attempts at marrying the space age to the steam era have proven quite successful. There is no doubt that many more advances will come in this area.

There are many other scientific disciplines pushing the paintball we know and love today toward an even more amazing tomorrow. So many, in fact, that it is impossible to cover them all adequately. It is amazing though how rapidly the science of paintball has progressed from a garage-tinkering hobby to the cutting edge of various scientific endeavors.

—SD

JOHN RICE **ON SAFETY**

Paintball has developed extraordinarily fast over a very short period of time. We've come a long way from the traditional little pistol that used to fire one shot and then required a reload. And everyone used to wear a completely unsafe goggle system. Nowadays you're going up eighteen shots plus, and the goggles are designed to withstand the impact of balls traveling 200 miles per hour in rapid succession. It's a whole new standard of safety for a whole new kind of game. As an industry, we've agreed to hold back on firing rates. My technology could take us up to thirty shots per second, but is the player ready for that? Is the safety equipment ready for that intensity? No matter what, safety needs to set the limit for the implementation of new technologies. On that, we should all agree.

Principles of Worr

Bud Orr

"My dad always said, 'If some guy built it, then you can fix it.'"

In 1953, Bud Orr learned about engine conversions from his father. In 1960, he worked for the U.S. Air Force as a jet fighter mechanic. In 1969, he started working for the Navy overhauling ships (literally, entire ships!). He took up scuba diving, and soon began learning about air flow, gas pressure, and soon began redesigning regulators and compressors. Then, in the mid-1980s, Bud fell in love with paintball, Much of what makes paintball what it is today is directly attributable to innovations pioneered by Bud Orr, founder of Worr Games Products.

ADAM COHEN: So how did you discover paintball?

BUD ORR: Well, one day I came back from vacation and my family wanted to go play paintball. My son wouldn't go unless I went. So, we all went, and basically, I think I rented a PGP at the time and I got shot up pretty bad. And, of course, I loved it.

ADAM: This is back in 1985?

BUD: Yes. And from that point on, we went ahead and went back the next weekend and I thought I could do better because I had thought about the game. The same thing happened, but I figured out why they were shooting at me. Every time I released a CO_2 to change it, they'd run up on me. They were listening carefully and knew when my gun was dead.

So, I went home that week and developed a little device that enabled me to vent CO_2. The following weekend I had more success. I'd vent it, they'd run up, and I'd shoot them. Then, I started modifying guns because I didn't have enough CO_2's. So, I made a manifold so I could actually bolt more CO_2's on it. I was into scuba diving at the time and designed some stuff for the scuba diving industry, so I had access to these little quick release devices. I used them to make it so that you didn't have to expend CO_2 until you pulled a lever.

So, I made a manifold, I bolted two of those on there, and I went out and played all day with two 2.5 ounce CO_2 cylinders.

ADAM: Up to this point, you were doing this primarily because you just loved the game?

BUD: That's right. I just loved it. It was an adrenaline rush. Up to that point... well, I've been a racer all my life. I'm real competitive as far as racing is concerned—drag car racing, sports car racing, boat racing, motorcycles, you name it, I've done it.

The adrenaline rush was just about like it was in racing, only it lasted longer. Just the thrill of the hunt and of being hunted. There's nothing like it, not to this day. Two hours of pure adrenaline rush.

I just started improving the guns. We went to stick feed and then I went over to Sat Cong village and I was a gunsmith there. And in late '86, I was shooting Annihilators. I was actually buying and selling them, and I couldn't really get them from the guy that was making them. He sort of laughed at my ideas for improving the gun. So I went home that week, designed in my head what I wanted to build, and prepared to put it together myself.

Autococker, in all its glory!

I'd been thinking about it for a long time because of all the problems that people had, and different types of play and different atmospheres of play.

ADAM: What were the central problems you wanted to solve?

BUD: I thought it was important to have a feed system on the gun, as well as a constant air system attached directly to the gun. I thought the gun should be closed so that you couldn't get sand in it. Stuff like that. I wanted to build a pretty accurate gun. I didn't like the idea that you couldn't change barrels.

I really didn't like the idea that you had a hose going to the gun from a remote CO_2 system. But, before that, I started to use what they call Ansel bottles; they're for CO_2 cylinders that are made out of steel. I'd mount those on the Sheridan rifles. A guy could play all day on a single bottle of CO_2.

Then I started refilling the cylinders at that point, and I designed an apparatus that we could transverse fill. I don't know that anybody came up with that before I did. Basically, I actually had the first commercial transverse filling.

And from that point on, I was building guns with all kinds of bottles hanging on them. Then I went home one night and I was watching "Miami Vice." Before I watched it, I went out and had a body and frame made in about two hours. After the show, I spend most of the rest of that night building the gun, which became the Sniper.

The next morning I finished it. I went to the Sat Cong village at Battondoon and shot the guy who had laughed at me in the butt. [*Laughs*]

ADAM: When was this, now?

BUD: That was late 1986.

ADAM: Wow. So in essence your first year of involvement with paintball was just one innovation after another.

BUD: Oh yeah, I never quit. It was just one thing

after another for a couple of years. It was neat. The technology was so young; there weren't very many innovative products available. A few people had some really cool stuff, but I wanted it to be more. I pushed the technology a few logical steps further. That's what the Sniper was. It was the first actual paintball gun, the first that was manufactured explicitly for paintball. As opposed to being modified for paintball.

Most of the guys took pellet guns from Sheridan, and they took paint markers... 007's that were made for marking cows... and I think there were a couple of other guns out on the market at that point. Players would take the top barrel off and put a barrel on it and use it for paintball.

I built that first gun. It was the first paintball gun with a direct feed; the first gun out with a closed bolt system that you could field strip. You could actually adjust the velocity without having to tear the gun apart to clip springs.

It was also the first gun to offer a removable barrel. It was one of the leaders in the pumps and stocks, where you had a stock come with it standard.

ADAM: So, within your first year of playing the game, you had started up a company for manufacturing and selling these guns.

BUD: Yeah, I founded Worr Games Products in 1987. It was Thanksgiving of 1987 when I actually incorporated the company, bought my first trailer, and started a business.

Then a year later, in 1988, my Dad was sick. I put in for a leave of absence, so I could spend some time with him. And then he passed away before I even got the time off. That was a bad break. So, I just took the leave the absence.

Now I had worked for the United States government for 22 years, overhauling navy ships in private shipyards. Got kind of tired of that. My wife made pretty good money, so we sat down and figured out that we could live off her paycheck if we needed to. So I just started manufacturing guns in 1988.

I had four months. Four months to make it or break it, you know? And it took off from that point. My daughter, a friend of mine, and my wife and I committed to it.

ADAM: So, you never turned back.

BUD: Our growth was amazing. It was just one innovation after another until 1991. Our company came up with the first speed limit. And we invented the first barrel plug, the first constant air gun, the first screw-in barrel. We had the first ammo box. Actually, we were neck and neck with another company, but when we started making them, we were the only one in the market addressing this need. Russell Maynard, who was the editor of APG at the time, and I made the 45 round ammo box happen.

We spent hours making this ammo box, so it would feed well. We figured it out and it was a huge hit. We sold over 500,000 ammo boxes. From there, we went on to speed ball.

ADAM: How did you come up with the idea for the barrel plug?

BUD: Out of necessity. Guys would come up to the window of our retail store, which we ran for about 5 years. My wife would take a gun from a guy and it would go off and just miss her. She's nice looking, blonde, blue-eyed, and I just didn't want to

see her get hit in the face with a paintball. So we actually came up with a barrel plug.

ADAM: So you invented it to protect your wife?

BUD: [Laughs] Yeah, but we knew it would be good for the market.

The original barrel plug was designed so that if you were shooting at 350 feet per second or under with a nine-inch barrel, the ball would not make it to the end of the barrel because of the air pressure. It would just cushion and stop the ball.

And then, in 1988, I was flying back to see a gentleman named Ray Gong. This man was spearheading a drive to legalize paintball in New Jersey. In 1988, if you owned a paintball gun in New Jersey and got caught with it, you'd go to jail. [EdNote: At the time, paintball was legal in 48 states. Only New Jersey and Massachusetts made it illegal. Currently, paintball is legal in all 50 states.]

So, Ray Gong, myself, Jessica Sparks, and Russell Maynard went to the Supreme Court in the State of New Jersey, and it took us two sessions to get an old law overturned so it was actually legal to play paintball in New Jersey.

ADAM: Cool.

BUD: Yeah, it was a battle, but we won. Anyway, I was flying back to meet with Ray, and I met some women and children whose fingers broke when they were hit with paintballs. Like I said, there wasn't a chronograph at the time. Very few people used chronos. The way they adjusted a gun's velocity was pretty crude. If the gun shot bark off a pine tree, it was shooting too hot. So, you turned it down and cut the spring until you shot and the bark didn't come off. That was supposed to be a safe level. Of course, people were still getting their fingers broken, which was intolerable.

I went to an orthopedic surgeon and asked him what were the average pressure level and types of pressures that fingers could withstand in terms of the impact of a paintball. He told me that the average would be about 12 pounds of energy.

I calculated the weight of the paintball and all that stuff and came up with 300 feet per second. Not that the gun shot very well at that speed. It was simply a rational safety factor; guns wouldn't break bones at that level. So, I was the one to come up with 300 feet per second, which is the paintball velocity at virtually every outdoor field. They turn it down even more for indoor fields, to about 270 feet per second or lower.

ADAM: From that point forward, the key challenge was developing guns that fire reliably and accurately at that speed.

BUD: You bet it was. And we even accounted for variations that might make the gun fire hotter all on its own. You know, people make mistakes, like setting their gun out in the sun. My gun, if it gets up over 1100 pounds of pressure in a chamber area, would fire at about 320 feet per second. But after 1100 pounds, the gun simply won't fire.

The weight of the hammer and the chamber pressure, the spring pressure, and the speed of the hammer are all designed to prevent the valve chamber from opening until the pressure reaches the level that fires at 300 feet per second.

We didn't have regulators at that point. Around 1990, Tom Kay, inventor of the AutoMag, and I solved that problem. Tom Kay and I are extremely good friends. We actually met in '87 or '88, and I

flew back to meet him, and we were going to do some projects together. I had the ammo project and he and I were both independently plugging away on the semiautomatic at the time. When I walked into his facility and sat down and talked to him, I was shocked. Right there on his desk was almost an identical copy of what I was working on.

He and I thought the same way. As a matter fact, the only difference was in the hammer. He used rubber bands to adjust the pressure, as far as pulling the hammer back into place, whereas I used an old beat up spring. That was it.

And, so we made a deal. I'd go off on ammo box, he went off on the semi. Eventually, I actually made my semi and sold it to PMI.

None of us had a lot of money back then. I helped him out and he helped me out. Tom still comes out once a year and we go over old times. There's nothing that we hide from each other. We're fierce competitors on the open market, but we're still really good friends. And I think we'll remain that way the rest of our lives.

ADAM: Tell us about the origins of the Autococker.

BUD: Well, in the early 1990s, semiautomatics were coming and, to be perfectly frank with you, I really didn't like that. Back then, I was trying to push on people what I liked about paintball. I thought the idea of semiautomatics would subtract from the development of paintball as a highly competitive, skills-oriented game.

Paintball was originally designed to highlight individual skills. The point was never what a player had in his hand. It's great that Hayes [Noel] came up with the paintball gun, but even he thought of the gun as a means, not an end. The game was originally about survival, and that's the way I always looked at it. The way the game forces you to improvise is so unique. I've actually thrown paint balls at people and got them out because I was out of CO_2. That's the thrill of it. Not firing tons of paint. Anyone can pull a trigger, but knowing how to do it so that you prevail is the real thrill.

ADAM: Suddenly it looked to you like the technology was going to upstage the skills.

BUD: Yes. And it has. The game I loved is hard to find. Whenever you can sit back and just hose paint at somebody, it takes away from the sport.

So, at that point, I didn't want to be a semi-guy. But Tom had brought out the automatic and, from a business perspective, I was just forced into it.

I had a bunch of ideas. I ran across a gentleman named Jamell, out of Sacramento. We put our ideas together and came up with the Autococker.

Jamell got out of paintball and I continued on with the Autococker. We're talking 1990, because I sponsored the Ironmen team that year. It was one of the first teams I ever sponsored, and they used the Autococker.

Up to two years ago, some of the guys on the Ironmen team still played with pump guns. There are actually point men who play with a pump gun. Some of them hated the semis, couldn't get used to them. And we're talking about amazing point men, guys who are doing a ton of shooting in every game.

The Autococker is actually a pneumatic system that I bolted on to a pump. If you take the pneumatic cocking system off, you have a top of the line pump on the market. The closed bolt system, which is a design of the Autococker, seems to have good range and consistency. Too many gun manufacturers fall short of that, even today.

Then we came up with regulators and regulating systems. That's the first one. Unique Sporting Goods brought out a design for an on-off valve that goes into cylinders. And it would be a nightmare to make any of those valves in quantity, so we came up with another design, and that's the on-off valve that's on the market right now. That's probably one of the last, really influential projects that we were responsible for.

ADAM: So, how would you describe the state of the Autococker today?

BUD: Great. If you look back at the history of paintball, this gun's back in all the magazines. It came out in the second or third issue of APG, and it's been in there ever since. It's outlasted all other guns on the market. I don't know of any gun right now—with the exception of the PGP—that was on the market 10 years ago.

ADAM: Have there been any modifications to it? Significant modifications in that time?

BUD: Every day. And all of the modifications that we've made on the Autococker will fit on the original gun. So, no matter what year's model you own, even if you bought one of the first ones, ten of which had no serial numbers, all of my modifications to date will fit on that gun.

That's what makes the Autococker like a 1911 Colt .45. It's a standard that ages quite well. And many people make a living off of making accessories for the Autococker. Modifications on it are unlimited. Every time I think I've seen them all, along comes something new.

ADAM: Is there anything you can share with us about the future of Worr Games paintball guns?

BUD: Sure. We're heading into electronics. We're already working on them. We're actually working on retro-fit kits for the Autococker so that it can become an electrically operated pneumatic system. Like everything else in this world, the gun is going to be computer-operated.

ADAM: Like the Angel.

BUD: Yes. If you really look at the Angel, it's basically an open bolt 'cocker, because they use a three-way. As a matter fact, the valve system in the Angel is identical to mine, just scaled down a little bit, which we talked about. I mean, they didn't copy it; what they've done is pretty great. They made it work.

ADAM: Do you still play the game, Bud?

BUD: Oh, yeah!

ADAM: And when you do, what are some of the accessories that you use with your Autococker? Are there any you can't go without at this point?

BUD: Not really. When I go out to play, I usually pull a new Autococker off the shelf, one that's ready to ship.

That's how I know whether my stuff is good enough for the public. If I see somebody who would like what I have, and I know he can't afford it, I usually give it to him when I'm done for the day. I haven't done that lately because most of the people out there that play nowadays can afford to buy my stuff, I guess.

It costs a lot of money to play nowadays, and that's annoying. When I first started, it would cost me $25 bucks a day, because when I started, paintballs were anywhere from 12 to 15 cents a piece, and we were shooting enamel paint.

So, when we went out and got hit with enamel paint, we had to have turpentine with us to get it

off our skin. And the safety equipment that we used back then? We wore sunglasses.

ADAM: Anybody lose an eye?

BUD: [Laughs] How we didn't blast our eyes out of our heads, I don't know.

ADAM: What do you think about the state of the game?

BUD: The survival part of it is just a great mind trip. I hunted animals for quite a few years, and I was pretty good. I never got skunked in all the years I hunted. I went to areas where they said there were no deer or antelope, and brought out my animal.

So, I classified myself as a pretty good hunter. And I often wondered what it would feel like... you know, I was in the military, so I've been hunted, but that's quite different. The sides were rarely equal, and if you got caught, you might die. Paintball provides an altogether different feeling.

When you're the hunter as well as the one being hunted, and it's not your actual life so much as your pride as a survivor that's on the line, it's just a great experiment. The experience is a test of survival skills and instincts. A bunch of people put themselves in this context where only one can emerge a victor. I haven't been able to duplicate it in any of the things I've ever done in my life. And I've taken my life in my own hands in many ways.

I've jumped out of planes, scuba-dived, participated in every type of extreme sport except bungee jumping. Paintball is just a greater thrill than any of those things.

ADAM: Do you believe that the game today is very different from the game you're describing.

BUD: Today's game can get a little weird. Referees blow a whistle to start the game, and people who don't even see anybody start shooting paint. It's literally impossible that they could hit anybody, but that's irrelevant to them. They are there to shoot.

Right now, there's no adrenaline rush for me unless I play with some of the veterans of the game. They don't shoot unless they have a clear shot and the time is right. These people who just start shooting at anything, who think the ability to shoot, not to hunt, makes them good, they're the ones who've taken over the contemporary game.

ADAM: You ever talk to kids about your way of playing?

BUD: Actually, yes. I was with some kids in New Jersey, and I taught them how to hunt. They took a whole new look at paintball; they felt the adrenaline rush I get from the game. They were turned on by the idea of a guy stepping over them who doesn't even know they're there.

ADAM: Is there any effort currently underway to promote paintball as a survival game?

BUD: I would love to change it back. You know, I love kids, kids are the backbone of our lives. And if I had my druthers, I'd like to take kids out and spend about five or six hours teaching them survival skills in the woods. Then you test those skills by putting them up against another group of kids that are equally trained and go play paintball the way it used to be played.

And if they want to use a full automatic, they would get only 200 rounds. I used to go out with 20 rounds on me, and take out four or five people.

The game was quieter, but no less active. It was more intense.

We used to crawl on our hands and belly over rocks. I'd be crawling... I could crawl right underneath someone... and before they even knew I was there, I got'em all! And I'm a big guy. That's the thrill!

Other times, I'd walk in on a group of people that thought I was on their side, which you accomplish by keeping your armband away from their eyes, so they can't see it. I'd take out 10 of them before getting hosed, but it was worth it.

ADAM: Are there plans to resuscitate this style of play on a widespread basis?

BUD: Yeah. I talked to Hayes Noel about it. Yes, I would say there are plans. Somewhere along the line, when I slow down a little bit from what I'm doing now, I'd like to be involved in that.

There are people that I know who do play this way now. They're renegade players. They take 30 people out in the forest with two cases of paint and play paintball the way it was meant to be played.

ADAM: This is "outlaw" paintball?

BUD: Yeah, 'outlaw,' 'renegade,' it's all the same thing. It's just about a bunch of people who are sick of going to a field where everybody just wants to hose everybody else. Sometimes it gets pretty bad. On some fields, you shoot a guy 15 times in the goggles and he says he's not hit. Some people can't deal with the most basic rule: if you're hit, you're out. Hold up your hand and walk off the field.

I've gone to seminars, talked to people and some of the older groups that used to play paintball, and they would love to see the old game mainstreamed. Some of us set up some games with pump guns that are played on an individual basis. We've offered a $10,000 purse for first, second, and third place.

There's 10 people playing, and you're against all of them. That's the way to play paintball.

ADAM: That's definitely old-school paintball.

BUD: Yup. That puts a whole new aspect on it. We used to play one on one. We used to play "hare and hound" at Easter time. They'd send a 'hare' running, and then release a 'hound' every 15 seconds. They were all against each other, but the goal was to eliminate the hare. So they're hunting someone who can shoot back at them, and they have to look over their shoulders, because every hunter has incentive to take out the other hunters as well. It was awesome. And I think they still do it like that in some places. But those are just scenarios.

We'd take Easter Day, get 30, 40, 50 people out there, and run two or three games, with everyone fending for himself. There's just not a rush like that. It's unreal.

ADAM: You and Hayes Noel are birds of a feather on this view of the game.

BUD: That guy is incredible.

ADAM: Have you played with him?

BUD: Never played with him, but have you ever met him? That guy is just absolutely top of the line. He's just a really neat, fun, individual. I don't know of anybody that could say anything bad about him. He's put me where I am, and I appreciate that. He just started paintball. I'm one of the people that followed in his footsteps when he backed out of it.

ADAM: If he hadn't played that first survival game...

BUD: ...I wouldn't be in business today.

You know, I had often thought about what he thought about, but I didn't know what to use. I was going to use blow guns or darts or slingshots. I always wanted to see if I could survive in the woods, with people chasing me around.

ADAM: Looks like you got your wish.

BUD: Sure did.

ADAM: I really appreciate your sharing your insights with us.

BUD: No problem.

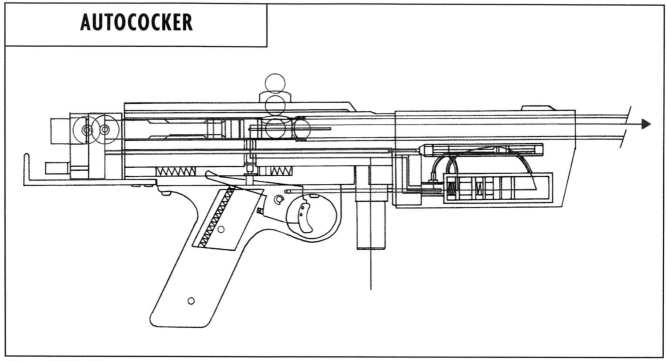

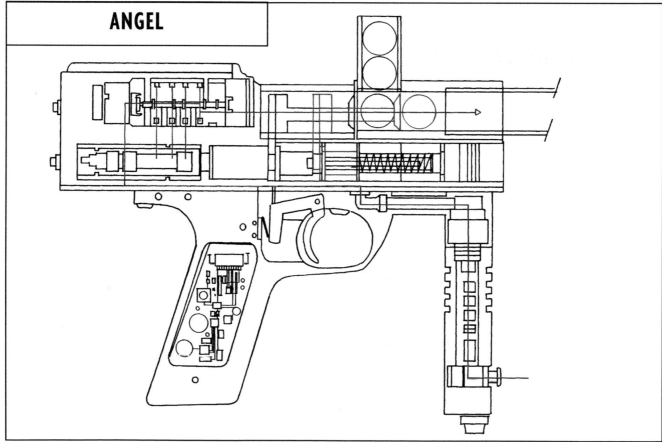

Red lines indicate the action of the bolt.
Blue lines trace the path of the gases.

GUTS

SHOCKER

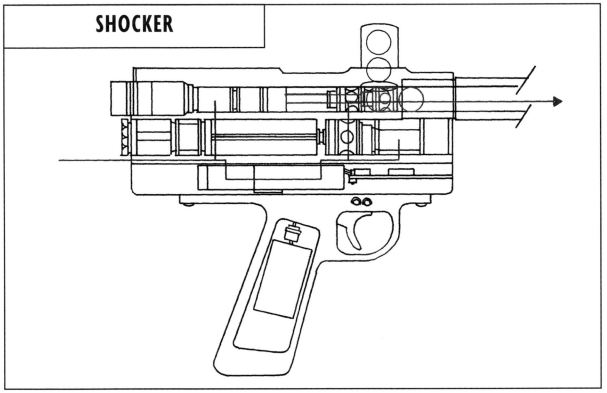

AUTOMAG

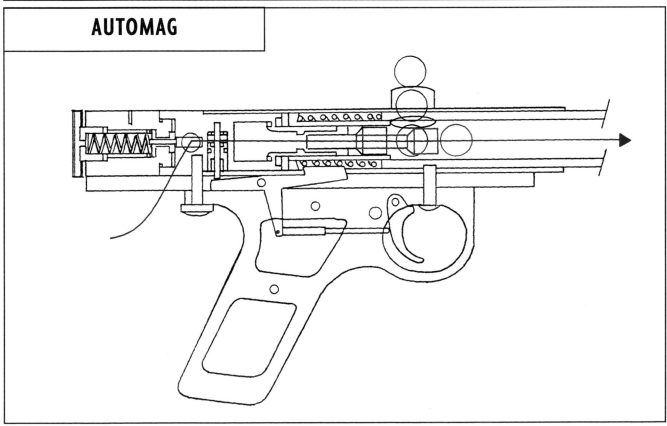

How the Angel Got Its Name and Everything Else You've Always Wanted to Ask This Man

John Rice graduated college with a degree in metallurgy and spent 12 years at TI research laboratories in Cambridge, England, and another 5 years at GE/GEC joint ventures based in England. He specialized in materi-

als technology, high vacuum and surface coating technologies for Joint European Toruss at Harwell Atomic Research. He joined WDP in 1994, working in their new product developments division, and signed on full time as Technical Director in 1995. At 35 years-old, John has been married for 13 years and has a 9 year-old child. His first gun was a Bushmaster, his favorite pump gun is the Sterling, and his first semi-automatic was the Automag.

John Rice and his gun, The Angel, are legendary in the paintball industry. One of the most coveted guns around, the Angel is the first electropneumatic gun to arrive on the scene.

ANDREW FLACH: Where did the idea for the Angel originate?

JOHN RICE: There are certain stars in paintball, players who are very skilled and fast on the trigger. Joe Public wants to be a star. So, I think, how can I make "Joe" a star? The first question in my mind was "how easy is it for 'Joe' to pull a trigger?"

I thought that if I could make it possible for anyone to pull a trigger real fast, as fast as someone who's super fit, it's going to appeal to that player because achieving something awesome will feel "easy."

Now, if you have something that's mechanical and there's a certain timing sequence to maximize the rate of fire, you have to be quite skilled in coordination to achieve the desired result. That's a disadvantage to some players, whereas it might be an advantage to others. So I wanted a leveler, I wanted everybody to have their 15 minutes of fame. That's where electronics come in.

ANDREW: Did you wake up one morning and say 'Eureka'?

JOHN: No, it wasn't as easy as that. If you could have seen the prototype you'd know what I mean. It was spread over about a 5 foot table—bits of valve over here, some electronics over there. Have you ever heard the term "Heath Robinson?"

ANDREW: Heath Robinson is a term? No, I haven't.

JOHN: "Heath Robinson" is English terminology. He was a famous artist who used to draw crazy machines to solve simple problems. Like America's Rube Goldberg. Our first products were like that.

ANDREW: In other words, it did its thing, but you couldn't fit it into a gun.

JOHN: Exactly. But we were thinking about how we were going to make this work. Some of the technology simply wasn't available at the time. That was a major hurdle. I was quite fortunate that, with my background in the industry, I could apply certain industrial technologies to paintball. My former research and engineering experience exposed me to a wide range of possibilities.

New types of materials and different ways of doing things. I realized early on that what I wanted to achieve with a paintball gun could only be achieved with electronics.

I had to take a lot of what the individual did out of their control. I just wanted them to point the gun and pull the trigger, I didn't want them to have to apply any further skill to that process. Basically, that's what the electronics do.

The Angel was born out of my desire, my frustration, my blood, sweat, and tears. And also out of the faith of people like Gerard Green. He believed that we could come up with a product that would work.

We targeted a niche market; the Angel is aimed squarely at the top pro player. It's made in England, and, as I'm sure you've heard, it's very expensive. That's the first thing people say: "It's expensive. Why should I pay that much money?" The answer is that making things in England is expensive. Our labor costs are very high. Machine costs and raw materials are more expensive. These facts, in conjunction with our commitment to R&D and next generation products, plus the level of customer support we offer, lead to an expensive product, but one with a great deal of value built into it. The consumer is receiving the most technically advanced paintball gun in existence.

Europe nowadays cannot rely on a mass market. I don't know if you're aware of how the European market works, but mass marketing in Europe is dead. We can't compete with Poland or Taiwan. So, we specialize. In Europe, everything's moving towards specialization.

ANDREW: Craftsmanship is a way of adding value.

JOHN: Exactly. So we set up the Angel, developed it, launched it, aimed at a very small niche, low production numbers, at the top end player. Due to it's success, it's actually cascaded down, which has surprised us. We're amazed at how many Angels we've sold. And we're actually seeing young kids buying them. 12-year-olds are hassling their parents to buy them. And yes, we'll build a rapport with the parents, offer them support. But that's amazed us.

Our product was not targeted at them. And you know, when you see a young lad come up to you, 12 years old, and he's holding his Angel up, it does knock you for six a bit. [*Laughs*]

One thing we recognized very quickly was that our product was moving across the pond, and to support customers we had to come to America on a regular basis. Because if you're asking someone to part with a lot of money and they say, "I've got a problem, where do I go?", you better be able to answer them.

ANDREW: So, what year marked the origin of the Angel?

JOHN: The first working prototypes that you could actually hold in your hand and play with appeared in 1995. That's when you could actually say "this gun looks like an Angel."

ANDREW: Who named it?

JOHN: Dave Poxon, our Marketing Director. Have you ever heard of a rock group called Saxon? It's a heavy metal group, early 80s, and he used to be its manager. He was into marketing, and he knew which way the music industry was going. He said "Angel is going to be a big word on the music scene," and he chose it as the name of our gun, too. Sure enough, records come out with "angel" themes and lyrics, and it became this new happening thing. That's his skill.

That's how the Angel name came about. It was called the Angel V6. We chose V6 because it sounds gutsy, earthy. In America they like V6. It was V6 because it's 6 volt, no other reason. Amazingly, we dropped the V6, but people over here still say, "Oh, I've got a V6."

Also, the Angel had another appeal. It's a little mysterious. A little sinister. A

little dangerous. You could turn a dark side to it. That's where the Dark Angel was born.

ANDREW: Double entendre.

JOHN: That's it. And it worked very well for us. So that's how the Angel got its name.

Another interesting bit of Angel trivia is the fact that on the packaging, the gun depicted is a left-handed model. The reason it is photographed this way is because I'm left-handed. It wasn't until very late into the design and production of the Angel that we spotted the oversight.

Andrew: So the early production models, the design models...

JOHN: ... are all left handed.

ANDREW: What is it that makes the Angel a unique paintball gun for the player?

JOHN: First of all, the shape works well. It's very sleek, very modern looking. That's come out of European styling more than American styling. In America, space is so free. Everything in the U.S.A. is big. Look at your appliances, look at your cars, look at your houses. You've got space, and you like to fill it. The Americans also like to bolt things on and add things because of this perception that there is no space restriction. In Europe, everything's got to be small. We made everything small deliberately.

People buy instant prestige when they buy an Angel. They're buying something that is European, that is new, that is unique.

Andrew: Tell us about the Angel's technical features.

JOHN: With the Angel, you can have a very short trigger pull. In fact, the first prototype triggers were so soft you could literally blow on them and they would go bang. People shot themselves a good deal. [*Laughs*]

So the trigger is very easy to use, everybody can pick up an Angel and achieve a very high rate of fire. They don't need the skill to do it.

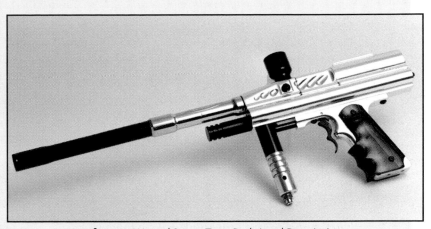

Manufacturer: Warped Sports **Type:** Dark Angel **Description:** Customized and modified Angel with double trigger. *Courtesy of Rocky Cagnoni.*

ANDREW: Now, when you pull the trigger you're activating a circuit?

JOHN: You're basically starting a sequence of events.

ANDREW: What is the sequence?

JOHN: The sequence of events is basically as follows. When I pull the trigger, I start an elaborate clock which now needs to drive electro-pneumatic valves and solenoid valves. And what we've actually got is a Japanese valve. We call it a "fourteen way valve."

It's called that because it has fourteen gas galleries. It's a very reliable valve. The Japanese have done an excellent job in miniaturizing it for me. What that then drives is a traditional mechanism, and although there are several unique features that we've patented in that mechanism, it's still using gas to fire a paintball.

Gas comes into the fourteen way valve and it drives a servo. A servo is how to get some movement using less force, like your brake servo on a car. If you didn't have a servo, you'd be pressing on that brake with all your strength to get an effect. The servo translates a mild force into a heavier force.

For example, if I have a very small piston, I could lift a 300 ton weight with my thumb. I'd only move it very slightly, but I could do it, because I could apply force over a very small area, the way a car jack works. It's mechanical advantage. That's what a servo does. A servo actually drives what we call the spool.

The spool changes gas direction, which drives a hammer forward, and that hammer will strike a valve. Just how long that valve is open for is controlled electronically. Controlling it electronically is extraordinarily efficient. This is all happening in sixteen milliseconds. Sixteen thousandths of a second! This eliminates the "chopping of paint."

ANDREW: And chopping paint is?

JOHN: It's where your bolt or your mechanism comes forward, and it literally chops the paintball in half, before it's properly positioned for firing. You can make guns shoot incredibly fast, but you haven't got a hope in hell of shooting paint. Because if a gun's shooting faster than you can feed it paintballs, it turns into an emulsion gun.

ANDREW: You're blasting out broken paintballs.

JOHN: So with the Angel what you can do is actually adjust the timing. Now, because I can control the timing of the firing mechanism through electronics, I can achieve a very high rate of fire. The Angel has the fastest rate of fire of any paintball gun available.

ANDREW: Which is?

JOHN: Currently we've kept it at 13 shots a second, but 18 shots per second capability is built into every Angel. And yes, it will shoot at that rate for those who have discovered it.

ANDREW: Semi-auto or full auto?

JOHN: Either. There's a set of dip switches on a chip inside the gun that changes the mode of firing. You have semi-auto, full auto, three shot burst, and a "zipper burst."

ANDREW: What is a zipper burst?

JOHN: Zipper burst was developed in reaction to what they called the "Turbo Trigger." Essentially, it's an eight round burst. It's purpose was to show the

Wire synchronizes electronic loader with firing rate of the gun.

farcical nature of some of the current definitions of a trigger action. But that's another story altogether.

ANDREW: Would you have specific loader systems that are recommended for use with this or do people widely use whatever they desire?

JOHN: The most popular system is made by Viewloader. It's a motorized system. However, the paintball industry is on the verge of the next big step, which is force feed.

The limiting factor with any of the current loader systems is gravity. Once you take gravity out of it, rate of fire can go sky high. Way above 30, even hundreds of paintballs a second. It's virtually unlimited, in theory.

THE AIR SYSTEM

ANDREW: The Angel is a compressed air gun, right?

JOHN: Correct. Carbon dioxide is a very harsh gas, and the trouble is it's stored in its liquid state. As it turns into gas, its temperature drops. The colder it gets, the less it wants to give off gas. I call CO_2 a "dirty" gas because it's slow to fill up, it freezes, it's not very temperature stable, and it's very abrasive. The ice crystals that form in it are actually physically abrasive to gun parts.

For running a paintball field, CO_2 is attractive. It's cheap, it's simple, because all you're buying are cylinders of CO_2, you don't have to have a high pressure air regulation system.

With the classic 12 ounce cylinder, you can get 2000 shots off under perfect conditions. Such are the thermodynamics of CO_2. That means you fire one shot, you allow the gas pressure and the temperature to recover, and then fire your next shot. Paintball guns aren't used that way, of course. Paintball guns are shooting faster and faster.

ANDREW: So, in other words, the CO_2 has a lag time between shots caused by the nature of the gas.

JOHN: Yes.

ANDREW: Because each shot costs pressure, and it takes time to get back up to pressure.

JOHN: Up to pressure and temperature. So you can take a CO_2 gun and fire it. The number of shots you get out is phenomenal initially, but things go downhill from there.

ANDREW: So compressed air was your vision from the start.

JOHN: Yes. That was the only choice, in my view. I wanted air, nitrogen. I did not want CO_2.

ANDREW: Now, I heard you use a term earlier, low pressure regulator? The LPR. That sounds like a scuba diving term.

JOHN: Because the Angel is pneumatically driven, I need a lower pressure to drive my pneumatics. My servo valve will not survive high pressure, so I needed a lower pressure to do that.

ANDREW: So you need something to stage it down.

JOHN: Correct. The LPR.

THE INFINITY BARREL

ANDREW: What kind of barrel systems do you use? Do you develop your own?

JOHN: We make our own barrels, which we call the Infinity Series. Barrels are such a personal choice. I could sit here and say Infinity barrels are the best barrel in the world and believe it. But in the end, it's very personal.

ANDREW: What are the unique features of the Infinity barrel?

JOHN: It's a step bore. Have you heard of step boring barrels?

ANDREW: No, tell me what that means.

JOHN: Step boring a barrel is an old system in the manufacture of real firearms for many years. Basically it's a barrel with two bores, each with a separate diameter. The smaller bore provides the acceleration and the wider bore provides guidance. The holes in the side provide a silencing effect.

Now, previously everybody's accomplished this step bore manufacturing process in a two part design. Our two bores are achieved with one tool. Traditionally, step boring required people to hone a bore of one diameter in the first tube, and another diameter in a second tube. Then the two tubes would have to be mechanically joined.

We actually achieve two bores with the same equipment. If you look down the barrel, you can actually see the two bores. Hold it at a distance, and you'll see something like a ring. That's where the two bore diameters meet. No seam is visible.

We don't hone. Some people hone barrels out, we don't. We use a technology that was developed in Germany, using special types of tools and special high pressure coolants. It gives us an edge that no one else has. I believed it was the best way to go. I don't have any misalignment problems involved with joining two points together.

THE LED DISPLAY AND THE FUTURE OF ELECTROPNEUMATIC GUNS

ANDREW: I notice there's a LED on the back of the Angel? What information does that give the player?

JOHN: Looks good, doesn't it?

ANDREW: Yeah.

JOHN: A cosmetic thing. Seriously, though, it's a safety feature. Somebody can see it from a distance and know the gun is on and capable of firing. It's a visual indication, too. When you pull the trigger, the LED changes color. The gun makes a bang sound, but it allows you to see that information.

ANDREW: Have you ever thought of putting a counter on the Angel?

JOHN: No comment. But, if you're asking me where paintball's going, I'll tell you where I think it's going. Electronics are here to stay. You're going to be hooking them up to your computers, you're going to have digital displays. You're going to have RS232 ports, infrared links. You're going to have user interfaces, you're going to have head up displays. That's where the sport's going.

ANDREW: High tech all the way.

JOHN: Technology is being applied to everything. People are timid about electronics initially. When we first launched the Angel, people said "Oh, it's going to be unreliable," or, "It's not going to work." There was a lot of negative speech about electronics. Electronics are used in every walk of life. Anything you do counts on electronics. That's a trend that's only going to get bigger. And soon, any competitive paintball gun will be electronic as well.

ANDREW: What's the next step for WDP? How long is this version of the Angel going to be around?

JOHN: No comment. [Smiling]

ANDREW: Why are you smiling?

JOHN: I could tell you, but then I'd have to kill you.

ANDREW: [Laughs]

JOHN: Just wait and see.

F/A THE DAY AWAY

Single-Action. Auto-Trigger. Pump-Action. Double-Action. Semiautomatic. Full-Automatic.

Paintball guns have evolved radically over the past eighteen years, driven by players' fervent desire for ever increasing rates of fire. This has become a source of contention, concern, and debate among members of the paintball community.

Back in 1981 and 1982, when this great game was just getting started, there were really only two gun choices: the side-cocking Nelspot, remembered by its users for the calluses it left on their fingers, and the rear-cocking Sheridan PGP. Both guns had to be recocked between shots using a rather complicated procedure. For the Sheridan, you had to turn the bolt a quarter turn, pull it back until it clicked, tilt the gun back, so the ball could roll into the chamber, tilt the gun forward, push the bolt back in, and then turn it back a quarter turn. For the Nelspot, you had to raise the cocking lever, pull it back, tilt the gun forward, tilt it back, push the lever forward, and then lock it in place.

It's hard to remember the procedures in correct order, let alone retain the mindset necessary to shoot someone two or three times using it! It's no wonder that players were considered to be paint hogs when they carried more than 50 or 60 rounds per game.

Rate of fire was not something that concerned those who played the game in its infancy. Waiting an hour for a single elimination was common. Forcing opponents to surrender was considered the highlight of the game. But then, what more can you hope for when you can only fire about three rounds per minute?

Missed shots, chopped balls, empty firing chambers, and general frustration led many players to concoct their own solutions to the problem, beginning with the pump. A relatively simply modification, the pump did away with the need to pull and turn the bolt. Shortly after, someone came up with the idea of the 'gravity feed,' which meant that it was no longer necessary to roll the ball into the chamber. Both ideas were combined and the paintball technological revolution was underway.

The new ideas caught on quickly; less complicated guns meant more people could play the game. More paint being fired meant that game site owners were making bigger profits. Start-up manufacturers now had hundreds of potential products and a new audience waiting for them.

Players quickly became obsessed with how many balls they could fire per second. One player remembered his/her course in basic firearms, shaved a gun sear, and created the auto-trigger, a device that eliminated the need to pull the trigger when firing. Your average player, someone who owned their own gun and played regularly, could now pump out four to five rounds per second. Legendary players were clocked at seven rounds per second!

The quest for a user-friendly gun now turned into a mania for increasing rates of fire. Before anyone could figure out how to make a semi-automatic, at least two companies marketed a double-action, the first pumpless paintball gun.

Unfortunately, the mechanics of a double-action (releasing the sear and resetting the bolt in one pull of the trigger) created a slower rate of fire, relegating these guns to the backwater of paintball technology. However, the first generation of semi-automatics was not long in coming.

First introduced around 1990, most new semi-automatics were technological disasters. They were prone to breakdowns and leaks, in addition to being poorly designed and sensitive to weather conditions. Manufacturers were rushing to supply a new demand.

The first protest against this increasing rate of fire made itself heard around this time. Probably due more to the bad performance of the new guns than to anything else, many tournament teams refused to use semiautomatics and lobbied tournament promoters to ban their use also.

This protest was short-lived with the arrival of the second generation of semiautomatics. They were more reliable, less complicated, and backed by some of the most respected companies in the industry. Seeing a trend in the making, many event producers offered 'open class' competition where any gun was welcome. High profile teams began endorsing them and semiautomatics quickly became the guns of choice.

Gun designers and experienced players had learned something over the intervening years; paintballs are only accurate within a very limited range. Beyond that range, luck plays a huge role. The only way to increase the chance of a hit is through volume and persistence. Once players realized this, the quest for increasing rates of fire swept all other priorities aside. The need for a fully automatic paintball gun had arrived.

The late 1990s ushered in the second introduction of the fully automatic. In 1985, Tippmann Pneumatics introduced the SMG-60 (later converted to the SMG-68), which could fire up to twenty balls with a single pull of the trigger. It met with mixed reviews from the players; some feared it and felt that it represented a safety hazard, particularly at close range, leading it to be banned from many playing fields and events. Other players had nothing but contempt for its users, after having learned that once the clip was emptied the user was vulnerable as the SMG could take well over a minute to reload. The gun itself was a good performer, accurate and very robust, but just a little ahead of its time.

Other companies, like Palmer's Pursuit Shop and Pro-Team Products, introduced novelty full-automatics around the same time. These were extremely expensive show guns that were designed more to demonstrate technical prowess than to create a marketable product.

It took over a decade for development to come full circle with the introduction of the electropneumatic paintball marker. Once you start running a gun with a microchip just about anything is possible.

In 1995, Tippmann Pneumatics introduced the F/A, a spring actuated full-automatic. It's only real drawback was that after reloading, the user had to crank the spring by hand. Later that same year, Smart Parts introduced the Shocker, an electro-pneumatic paintball gun with three modes of fire: single shot, three round burst, and full automatic. At the same time, Airgun Designs unveiled the Reactive-Trigger Automag (RT) and WDP from England introduced the Angel, another electropneumatic equipped with multiple modes of fire. Shortly after the introduction of these new guns, the rate of fire debate began and has been going strong ever since.

Smart Parts engineered an after-market upgrade for their gun called the 'Turbo Board,' which was able to anticipate the user's highest firing rate and then reproduce that rate, even if the user was pulling the trigger at a slower rate.

Although not truly fully automatic, the RT was dragged into the same category of 'super-semi' because of its ability to fire at very high rates with little intervention by the user. The Angel was also classed as a 'super-semi' because it had the ability to replicate the performance of the Shocker and RT.

The electropneumatic paintball guns are amazing performers. In fully automatic mode, they can put out a total blanket of fire. Two or more of these guns used by experience players can virtually shut down an entire field of opponents.

Yet while at first enthusiastic about the ability to shoot more paint—half the fun in paintball is pulling the trigger—players have begun to complain about getting hit. Field owners have become concerned over their insurance liability and the loss of customers due to the perception that, "playing at

Getting ready for a game

Guns

that field will get you lit up." Goggle manufacturers are asked if their lenses and frames can withstand, "multiple impacts in a short period of time." Paintball technology has, in a way, become a victim of its own success. The gun manufacturers give the players exactly what they are looking for, but maybe not exactly what is needed for the game to thrive.

Is it safe to subject players to a situation in which they can be hit by up to sixteen rounds per second? Does paintball need to limit its technological growth? Is there such a thing as a reasonable limit for high rates of fire?

Some members of the paintball community advocate a self-imposed rate of fire limit of thirteen and half rounds per second (the current high without electronic assistance). Some also recommend such artificial fixes as a three round limit, which means that players must stop and check on their opponents' condition after firing three rounds. Others are making suggestions for new rules such as an engagement range limit, the separation of players into classes based on their guns, or limiting the amount of paint that an individual can carry.

These solutions are impractical, so it is doubtful that any of them will find widespread acceptance. Players will continually seek to enhance their technological edge. The bottom line is that if they can't do it on the commercial paintball fields, they'll do it on private fields. Players, regardless of their stripe or 'the truth', love to boast that their rate of fire is better and faster than everyone else's. Silly? Yes. A reality not likely to change anytime soon? You bet.

A three round shot limit is completely impractical; new players can barely remember how to pull the trigger, let alone stop themselves after three counts to inquire about the status of the person who is shooting paint at them. All it takes is one player to decide that he/she will fire four shots before checking. Furthermore, there is absolutely no way that a referee can keep track of how many rounds different players have fired at any given time.

Any rule that does not take into account the natural way that players participate is bound to fail. Players do not carry signs saying, "I surrender," which automatically deploy whenever an opponent gets within a certain distance. New players, who are the most likely to order the guns with the highest firing rate, and then complain strenuously about getting hit too much, resort to instinctive responses during the game (e.g., holding the trigger down and firing as fast as they can at anything and everything that moves, or just hiding when they get hit and getting bunkered for their choice). Such responses do not follow rules.

Fields can try to organize games based on technology, but the reality is that few fields ever have enough players in each category or class to make this economically viable. You can't ask paying customers to play with two or three other people based on the type of gun they purchased. After a few days without much competition, they'll find somewhere else to go.

As time progresses, the industry will come to realize the truth about the recreational sport's business: paintball companies are firmly in the business of giving the customer what they want. It is a field's business to provide a fun and safe experience, without the customer having to be confused by artificial rules and restrictions whose use and enforcement are dependent upon them. If pain and multiple hits are customer concerns, products which reduce the impact should be introduced, or a lower velocity limit should be imposed.

The irony of this situation is that lots of paint being fired translates into industry success. Because of that incentive, the rate of fire will be difficult to limit. If it's possible to create a paintball gun that can shoot one thousand rounds per second, someone is going to build it, someone is going to buy it, and someone is going to get shot by it. The demand underlying this trend pretty much obliterates all other considerations, unless safety issues are not properly addressed.

The only real question concerns how the industry is going to respond responsibly and effectively to emerging technologies. Will the new super guns be embraced by commercial fields, where their use can be controlled and supervised, or will they thrive in the riskier, uncontrollable private field arena?

No matter how the industry responds, paintball players need to consider that the game is really not about the paintball gun. Yes, obviously, the gun is a key tool, and there's nothing wrong with wanting the latest and greatest semiautomatic. But using any paintball gun prudently is a responsibility that ultimately falls to the players of this game. If you love the game, hopefully you'll take that responsibility seriously and insist that your fellow players do so as well.

—SD

EDITOR'S NOTE: As of August 8th, 1999, several of the major gun manufacturers agreed to establish a voluntary moratorium on the manufacture of full-automatic paintball guns, and further agreed to limit the upper rate of fire of all semiautomatic paintball guns to a maximum of 13 rounds per second.

Left: Adam Gardner, Right: Bill Gardner

GETTING TO KNOW THE SHOCKER

ANDREW FLACH: What's the story about the Shocker?

ADAM GARDNER: Many of our ideas come out of the fact that we play at the highest level all the time and we're constantly looking for the edge. The edge in racing can be quite small, but at the highest levels, a small competitive advantage makes the difference.

I'm head of the product development team, and what we are always looking for are ways to improve the gun so that my game is improved. If my game can be improved, then everybody else's game can be improved.

In building the Shocker, we've integrated the best concepts: minimum ball breakage, long range accuracy, aesthetics. These are the things serious paintball players want. Add to that, it's the first electropneumatic paintball gun. Other people will argue that, but the bottom-line is, we have the patent on it.

ANDREW: Can you explain what that term means? Electropneumatic.

ADAM G: Guns all involve timing. Timing means that the bolts have to operate in such a way that a ball is dropped, a bolt moves forward, and a gun fires. Pretty simple process that really doesn't change from gun to gun, except in terms of performance.

We brought in electronics because they are precise. Mechanical timing can't be held to the same standards in terms of timing. We combine two solenoid valves together with digital electronics. Solenoid valves are electrically fired valves. The result is extremely good control over the timing of the way the gun fires. This adds tremendous performance consistency and the possibility of new features.

On the mechanical side, we wanted the lowest pressure, longest range, most accurate gun we could find. And with low pressure comes minimal ball breakage, because there's not as much energy exerted against each ball.

Then there's accuracy. The gun is unique in that there's no anti-doubler. Most guns have anti-doubler devices—these are devices balls settle into and rock against. Without an anti-doubler, what happens is, if you hold the bolt open in the back, two balls can roll in. The anti-doubler prevents the second ball from rolling in. But under rapid fire, you still have to push the ball past it. Not on the first shot, but on the following shots.

The Shocker uses only timing to hold the ball. We never push it past anything. So, there's no little ball bearing, or spring. Nothing is pushing sideways on the ball as it's firing.

Beyond the super low pressure and everything else, we're also not interfering with the ball shot to shot. The accuracy level we've been able to achieve with this gun is beyond anything we've ever seen.

Again, the reason for all of this is that I want to go out and win my paintball games at the highest levels of competition. I'm not saying, we're not here to make money because we are, of course. But I think that we're in this business because we love the game, and that ensures that we'll promote new technologies that make a difference in game play, not merely in profit margins.

ANDREW: Was there one concept you started with when developing the Shocker?

BILL GARDNER: Low pressure. I determined early on that low pressure was absolutely necessary. Low pressure was the primary concept. And then, electropneumatics. The concept was to combine low pressure and electropneumatics.

As I saw it, that was the way to make better guns. Bringing those concepts together opens up more opportunities for developments in paintball gun technology. More components can be used at low pressure than at high pressure. Things don't wear out at lower pressure. Your gun will last longer, and parts will last longer, too.

ANDREW: How long did it take to develop this idea?

BILL: Two years, at least, and lots of money, effort, and designs that weren't right. These designs look simple only after they're done right.

ANDREW: What are the Shocker's features?

BILL: It likes to shoot consistently and it doesn't break paint. It's got three fire modes: three-shot burst, single shot, and fully automatic. It's one of the only guns you can fire consistently fully automatic without breaking paint.

There's also another very controversial feature that it has, which is called a Turbo Board.

ANDREW: What's a Turbo Board and what does it do?

BILL: The average player can only pull their finger at a specific speed. And everyone wants to shoot fast. You've got a lot of people who are dexterous and can shoot very fast. So we developed a technology called Turbo. It's a trigger enhancement. You still have to move the trigger full speed, and you still have to fire, but it allows you to achieve better consistency than you could without it. It's not so much fire rate, but consistency.

And when the Shocker first came out, the fire rate was 11.2 shots per second, which is fast. Anyone could pull the trigger and fire at that rate. It's not a fully automatic gun, it's a semiautomatic gun.

ANDREW: Where does that fall into the rules?

BILL: For a year, we've been fighting with the various rule-makers to determine what's legal and what isn't. And what they've come down to now is they say, "You can use your Turbo Boards if you want to, but we're going to limit your fire rate to 9 shots per second."

ADAM G: So that's fine with us. That's what I use anyway. And yet, there are other guns that use very light touching methods that can shoot 13 shots a second. So, it becomes a matter of semantics. In other words, if I'm shooting 11.2 shots a second with turbo, and you're shooting 13 with a light trigger, what's the difference?

We can do things that make it a really unique gun. What we've done with this technology is make the first three shots normal fire, so you can aim them. After the third pull, you kick in the enhanced mode and you can sustain a faster rate of fire.

ANDREW: In terms of the electronic circuitry, one of the things that came up when we spoke to the guys out at Skirmish was that the older guns are easy to maintain. With all the new circuitry in here, is the Shocker something that you can foresee a recreational player having?

BILL: 85%–95% of our sales are recreational. We had mothers phoning up here for that gun, and we sold out and sent them to one of 30 dealers that we hoped had guns in stock. These are strictly recreational players, 13–16 year-old kids.

ADAM G: People want exhilaration. Especially the new generation. Kids love fast firing guns. They love things that fire fast and move fast and shoot fast.

ANDREW: I'm thinking more about just the sophistication of the technology. In other words, like circuit boards.

ADAM G: See, electronics scare people. People who don't understand electronics assume difficulties and problems come with electronics. The bottom line with electronics is that they're dependable.

I'm not going to say to you that this is as dependable as a pump gun, because I'm sure it's not. It's much more complex than that. We're moving the bolt 11.2 times a second. We have a lot of things going on. In the end, we're a service oriented company.

If you have problems with your gun, we aim to get it back to you within a week. Sometimes we can't meet that, but we usually do. We train our dealers. Everybody can come in and take our training session. And the sport has professionals, like golf pros, who run shops all over this country.

Then there are user-support groups. Go to the Shocker web page and you'll get a feel for the community of users surrounding our product. The site just evolved on its own. It's got pictures of every way to fix the Shocker, constant discussion about the way it works, full blown color pictures.

ANDREW: I'm very impressed with the gun. Having just seen and test fired it, I'm thinking this is pretty cool. Seven hundred bucks is not small change, but I'm tempted.

BILL: There's something you've got to understand here. Unlike any other gun out there on the market, you get a top of the range barrel with it.

Plus, you get one of the best regulator systems with the gun, and the gun does not rely on anything else for velocity.

I think what you're getting at is, why would the average recreational player pay $600–$700 for a gun?

ANDREW: No, that's easy to see. People get caught up in the things they love, and you're catering to their desire to own some of the finest equipment available for their hobby. I mean, the Shocker is fun times 20.

BILL: You figured that out in five minutes?

ANDREW: My only question is, if I drop it or it gets dirty or muddy, can it stand the abuse? Will

these cutting edge, finely tuned components stand up to intense, real world use.

ADAM G: We played last year with these guns in Vegas. Vegas is the worst scenario—desert conditions, desert winds.

We're usually sick for two weeks afterwards because you can't talk from the dust getting in you. But these guns can handle it. The guns have a special coating so you can almost submerge them. We don't recommend that. The point is, they can take the punishment.

ANDREW: Out at Skirmish, there are places where you can easily drop this into a creek.

ADAM G: It's a good question in general for players. There's certainly different levels of maintenance. The bottom line is any of your top guns require higher levels of care than your other guns do.

And you have two types of people. You've got the people who are willing to do it, and you've got the people who aren't. The people who aren't, they send it somewhere and incur the expense of having someone else deal with it.

The people who are willing to maintain their guns, they do the cleaning themselves. Frankly, it's not hard. People who would never imagine themselves working on a paintball gun manage to do it pretty well. But, no matter who you are, we recommend buying the gun from people who support their product.

You'll avoid frustration if you have a place staffed by knowledgeable people who can help you out.

All guns need a certain level of service, and the electropneumatic guns are no worse than anything else. But they are newer, and that means not as many people know how to work on them right now.

Within two years, probably every good field and dealer in the country will understand how to work on the Shocker. Some of the older guns have been around for so long that we all know how to work on them here, because we worked on them for years.

ANDREW: So if I spend this much money on such a sophisticated piece of equipment like the Shocker, can I really play hard with it?

ADAM G: The answer is yes.

ANDREW: Is there anything else you wanted to add about the Shocker in terms of unique features, concepts, a funny story? Anything?

ADAM G: Well, the only thing I want to add is what you just said a few minutes ago. This always happens with the shocker—the fun factor. You grab that gun and shoot it... and then you keep shooting. It's hitting the same target in the same spot, and that experience is ultimate. The gun is easy for us to sell. "Here, just shoot it."

Anytime you do something well, whether you play football or play piano well, whatever it is that you excel at, there's going to be a group that loves you and a group that hates you.

We're the people who do things well. As you go around the country, you're going to find a whole group that hates us. We go out and beat the heck out of a lot of the top teams in the world and they're all connected to the dealers and the distributors and the stores. They definitely don't like us.

We're beating them in paintball, we're beating them in the market, we're beating them everywhere. So, you'll have a very mixed reaction. But what I can tell you is that if you put that gun in the hands of anyone who can afford it, and they get an opportunity to use it, they're going to have more fun in that day of play than they ever had before.

In our opinion, they're going to have more fun because we have built the Shocker around the idea of consistent velocity and consistent controls. It's fun and safe in one package.

ANDREW: Do you find people shoot the Shocker with a remote air system more than an on-gun system?

ADAM G: All of the pros used to use remote. And then staying in bunkers and everything like that became more important. Tightness became more important. The ability to shift hands with the gun and speed and things like that became more important.

So, all the pros stopped shooting remote, and when that happened, so did everyone else. It's a funneling effect that influences everybody in the industry. Kids start saying, "Well, you know, that guy on team X doesn't use remote. Look how he bunkered that guy."

So, what you'll see is that you'll have this very influential group of professional players, and they lead the sport in one direction. And then you'll have all your manufacturers down here, and they just look at them as expensive people that they have to pay to use the products. Of course, they want everything for free. And that's all true.

Again, what's unique in our case is that we're in both places at the same time. We know that what we need is something people will want, and we take that pretty seriously.

What was the original question? I'm sorry.

ANDREW: It was a good answer.

Shocker Cleaning & Basic Maintenance

This section is provided to show one player's cleaning procedure for an electropneumatic gun, following a day of recreational play at an outdoor field. Please consult the instruction manual that the manufacturer provides for guidelines specific to your gun.

After a day of play at the field, a rainy day at that, Sarah Stevenson shows us how she cleans her Shocker. Keep in mind—this is an unrehearsed cleaning session. Anything can happen!

SUPPLIES NEEDED:
   Cloth towel; rubbing alcohol; squeegee; Phillips screwdriver; Allen wrenches; awl; dental pick; cotton swabs; lubricant (Dow 33 silicone grease); paper towels; rags.

Never use oil or Teflon tape!

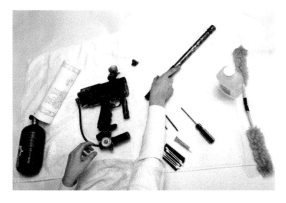

1. Take the hopper off and set it aside. Remove the powerfeed plug from the loader elbow and set it aside. Remove the 60 cubic inch tank by unscrewing it from the regulator.
The tank valve can be run under warm water to remove paint and dirt.

2. Remove the barrel by unscrewing it.

3. Turn the gun over, get a good grip on it, and remove the air hose. It is held in place with a pressure fitting and is removed by pushing in on the hose while holding on to the fitting. It should pop right out. This hose supplies the air from the MaxFlow fitting to the gun.

4. Use an Allen wrench to remove the Max-Flow cradle, which is held in place with two Allen bolts. Use a little elbow grease if needed.

5. You will notice there are two suction connections with o-rings.

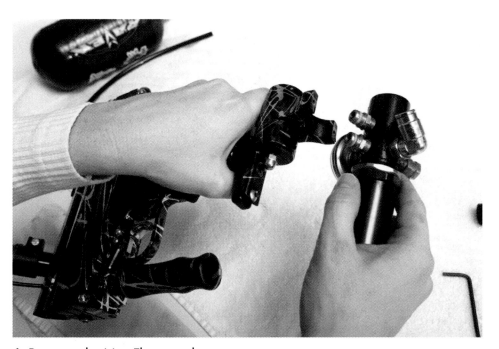

6. Remove the Max-Flow regulator.

7. Now we begin removing the bolt assembly. In a counterclockwise motion, twist the knob on the back of the gun that retains the bolt cylinder.

8. Remove the bolt assembly by pulling it out. This is the bolt that pushes the ball out of the gun. Lay it aside for later cleaning.

9. Use a chamois squeegee to clean the barrel housing.

10. Use alcohol impregnated cotton swabs to thoroughly clean the barrel housing area. Any dirt or debris left behind can cause the gun to malfunction.

11. Clean the feeder tube assembly with your chamois squeegee.

12. Clean the Powerfeed plug by wiping it down with a rag.

13. Clean the barrel with the squeegee.

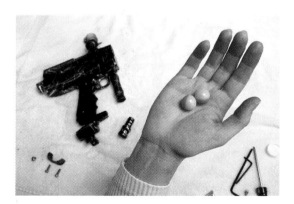

14. Here's a very real reminder about why you should not work on your gun with the air supply attached. During this cleaning, we found two balls still in the system!

15. Now let's turn our attention to the regulator. First, wipe off the excess dirt.

16. Follow that with a more detailed cleaning using cotton swabs and alcohol. Note that dirt is everywhere, including threads, openings, and crevices. Care should be taken to remove it all.

17. Carefully remove grains of dirt from the suction assembly by using an awl. Also use the awl to remove dirt from the cradle.

18. Using the Phillips screwdriver, remove the grip. Since this is an early model, we need to access the battery compartment to disconnect the batteries. Newer Shocker models feature an on/off switch.

19. Disconnect the batteries by pulling apart the connection. Do not grip the wires when disconnecting the battery. Only grip the connectors!

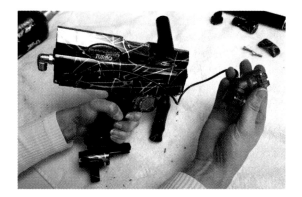

20. Replace the battery in the housing, leaving the wires disconnected. (Remember to reconnect the battery next time you want to play!)

21. Remove the air assist elbow. The air assist applies gentle air pressure to keep the paintballs moving down the elbow into the breech.

22. Wipe down the gun from top to bottom,

23. Clean the air assist elbow with your squeegee.

24. With cotton swabs and alcohol, clean the threads and seating area where the air tank attaches to the Max-Flow system.

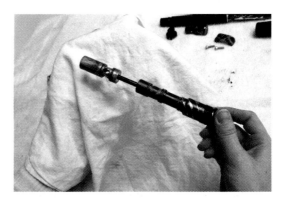

25. Wipe down the bolt. Remove all old lube and dirt.

26. Use a dental pick to clean the holes in the bolt. Get the old lube out before applying new lubricant.

27. The opening at the end of the bolt can get jammed full of paint and broken balls every time you push your squeegee down the barrel to clear a jam. Make sure you clean it out well.

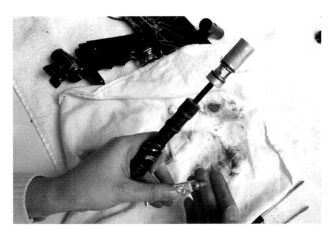

28. Apply a small amount of Dow Corning 33 Silicone Grease to your finger tips and then spread the lubricant throughout the bolt assembly. Movement of the bolt should be free and smooth.

ALMOST THERE...

29. Take care to lubricate all areas where parts of the gun come together—especially o-rings and metal-to-metal contact areas. The lubrication will help make the Shocker easier to disassemble next time.

30. The disassembled Shocker with maintenance and cleaning equipment.

—SS

Choosing a Barrel

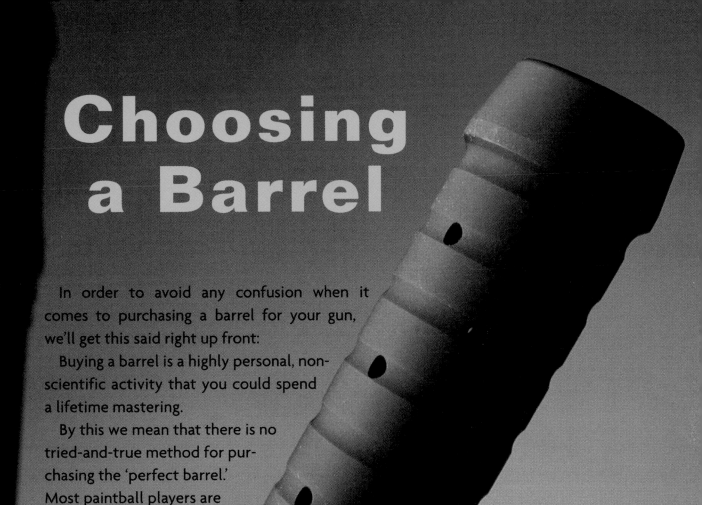

In order to avoid any confusion when it comes to purchasing a barrel for your gun, we'll get this said right up front:

Buying a barrel is a highly personal, non-scientific activity that you could spend a lifetime mastering.

By this we mean that there is no tried-and-true method for purchasing the 'perfect barrel.' Most paintball players are absolutely convinced that they already have the perfect barrel—namely, the one screwed into their gun when they buy it. If this were true, if each gun came packaged with the perfect barrel, then there would be no need to purchase an aftermarket one. That brings us to the critical question:

Is there a need to purchase an aftermarket barrel? The answer is yes... and no.

Most guns are purchased with a 'stock' barrel. Originally, the 'stock' barrel was all you could get. Most gun manufacturers made and continue to make fine barrels. However, once removable barrels arrived on the scene, which not only promised superior performance but were definitely far easier to clean, somebody was bound to make an aftermarket barrel that actually was 'better.' Major growth of demand for aftermarket barrels soon followed. As a result, most gun manufacturers have stopped making expensive stock barrels and instead provide a basic one for you to use until you can go out and purchase a 'perfect' one. Today, there are at least twenty (if not 40) different barrel brands.

But it doesn't stop there. Each brand of barrel has to have a different model for each different gun on the market. Add to this the fact that there is no industry standard when it comes to the manner in which a barrel is attached to a gun, and you have a huge number of barrels available across a wide range of prices. Most are threaded (like a screw), but there are several models which use a 'twist-lock', and several which use a pressure fit.

Barrel Length Counts

Most everyone agrees that you need at least 8 inches of barrel to make the most effective use of the gas and to give the ball some accuracy over decent ranges. After that there is virtually no agreement. Barrels come in lengths ranging from 8 to 18 inches. The length of a barrel also affects the issues of gas volume and pressure: guns with very low operating pressures will require a longer barrel.

Barrels are also made out of several different materials. Aluminum, brass and stainless steel are the most common, but you also can find carbon-fiber barrels and mixed-material barrels. Different inner-coatings also have been added (teflon, for instance), as have various forms of rifling. Barrels can come with 'muzzle breaks,' spiral rifling, gas porting, and a whole museum's worth of external patterns, sculpturing, and colors.

The barrel's inner diameter also varies. This might not seem to make sense. After all, a paintball is .68 caliber, right? Well, in fact, that's not entirely true. The *ideal* paintball is perfectly round and exactly .68 inches in diameter, no matter where you measure it. A real paintball is anywhere from .65 to .70 inches in diameter, sometimes oblong in shape, with a seam around it. In other words, it's far from a true sphere. Paintballs are commonly referred to as small-bore (.65 to .67) and

big bore (.68 to .70). Because of this, the inner diameter (or ID) of a barrel can vary from as small as .685 to .692. Admittedly, this is a relatively small difference—but when it comes to performance, it's a critical one.

Every paintball barrel manufacturer out there will say that the most important factor in choosing a good barrel is picking the right paint. After that, they'll say that the 'fit' between your barrel and the paint you are shooting is the next most important thing. They're right.

Of course, there are the ambient or 'local' conditions, things such as temperature, humidity and air pressure, that also affect performance: the barrel you use today with such amazing results may

belong in the bottom of your gear bag tomorrow, even if you are shooting the same gun, with the same paint at the same velocities as the previous day. The differences in performance may be due entirely to the changing play conditions, and they aren't necessarily your barrel's fault.

No one who plays paintball for any length of time always shoots exactly the same paint each and every game. Paint varies from brand to brand

(and from batch to batch). In order to counter this, most serious rec players have adopted the strategy of collecting a variety of barrels, in different lengths, with different IDs, made out of different materials, so that no matter what paint they are shooting, they will always have a barrel that makes a good match.

The general rules of thumb when buying a barrel relate to the ID, the length, the material it is made from, the presence or absence of rifling, porting and breaking, and the barrel's aesthetics.

Fortunately, you can be a little more discriminating (although you will probably end up with your own barrel bag eventually). When it comes to ID, most companies tend to make one to three different 'bores' (the tube inside the barrel is the bore). These bores generally correspond to a 'tight', a 'medium,' and a 'loose' fit. Tight bores are for small bore paint, loose bores are for big-bore paints and medium bores are for everything in between. Brands that only offer one or two bore sizes usually make a tight and a medium, since most paint tends to be small these days.

Try and settle on a particular brand of paint to use most of the time. This might be a brand offered by a local retailer, the brand of paint sold at your local field, or the paint recommended by local experts. Find out what 'size' this paint is (call the supplier if you have to). Your general-purpose barrel should have an ID which matches this brand of paint, since this is what you will be shooting most frequently.

Material really has only one determining factor, and that is its weight. The lightest barrels are generally 'composites' (carbon fiber) and aluminum, although some companies are doing amazing things with stainless steel. Brass is next in weight, followed by most stainless steel barrels. (Don't forget that the length of a barrel also contributes to its weight.) The smoothness of a barrel's bore is an important factor. The smoother it is, the less friction will be experienced by the ball as it travels through the barrel. All of the materials mentioned have roughly the same smoothness factor, so this is not a huge consideration. Sometimes smoother surfaces actually create greater drag. This is exactly why choosing a barrel is an art, rather than a science.

When it comes to porting, breaking and rifling, it's probably anybody's guess as to which implementation creates the best range or accuracy. Rifling is a technique borrowed from firearms technology. A helix of ridges and grooves is cut down the length of the inner surface of the barrel. These are used to grab the soft body of a bullet and cause it to spin. This gives the bullet greater stability in flight. Unfortunately, paintballs are not solid, aerodynamically shaped objects, and conventional rifling can't be used because it would rip and shatter the paintball. Nevertheless, barrel makers have come up with at least three paintball versions of the same thing, none of which work by 'spinning' the ball, but which can aid it in other ways. Polygonal Progressive Rifling (Armson) barrels have twenty-eight blunt-edged lands (the ridges of rifling) which curve down the inner surface of the barrel. These provide a greater surface area for the ball to seal against and help stabilize the ball as it leaves the barrel. Spiral Porting (Smart Parts) uses a patented external version of rifling. Two lines of 'ports' (holes drilled through the body of the barrel) are created down the length of the barrel in a spiral. This relieves pressure behind and in front of the ball and allows the ball to make a smooth transition to the air. Straight Rifling (J&J) uses four straight lands cut down the length of the bore to provide greater stability and better control of the ball as it moves through the barrel.

Most barrels, however, are 'smoothbore' barrels; they have no rifling of any kind. By the way, players have had tremendous success with all bore styles.

Guns

Muzzle Breaks are another adaptation from 'real guns.' They are typically used to suppress noise, reduce pressure at the muzzle (when the gun is fired), and suppress the 'flash' coming from a barrel. In paintball guns, it is generally believed that a muzzle break will aid the ball when it makes the transition from the barrel to still air. Muzzle breaks can be found on a wide variety of barrels.

Porting is generally used for its sound-suppressing qualities. Small holes (of varying number and size) are drilled down the length, or a portion of the length, of a barrel. These are not cut in a spiral (like the external rifling), but in straight lines. Sometimes slots are used instead of round holes.

And now we come to length. Determining the ideal length for a barrel is the biggest source of controversy when it comes to barrels. Some people swear by long barrels, some by short ones. Some are convinced that thirteen inches is what you need, while others think that sixteen inches is the mandatory minimum. The truth is that only a gun's manufacturer (or someone who works closely with a particular model) knows what the 'best' barrel length for that gun is. In general, you need the length of a barrel for two things.

- First, it needs to be long enough so that an optimal amount of gas will get the ball up to the desired velocity.

- Second, it should be long enough to give the ball some accuracy in its flight. However, if a barrel is too long, it will slow the ball back down again.

Unfortunately, these factors vary from gun to gun. The most efficient barrel, in terms of gas use, is one that is exactly long enough, and no longer. This may not be the same length as is required for the desired degree of accuracy, so choosing a length becomes the art of balancing these two goals within a range that is good for that particular gun.

Usually, an inch or two in either direction won't make a tremendous difference: if your gun 'needs' a twelve inch barrel, you'll still get good performance out of a ten inch barrel or a fourteen inch one.

The basic rule of thumb regarding length seems to be that if you are planning on playing up-front and personal (close to the other team), you want a shorter barrel so that you can 'tuck in'; and it will give you the kind of accuracy you are looking for with short to medium ranges. If you are planning on longballing (shooting long distance), you'll want a longer barrel to increase your sight radius and achieve greater accuracy. Remember to keep in mind that these are relative lengths, based on the kind of gun you are shooting.

A barrel's look is nearly as important as everything that has gone before. If your barrel looks cool, then you look cool, and it hardly matters whether you're hitting anything or not! WOOO-HOOO! (Just kidding.)

Most barrel manufacturers have developed distinctive styles for the outer surface of their barrels. Grooves, cuts, slashes, stippling, bumps and ridges have all been cut into barrels. Then there's color; you can get a barrel in just about any color you can imagine. Other manufacturers have begun to add graphics to their barrels and feature things like flames and skulls. Your typical macho-stuff can be found in virtually infinite variety from the tasteful to the tasteless. Chances are, whatever look you want, you'll be able to find a barrel to match it.

When you finally do go to purchase a barrel, remember to take along the information you've gathered about the kind of gun you are using and the paint you'll be shooting, remember that no barrel lasts forever. Think of your first barrel purchase as the beginning of a long and rewarding learning process, and save up your money so that you can afford to buy the next best thing.

A Brief Overview of Choosing an Aftermarket Barrel That's Right For You!

ANDREW FLACH: What does the barrel have to do with the game? Why should I consider an aftermarket barrel?

BILL GARDNER: Keep in mind that the gun manufacturers have a lot of competition, and they put very little money and effort into their barrels. Most stock barrels are not much more than a piece of aluminum with a hole in it.

And the manufacturers know that the players are going to want to go buy an after-market barrel anyway. So, it's probably the number one accessory out there for paint guns and the one where you'll see a big difference.

There are some accessories you can buy that will improve performance a little, and there are some that will do a lot. The barrel makes a big difference in performance.

ADAM GARDNER: There are basically two types of players. There's the person who really doesn't care, technically, about how the barrel works. They see that it shoots further and more accurately, and that's what they want. Results. Others are more technically inclined and want to know the theory behind the barrel and why it shoots better.

BILL: First, I have to sell you on a theory. Originally, everyone thought that a ball coming out of a barrel at 300 feet per second would travel exactly the same distance, with the same characteristics as any other ball coming out of any barrel.

The thing that they're forgetting about is aero-

dynamics. You know, not everyone realizes that balls change shape as they're flying through the air. They're gelatin, so they distort. Beyond that, even fewer people know how to make barrels that enable a paintball to travel further and more accurately. There's a lot of science behind this.

What that means is, if you have a barrel that's too tight for your gun, gases will hit the ball too hard and distort it, squeezing it and changing its shape dramatically. This decreases its aerodynamic power.

When a paintball gets slammed with the gases, it gets crushed, and then as it flies through the air, it's expanding and contracting with the initial energy that hit it. The softer you hit that ball, the less you distort the shape, and the more aerodynamic it remains during its flight.

Now, that's what we call low pressure. At Smart Parts, we aim for a low pressure approach, delivering a high volume of gas at a low pressure, thereby creating less of a distortion on the ball.

So, first, that brings you to the gun. You have to

go to the guns before you go to the barrel. There are two basic types of guns-there's the blow forward gun, meaning the bolt is open and the ball sits in there and when you fire it, the bolt closes, hitting the ball and firing the gun.

And then, there's a closed bolt gun. In a closed bolt gun, the ball's in the breech with the bolt closed behind it.

So, the difference is the bolt's position when you fire. And the other difference is that the open bolt guns for paint ball need to have a ball retainer, to keep the ball from prematurely lodging itself in the barrel.

And since the paintball is held in place by the ball retainer, we recommend a barrel where the ball will roll right out of the gun, if the ball retainer weren't holding it in place. And the accuracy and consistency will be there, if the barrel is just slightly larger than the ball.

Now, in closed bolt guns, you don't want that. You want a situation where, if the ball sits in the barrel, you can very lightly blow it out with a light puff of air.

ANDREW: And it should not roll out?

BILL G: It should not roll out. If it does, when you go to shoot somebody, you'll lose the first ball and you'll have to fire twice.

ANDREW: What about rifling?

BILL G: As far as rifling goes, we patented the rifling on our barrels. It's probably what made our business successful. We do spin the ball.

The Smart Parts barrel puts a very light spin on the ball. It's not disruptive. And what it does is, if you have a bell curve or distribution and you fire other than Smart Parts barrels, you'll find that when they reach the end of their energy curve, when they're way out there, they can fall in any direction. They can drop left, they can drop right, they can drop randomly—it's a random pattern.

But the Smart Parts barrel, you'll find that the end of its trajectory, it will generally always fall in

one direction. That gives you a little bit more control over that flight path. A competitive edge.

ANDREW: How about choosing barrel length?

BILL G: Well, related to the gun, again, and this is going to be a slightly different concept. Beyond open bolt versus closed bolt, you have high pressure guns and low pressure guns.

A high pressure gun is a small chamber with a lot of pressure. When you fire the gun, it imparts the energy very quickly on the ball. So, I like to call it large baseball bat versus small one. You want to hit 300 feet per second with a whiffle ball bat, you're going to swing the thing really hard.

If you want to hit 300 fps with a nice, big wooden bat, you know you don't have to swing as hard. So, the high pressure/small chamber guns

don't need as long a barrel to get the velocity up to two or three hundred feet per second.

The bottom-line is that low pressure enables you to use more of the barrel length. You'll find, though, that the average barrels will be 12–16 inches. That's what everybody's comfortable with. A lot of recreational players use an 18-plus inch barrel. It's fine for fun, but as far as maneuvering in your bunkers, you're knocking into things all the time and it's very difficult to change directions.

Regarding the choice of the barrel and the barrel

length: the guns favoring lower pressure can use a short barrel, but will appreciate the extra expansion area of a longer barrel to move the ball steadily rather than abruptly up to top speed. Less distortion equals more accuracy. It's all a matter of keeping that ball aerodynamic.

So, if you've got a gun that's hitting so hard you're breaking paint, then what you can do is turn your velocity down and increase your barrel length.

For example, during the summer, you may shoot all day long and not break a ball. But when the temperature's cool, the balls get a little bit more brittle, you find yourself shearing paint. One of the things you can do to alleviate that problem is to go to the long barrel. Now, your velocity's gone up, but you can turn down the pressure.

On the tournament level, barrel length becomes an issue of ergonomics. "Can I move quickly in my bunkers?" For front line players, they don't need quite as much accuracy as back line players, who'll tend to use a longer barrel.

But in terms of the recreational player, it's also a matter of "which barrel makes my gun work in the most conditions." Too short a barrel will definitely lead to accuracy problems.

ANDREW: What about unusual barrels, for special playing situations?

BILL G: We make a huge variety of barrels. People love gun barrels that look good. You know, cosmetics is important in this sport, almost as much as it is in skiing or snowboarding. I guess if you break it down and you ask yourself, "What gun do I have? Is it high or low pressure? Is it closed or open-bolt?" Those are the critical, first questions.

Then you say, "Okay, what type of bunkers do I play? Do I want a short barrel where I can maneuver very quickly, or do I want a longer barrel with a little bit more accuracy?" And then you start to ask, "What conditions? Am I playing in the winter, the summer? Am I breaking paint? Is my paint in good condition?" These types of questions usually lead people to buy a series of barrels for their gun that fit the various conditions they encounter as a player.

And then the other big question involves the cosmetics. "If I look good, I feel good, and if I feel good, watch out!" So, you say to yourself, "Well, do I like purple splash?"

So, certainly looks matter in your choice of barrel.

It Ain't Just Paint

Have you ever eaten a bowl of jello? Maybe it had whipped cream on top, or fruit buried in it. Did you ever watch it wiggle and shake? It's not possible that there is anyone in the world who hasn't at least *seen* jello.

Well, if you haven't then you must be the only person on the face of this planet who hasn't seen the substance paintball shells are made of.

It's called gelatin and it was invented circa 1900 as a 'neutral' food that could be added to just about everything and flavored to taste like just about anything. For a brief period, it was a popular delicacy, reserved for kings and queens and aristocrats.

Today, of course, gelatin no longer holds such a lofty position— definitely not in its capacity as the shell of the humble paintball. It's no longer a privilege to eat gelatin—although doing so won't harm you. Gelatin has been run through some pretty high-tech processes that make it just strong enough to be shot from a gun, yet brittle enough to break when hitting cammo'ed paintballers more than 100 feet away. Nonetheless, gelatin is quite digestible. (As any newbie will attest!)

Gelatin is created by 'rendering' the soft tissues, hooves, bones, and other unmentionables left over after a pig or cow has been prepared for market. During manufacture, sorbitol (a preservative), some glycerine, and starch (to give the shell 'body') are added to the mix. At the end of this process you get long, thin, sticky sheets of gelatin.

Using a process originally developed for the pharmaceutical industry, these sheets are then used to mold the shell of the paintball. As the sheets of gelatin are fed through an encapsulating machine, they pass through a reservoir of fill or paint. The two halves of the ball seal together and the entire paintball is left to dry.

The inside of the paintball is what really counts, though. Because gelatin wants to absorb water (just drop one in a glass of water and watch it swell), the 'paint' inside can't be water-based. In fact, during paintball's formative years, the paintball fill was oil-based.

Over the years a 'water-soluble' paintball was developed that replaced the petroleum-based oils with mineral, vegetable, and fish based oils. The most commonly used natural oil is polyethylene glycol. To this are added starch, which serves as a thickener, and water. Artificial, non-toxic dyes are used to provide color.

Everything that goes into a paintball is edible, non-toxic and completely biodegradable.

If it weren't for the taste, you'd be tempted to eat them.

—SD

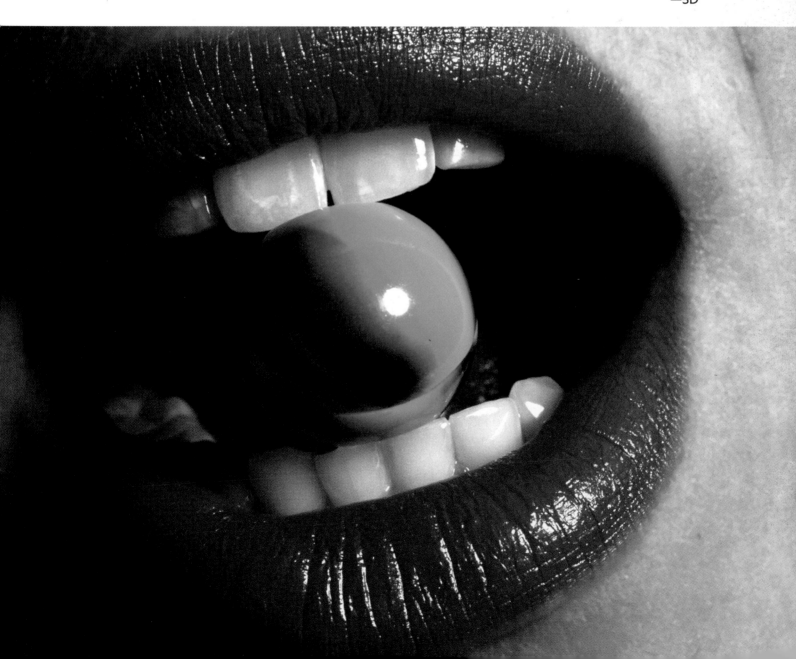

RON OLKO, TECH REP FOR AIR AMERICA, SPEAKS WITH STEW SMITH AT THE 1998 WORLD CUP ABOUT HIS COMPANY'S AIR SYSTEM:

STEWART SMITH: To start, what are you cleaning the regulator with and what are your lubricating it with?

RON OLKO: Just wipe it off with a rag or paper towel.

STEW: No solvent?

RON: The only solvent that you'd want to use at all is maybe a little bit of rubbing alcohol. Rubbing alcohol works really well because it doesn't promote rust. It cleans up the paint and it evaporates. You don't want to use too much alcohol on the regulator though, because it can ruin the o-rings. But generally, you just wipe it off. You very rarely need any type of cleaning fluids.

You get all the paint off, any broken shells that may be in there, and then you lubricate it. Really, one of the best lubricants to use is automatic transmission fluid. It's readily available, and it's not corrosive on the o-rings. You want to avoid most real firearm solvents. Those are terrible, because they're meant to break out carbon deposits in guns, and there are no carbon deposits in here. What ends up happening, if you put that on a paintball gun, is it attacks the o-rings, causing them to swell and break down. When the o-rings get damaged, you get leaks, and they're a problem. You want to avoid that.

You also do not want to lubricate with any type of aerosol, WD-40, or something like that. That's very bad. WD-40 is so thin, the o-rings will absorb it and swell up and cause the gun to jam.

BASIC FIELD STRIP

RON: As far as basic service and trouble-shooting goes, if there's a problem, check out the

whole valving. It's either dirty pins, springs getting compressed over time, or dirt where it shouldn't be.

STEW: What are some indicators that those items are dirty or something's wrong with them?

RON: You'll have erratic output. High or low pressure swings. You have two gauges on the system. You have your bottle pressure, your high pressure gauge. This tells you your unregulated pressure. Then you have a low-pressure gauge that shows you when there's a load on the system, what your output pressure is. As you pull the trigger, and cycle the weapon, you'll see the needle deflect or bounce. If there's a slow recovery from that deflection, that means there is a problem. If you see the needle swing past your set pressure, and it keeps climbing, that's another indicator that the valve pin is not seated properly. The system is not regulating the pressure correctly. Any kind of leak, however small, will affect your pressure. When I take the regulator apart, I'll show you the piston. There's an o-ring on it that can get dirty or worn or harden over time and cause a breakdown. It's a little thing that can make a big difference, and it's easily consumer replaceable. We've made this a very simple and user-friendly system.

STEW: Looks like it's no more complicated than regular scuba gear. It might be a little more difficult.

RON: No, actually, for the average paintball player, this is probably easier to maintain and troubleshoot than a scuba system. It's best, though, especially in situations like this tournament, to leave repair to technical representatives, which is why we're always out here. We come out early. We stay late. Make sure players get quality service, make sure things get done right. A lot of consumers outside the tournament circuit don't have direct access to tech support, and don't

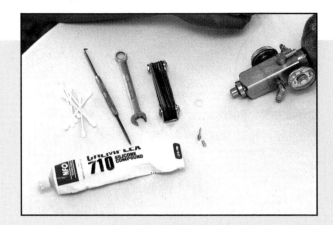

have the knowledge base. So, you'll see them putting black rubber o-rings in there which may last for one cycling of the gun and then blow apart, or they wrap teflon tape around internal portions of the regulator. They're thinking, "Hey, it stopped leaking, so it must work, right? Wrong. That's why a step-by-step process like this is really important. Our air system is very easy to maintain. We try to educate our customers. They get an operator's manual that outlines these same procedures, how to troubleshoot.

STEW: For the basic servicing of the Air America system here, what tools do you need to have?

RON: The main tools you need to do any consumer level maintenance would be a set of hex keys, a main set of 16ths, 5/32nds, a pick or o-ring tool, and a 7/16ths open-end wrench. That'll perform 99% of the maintenance. Q-tip swabs and some rubbing alcohol to clean out dirt and debris, and a lubricating oil or grease.

STEW: Any one in particular for lubrication that you recommend?

RON: What shouldn't you use? A lot of players use vaseline, or auto grease on the piston. Any kind of grease other than this silicone lube I'm using collects dirt. Lightweight motor oil will work fine, as well as gun oil. Any of these can be used to perform routine maintenance and lubrication. In addition to the piston, we also put oil on the mainspring, also called the spring pack. It's a series of stacked concave disks that doesn't look much like a spring, but the concave disks working against each other provides a spring action. If you don't keep it lubricated, and the disks become corroded, it increases friction and the spring becomes less effective or erratic, and pressure adjustment becomes difficult. So we put a light coat of oil on that spring, which I'll show you when we take it apart, and a light coat of oil on the piston o-ring.

STEW: So you can use petroleum products to lubricate it?

RON: We'd rather the consumer use a urethane-friendly lubricant, a non-penetrating type of lubricant. Over time, the o-ring will become hard or swell and tear if they use distillate-type lubricants. This silicone compound we just started using is an industry standard o-ring lubricant. We find that it works very well. But it's not readily available to all of our consumers. So I recommend a light lubricating oil, friendly for urethane products.

AIR VS. CO$_2$

STEW: So why air and not carbon dioxide?

RON: Carbon dioxide is a compressed liquid gas. It's more unstable than air and very susceptible to temperature changes. Since it's a liquid, we have a problem. Even with an anti-siphon tube, when a player tilts his bottle down, he is going to get some liquid up into the hose that can cause the gun to freeze up. At a minimum, you'll get hot shots in excess of 300 feet per second, which can be potentially hazardous. With the anti-siphon bottles of today, the technology has advanced to the point where it is safer, but there are still problems. There are always temperature fluctuations. Not to say that CO$_2$ is a bad way to do things, you just have to be aware of how it works. The majority of the entry level paintball guns and field owners still use compressed CO$_2$ because it's more affordable at this point. Due to the materials and labor that are involved, our compressed air systems are a lot more expensive than buying mass-manufactured 12-ounce or 20-ounce CO_2 bottles, which you can pick up for 40 or 50 bucks, depending on the size of the bottle.

STEW: Does it help with cyclical rates of fire? Remember we were talking about using the Shockers and the Angels. They wouldn't use carbon dioxide, would they?

RON: A low-pressure gun needs more volume. Volume is a big deal. One player in a 10-man competition, two 5-man teams going at it, can go through up to 2500 rounds in one game.

The guns vary. Take an Autococker, for example. There are so many after-market products that change the flow dynamics and the volume characteristics that are available for that gun. The average shot count for an Autococker with a 4500 psi system may be 1600–1800 shots per fill. Variations in barrels and different types of actuating mechanisms will affect performance. Different manufac-

turers recommend different volumes. So, we say the average is probably about 1800 shots for this system here. But when you get into a Shocker, with its high-rate of fire and particular volumetric efficiency, it's not going to work for a player who wants to shoot 1800–2,000 rounds. That type of gun typically eats more air than others.

STEW: What do they use to get the volume they want?

RON: They use CO_2. We can use this same type of bottle with a CO_2 valve. The threads are standard. So they can get more with the CO_2 in this same sized bottle than you would with compressed air. There's a trade-off, because now you're carrying around 30 ounces of CO_2 in a heavy bottle. We looked at that added weight, at the risk level involved with carrying that around, and went with compressed air.

DISASSEMBLY AND BASIC MAINTENANCE OF THE REGULATOR

1. The first step in disassembling the regulator is to remove the locked tournament cap that holds the regulator adjustment nut in place.

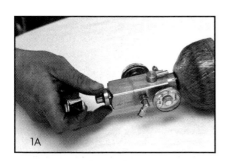

STEW: Can you describe the relationship between the regulator adjustment nut and the tournament cap?

RON: By turning the regulator nut with a hex key, the outgoing pressure is increased by turning it in a clockwise motion and decreased by going counter-clockwise. The tournament cap is locked down, so when the system is not under pressure, the regulator nut does not move. It's called a tournament cap because without it, you would be able to adjust the regulator pressure during the game and increase the speed. This would allow you to get further down the field, but you'd be shooting at other players with a hot gun, so it became a standard rule within the NPPL to have a locking tournament cap on your air system. With the locking cap, you won't be able to increase your pressure on the field and then leave it with a lower pressure.

STEW: How does being able to adjust the pressure affect the gun's performance?

RON: Each gun operates at a different pressure which affects performance. By adjusting the pressure, you're modifying it for that type of gun. Automatic style requires 600–900 psi to operate, depending on what type of valve work has been done to the gun. Standard Autocockers require anywhere from 375–500 psi to operate. This allows you to adjust the air system to whatever inbound pressure your gun requires.

STEW: And then the tournament cap locks that setting?

RON: The tournament cap locks that setting down, so when the air system is de-gassed, there's pressure on the adjustment nut. At that point, when you have to empty your tank, or it is loose in your gear bag, the nut won't float around and change the pressure setting.

2. The second step is to remove the regulator adjustment nut. As we remove it, the mainspring (the spring pack) comes out with it.

2A

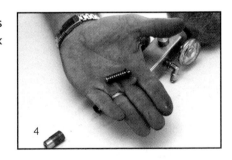

2B

3. Remove the mainspring from the regulator nut. Remove the piston from the piston bore.

3A

Stew: Can regular players do all of this? Ron: Yes.

3B

4. Inspect the mainspring for tightness in the disks, corrosion, and check the lubrication.

4

5. Check the o-ring on the piston for any obvious nicks, cuts, scratches, discoloration, water saturation, or swelling. Replace the o-ring if necessary.

5

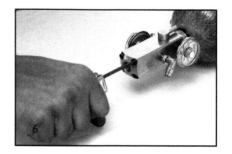

6. Take the piston housing off and inspect the regulator seat for any clues to problems you may have been experiencing. This is where we get into the regulator a little further than we would during regular maintenance. Troubleshooting a problem like broad swings in output flow, which may indicate a failed valve system, requires us to perform this inspection.

7. Inspect the white seating material (the little, white, plastic washer). Look for dirt, or the center hole appearing oblong instead of round, which would indicate that the pin is travelling in a direction that it shouldn't be. Then remove the regulator seating material from the piston housing with a pick.

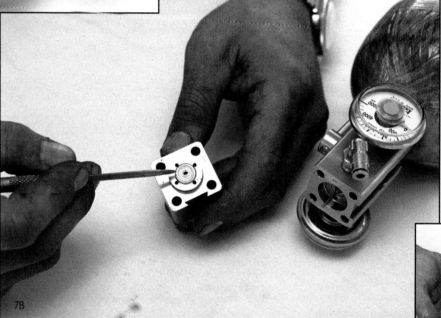

8. Using a clean rag or preferably a cotton swab with a little bit of rubbing alcohol on it, clean all the mating surfaces of debris and oil. Pay close attention to the area that the regulator seat fits into.

The Complete Guide to Paintball

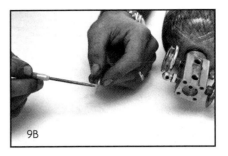

9B

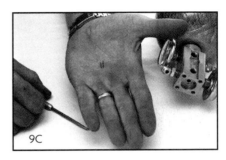

9C

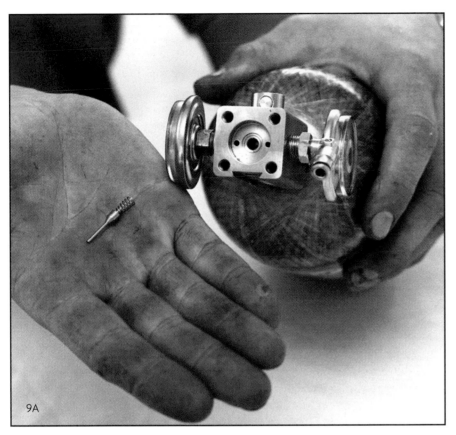

9A

9. Remove the regulating valve pin and the cone spring from the gas distribution body. Inspect them for any damage. Over-adjusting the regulator nut can bend the valve pin shaft. Make sure that the pin is straight and not marked up, and check that the cone spring isn't compressed or stretched due to improper installation. Watch for the natural compression that occurs with time and use.

10

10. Now, with a clean cotton swab or rag, clean the internal surfaces of the gas body, removing any debris, oil, or moisture.

11. This is as far as we go. After making sure that all of the surfaces are clean, we're going to work backwards and reassemble the regulator. The regulator seat (white washer) that we removed is made of hard urethane and can be used only once. It's a compression fitting. The two halves of the regulator, the gas distribution body and the piston housing, have sealing beads that make an indentation on the seat. Once you separate the two parts, the regulator seat needs to be replaced with a new one. Place the disk in the recessed area of the piston housing.

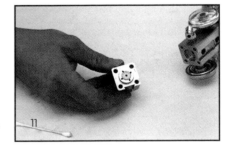

11

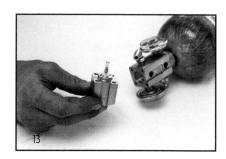

13. Replace the cone spring by fitting the tapered end on the short back-retaining shaft of the valve pin.

12. Now replace the valve pin by inserting the long shaft of the pin down through the regulator seat.

14. Firmly re-seat the piston housing on top of the gas distribution body. Fit the wider end of the cone spring into the recessed retaining pocket for the valve pin. Reinsert the four retaining screws. Take an Allen wrench and tighten the screws down gradually in a diagonal pattern. Tighten the opposite corners to evenly compress the seating material between the two halves. Tighten so that there's no gap between the piston housing and the gas distribution body, nice and snug, not over-torqued, but not just hand tight.

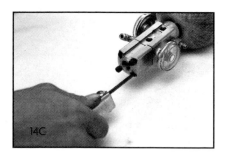

15A

15B

16

15. Lubricate the piston with a light coat of oil or silicone grease, and re-insert it flat-faced down, open end up, into the piston housing.

16. Insert a lightly lubricated mainspring into the piston.

17. Thread on the regular adjustment nut over the mainspring. At this point, we fill the bottle with nitrogen or compressed air, testing the regulator for any leaks.

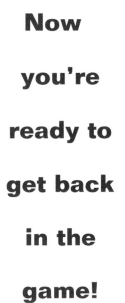

Now you're ready to get back in the game!

17

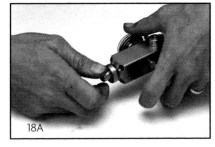

18A

18B

18. Thread the tournament cap onto the regulator adjustment nut. Set your outgoing pressure using an Allen wrench, and lock down your tournament cap. Tighten its retaining screws.

LIKE A ROCK

Dennis Tippmann, Jr.

STEWART SMITH: Tippmann is the first name we heard of when we started out to make this book. How long have you been in the paintball business?

DENNIS TIPPMANN, JR: I've been doing this since 1986. So, it's been 13 years now. I don't know of any bigger companies in this industry that are older than we are.

STEW: As an established leader in the paintball industry, how do you explain your success?

DENNIS: We keep improving the quality and the price point of our products. The mass market volume sales we do enable us to do this, and our commitment to improving upon our guns in ways that are cost-effective for us and our customers keeps us ahead of the game.

STEW: Your guns are definitely affordable.

DENNIS: We make valuable guns that simply perform reliably and consistently over time. They're easy to maintain and we support our products very aggressively.

STEW: Your guns are also unique in that you diecast them in aluminum.

DENNIS: That's right. It definitely saves us money because we can avoid the more expensive class of machining.

STEW: Do you find the diecasting durable?

DENNIS: Oh, yes. Basically, it's the same material. Diecast aluminum is very tough.

STEW: How do you explain the popularity of your guns with field owners?

DENNIS: Rental places need our expertise. They need good, reliable, affordable guns, and they want the best CO_2 system guns they can buy. One thing we've always been good at is mak-

ing great CO_2 guns. The rental guys need parts and service, too. That's another thing we do well. We get parts to them quickly. We offer one-year warranty on all our equipment. Because renters are more abusive and the gun gets used everyday, our support of fields is critical to their success.

They need a gun that's extremely durable, and a company to back it up. That's why they use our equipment.

STEW: Tell us about your Tippmann Model 98.

DENNIS: Sure. Our guns have always been solid, but we want to start introducing some of the high end advances to the mass market. Model 98 brings an advanced trigger system to the masses. Real high end guns go out of their way to build really good trigger systems, so that's where we've started. We've made the trigger really light on this gun, and it shoots very fast.

STEW: It's a reactive trigger?

DENNIS: Yeah, we call it the hyper-shot trigger. A light trigger with great response pressure. You see, on some guns with light triggers, the trigger doesn't swing back after you fire. We don't have that problem. The Model 98's return pressure gives you "lightness" speed and control.

STEW: So can you take the stock 98 out of the box, and add on bit by bit until you're up to a tournament level?

DENNIS: Yes. Absolutely. In fact, there are companies right now that are buying these receivers off us raw and doing stuff like this to them because we diecast that receiver. We don't have much money invested in the receiver anymore. So they're buying the receivers and making a number of little jazzy modifications to them. Double triggers and stuff like that.

As we're doing a lower-priced gun, we have the volumes real high. We can afford to diecast it. And then they can take that same diecasting, go and modify it, whatever they want.

STEW: Are you in any retail stores?

DENNIS: Wal-Marts and K-marts are what we're looking at right now. The guns are actually in Dicks, which is a sporting goods store, and some Sports Authority stores carry them.

STEW: What is an expansion chamber?

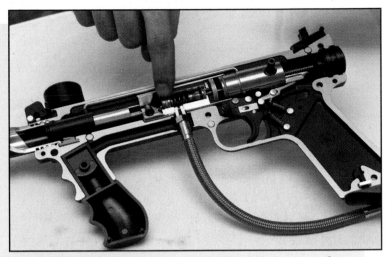

Dennis Tippmann, Jr. points out the CBX valve in this cutaway of a Model 98.

DENNIS: This is the first upgrade you would perform on a Tippmann Model 98. A lot of players put a barrel on right away and expansion chamber kit next.

Because CO_2 pressures go up and down, sometimes you'll get liquid CO_2 in your gun. Liquid CO_2 can be hard on a gun. You point your gun down, the liquid enters your gun and it responds by shooting really hard and erratic. The expansion chamber helps eliminate this effect. It makes it harder for liquid CO_2 to form and get into the valve of the gun. So it's just a way of making CO_2 work a little bit better.

STEW: Tell us about how your gun works.

DENNIS: When you pull the trigger on the gun, you release the bolt, and the rear bolt is connected to the front bolt. That'll shuttle a ball into the barrel. Now when the rear bolt gets clear forward, it hits the valve. When the valve is opened, pressure goes two directions. A very little bit goes to recock the gun, maybe 10%. The rest of it goes around the valve and shoots your ball. A little bit of pressure comes to the rear bolt, and recocks the gun. Normally, you wouldn't even be able to let off the trigger by the time the gun's recocked. The sear hits the back of the trigger, and then you let out the trigger and it reengages the top of the trigger for the next shot. There's a latch to hold the ball in place so it doesn't roll out your barrel until the trigger is pulled.

STEW: This latch is a piece of rubber?

DENNIS: Yeah. So, it's really a pretty simple system.

This is what they call a blow-back system. The bolt's blown back. There's two other systems. The blow-forward system, like your automatics, and the closed bolt system, which is like a pump gun with an automatic pump. What they mean by closed bolt is that the bolt's forward, ready to fire. When you pull a trigger on a closed-bolt system, the bolt's closed. That means the bolt has already shut the chamber off. When you set the gun off, the ball's already in the barrel.

So the closed-bolt is like a pump gun, with an automatic pumper on it, like your Autocockers.

STEW: Autocockers are closed bolt?

DENNIS: Yeah. Automags are blow-forward, and mine are blow-back. Tippmann actually invented the blow-back system. We've got the patents on it.

STEW: The most efficient use of air would be the blow-back system?

DENNIS: They all run pretty neck and neck. I think the Model 98 is extremely efficient. But right now, I'd say probably the most efficient system besides this gun would be your closed-bolt system, which is found in Autocockers. They're extremely efficient because of the way they use the exact amount of air needed to cock the gun, and the exact amount of air needed to shoot the gun. Since the systems are all compartmentalized, it's easier for them to achieve high levels of efficiency. It took us a lot of tuning to get to that level. So Bud Orr's guns have been efficient for a long time.

And the next level we'd step up to is the CBX valve. It's our high performance valving system, and we're sure players will notice its advantages, particularly its reliability.

STEW: And this is something that you developed?

DENNIS: Yes. I do all the drawings. I make the prototypes. My father and I sit down and go over the designs before they're made. Some of the other guys actually cut some of the prototype parts. Some of our prototypes are cut out of solid aluminum. I'll draw a 3D model of the gun on my computer, which then actually talks to a milling machine. It writes a tool path that'll cut that shape out of a block of aluminum. So those prototypes are made out of solid aluminum. And that same software can be used to make a mold.

STEW: You have a family business. That's wonderful.

DENNIS: Yes, as far as design and conception. Yes, it really is.

STEW: Thank you for sharing your time and insights.

DENNIS: It was a pleasure.

Cleaning of a Tippmann Model 98

KEEP IT CLEAN

This is an ad hoc cleaning, the kind most recreational players will do after a solid day of play. Keep in mind that proper care and maintenance of your paintball gun will provide you with many years of reliable and safe fun. Of course, some people will leave their gear in a bag and worry about it tomorrow... but why should you?

You've made an investment in your gun and part of that investment is your time. Take the time to clean your gun after a day at the field.

I performed the following gun cleaning on a Tippmann Model 98 with a Lapco barrel.

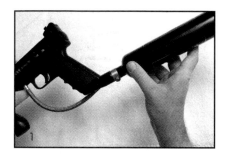

1. Remove the air tank first by turning slowly to release the pressure. Shoot the gun a few times to degas the entire air system. Note: shoot into a garbage can or cardboard box. Never into the air or at someone. And not with the barrel plug still in the gun.

2. Repeat this process, turning the air tank, and degassing the gun, until the bolt flops forward. This is an indication that it's okay to remove the air tank fully. The reason to take this care and not twist the air tank off fully in one go is to protect your o-rings.

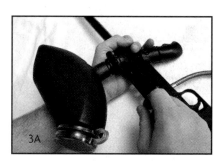

3. Using an Allen wrench, remove the loader from the feed neck by loosening the retaining bolt. Unique to the Tippmann feedneck is a set of "teeth" that grip the throat of the feeder. Don't try to yank the loader out. Loosen the retaining bolt (be careful not to lose the nut), and remove the loader when it pulls freely.

4. To clean the loader, stick your pinky in the feed neck, and check for paint. If it comes out dirty, wash the loader in the sink with some warm water.

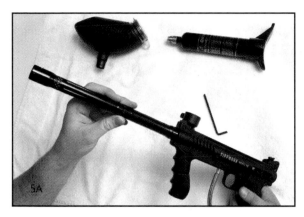

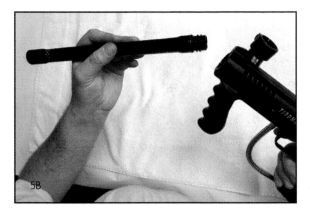

5. Remove the barrel. Notice the "fat" threads, which are due to the unique die casting techniques used in manufacturing the Tippmann 98. It takes just a few twists to remove the barrel. You'll clean it in a few moments.

6. Swing away the feed tube by depressing the front sight. This exposes the face of the bolt.

7. Examine the bolt area for paint residue and wipe it clean with a cloth.

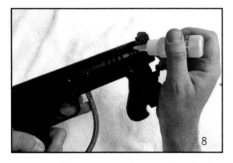

8. Apply some oil to the bolt through the exposed breech. Pull the cocking knob back and dry fire it a few times. This distributes lubricant to most exposed bolt areas.

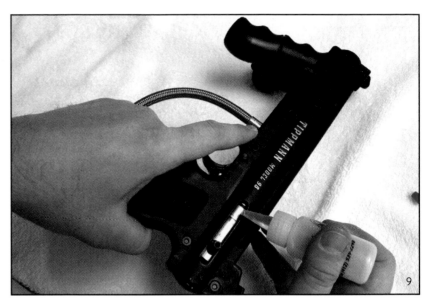

9. Pull the bolt back and apply oil to the back portion of the bolt. Dry fire the gun several times to distribute the lubricant.

10. Apply oil to the o-ring on the bolt. One drop on each side. Again, dry fire to lubricate.

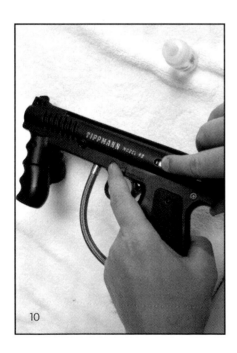

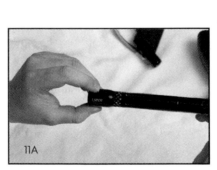

11. Paint accumulates in the holes of the Lapco barrel. To clean the barrel, find a sink and rinse out the gunk.

12. Pour a little cleaning agent into the barrel, rotating the barrel in your hand as you apply the solution. Here, I used Armson cleaning solution.

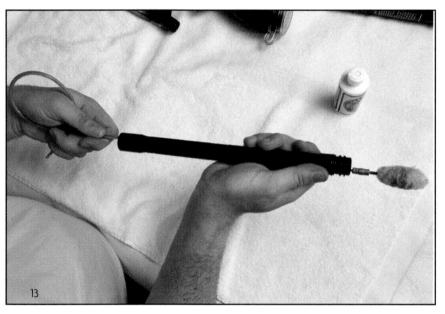

13. Using a cable squeegee, scrub the inside of the barrel. Run the cable end of the squeegee through the firing end of the barrel and pull; this will draw the soft end of the squeegee through the barrel. Repeat the squeegee process a few times.

14. Rinse the barrel again in the sink to remove the cleaning agent.

You're done. Ready for another shot at paintball glory? Reassemble the gun, reversing the process described here. Take your time and do it right!

Is It Safe?

PAINTBALL—THE SAFEST SPORT IN THE WORLD

The latest insurance information on paintball rates it safer than football, bowling, and statistically safer than staying in your house.

SO WHAT ARE YOU WAITING FOR?

Paintball is an exceptionally safe sport. The reason paintball is so safe is that the safety precautions have been evolving as fast as the game has been evolving. Safety equipment is vital to paintball, and should never be ignored no matter where you play.

AGOG ABOUT GOGGLES

Paintball goggles are highly specialized for the sport and must pass strict ASTM standards for paintball lenses. For example, paintball goggles must be able to absorb the impact of a paintball moving at over 400 feet per second (that's over 270 mph!) fired from less than one meter away. Many new players assume they can wear ski goggles, tank goggles, shop glasses, sunglasses, or shooting glasses. This assumption is completely erroneous, and therefore extremely dangerous! Paintball goggles are designed to absorb impacts that would shatter other goggles or dislodge them from the wearer's eyes. Your eyes are the only bodyparts that you rely on and regularly expose during the game that can be catastrophically injured by a paintball; whenever you're around paintball guns, don't trust anything other than paintball goggles to protect your eyes.

Paintball goggles are also designed with the game in mind. They have a wider peripheral vision than other styles of goggles. Many styles can be worn over glasses. There are "thermal" systems available to help prevent goggles from fogging up. You can even get fans to blow in fresh air to help prevent fogging. Goggles also have attached face shields and ear armor, which you are required to wear at most fields. There are several styles and colors to choose from.

You must wear your goggles at all times when you're on the playing field or on the target range. Even when you're eliminated, you don't want to remove your goggles until you're in the staging area and off the fields.

Plug It Up

After goggles, barrel plugs are the most critical safety equipment you'll need to be in the habit of using. A barrel plug is a device you stick onto or into the open end of the paintgun's barrel when you are off the field. This device prevents a paintball from coming out the end of the paintgun's barrel. *When used with the mechanical trigger safety switched on, the barrel plug makes it safe to remove your goggles in a "goggles off" area.* Just having the safety on is not as "safe" as it appears. Using a barrel plug is a visual way to show your paintgun won't hurt anyone, and if anyone forgets to put one in their gun, you should tell them to plug it up immediately.

Every player must use paintball goggles and a barrel plug for their paintgun. More than any others, these two pieces of safety equipment make paintball safe for players.

There is one more vital piece of safety equipment that every good field uses regularly, and will make available for your use when you bring your own equipment. A "Chronograph" measures the speed of a paintball as it comes out of the barrel of a paintgun. In the early nineties, the IPPA (International Paintball Players Association, now disbanded) helped create a standard of 300 feet per second (300 fps) as the safest maximum speed for paintballs coming out of the barrel. This has held ever since. For indoor paintball, the top limit is usually lowered to 270 fps or less, depending on the field size. Higher velocities are unnecessary with smaller fields. If you have your own equipment, you will need to adjust it to get under the field speed limit.

Know where your gun's safety is and always use it. But don't stop there. Insert your barrel plug to ensure maximum accident prevention.

Safety—Above and Beyond

There is more safety equipment you can use as well, but it is not mandatory. (Read: common sense indicates that using additional equipment goes above and beyond the essential safety requirements.) This is effectively the point at which you can exercise your personal preference to accessorize for further safety. Some items make good sense to use. Men should wear a cup. Women should wear fem-guards to protect "soft spots." If you have bad ankles, wear shoes with ankle support or wear a brace if necessary.

If you have bad joints, or you don't like the idea of crawling on rocks and twigs, you can wear knee and elbow pads. Many styles are available, and

many are paintball specific. If you slide a lot you may want knee/shin guards. If you crawl a lot, then elbow pads would be a good idea. It's all about wearing what you are comfortable moving around in. Wearing loose clothing will also help absorb some of the impact of a paintball. You don't want to go overboard, however. If your clothes are too baggy, you'll have a hard time moving around.

Other products are available for personal safety, such as neck protectors, hard or soft armored vests, gloves, head wraps and protective caps. Some people think you can't be too safe; others feel like they sacrifice agility and actually become more vulnerable to getting hit when they wear these extras. You'll have to make up your own mind about these items.

But, if I ever catch you not wearing your goggles on a paintball field, I'll tackle you.

—RR

NOTE: We included this article on safety in the GUNS section because paintball guns should not be discussed independent of safety gear. Read on to learn more about the assorted paintball gear you need to play this game.

PART 3
GEAR

To Thine Own Paintball Goals Be True

How to Make Sure You Have What You Need To Enjoy This Beautiful Game

The best way to choose your equipment is to analyze what kind of player you are, figure out where you're going to use the equipment, research the quality versus pricing issues, and then, *and only then*, spend your hard earned dollars accordingly.

Equipping yourself to play paintball is easy these days. Almost too easy. You basically have three choices: use what the advertisers say you should use, purchase the most expensive thing on the shelf, or get what your local dealer happens to have in stock today and "really likes." In reality, many players use one or another of these purchasing methods to equip themselves or their teams. That's sad, because it rarely leads to an optimal purchase.

Caveat Emptor!

The only way to make sure that you have the equipment that's right for you is to become an informed consumer and think for yourself. One of the ironies of living in the information age is that we now have access to unprecedented quantities of data, which makes isolating quality information relatively harder.

The information in this section is meant to help you gain a complete understanding of the air systems that you'll want to use with your gun. You'll learn that making this selection is directly related to the kind of paintball player you want to be.

While this is not exactly a buyer's guide to paintball paraphernalia, my goal is to furnish you with a sense of direction when you start considering your key paintball purchases.

PRESSURE SYSTEMS

There are two basic kinds of paintball pressure systems or 'propellant sources' available for use with paintball guns. These are generally referred to as CO_2 (carbon dioxide) tanks and high-pressure or nitrogen systems.

Carbon Dioxide—Feeds Plants and Propels Paintballs

Carbon dioxide was the original propellant of choice for paintball. Small pressure bottles, holding 12-grams of gas (hence the name 'twelve-gram') were available for use with BB and pellet guns and were adopted for use with paintball guns. Several years later the idea of using larger pressure vessels, containing as much as 40 ounces of gas, was introduced. These systems allowed a user to shoot sev-

Old-school wristband 12-gram carriers.

eral hundred to several thousand paintballs without having to replace propellant sources and acquired the name 'constant air.'

Contrary to what some people believe, carbon dioxide is not a toxic chemical. It exists in fair quantities in the Earth's atmosphere and you exhale some every time you breathe. Nor does using a carbon dioxide system contribute to the green house effect: all of the CO_2 used in paintball systems is originally taken out of the atmosphere.

CO_2 has some physical properties that make it a good propellant; at the pressures and temperatures normally at play in a paintball gun, the gas can exist as a solid, a liquid, or a gas. This property allows a large amount of gas to be stored, even when using relatively low pressures. (CO_2 systems are generally considered to have working pressures of 800–1200 psi.) It is also a relatively dense or 'energetic' gas, which means that you get a lot of oomph out of just a small amount.

On the other hand, **one major drawback of using CO_2 is the fact that it can exist as a liquid, gas, or solid, literally at the same time, inside**

Gear

your pressure tank. This means that when the valve is opened, you sometimes get liquid CO_2, sometimes you get gaseous CO_2, and sometimes you get a mixture of both into the gun. This can cause wildly fluctuating velocities and ruin shooting accuracy. Additionally, some guns will become frozen and experience a drop off in velocity when rapid-firing occurs; each successive shot chills the gun further, sometimes causing it to malfunction or cease operating entirely. Finally, CO_2 systems are susceptible to negative effects from local temperatures; specifically, the colder the outside temperature, the less energetic CO_2 is. In such a situation, you're losing bang for your buck.

Constant air systems come in a variety of tank sizes and in several different configurations for attaching to your gun. Tanks can be purchased ranging in size from 3.5 ounces (the amount of gas the tank holds), 7 ounces, 10 ounces, 12 ounces, 15 ounces, 20 ounces and 40 ounces. Gun hook-ups are generally named after the manner in which they attach to the gun; consider the following.

A *back-bottle* system screws into an adapter mounted at the rear end of the gun.

A *bottom-line* set-up uses an adapter fitted under the grip.

A *vertical bottle* screws into a fitting underneath the barrel at the front of the gun.

A *California-style* bottle attaches the gun to a stock and uses an air hose to connect the tank to the gun.

High-Pressure Air (HPA) and Nitrogen, Alternative Paintball Power Sources

High-pressure air and nitrogen systems utilize normal atmospheric air (a combination of nitrogen, oxygen, carbon dioxide and some trace elements) or pure nitrogen. Once again, this is not a toxic gas. In fact, nitrogen is the gas that makes the sky look blue.

Unlike carbon dioxide, air (or nitrogen) exists only as a gas at the pressures we use it for in paintball. This has the potential benefit of decreasing the shot-to-shot variation in pressure, thereby producing more accurate shots.

On the other hand, neither of these gases is as *energetic* as CO_2; the number of shots you get is less than you would get from a similar amount of CO_2. Therefore, to make their use practical, the pressure these gases are stored under has to be significant, far higher than that used to store CO_2.

Today, two basic nitrogen system models are used: The standard 3000 psi system and the 'tournament level' 4500 psi system. The benefit of going with the higher pressure is that you can store half-again as many shots in the same volume. Unfortunately, as of this writing, the paintball industry has only just begun to adopt HPA systems. The ability to fill 3000 psi tanks is not universally available and the ability to fill 4500 psi tanks is relatively scarce (except at tournaments and other major events).

HPA and nitrogen systems are referred to as 'regulated' systems. Why? Well, the pressure stored in the tank is much higher than the pressure used by the gun when firing a shot, so a device (the regulator) must be used to reduce the tank pressure to the gun's working pressure.

Several different makes and models are available, each of which uses different regulation systems and different methods for attaching to the gun. The most typical arrangement is a *cradle system*, which mounts the tank underneath the grip, and is connected to the gun via a high-pressure

Check out all those guppies. Smart players don't get caught short on paint.

line, or a *remote system*. Players carry the tank in a pouch mounted on their backs or at waist level, and a pressure hose connects the tank to the gun.

When choosing a propellant system for your paintball gun, the first question you need to answer is...

DO I NEED A HIGH PRESSURE SYSTEM?

If the information on high-pressure systems confused you, and you're really not sure what it all means, the answer should probably be, at the very least, "not yet." Plenty of players have a perfectly wonderful time never using high-pressure.

The bottom-line is that you shouldn't pay for advantages that are negligible in the games you're playing. There are reasons why manufacturers offer high-performance options, and those reasons rarely overlap with the average player's priorities.

On the other hand, if you are a fiend for performance, or live in an area where you play in the cold (below 50° F) most of the time, then you can benefit from using a high-pressure system.

If you choose to go with CO_2, make sure that the model of gun you are using will operate efficiently on this propellant. Some guns are made specifically to use liquid CO_2, and therefore you will need to provide this kind of propellant. You will also need to determine the size of tank you should purchase: heavy shooters ought to carry a larger tank (15–20 ounces), while players who shoot less can get by on a smaller one. Especially for cold play days, remember that it's best to have several tanks on hand which can be filled and stored at room temperature for later use.

BRING ON THE PRESSURE

If you've made the decision to obtain a high pressure system, you need to answer two more questions.

Do the Fields and Events Where You Play Provide High Pressure Fills?

The answer to this is probably yes (although not necessarily for 4500 psi systems: these systems can be used with 3000 psi fills, you'll just get fewer shots per fill). More and more fields, and just about every big game and tournament, either already provide high pressure fills or will be in the 21st century.

The next question, and this isn't the first time we've brought it up, is...

What Kind of Player Are You?

For our purposes, players break down into three basic groups in terms of the environments in which they play the game. There's the tournament player, the "serious" recreational player, and the casual player. I'll deal with tournament players first.

Tournament Players

The "position" you play on the field virtually dictates the kind of gear you should be carrying. Yes, there's room for variation, but the pro is counting on team action and is playing a specific role in the team's use of tactics, so not every team member has to be equipped to the teeth.

Here, again, tournament players can be divided into three player types: *front, utility and cover*. Even if you are not a tournament player, you should consider the following descriptions of playing styles and see how you match up.

Front players are the ones who break out of the station with the intention of achieving a forward field position. They've got to move fast and need to have versatile skills. They never know what contorted position they're going to have to fit themselves into to make shots and stave off elimination.

Cover players provide direction, coordination, and cover fire for the front players. Cover players need to be able to shoot volume.

Utility players are players who are able to fill both roles, but their game plan is not to concentrate on either one particularly. They need to be able to move, they need to be able to shoot, and they're usually changing positions quickly. Some teams call these players "wingmen" or "support" players.

Front Players

Since speed, weight, and size are at a premium for the front player, I recommend that these players use a small bottle, on-gun system. They're usually going to be "tucking in" throughout the game, drawing fire rather than shooting, so a small system will provide enough air for the several hundred shots they may need to take. The configuration for mounting the bottle on the gun ought to allow front players to use it as a stock, since aimed shots are critical for them. This player definitely benefits from a compact mounting configuration.

Cover Players

Cover players, especially the *hosers* out there, ought to be carrying a large bottle remote system. This player needs the capacity, since chances are his job is to shoot *beaucoup* paint. Keeping the bottle off the gun gives the player more mobility, especially when firing longball style; besides, most large bottles are, in all practicality, just too heavy to mount on the gun.

Utility Players

Utility players need both the mobility for speed and the capacity for shooting. A large bottle is recommended, but this type of player ought to think seriously about mounting it on the gun, because he just might end up *filling in* at a forward bunker. The large bottle makes the gun a little more awkward when you're moving, so I recommend experimenting in a few games with a remote and an on-gun configuration to see which works better.

Serious Recreational Players

The serious *rec* player comes in several types as well. There's the "for-fun-team" type, who ought to read the above tournament player section for our recommendations.

Then there's the regular "no-team" player, the player with a few friends who is a regular at the local field.

Here, the choice of bottle is actually a combination of the type of role this player likes to perform and the type of field that this player usually frequents. If the field is a long distance from the nearest fill facility (or if the field has no fill facilities), then the larger bottle is called for because it gives the player more games without having to reload.

On the other hand, if fills are readily available (and relatively inexpensive), then you'll want to get the kind of system that best compliments your playing style.

While it's true that some folks do shoot a lot of paint in rec games, most of the time the games are of short duration, so more often than not a smaller system will do.

Scenario game players will most probably want to go with a large bottle remote system. These players are usually out on the field for several hours at a time. The large bottle will support this, and its remote configuration lets them keep it out of the way.

Casual Players

Most casual players rent their equipment, but for those who don't, a small, on-gun system is probably the best choice. More often than not, they don't need the volume capacity of a large tank, and usually they're also looking to stretch their paintball dollars.

When you're just starting out in paintball, it really makes no sense to make any purchases. Play at different fields and use different guns and air configurations.

Indoor games and speedball games almost always dictate a small, on-gun system. The games are over fast and space is at a premium in both formats, as is speed. Because of these facts, a casual player's rental equipment is only marginally less effective than a rec player's owned equipment (though, of course, this is going to vary from field to field).

> *Again, it really comes down to the player's skill and good fortune.*

ULTIMATE CHOICES

If you are serious about paintball and play with some degree of regularity, you'll probably find yourself in need of several different configurations, and will most likely end up obtaining both a remote and an on-gun set-up, as well as a large and a small capacity bottle. This might sound like a sales pitch, but in reality, matching your system to your playing needs does help your game. Without both types of bottles and both types of mounting rigs, your options are limited.

SAFETY

High pressure *sounds* more dangerous than the carbon dioxide-powered, lower pressure systems. In fact, many of the high pressure systems out there have been tested to meet military specifications and are designed in such a way that a catastrophic failure of the system will *not* result in rockets or shrapnel. In this respect, it's possible to say that high pressure systems are actually safer than carbon dioxide systems.

However, with high pressure systems, you are dealing with pressures three to four times greater than those in carbon dioxide systems. So one safety requirement is clear...

DON'T FUTZ AROUND IN THE BASEMENT WITH A HIGH PRESSURE SYSTEM!

• With a high pressure system, as with any pressure system, you must always depressurize the system when storing it.

• If you are using a remote with your system, make sure that your hose is always under control.

• Finally, do your homework. Before you buy one, find out if the system you want to purchase meets the U.S. Department of Transportation (DOT) burst and hydrostatic test requirements. A legitimate system must be able to contain pressures four times its working pressure.

HIGH PRESSURE SOURCES

Eight companies currently manufacture and sell high pressure systems in the paintball market. First into the market were Air America, Air Power, Govnair (UK), Paintball Mania Supplies, Smart Parts, Pro-Team Products, and Pursuit Marketing Incorporated, all of whom offer high pressure systems in various configurations, for both on-gun and remote set-up.

Beyond the position you play and the various features of individual systems, high-pressure tanks come in two varieties—preset regulators and adjustable regulators. The difference is that the output pressure of pre-set regulators can't be adjusted by the user, while adjustable regulator systems can be.

Most guns and most players—except for those playing at the tournament level, or those who are performance gurus—can do just fine on preset systems. Some systems from PMI (Crossfire) and Paintball Mania Supply (Micro-reg system) are preset systems and can be obtained for a lower investment than adjustable ones.

Pro-Team products recently introduced a low-price adjustable system (Millennium Series) and adjustable regulator systems are also available from Govnair (MAX Attack), Air America (Armageddon, Apocalypse, and Raptor systems), Smart Parts (Max-Flow), and Paintball Mania Supply (Mini-reg).

—SD

BACK PLAYER

The back player usually carries the heaviest load. This player is responsible for most of the cover fire for his teammates. He usually is the eyes of the team and is responsible for relaying the opposing teams' movements. The back player will usually control his team's movement on the field. As an example, in 5 man paintball if the back player is aware that 2 players have been eliminated from one side of the field he may move his front men on that side further up the field. This player usually spends the entire game yelling codes and raining paint. For this reason, his equipment should be chosen for maximum distance and firepower. His pack should carry a large amount of paint. (Keep in mind that if you carry a half case of paint but can only shoot 800 rounds your extra paint will be useless!) Not all game situations require huge amounts of paint. Use common sense. If you are playing a 5 minute game on a speedball field, 1200 rounds of paint is overkill. Your teams game plan may also influence the amount of paint you carry. Some teams sit back and wait for something to happen while others go out and make things happen. If your team averages a very short game, carry less paint. If they sit in bunkers until the last 30 seconds you may need to carry more paint. Again, keep in mind that if you are going to carry it, you should have enough air to shoot it. The back player will find it helpful to be able to shoot left and right handed. In most cases the largest bunkers are at the back of the field. That does not mean that this player has the luxury of hanging the entire left side of his body out while trying to shoot right handed out of the left side of the bunker. It may also be helpful to have the ability to shoot with more than one finger. If you have to give cover fire for an extended period of time your index finger may appreciate a brief rest. The job that the back player does is not the most appealing job on the field to most players. That fact makes this a hard but important position to fill.

The Key for Mark Smith's Illustrations

1. Baggy Uniform—should be loose for flexibility and to deflect paint
2. Baggy Pants—the looser the pants...
3. Cleats—should be comfortable
4. Stripes on Cleats—any color on feet may draw attention to you, especially when crawling, color them black
5. Elbow Pads—under uniform (optional), lightweight and comfortable
6. Knee Pads—should be soft and comfortable, covering knees and shins, should not restrict movement
7. Hat—soft fabric helps with hard hits and may deflect paint
8. Rubber Visor—keeps sun out may deflect paint
9. Ear Protection—prevents ear damage
10. Rubber Lower Mask—when selecting a mask make sure the lower half is rubber and not hard plastic
11. Thermal Lens—helps prevent fogging during play
12. Squeegee—for quick barrel cleaning, comes in several lengths, should match barrel length, can be placed in knee pads, placed on a string around the neck or various other locations for quick access
13. Battle Swab—for cleaning hopper necks and barrels
14. Back Pack—should be sized appropriately for the position being played, should be comfortable, avoid a pack that places all those hard loaders down an exposed side of the body but make sure that you can get the loaders out
15. Velcro Waist Strap—avoid plastic or metal, hard surfaces break paint
16. Suspenders—use to help balance a heavy load of paint, should have soft connectors
17. Gloves—protect and hands and may deflect paint
18. Viewloader—choose one that is appropriate for your gun type and the amount of paint you want to have available, remember that this will greatly affect the weight of your gun
19. Battery Operated Feeder—keeps paint flowing efficiently into the gun
20. Timer—absolute necessity, keeps you aware of when the game is over or the one minute warning is up
21. Codes on Lid—the lid of your Viewloader is a good place to apply a sticker with codes that are difficult to remember
22. Codes on Inside of Lid—good place for a backup set of codes
23. Viewloader Lid Left Open—allows you to load while continuously firing at a target during a crucial time of the game
24. Bottle on Gun or Remote Line—front or mid players should stay away from remote lines, they become tangled and slow running, some back players choose a remote line to reduce weight of the gun
25. Drop Forward—moves bottle forward and makes gun shorter
26. Adjustable Drop Forward—allows bottle to be moved forward or backward to make gun shorter or longer
27. Air Intake Cover—keeps dirt out of your bottle
28. Bottle Pivot Adjustment—allows bottle to be twisted to one side or the other, may make gun smaller
29. Shroud—covers 3 way valves on an Autococker, saves on cleaning
30. Barrel—should be rifled, should be chosen with length determined by the position you play, example: a front player usually does not have to shoot the distance of the field and benefits from small size in a tight bunker
31. Lightweight Barrel—reduces weight of gun
32. Handgrip—steadies gun for a more accurate shot
33. Extra Loaders Taped Together—can be carried to a bunker, allows you to carry extra paint without adding weight to your back
34. Cup—crucial in importance, second only to a mask. Unfortunately many players neglect this, they are the ones that are carried off the field
35. Armband—given by the judge before the game, make sure that it is comfortable and does not restrict movement

key on page 177

MID PLAYER

The mid player tends to be a fill-in man. He will usually start the game in front of the back player and behind the tape runner. This player needs to be very versatile. In any given game he may start as a "back player," move in to his middle position, and then jump in front of the tape runner becoming the point man. He is crucial in relaying codes from the back player to the tape runner and vice versa. This player's primary job is to keep the tape runner alive and in the game. It is important to keep in mind that the tape runner is often under heavy fire and unable to look or shoot. This is where the mid player steps in. He may give cover to allow the tape runner to get up or he may merely talk to the tape runner to keep him comfortable. For example, it is very comforting for the tape runner to know that someone is watching over him. The mid player may constantly repeat: I've got your front or everything is okay. By the same token, if the mid player is forced to turn his attention elsewhere, he needs to let his teammates know this, also. The mid player's gun is usually smaller than that of the back player. Keep in mind that flexibility is very important to this player. If the back player or the tape runner is eliminated, he may be called upon to assume those roles.

Gear

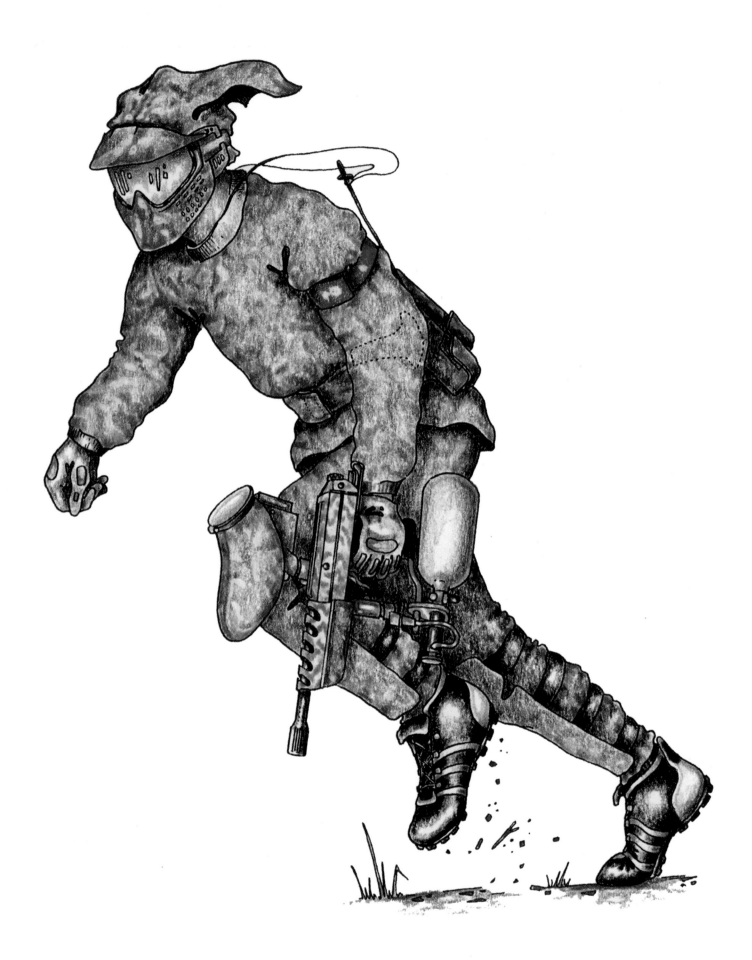

key on page 177

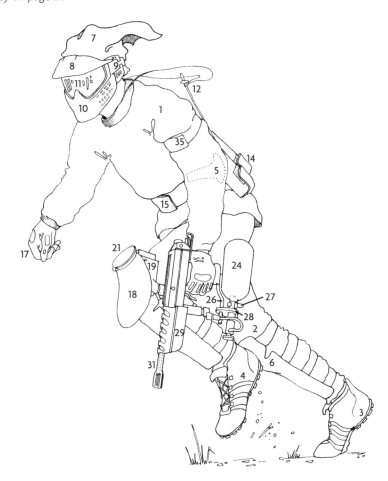

TAPE RUNNER

The tape runner should carry the lightest load and be your fastest runner. This player usually takes the most aggressive position on the field. This positioning usually makes him a big target. He is the guy that the back player on the opposing team is dumping all that paint on. He will usually shoot the least amount of paint and should, therefore, carry less than the mid or back player. This is the player that is most often called upon to go bunker someone or sacrifice himself. His primary job is to get into his bunker, make himself small, and find a way to shoot effectively. At the start of the game he should be conscious of where his gun is in relation to which direction he is running. As an example, if he is running to the left, and he carries his gun in his right hand, he is giving the opposing team a nice, hard target. If, however, he carries his gun in his left hand his body helps cover it. This can be made more or less effective depending on how you swing the gun. The closer you keep the gun to your body the more effective this will be. Do not fool yourself into thinking that you are going to run and shoot. It will slow you down, and it would be extremely unusual for you to hit anything. The tape runner should have the smallest and lightest gun. He will be trying to live and be effective in the smallest bunkers. For this reason, he should be very conscious of what he carries. Only truly necessary items are worth taking in.

Gear

AFFORDABLE
Invaluable
Paintball
Paraphernalia

GET THE BIGGEST BANG FOR YOUR BUCK

Here's a list of simple, low-cost necessities you can purchase that will add to your enjoyment of the recreational paintball experience. Most items can be purchased at general merchandise stores, like Wal-Mart or K-Mart, at sporting goods stores, or at military surplus outlets.

1. A decent pair of ankle supporting shoes. High top style cleats are the best.

2. A pair of gloves. Can even be gardening type gloves. Less than $1.00 a pair. Cut the fingertips off. Bicycle gloves are great, too.

3. Knee Pads. The only way to slide.

4. Elbow Pads. Crawl without pain.

5. A good watch with a timer function or a kitchen timer. To keep track of time elapsed during games. Glue it to your loader's lid.

6. Fleece shotgun swab. A 12 gauge for barrel-cleaning.

7. M16 Ammo Pouches and belt.

8. Wool cap, to protect your head from close range hits.

9. Camouflage BDU pants and top. These come cheap if you buy them used.

10. MRE's (Meals Ready to Eat) In case you get hungry during those long games.

11. Toilet paper. It's a messy game, after all.

12. Military helmet storage bag, for your goggles.

13. Insect repellent with DEET. Avoid Lyme disease and keep away the bugs.

—SD

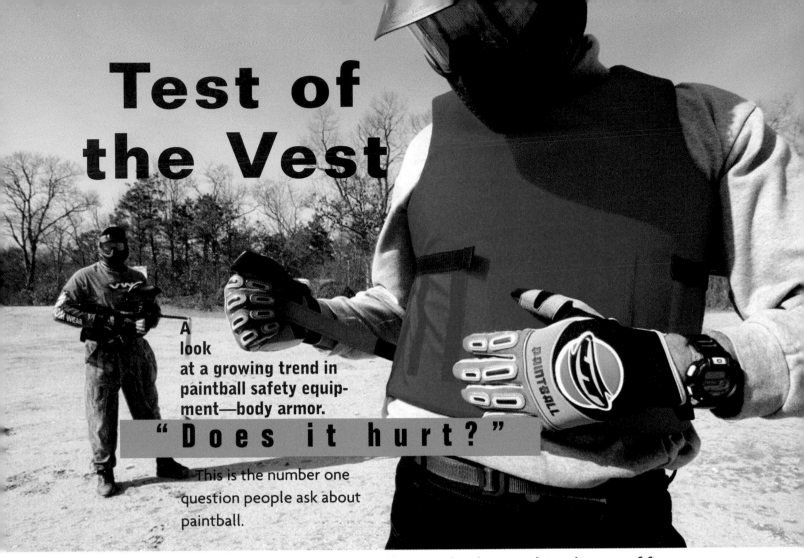

Test of the Vest

A look at a growing trend in paintball safety equipment—body armor.

"Does it hurt?"

This is the number one question people ask about paintball.

With the increase in paintball gun technology pushing the rate of fire ever higher, there is a definite need to provide players with safety equipment that can handle these new conditions. And as more people get into the game, why hurt 'em?

Rose and Dan Drewek have a deep love of paintball that goes beyond playing. Their dream is to have a profound impact on the industry by promoting safety. In 1993, they opened an outdoor paintball field in Canada. In 1996, they opened a retail store to better serve their customers and promote the sport. In 1998, they opened an indoor field.

Rose and Dan have been involved in paintball for 13 years. Dan has always been a tournament player, and has developed a number of local tournament teams. Dan currently plays for the Focus International factory team on the amateur circuit.

"I once had a child cry from the sting of a paintball at his own birthday party," explains Rose Drewek.

"I began to wonder if there were a way to run things so that people didn't have to be afraid of being hit by paintballs."

With this in mind, Paintball Encounters teamed up with Extreme Adventures, a Canadian manufacturing company, to develop a safety vest. They wanted to maintain authenticity and realism for players. They designed the vest to be the most universal piece of equipment available, next to a goggle system, and called it "The No Flak Jack."

Designed for both players and referees alike—in fact it was selected to be the safety vest worn by the referees at Skyball '99—the No Flak Jack is constructed of heavy Cordura material and is padded with closed cell foam. Two models are available: a recreational vest, which features a removable neck guard and an optional crotch protector (see *A Case for A Cup* and you'll know why this is a good idea), and a field rental version vest, which offers similar protection with a stripped-down design.

We decided to put the utility of a safety vest to the test as part of our field trials for this book. We wanted to see first hand whether the No Flak Jack lived up to the promises of its inventors.

A SIMPLE TEST

Our test was simple: four shots to the back and four to the front from ten feet away. Rob was shooting his Viper. Needless to say, I was reassured by Rob that he'd hit the target every time. This was good news, since I was wearing the vest.

Wham! Wham! Wham! Wham! to my back they came. The third shot landed on top of the second, right in the middle of my right shoulder blade. The impact was felt-in fact, the third shot did sting.

I turned around 180° and Rob repeated his marksmanship skill four more times to my chest. Wham! Wham! The second shot threw paint onto my goggles. Wham! The last shot was a bounce, no break. Pain factor? None.

Removing the vest, there were no obvious welts, just a little redness. Twenty-four hours later where normally bruises would have appeared, there were none.

No marks. No welts. No soreness. Pretty Cool!

Since that day, I have worn the No Flak Jack under my coveralls on the field. I have been wearing the field rental model, because I like the design. Being a big guy, the straps tend to be a bit short, but nonetheless the vest does the trick.

Our conclusion: wearing a vest is an excellent safety precaution, especially as more and more kids are getting into the game. A close shot to the kidneys can indeed cause injury, so why risk it? If I had kids, and they played paintball, I'd make certain they wore a safety vest in addition to their goggle protection. It's a small investment (under $100), and well worth every penny to live to fight another day!

—AF

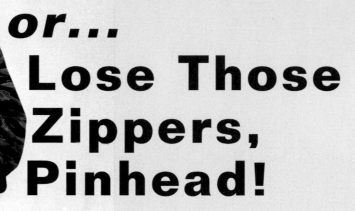

or...
Lose Those Zippers, Pinhead!

AN INTERVIEW WITH GRAHAM EASTON AND ADAM GARDNER

ANDREW FLACH: Head to toe, what does the well-dressed player wear? Obviously, you're going to wear a pair of goggles. Would you wear a hat underneath your goggles?

ADAM GARDNER: I recommend it. As far as I'm concerned—the NPPL says you can pretty much put a pillow on your head, if you want to.

The point is that head protection is certainly something that I think is a good idea, and I think a garment of some sort on the head is a good idea, whether it's specially designed or not. I wear just a woolen winter hat. It doesn't hurt as much when you get hit in the head.

When it comes to clothing, we dress in layers. First, a long sleeved shirt. If you wear a T-shirt on the playing field, you're going to get a lot more bruising than if you wear a long-sleeved shirt. I strongly recommend a turtleneck because a turtleneck protects the front of the neck to some degree, and it certainly is a lot better to get hit in the neck if you're wearing a turtleneck than it is if you are not.

GRAHAM EASTON: And on top of that a loose fitting pull-over sweatshirt. One that's baggy and not tight to the skin. This will improve the odds that paint will not break when it hits you.

You don't want something that's super tight to the body because then the clothing tends to transmit the energy of the paintball to your skin. If your clothing hangs a little bit looser, it will absorb more energy before the paintball hits you.

Wear a top that doesn't have buttons, either on the sleeves or on front.

Buttons break paint. Elastic necks and cuffs are ideal. When you're crawling or moving through brush, you don't want your sleeve riding up your arm. Elastic will keep it where it should be. You can move, but you're not tight, you're not restricted. That's how you want to play.

The same holds true for your pants. No belts, no fly, no zippers. I would suggest something like stretch pants underneath the uniform as well-biking pants or long underwear. The undergarment should be tight, but then your second (outer) layer should be loose and baggy. You want to wear something that's soft and smooth and doesn't have a lot of zippers and buttons that are going to break paint.

ANDREW: Of course, you need something to carry paint. What do you recommend?

ADAM G: You'll find that the players have different budgets and different amounts of paint that they intend to shoot. A lot of your back line, bigger guys carry just as many rounds as they can carry. And then small kids and front-line players carry different amounts of paint in harnesses designed to accommodate them. One of the challenges is finding a harness that is comfortable to wear and that doesn't twist around to the front side of your body during a game.

GRAHAM: A good harness is one that will provide support to the lower back, as well.

ANDREW: What do you suggest you wear on your feet?

ADAM G: You have to be able to run to play paintball. If you go out there wearing your typical steel-shank army boot you won't be able to run. The best choice is a supportive high-top cleat.

Something to consider is the surface you'll be playing on. When you go into an indoor field, you are better off with a high-top tennis shoe. If you wear your cleats and you're playing on a cement floor, you'll start skidding.

One of the other things I can recommend highly: neoprene socks. It looks like part of a diving suit that's worn over the foot. In paintball, in various conditions, your feet get wet and cold,

depending on where you are in the country. And even if they don't get cold, the neoprene sock prevents your ankles from twisting. It almost works as an extra ligament. We haven't had an accident in five years.

The negative side is they smell.

GRAHAM: When you lace your boot up, the neoprene sock almost conforms around the boot. So, it's very, very tight, very comfortable. And as the day goes on, you can just feel the support. I don't get swollen ankles anymore.

On your shins and knees, wear a nice pair of pads to protect yourself in case you slide or in case you accidentally fall. Obviously, everybody knows how painful it is to hit your shins or get a bruise on your knee, so why risk it? Protect your legs.

ADAM G: In paintball, you're always sliding. It's like football or baseball. When you run in, your gun's up, you're shooting and you hit you knees and you tend to slide in. And there are lots of things on the ground that really hurt when you slide into bunkers. So knee/shin pads are important.

ANDREW: Do you wear something like that to protect your elbows?

GRAHAM: I wear an elbow pad because I'm on the ground a lot. Indoor players tend to wear plenty of padding because they are playing on harder surfaces and the bunkers are of man-made materials. Outdoor players tend not to wear elbow protection. Unfortunately, they can be uncomfortable. It's a decision people make for themselves.

At least, wear gloves. Either full-fingered or fingerless gloves. They really help.

ANDREW: What about something like a Camelback or any of those water bottle things? Do you see a lot of that being used?

ADAM G: You mean carry a water bottle while you're playing? Paintball generally doesn't last that long in terms of an individual game to concern yourself with hydration during the game. Except during longer, scenario-type games.

It's important to drink plenty of water before games and between games. Some people don't and they get dehydrated. Being dehydrated can zap your energy, no matter what you're doing, but especially when you're exerting yourself.

It's very rare that you're going to play for hours without a break. When you have the opportunity to drink between games, do it. Speaking of hydration, a lot of people in the warmer climates feel that the less clothes you wear, the less dehydrated you'll get. It's actually the opposite.

If you wear a thin layer of clothes, the moisture on your skin is evaporating constantly. One of the most important things you need in deserts is a full winter jacket. You know those Middle Eastern robes that look so light? They just flow in the wind? Well, they're made of thick wool. They actually help preserve your body's moisture within the folds. The same principle is at work if you're dressed appropriately for paintball.

The hottest temperature at a tournament we ever played was 122 degrees in L.A. Heat is a problem with paintball. When it's this hot, cover yourself up, cool down, and drink plenty of water. Simple stuff, but it's easy to neglect.

ANDREW: Sounds like a day pack is needed to get your stuff to the field.

ADAM G: Paintball players are not carrying just a little bit. They are carrying a ton of junk. You've got a harness, you've got a few loaders of balls, you've got a case of paint or half a case of paint, you have

a gun, maybe a back-up gun. You have shoes, socks. They're packing a suitcase, not a day pack. Paintball is equipment-intensive, like golf.

ANDREW: So, another piece of gear is a decent gear bag.

ADAM: Sure. One thing kids do is use those wheeled coolers, the kind you find at the local K-Mart or Wal-Mart. They make a very good, inexpensive way of getting your equipment around because when you go to a paintball field you have to haul this stuff to where you're playing.

THE BEST WAY TO HIDE YOUR FACE

ADAM G: Goggleflauge was invented by George Davidson of the All Americans. In it's simplest form it's a great way to disguise your goggles. But it's more than that.

In paintball, one key to success is spotting your opponents and taking them out with a clean shot before they have a chance to do the same to you.

Why not take a little extra precaution and hide your face more carefully? After all, your round head provides an excellent target for the enemy. Your glinting goggle lenses call to him to put a nice shot between your eyes.

Why present a clear target? You've got your cammies on, right? Add on some Goggleflauge and you'll stay in the game that much longer.

If you use your Goggleflauge properly, you can slowly work your head up to a crack in the bunker you're hiding in and look right at your opponents without them even seeing you. A major advantage, I think you'd agree.

Another advantage of Goggleflauge is that it softens the blow. It may cause a ball or two to bounce off (and you know they don't count unless they break), but more importantly, if you get hit in the face at point blank range and you're wearing your Goggleflauge, you'll be a much happier player.

You know how your goggles have little holes in the plastic face guard? When a ball hits there it breaks into little pieces which fly at about 150–300 feet per second if you're hit within 5 feet. And when those innocent little pieces hit your skin... there's an ouch factor.

With your Goggleflauge, you may still feel it a bit, but it won't hurt as bad. That's a promise from the manufacturer.

If you've been eating paintballs by the bowlful, it's time to invest in some Goggleflauge, don't you think?

THE CASE FOR A CUP

Andrew Flach Recounts a Personal Moment of Humility & Discomfort

To wear a cup or not wear a cup, that is the question. Of all the answers I've sought in the process of putting together this book, it is the most mercurial of them all. Some people swear by cups, others swear against them, saying they're too uncomfortable and restricting. Many players who never wear them can recall situations where they wished they had.

The first time I ever played paintball was at an indoor field called Dark Armies in Indianapolis, Indiana. As we went through the check-in procedures and briefing, we were informed that protective cups were available for purchase at $7 each. I skipped the additional investment and threw my extra bucks into more paint and a gun upgrade, naturally.

Wouldn't you know, in the early moments of my very first game, as I leaned stealthily out of a doorway... Wham! Wham! Wham! Three "precise" shots right in the crotch. Kinda took my breath away. "I'm hit. I'm hit," I cried, hoping to end the flow of balls to my already sore area. The shooter stopped, and I hopped out-of-bounds.

The lesson: paintballs can hurt.
My advice: wear a cup.

Lock & Load

Paintball loaders serve one purpose: to feed more paint into a marker more efficiently. The first "Loaders" were tubes that were a permanent part of a paintball gun. To load a paintball you had to rock the gun to roll a paintball into the open breech, and then cock the gun. "Rock-N-Cock" loading systems like this are still evident in Stock Class paintball guns like the PGP, Phantom SC, and P-68SC. Many players added a "speedloader" to these guns to add another tube, and another 10 paintballs.

The widespread desire to carry more paint in a gun led to a simple "Stick Feeder." It was essentially a PVC tube attached to a PVC elbow that was designed to come off the back of an on-gun feed tube. A sock holder prevented the balls from rolling out of the top. It was usually designed to hold another 10-15 paintballs. Anything longer was too much of a target. Later, when direct feed guns were introduced, many players still used a stick feeder for quite some time.

The Idema Combat Systems vest, filled with with tube loaders. Introduced 1988 — Discontinued 1991.

Many people made "Home-brew" loaders from all sorts of objects. The most popular was an old oil can cleaned out, the top made into a lid, and placed onto the neck of a paintball gun. "D.A.M. cans" were a mass-produced version of the oil-can loaders. This design eventually lead to the mass-produced "Worr Games Ammo Box." This box held 45 paintballs, and had an opening for tubed paint (as in 10 round tubed paint). The WGP ammo box had the advantage of being smaller and more streamlined than the oil-can style of loaders. It was an instant hit.

Larger loaders were introduced very quickly. The first was the "Whaler," which resembled a large sausage tube with "Magic Fish Lips" (no, I'm not making this up!) to aid in faster loading. The need for a better loader was answered by Viewloader, a company that introduced a modular 90-round hopper simply called "Viewloader." It had a clear flip lid, which was easy to look into and to load on the fly.

Viewloader also made 45-round hoppers with which one could fill this new loader. Other companies used this same principle to create a plethora of 100–150 capacity loaders. This was the norm, with a few larger loaders becoming available.

The only problem with all this was the paint. Many paintball guns wouldn't create enough of a 'kick' to move the paint around, and jams were common. Imagine having to shoot five times, shake your gun, shoot another 5 times, shake your gun, and doing this all day. Players wanted a solution, and Viewloader delivered one.

Viewloader created the first patented agitating loader, the VL-2000. It works by placing an electronic eye in the feed neck that tells a motherboard to rotate a paddle to move the paintballs around in the loader. They originally designed it on their 200 round loader, but with time and research it's become streamlined and efficient. Many players agree that the 200 round loader is the best for size, weight, and capacity.

The latest in high-technology is based on the VL-2000, called the "VL-2001." It's an electronic loader that you plug into the gun itself. The motor rotates and agitates the balls at a predetermined trigger pull. Electropneumatic paintguns like the Angel or the Shocker use this kind of loader, as the guns themselves are electronics-based.

Other loaders are still available. For example Indian Springs makes a 125 paintball hopper that's well suited for pump guns, if you're into vintage old-school play. Many other companies and loaders exist as well. Keep your eyes open for the next best thing—force-feed. But for the time being you have many excellent loaders to choose from.

-RR

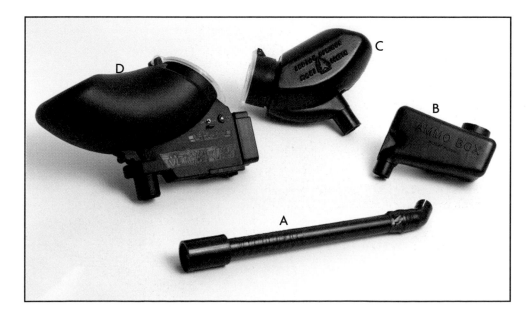

Brief History of the Loader

A. 15 round stick feeder

B. Worr Games Product Ammo Box

C. Indian Springs 120 round loader

D. View Loader Revolution, Brass Eagle, with VL timer

Squeegees in a Nutshell

The Fine Art of Squeegee

WHERE TO START

There are two basic styles of squeegees on the market. Picking one is a matter of objective necessity and personal preference. Both clean out your barrel very effectively, but you may like one more than the other.

The first style is a "Stick" squeegee. "Stick" squeegees are long plastic tubes with a rubber disc at one end, and a spring-style action at the other end. To use this effectively, you push down on one end to push the rubber disk out. You need to flatten the disk out, and push it down the barrel.

When you release the top spring, the disk comes flat against the plastic tube, filling the barrel. When you pull out the squeegee, it pulls broken paint and shell out with it. Many styles have a cloth on the opposite end, with which you can clean any residual paint out of your barrel.

The other style is a "Pull Through" or "Cable" squeegee. The cable style has several disks on a cord, and sometimes a fluffy "Swab" on the end. To use one, you need to remove the barrel from the paintball gun. You place the end without the disks in one end of the barrel, feeding it to the other side. You then pull on that end to bring the disks through the barrel, cleaning out the paint in your barrel. The "Swab" removes anything that may be left in the barrel, making one clean sweep.

Both styles have advantages and disadvantages.

- Stick squeegees are easy to use and you'll be done in a jiffy, but they may not clean the barrel as effectively as a pull through.

- A pull through can't be used on some styles of paintball guns with "Fixed" (non-removable) barrels.

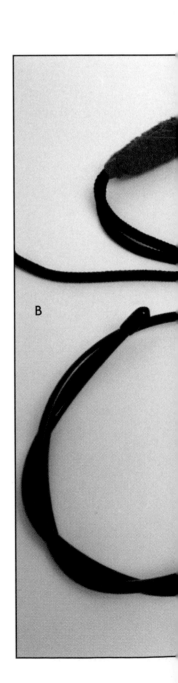

B

- Pull through squeegees can be folded, and fit into your pocket.

- Stick squeegees are bulky.

After squeegeeing your gun, you should clean off the disks. Placing a stick squeegee in the back of your knee and wiping it clean is a fast way to do this.

A. Straight Shot
B. Jerk
C. Battle Swab®
D. Power Squeegee
E. Barrel swab

-RR

If you borrow someone else's squeegee, it's good form to clean it off before you return it.

"PAINT IN THE HOLE"

DENNIS TIPPMANN, JR.: Paintball grenades are made of surgical tubing, which is like rubber tubing. Basically, we pump up this heavy-walled rubber tubing like you would a water balloon. It takes about 100 pounds pressure to pump these things up. Once they're pumped up, we put two balls in the end. The two balls are positioned right up by the neck that's holding all the paint back. Now the remaining chunks of tubes are sticking out there. We've pulled it and we put a cap on, and we put a pin in that keeps the balls in place. During a game, you pull the pin on the grenade (some guys pull the cap off, it really doesn't matter) and throw it. As soon as it hits the ground, the cap just pops off. The impact pops the two balls out and they just spray in any and every direction. They spray all over the place, and you'll get fully painted if one lands near you.

If someone threw one in the middle of a 100 square foot room, there would be speckles and quarter-sized splotches along all of the walls. So, yes, this can be a pretty powerful part of your paintball arsenal.

Sights & Scopes

All you have to do is line up opponents in your crosshairs and pull the trigger! It's that easy, right?

not quite...

THE HARD CORE TRUTH ABOUT SIGHTS & SCOPES

Many players use sights or scopes on their paintball guns to help improve "accuracy." I've seen some very impressive 20x-scopes placed on all sorts of paintguns. But do they really help your *accuracy*? Well, yes and no.

A paintball is not a bullet. Therefore, the accuracy of a paintball cannot be guaranteed. A paintball is filled with liquid, so all sorts of variables affect what happens to it once it's shot out the end of a barrel. The wind can catch it and blow it round. Extreme high velocity can make it unstable. Even the paint can influence your accuracy. Other things that affect the path of a paintball include:

*   The gun and barrel brands and how they match-up.

*   If your paint is dry or dimpled or wet.

*   If your barrel has broken paint in it.

The Complete Guide to Paintball

- The phase of the moon. (Just kidding, but you get the point. Many things affect your paintball's path!)

Adco Hot Shot, Adco vision 2000

Where a paintball is going to go is often an unknown. So, the scope usually out-performs the paint. This isn't to say that a scope or sight is useless. I've had a lot of success using them on my personal paintguns. You just need to understand a few guidelines for the use of these accessories so that you can optimize your experience of them.

HOW TO USE SIGHTS & SCOPES TO IMPROVE YOUR GAME

My opinion is that scopes have limited usefulness. Why? Magnification interferes with your aim. Your magnified perspective will usually be further ahead than the ball will travel. That said, I grant that sights and scopes are useful for looking downfield in the larger "big game" formats of paintball. In other words, use the magnification to look a couple hundred yards ahead to see if your competition is moving around out there, where they're headed, things like this. Of course, opportunities to do this are few and far between for most people. In most cases, you want a sight with no magnification that simply puts a "dot" in space.

Once you've gotten your sight, you want to "Dial it in." What is *dialing*? In an ideal scenario, realize that a sight can only tell you where the barrel is pointed, not where your paint will eventually go. A little experimentation will tell you where paint is likely to go when you're aiming at something within a certain range. If you can hit a pie-plate at 75 feet, you can calibrate or 'dial' your sight so that it will reflect where the paint usually goes at that dis-

Smart Parts HI VIZ

tance. This takes some time and patience. I like to dial in at 75–100 feet, as most of my shooting happens within that range.

In regular "toe-to-toe" play, you usually don't use sights. I find myself just shooting and following where the last ball went, or using the barrel itself as a large point sight. For long angle shots, or for ambush situations, sights work very well. My personal technique may not work for everyone, but it's worth trying.

Place the dot on your opponent's chest area. If a ball drifts in most any direction, it will still probably hit them. I like to keep both eyes open for a stereoscopic view, but some prefer to close one eye to concentrate on the shot. Either way works well. Then, simply pull the trigger in the same way that you would any other time. Don't change that detail, because if you do it won't "feel" right and you probably won't hit the person. Paintguns have no recoil, so slow trigger pulls aren't necessary. In some cases, it may not give you the best shot. Some players put a short "string" of 3 balls on a target, but sometimes that's not necessary.

Using a sight or a scope may or may not improve your game. Your best bet is to invest in an inexpensive sight to try it out. If it helps your game or you just really enjoy using it, you'll find no shortage of variety in terms of available scopes and sights.

—RR

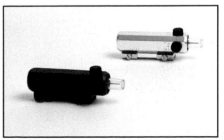

Armson/Pro-Team Products
Pro-Drop Red Dot

PART 4

DRILLS

Warm Up Play Hot

Prepare Your Body to Optimize Your Game Play

After interviewing some of the top paintball players and paintball field owners in the world, it was apparent that many of the injuries that occur during a paintball game could be easily avoided by a moderate level of fitness and flexibility. In fact, the two biggest injuries are ankle sprains and muscle pulls (hamstrings and lower back). The ankle injuries can be decreased by wearing proper shoes such as high top cleats and a few basic calf exercises and stretches. The hamstrings and the lower back can also be strengthened by a easy routine of stretching and exercising. This chapter is devoted not only to preventing the most common injuries in paintball, but to assisting adventurous paintball players in becoming more flexible, faster, stronger, and healthier. Follow this step-by-step stretching program during the week and you will be able to splat your opponents with ease during the weekend paintball games.

Stewart Smith graduated from the United States Naval Academy in 1991. He then spent four years on SEAL teams, after which he was put in charge of the physical training and selection of future BUD/S candidates. Stewart currently runs the getfitnow.com family fitness center in Severna Park, Maryland.

WARMING-UP

Warming up prior to stretching, exercise, and playing paintball is absolutely crucial to injury prevention. You will find that your muscles are more flexible and react to stretching far better after a brief 5–10 minute warm-up. Do this by walking, jogging slowly, riding a bike, or doing 50 jumping jacks.

The objective is to get your heart pumping above its normal rate, which will increase the blood flow to the muscles that you are about to stretch and use. Stretching is not only the best way to avoid injuries, but also the best way to prepare yourself to get tight and small behind a bunker, and then explode in a sprint on the attack. Regardless of your age, paintball is a vigorous and challenging sport that will test your stamina. To take your game to the next level, give your body the attention it needs, and follow these simple guidelines.

YO!

We'll be covering only stretches in this book, so we encourage you to check out our workout resources for the active sports enthusiast by visiting the GetFitNow.com web site. As most of our workout books are derived from the finest fitness regimens in the world, those of our United States Armed Forces, we are certain that you will find them extremely helpful in training to become the ultimate paintball warrior!

S T R E T C H E S

UPPER AND LOWER BODY

Arm (Shoulder)

Drop your shoulder and pull your arm across your chest. With the opposite arm, gently pull your arm across your chest and hold for 15 seconds. Repeat with the other arm.

This stretches the back of the shoulder and muscles that attach the shoulder blade to the upper part of the back. This is the very root of most tension headaches. Keeping these muscles flexible will help prevent injuries caused by running and falling to the ground when you are seeking cover from incoming paintballs.

The Most Advanced Piece of Machinery in Paintball? Your Body.

Arm Circles

Rotate your arms slowly in big circles forward and then reverse. This will help prepare your shoulders for pushups, dips, and dumbbell work.

Triceps into Lateral Stretch

Place both arms over and behind your head. Grab your right elbow with your left hand and pull your elbow toward your opposite shoulder. Lean with the pull. Repeat with the other arm.

This stretch prepares you for the dumbbell triceps exercises, pushups, and dips, but also helps stretch the back muscles. This is a very important stretch for upper body exercises!

Chest

Stand with your arms extended and parallel to the floor. Slowly pull your elbows back as far as you can. Hold for 15 seconds. Do not thrust your arms backwards. This is a slow and deliberate stretch designed to prepare your chest for pushups, dips, and other shoulder/chest exercises.

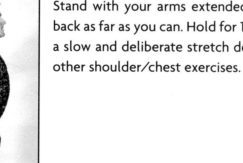

Shoulder Rotations

Rotate your shoulders slowly up and down, keeping your arms relaxed by your side. Your shoulders should rotate in small circles and move up and down in slow distinct movements.

Stomach Stretch

Lie on your stomach. Push yourself up to your elbows. Slowly lift your head and shoulders and look up at the sky or ceiling. Hold for 15 seconds and repeat two times.

Hip Rotations

Place your hands on your hips and slowly rotate your hips in big circles clockwise and counter-clockwise for about 15 seconds in each direction.

**In a game where a miss is as good as a mile,
an extra show of agility,
degree of flexibility, or burst of speed can make the difference
between Triumph and Defeat!**

Thigh Stretch On Ground

Lie on your left side. Pull your right foot to your butt by grabbing your ankle and hold it with your right hand. Keep your knees close together and hold for 10–15 seconds. Repeat with the other leg.

Calf Stretch / Achilles Tendon Stretch

Stand with one foot 2–3 feet in front of the other. With both feet pointing in the same direction you are facing, put most of your body weight on the leg that is behind you, stretching the calf muscle.

Now, bend the rear knee slightly. You should now feel the stretch in your heel. This stretch helps prevent achilles tendonitis, a severe injury that will sideline most paintball players for at least 4–6 weeks.

Hamstring Stretch

From the standing or sitting position, bend forward at the waist and touch your toes. Keep your back straight and slightly bend your knees. You should feel this stretching the back of your thighs near the connection of the leg and butt. Now, slowly straighten your legs, feeling the stretch travel down your leg and behind your knees. You have just stretched the entire hamstring. Hold both the straight leg and bent leg stretch for 15 seconds each.

Most people pull their hamstring at the top part of the leg (where it connects to the buttocks). By simply bending your knees while stretching, you will decrease your chances of suffering the most common injury to paintball players.

Groin/Inner Thigh Side Stretch

Stand with your legs spread and lean to the left. Keep the right leg straight while pointing the toes up. Repeat on the other side. This will help prevent groin strains, another common injury to paintball players who play speedball and games with a similar fast-paced tempo.

Hurdler Stretch

Sit on the floor with your legs straight in front of you. Bend your right knee and place the bottom of your foot on the inside of your opposite thigh. With your back straight, lean forward in order to stretch the back of your legs and lower back. Hold the stretch for 15 seconds, switch legs, and repeat.

Ilio Tibial Stretch

Sit on the ground with your legs crossed in front of you. Keeping your legs crossed, bring the top leg to your chest and bend it at the knee so that your foot is placed outside of your thigh. Hold for 15 seconds and repeat with the other leg.

You should perform this stretch before and after running. This will help prevent very common over-use injuries in the hips and knees.

Knees-to-Chest

Lie flat on your back. Pull your knees to your stomach and hold for 20 seconds. You should perform this stretch before and after any abdominal exercise.

As you may know, the lower back is the most commonly injured area of the body. Many lower back problems stem from inactivity, lack of flexibility, and improper lifting of heavy objects. Stretching and exercising your lower back will help prevent injuries to this extremely sensitive area.

Butterfly

Sit on your buttocks with your knees bent and the soles of your feet together. Grab your ankles and place both of your elbows on your inner thighs. Slowly push down on your thighs.

AND NOW YOU'RE READY TO RUMBLE

Underestimating the stress you put on your body when playing this game is a surefire way to get injured or develop chronic aches and pains. If you do these stretches every day, and always perform them before playing paintball, you will be doing yourself a huge favor.

Stewart Smith's Paintball Workout is available on our web site, GetFitNow.com, for those of you interested in the achieving the highest possible performance.

PAUL FOGAL ON FITNESS
Fitness Does Matter

"I think one of the beauties of paintball is that just about anybody can play because you can play to your level of fitness. If you're scared or you're slow or you have a disability or something, you can play a static defense. You can guard the flag. You can be a central source of communication. You have options people who aren't in the best shape don't have in other sports. And if you happen to be in great shape and you're real aggressive, then you can go out on offense and you can run.

It certainly helps to be in some kind of shape, because then you really have your choice of how you want to play. And, of course, small, quick people definitely have an advantage. It's harder to hit a quick and small target. You don't have to be in particularly great shape to enjoy paintball, but the better shape you're in, the more options you have."

Stretch out and you'll feel better before, during, and after you play!

Tactical Drills for the Beginner

TO KICK ASS, YOU MUST DRILL!

Our goal in this chapter is to teach paintball playing basics. Of course, you can tailor paintball tactics drills as you see fit. The key is not merely to practice, but to practice the right things.

FIRST THINGS FIRST

Chronograph your paintgun to 285–290 feet per second (fps), the appropriate outdoor playing speed.

Each drill is a scenario. The object of each scenario is similar to what you will face on a normal playing day in both recreational and tournament play. Once you know the moves, you can repeat them with minimal effort. Think of them as "katas" of sorts.

Each drill should be performed from "both ends" if applicable. The idea is to combine all of the aspects of the game into your individual game. Even in a team setting, your individual moving, shooting, and communication skills will make or break a game.

SHOOTING DRILLS

You'll need the following supplies: Paper Plates (pie tins, frisbees, etc.), a stopwatch.

Obstacle course

Object—Run the course as fast as you can, hitting all the targets as you do so. This is a sample course, feel free to adjust it to your conditions and playing field. Just remember that the course should resemble a playing field as accurately as possible.

- On breakout, hit a 100 foot target

- From a bunker position, hit 75' and a 50' targets

- Run to new bunker, shoot a 75' offhanded shot (lefty for right-handers, righty for left-handers)

- Run to new position, shooting at a positioned plate as you pass it. (This is called bunkering or a 'takedown').

- From new bunker, take offhand 50', 75' shots, then regular hand 75', 50' shots.

- Take a 150' long shot from new position, then turn around for a 25' close shot.

- Stop watch at flag station bunker. Repeat the course until you improve your time and accuracy. Then change the course to give yourself a fresh challenge.

A SIMPLE RUN & SHOOT DRILL

Another simple Run & Shoot Drill is to set up a series of targets (in this case soda jugs hanging from a rope) and run past them, shooting as you go. Your motion, as well as the swinging of the jugs makes this a particularly challenging drill.

Of course, you do have options...

Two player option: Follow the same course with a player shooting at you as you run through it.

Team option: On the same course, one player moves while the second gives cover fire. When the target is hit, the second player leapfrogs to the next position.

Pressure option: Same course, teammate runs course behind you. If you do not hit your target before your teammate does, your teammate is allowed to shoot you to get you to move.

BACKFOOT TACTICS DRILL

Timed Offense/Defense

Needed—At least 2 players, position of defense (such as a flag station or a building), flag, stopwatch.

Setup—3 attackers to 2 defenders *or* 2 attackers to 1 defender

Scenario—For each defender, put 1 minute and 30 seconds on the clock.

Goals

- Defense must prevent a flag pull.
- Offense must grab the flag and get away clean in the time allotted.
- Offense may set up anywhere beyond 150 feet of the defensive flag.
- Defense may set up anywhere within 150 feet of the flag, the closer the better.

Lessons

Offense—Must be aggressive when the numbers are in their favor, and learn to push hard under time pressure.

Defense—Learn how to be patient and kill a clock when outnumbered. Survival is the key, and staying in the game under pressure is hard.

This drill can also be used to simulate defending an opponents' flag station while they are trying to bring your flag in for a win. For this, do 3 on 1. Your solo guy gets a minute to set up. The aggressors have 2 minutes to hang the flag.

WORKING WITH BUNKERS

All bunkers "work" (or *are worked*) in the same manner. Flat-sided ones are easier to demonstrate on. The drills I'm highlighting here apply for use of trees, brambles, or any similar protection.

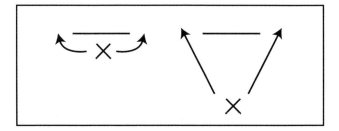

Take A Few Steps Back To Gain Perspective and Expand Your Field of Vision and Kill Zone

Get back if you can. You can cover more space with less effort.

Be Unpredictable

Move around in a position, because "Jack in the Boxes" get hit.

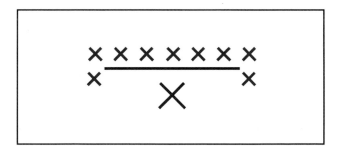

The little red markers represent all of the potential angles from which "X" can pop up and take shots at his opponents. Being unpredictable keeps your opponents waiting for your next move.

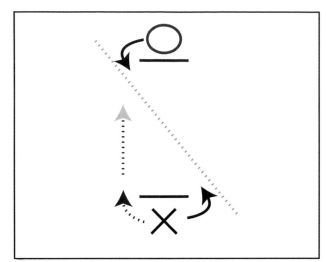

When "X" sees that "O" keeps emerging from the left side, he suspects his opponent is right-handed and relies too much on firing from the same place. They exchange fire along the pink line several times. Then, by shifting to the left side of his bunker and using his left hand, "X" surprises "O", and gets the elimination. "X" is right-handed, but he practices left-handed shooting to gain the advantage in scenarios like this one.

Downfall of the "Right Hand" Conspiracy

Actually, what we're talking about here has absolutely nothing to do with a conspiracy. It just happens to be the case that most people are right-handed and have a natural propensity to favor the right side of their bunker. From your perspective, that means most opponents will be emerging from the left side of their bunker. If you practice shooting with your off hand, you can make better use of your cover to eliminate your opponent.

This is pretty powerful knowledge, but you need to practice taking advantage of it!

Go *the other way and take opponents out before they know what hit them.*

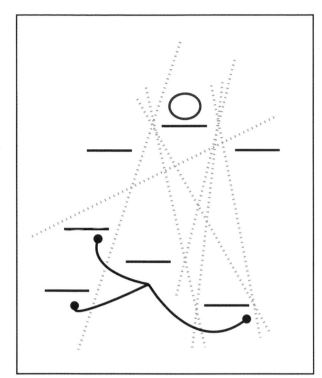

By moving behind different bunkers, even moving backwards, "X" is able to attain new angles of attack against "O." The dotted lines are shooting lanes that "X" can take advantage of if he's willing to take new positions.

Be Dynamic—Move From Bunker to Bunker To Gain New Angles of Attack

Use all the space you have available, even if it means falling back or shifting sideways. One person can take up a lot of space.

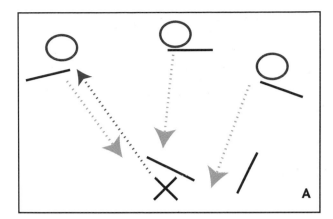

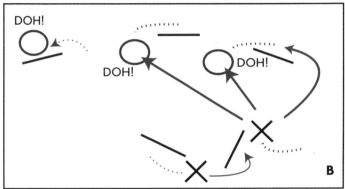

(A) "X" is in a tough spot. One moment, he's occupying two opponents. The next, he finds himself wide open to a flanking "O." While calling for support from teammates, "X" must act fast to maintain his position, using fire to literally "cover" his own position. This can't last for long!

(B) With support from a stealthy teammate who heard his coded plea for assistance, "X" is able to turn the opponents' perception of his weakness against them. As they move in for the kill, they are taken out by "X"'s flanking teammate. Now it's 2-on-1 in favor of our resourceful team "X" who quickly take new positions. *Never give up!*

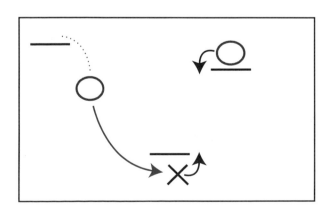

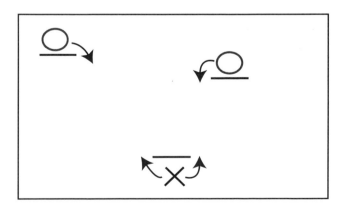

"X" is focused on the "O" right in front of him. This is exactly what Team "O" is counting on. A preoccupied "X" is easy to flank, as we can see from the first diagram. "X" is about to become "American History X."

A more mature "X" is moving in his bunker and looking for enemies on all sides. Here he has a good chance of keeping two opponents at bay, even taking them both out. Observe that if "X" has practiced using both left and right hands, he'll be more effective at keeping his opponents on their heels. Never stop moving behind your bunker. "X" should also communicate that he has two "O"'s in from of him and try to turn the tables on them with help from teammates! "X" may also want to try 'taking a few steps back' to facilitate handling this relatively precarious situation.

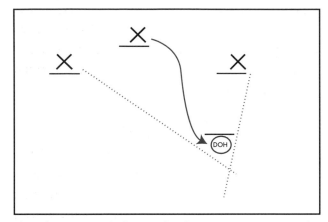

The Ultimate DOH! This is what happens to someone who doesn't communicate and doesn't play as part of a team. Or someone on a team that has been demolished!

If you're the only one left, and you find yourself completely overwhelmed, you still have options. As you can see, if "O" doesn't move, he's a goner. May as well try to take out as many of the opposition as he can!

**Avoid tunnel vision!
In a bunker, keep looking and shooting
both ways to keep your enemies at bay.**

**Look for natural holes in cover
(like barrels) and shoot through them.**

HERO TIME!

DELUSIONS OF INVINCIBILITY CAN BE USEFUL

Sometimes you need to act in a manner that others will perceive as incredibly daring and maybe even a little crazy. But in reality, a grand (or gutsy) move can blow open a game. Your opponents may fall into the trap of expecting you to be as cautious as they are. Suddenly, you're heading for an extremely aggressive position. They may get distracted by your audacity and pause before responding. If you pull it off, they'll feel demoralized and may be inclined to become preoccupied with your ominous position.

"I can't believe that guy just did that. What's he going to do next?"

These are just a few of the questions that you can implant in the minds of your foe with a bold move!

Another benefit of this is that it takes the heat off of your teammates, who should be able to take better positions while the other team is second-guessing itself. Of course, you should scream at your team to do this if they're not responding promptly.

Aggression can be rewarded, as long as you are in control and know what is going on.

DRILLING FOR DOUBLES

Coordinating your game play with one other person makes you a double-threat both defensively and offensively. The following drills will enable you to practice basic coordination techniques that can lead to dramatic results in games. You'll take a couple of steps closer to an elevated understanding of paintball when you practice working in teams. Drilling 2-on-2 is a great way to work on coordinated offense and defense.

Low Man Approach With Cover

High man supplies cover by shooting over crawler. Crawler takes new position and shoots opponent.

Flank'em

One flanks left while other teammate shoots to keep opponent occupied and down. Flanker shoots opponent from new position.

Overbound

One moves, the other takes his place. This is called displacing. Keep moving up like the ends of a centipede.

Bait and Switch

Direct an opponent to one side of a bunker by shooting at one side consistently. It's human nature to move away from incoming fire, so this is likely to work. The opponent is likely to use the other side to "return fire."

Keep paint on the side your flanker is approaching to prevent your opponent from returning fire to that side and discovering your flanker. You are the bait. Your opponent will be flanked and eliminated in no time.

Overwhelming force

Having superior numbers does not guarantee victory. A patient and skilled opponent will pick your teammates off one by one if you're not careful and methodical about eliminating him. The idea is to get angles. The more sides of your opponent you shoot at, the less chance he has to hide behind cover to avoid you.

DO IT AGAIN!

Drills can be fun, but they are not ends in themselves. The point of doing drills is to improve your response to live game situations. **There's nothing as satisfying as bearing witness to your own improvement in paintball. The shortest path to that uplifting experience is a balance of frequent drilling and playing.**

—RR

COMMUNICATIONS AND CODES

Communication on the paintball field is vital to winning.

Lack of communication spells defeat for your team. If the other side has equal skills and is communicating better than you are, you'll be counting far too much on luck to win. Whatever methods you choose, pick a system that is easy to follow and remember. In the heat of the game, you can always rely on plain old English, but codes can be faster if used well, and they can confuse your opponents!

There are plenty of things to communicate on the field:

- The Status of Your Team-what are you going to do; what's your team's status
- The Status of Your Opponent's Team-what are they doing; what's their status
- The Status of the Overall Game-how much time is left; how many players are left
- Field Locations-where is everyone
- Junk Codes-designed to throw off the opponent, they are meaningless

Verbal Codes

These are faster to communicate than visual signals

Here are few examples of verbal codes (and their meanings) that have been developed by actual teams:

Fishing - I've got a gun jam
Sunshine Red - Everyone shoot right
Sunset Blue - Everyone shoot left
Going Shopping - I'm off to "bunker" someone
Mickey Says - Indicates how much time is left in the game. "Mickey Says Three" means there are 3 minutes remaining in the game.
Exxon - Reloading
Juice - The Flag
Visa - Attack (As in "Charge!".)

Field Locations can be identified by memorizing a simple grid describing rows and columns, or a clever code system. Draw a grid with an "x" and "y" axis dividing the field into 4 quadrants. Then, draw horizontal lines to delimit 6 "rows." Use colors to divide the field down the middle. "Red3", for instance, might describe a bunker in the 3rd row on the left side of the field. "Blue3 would indicate the same row of bunkers on the right side of the field.

A more complex system, but one which might be easier to remember, can be based on the map of the US, the hands of a clock, or the locations of stores in a shopping mall familiar to your team.

Make certain all players on your team know your code inside-out! You can tape a copy of the day's codes to the inside lid of your loader.

Codes can be based on a number of different schemes: car types, breakfast cereals, animals, cartoon characters...anything goes so long as it's easy to understand.

Here's a code based on airline travel:

Passport - The flag
Lost My Luggage - Gun Down
Found My Luggage - Gun Working Again
New York - The Right Tape
LA - The Left Tape
Flight Delayed - Reloading
Cancel the Ticket - Bunker someone
Disneyland - The Opponents Flag Station
The Gate - Your Team's Flag Station
In-Flight Movie - Your team has the advantage
Airline Food - You are in a bad position and could use some cover
Buckle Seatbelts - Everyone attack
Emergency Exit - The flag is in jeopardy

Obviously, codes can add a fun dimension to your game. Why not make up your own code and try it out with your friends!

Sarah's Drills 2Die4

Here are a few suggestions for drills
from an expert at drilling,
Sarah Stevenson of 2Die4!

Anyone can participate in paintball at any level regardless of size, sex, color, creed, beliefs, habits... basically, it's an open party. You don't even have to own your own gun or equipment! However, if you want to be any good at this game, you have to develop certain skills. The old adage about practice making perfect is as true in paintball as it is in any endeavor.

Paintball is a sport in which you cannot look at your opponent and assess them merely on a visual basis. This is primarily a marksmanship and reaction-type sport. So your opponent doesn't have to be the strongest nor the fastest adversary to beat you. How do you gain an edge in this game? You must be tuned in to the game, have a full knowledge of your equipment, and play within your own physical abilities.

The whole idea of drills is to help improve your reaction time and target shooting ability. The following drills work very well with a few basic supplies. You will need the following items at your disposal: empty milk jugs or coffee cans, rope, and a stop watch.

Target Shooting

1. Place 3 targets approximately 15 feet apart and at different heights (place on top of bunkers and hang from trees).

2. Walk approximately 25 feet away and face away from the targets.

3. Count down, 3-2-1, spin, drop to one knee and (shooting only three times at each target) shoot left, center, right.

How many shots did it take to hit the targets? Which one was easier to hit than the others? After you have done this a few times, change the placement of the targets and your distance (either closer or farther away) and repeat it for a while. This drill will help you with your speedball reaction time. When you have two players running at you and they are spaced apart, you won't hesitate to take them on and you'll have success.

Snap Shooting

1. Again, place a jug on top (or on the ground to one side) of the bunker.

2. Place yourself behind another bunker just opposite the target. Crouch on your knees and raise your gun to your shoulder, leaning close to the edge you wish to shoot from. Lean out very quickly, shoot no more than twice, and come back in to your bunker.

3. Repeat until you hit the target.

How many attempts did it take to hit the target? Now, start again, only this time lean out the *opposite* side from the one you did before. Practice right and left snap shooting. This is a *very* important drill. This exercise will save you more times than you can count. It applies in either woods play or indoor speedball.

One-on-One

1. Two players take the field at opposite ends, set your clocks for 3 minutes.

2. Face away from each other *completely* (gun and all)!

3. 3-2-1, GO! Turn and try and take out your opponent as quickly as you can!

The technique this drill practices helps players try and "rule-the-field." You must take control of the opposition as soon as you come out from your flag station. Start shooting at them, follow where they run to, and *do not let them come out from their bunker to shoot at you*! As you keep their head in their bunker, you attempt to move up the field (never taking your eyes off their position), keeping other bunkers between you and your adversary.

This does not mean that you must shoot at them all the time, but you must be prepared. Your gun should be raised at all times so you can shoot every time you see them move. Soon, you will be close enough to slow down your rate of fire, minimize movements, and watch for them to come out. Then, "WAP!" you got 'em!

After you practice this for a while, try a few two-on-one's, two-on-two's, three-on-one's, etc. This will help build you up to what it is like in a tournament level competition.

RUN & SHOOT

1. Set up a jug on top of a bunker or hang from a string to add motion and increase difficulty.

2. Walk approximately 15 yards away, face away from the target.

3. 3-2-1 countdown, turn and run, holding your gun in an upright position, and shoot at the jug.

At what point did you hit the target? How many shots did it take? Another twist to this is to put the jug in different positions—on the ground either to the right or left side of the bunker, "peeking" through a hole in the bunker, etc. Set up realistic scenarios and run through them until your accuracy and time improve.

Keep practicing and you'll earn the respect of your fellow players!

DRILLING FOR VICTORY

SNAP SHOOTING DRILL

If you have been placed into your bunker and cannot come out, snap shooting allows you to take one or two shots to get your opponent back into his bunker, giving you an opportunity to get out. It is important not to come out from the same spot twice in a row. You change the spots you come out from so opponents won't know where to expect you.

When practicing snap shooting drills, make sure you have someone there to point out areas you are leaving exposed (e.g., your hopper or elbows and knees).

GOOD FORM IS CRITICAL

Left, right, center, it doesn't matter where you come from as long as you never repeat the same pattern twice.

RUNNING MAN DRILL

The purpose of this drill is to learn how to shoot into the empty space that a target is going to enter just in time to hit it. This is called *leading*.

Use a live moving target—with that person's consent, of course—and stage it so he or she is running perpendicular to your position. Lead the person by putting a stream of paint into the direction they are moving, or over the bunker they are heading toward.

It is good to start at a distance of 100–150 feet. Shoot about 10–15 feet in front of your target, and have that daring soul run his or her fastest. There's no time factor in this exercise, but try to limit the number of rounds to about 20 per drill before starting over.

Drilled Running Man

The Complete Guide to Paintball

By increasing the angle of your barrel, you will be able to increase the distance your paintballs will fly. At some point, of course, you shorten the distance the paintball will travel, but increase the slope of its descent.

LONG DISTANCE SHOOTING DRILL

When practicing long distance shooting drills, set up a target 200–210 feet in front of you. Limit the number of rounds in the hopper to time the drill and the number of shots you take. This drill teaches players how to control the arc of their ball so they can get the maximum range out of their shooting skill. Being a long distance shooter with accuracy is a fast track to leg-endary status in paintball lore.

At 200 feet, paintballs don't break that easily, as Steve points out. The longer the ball is in the air, the less energy it will have on impact.

Hopper Loading Drill

Learn to load your hopper without taking your eyes off the action. At first, perform this drill with an empty hopper and empty guppies. Get the motion down first before using paint (to avoid getting it dirty). With one hand holding your gun, perform your loading routine as follows:

A. Pop your loader's lid open.

B. Reach behind you and open your velcro harness.

C. Firmly grab a full guppy and bring it forward.

D. Pop the guppy's lid with your thumb.

E. Dump paint into your loader.

F. With the bottom of the now empty guppy, flip the loader's lid closed and snap the lid tight.

G. Toss the guppy aside and resume firing.

NOTE: This should be one smooth continuous motion. Practice until you get it right! Practice while you watch your favorite television shows and time yourself.

Blind Shooting Drill

There are times in a game where you are shooting without a clear view of your target. In these cases, you are "shooting blind." Blind shooting can be an effective shooting technique. The key is learning to identify a reference point that you can see from your firing position that relates directly to your opponent's position. This way you can stay safe in your bunker while you rain paint down on your opponent's head. He'll get dumped with paint and you can move on to your next unwitting target.

To practice, you and your buddy face off in opposite bunkers. From a quick peek, see if there is an object directly in line with their position. In this sequence you'll notice a tree directly behind your opponent's position in the background. Now, from the safe haven of your bunker, lay a stream of paint in the direction of the tree without overexposing yourself to return fire. Change the angle of your barrel to increase or decrease the range of your fire. By getting used to the feel of blind shooting in this manner, you'll increase your chances of survival, and become more of an offensive threat.

Out of paint?
Keep shooting anyway. The sound will keep your opponents' heads down while your teammates gain advantageous positions.

Out of air?
Throw paintballs. Heck, it'll keep them guessing and one just might break!

PART 5

TACTICS

A.C.T.

Rob Rubin's Customized Approach to Essential Paintball Tactics

"GETTING" PAINTBALL

When you first start playing paintball, you're literally bombarded with suggestions, advice, and ideas about the game. As is the case with most new players in any sport, it's easy to get overwhelmed just trying to keep up.

There's an easy way around "Information Overload."

You see, I've done a little work to fix this problem. And the good news for you is that paintball can be boiled down to a simple formula that's not only easy to remember, but even easier to carry out.

I call this "The Triad." It will carry you very far in your pursuit of paintball fun. You see, the game is only fun up to the point of elimination. Learning tactics is about learning how to stay in the game.

And the core of paintball tactics is the Triad.

Here it is.

A.C.T.-UNG Baby!

"Angles" "Communications" "Teamwork"

These are the three basics of paintball, "A.C.T." for short. That's all you need to know. This may sound simplistic, but even professional teams are always working on these three basic principles. Forget the gizmos, forget the gadgets, forget the tech-talk. These are the nuts and bolts of the game. If you want to be somewhere between competent and excellent at paintball, you must master "the Triad."

Why "The Triad"?

Much like a tripod, this particular trio of paintball skills works only as a whole. When you play them all, you get a whole game. It's easier to explain how they interconnect by looking at them in reverse order.

Do It For the Team

Teamwork can be as complex as 10 players moving as one mind, or as simple as finding a buddy and moving together up the tapeline. A second pair of eyes is invaluable, and a second shooter on a target can be the difference between wasting your time and eliminating your opponent.

Teamwork doesn't mean you're on top of one another, but it does mean you're working together for a common goal. One player is shooting at the opponent, the other player is advancing on him. That's great teamwork. One player is yelling positions, the other players are listening and moving accordingly. That's effective teamwork.

You can even have teamwork when you don't know anyone you're playing with!

In open fields or speedball games, I'll be the fool yelling his head off about where I saw players running to, or where they have people positioned. Why? Someone has to, and it may as well be me. Something as simple as "3 right, 4 left, 2 center" tells your team how they stack up against their foes. *Communication accomplishes teamwork.*

Communication = Effective Yelling

Sure, anyone can yell their lungs out. But it's effective yelling that makes the difference. Remember that teamwork thing? Here's the second part of it—communication.

Once you've buddied up, or you've decided to be a 'caller,' don't be shy. If you need some help, a simple "Help here!" gets the message across. You can get someone to move up to help you, or flank around to eliminate the opposing player who's shooting at you, and a lot of other things too.

New players often try to be 'stealthy,' and that works up to a point. One of my rules of thumb: "Once the other team shoots at you, don't bother trying to hide anymore." They've spotted you. It's useless to hide now. What you want to do immediately is get another player to help you out. Give them as much information as you can. For example:

"There are two guys in that bunker! Can you swing around and shoot them?" This brings us to the third leg—angles.

Angles

The term 'angles' covers moving, maneuvering, crawling, leaping, getting skinny behind a tree, and getting into a bunker so the other team can't occupy it.

Paintball is partially a game of real-estate, and getting angles is the way you use real-estate effectively. As an individual player, you want to take advantage of opponents who get 'tunnel vision' (players fixated on what's in front of them) by moving up on their flanks. A tree can only protect from so many directions at a given moment. The key is getting to an angle that renders your opponent's tree useless.

Your most frequent use of angles is to support your teammates. Most shoot-outs take place head on, meaning face to face. The idea behind 'angles' is to get to the side of your opponent while your teammate keeps your opponent's attention. After you make that key elimination, your teammate begins to move up while you support his advance similarly.

Pretty cool, isn't this?

You may already be starting to see the pattern. You can't "do" one part of the Triad well without doing the other two simultaneously.

- If you don't communicate, your teammates won't know you need them to take a better angle on the player shooting at you.

- If your team won't move to better angles, your teamwork breaks down and you get eliminated quickly.

- If you don't work together at all, you'll find the day frustrating, because your team won't communicate and move together in any way.

A.C.T. is a simple formula, and it encompasses the essence of what you need to do to qualify as a great player. It's also adaptable to your later paintball games as well. The concept of "Angles" includes 'back doors' and 'key bunkers' and seeing holes in your opponent's line. Simple "communications" later become your team codes. And "Teamwork" becomes the backbone of your game.

Putting It All Together
Eventually you combine the elements of the Triad into complex "Swing" moves and "Sweep" maneuvers.

For example, the "Two Man Swing" uses all of "A.C.T." in rapid order. Your buddy starts by telling you the opponent's position (communication), you start shooting to keep your opponent's head down (teamwork) as your buddy moves up (angles), you continue to feed your buddy information about where the opponent is (communications/teamwork) as he slides into his new position (angles). Your buddy begins to shoot (teamwork) and tell you where the opponent is leaning out of (communications) as you move up (angles) to get the elimination.

All of this may occur within ten seconds.

For now, don't worry about achieving that level of play. It takes practice, a good memory, and adventurous spirit to get good at this game. All of that takes time.

For now, have a good time! Enjoy yourself! Try to remember to "A.C.T." Write it on the back of your hand if need be. Talk to your teammates about it, too. It's something that everyone and anyone can do with a little effort.

—RR

Once you have the Triad down, you'll be amazed how fast it can improve your game.

Opening Moves

Military strategy and tactics and paintball, for the most part, do not mix. Military jargon has been adopted by players out of convenience, but the principles of war do not really apply to the game. However, there is at least one aspect of paintball that mirrors almost exactly its military counterpart—the use of surprise.

Napoleon (among many other legendary military commanders) believed that the effect of surprise is the equivalent of having an army ten times its actual size.

> Surprise is a critical aspect of tactics and it comes in two flavors—complete surprise and plain vanilla surprise.

Complete and total surprise is an elusive, ideal kind of thing, which doesn't really exist in paintball. At the very least, the other team knows the terrain, your objective, the size of your team, the length of the encounter, and when the contest will start. That's quite a bit of handy information. You can, however, achieve something close to complete 'paintball' surprise, but only at the very beginning of the game.

AT THE BREAK

It is only during the first few crucial seconds that the other team
has no idea where you are going to
go or what you are going to do.
Once the game starts, after no
more than about 30 seconds, the
other team will at least know
where a few of your players are.
This is one reason why good teams
and players spend more time figuring out their initial move than
any other part of the game. The
'Break,' the moment at which a
game begins, is your only chance
to catch the other team with their
pants down around their ankles.

After those first few seconds
have passed, you can only hope to
achieve vanilla surprises; these
would be things like suddenly
moving players from one side of
the field to the other, a crawler
getting into the midst of the other
team's positions and spreading
havoc, or a sudden push on a section of the field.

THE FIRST STEPS

The start, or opening move of a
game, is an all or nothing affair,
just like an opening move in chess.
How you begin determines the
entire outcome of the game: the
countermoves your opponent
makes and your counters to those
countermoves, *ad infinitum*.

Two very important factors are
set at the beginning: what terrain
you choose and how you use your
players, assuming you are the
team captain. You can decide to

take positions deep into the field (seizing portions of your opponent's half of the field); you can take terrain at the fifty (the mid-way point); or you can play the terrain 'short'—that is, take much less than your 'half' at the outset.

How you use your players depends partially (but not entirely) on the terrain itself, but more importantly it depends upon the tone of the game you wish to play. Playing an aggressive game generally means that you will commit most or all of your players from the beginning. Committing players means (1) you have given them a job to perform that will occupy all of their effort, and (2) it will be extremely difficult to position them. Playing a defensive game means that you will commit few to none of your players. And, of course, there is the very common tactic of taking those positions that must be taken and then waiting to see what happens, which is essentially a 'middle' strategy.

The three basic methods of playing the terrain and the three basic ways in which you use your players can be mixed and matched for an almost inexhaustible variety of game plans. Some real-world examples may serve to illustrate this.

- During an NPPL tournament game in Chicago, Bob Long sent one of his players to an aggressive location, well over the fifty, on his left tape—an aggressive, deep-field position. He then had that player tuck in, knowing that the other team would be forced to try to take him out. The final outcome was that the Ironmen's opponents lost four players in trying to eliminate the one player Bob had committed.

- At an NPPL in Boston, Renick Miller's Aftershock committed one player to a kamikaze charge down one tape, merely to attract the attention of the other team; this player was covered by two players on that side of the field who moved to about the fifty and then dug in. Meanwhile, the remainder of the team had been sent to the fifty across the middle and other side of the field in a 'waiting' posture. Once they saw the other team commit to attacking the sacrificed player, the Aftershock players in the middle pushed.

- At an NPPL World Cup in New York, the All Americans received the disadvantaged side of the field and were *forced* to play in a defensive posture from the beginning of the game; they committed no one to any specific action, but remained loose and mobile, stretched across the field just shy of the fifty, until opportunity came knocking. One bunker move led to another, and they handily won the game.

All of these plays were programmed from the outset of the game, based on the terrain, what the competitors wanted to achieve, and who their opponents were. These opening moves also were based on an honest evaluation of the limitations placed on each team, limitations created by the skill level of their players, by the nature of the terrain, or both.

Let's review the basic advantages and disadvantages of each of these strategies.

PLAYING THE FIELD

Aggressive—Deep Penetration

- Advantages—Surprises the other team, happens very quickly, adding confusion to the mix, and ends a game (one way or the other) quickly.

- Disadvantages—Concentrates a lot of your players in exposed positions; requires you to have 100% aggressive players; must be carried through no matter what, and ends a game (one way or the other) quickly.

Middle Ground—"Taking the Fifty"

- Advantages—As much terrain is taken as possible, without undue risk to players.

- Disadvantages—The other team knows (or should know) all the angles and how to play this area of the field better than just about any other area of the field.

Defensive—Playing the Field Short

- Advantages—Players can get set in position very quickly. Opponents are dealt with on terrain which is less familiar to them; typically opponents will not know shooting angles and will not have any pre-set positions to use.

- Disadvantages—Very little room for maneuver. No place to retreat. Usually restricts players to 'reacting' to opponents' moves.

In general, determining what 'mix' of playing styles to use depends upon what you and your teammates want to accomplish, and how much (or how little) the terrain of a given field will support those opening objectives. It would be foolish to overextend your players past the fifty, if there is nowhere for them to go once they get there.

The objective of an opening move is to prepare your team for the anticipated actions of your opponents and/or (and this is an important distinction) to place your players where they will be able to support your plan for the remainder of the game.

In order to practice these kinds of opening moves, you should constantly look for fields and games that will allow you to test different openings. For example, you can find the fast players on your team (or in your group) and, when playing on a field that has good cover over the fifty yard line, create a plan that pushes some of those players into that cover. Set the remainder of your players in positions that will support the forward players—some shooters who can pick off the opponents who will try to take your forward players out, some defenders on the other side of the field in strong 'hold' positions, a small reserve of players who can follow up on any push that your forward players may make.

On a field that offers good cover on your end of the field, practice setting up an ambush and playing the field short.

If you don't have any idea what a full-bore charge down one tape is like, pick a good field and give it a shot.

If you are playing tournament ball, remember that the number one rule for opening moves is to 'play the field,' not your opponents; it is far easier to analyze terrain before the game than it is to guess what your opponents will do.

-SD

Smart ideas work, bad ideas don't.

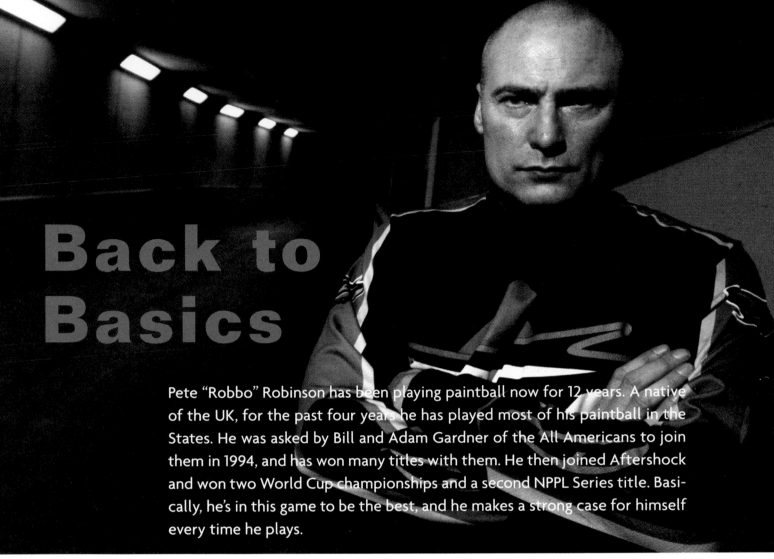

Back to Basics

Pete "Robbo" Robinson has been playing paintball now for 12 years. A native of the UK, for the past four years he has played most of his paintball in the States. He was asked by Bill and Adam Gardner of the All Americans to join them in 1994, and has won many titles with them. He then joined Aftershock and won two World Cup championships and a second NPPL Series title. Basically, he's in this game to be the best, and he makes a strong case for himself every time he plays.

As US editor of the hugely successful *Paintball Games International Magazine,* he has written well over 100 articles spanning ten years of playing professional paintball. He was also voted the World's Best Player in 1996. It's definitely time to tune in.

THE ONLY WAY TO PLAY PAINTBALL IS TO STAY IN THE GAME

In paintball, there are many people who have opinions about how the game should be played. You will hear and read about numerous theories and approaches, most of which are either unworkable or pretentious.

The game of paintball in its most basic form is the art of eliminating opponents without getting shot. *The definitive attribute of a good player, therefore, is his or her ability to stay in the game and eliminate opponents.* You will notice that I put *staying in the game* first. That has to take precedence over all else in the game of paintball. What is the point of being the best shot in the world when you're standing on the sidelines?

It may seem simplistic to say that to become a good player all you have to do is think about staying in the game, but it is neither simple nor easy to keep yourself in the game on a consistent basis.

At this point, let's clarify a few points. The techniques I will be discussing are wholly applicable to all levels of paintball. Whether you are a first time rec-baller, amateur, or pro matters not.

THE TECHNICAL AND THE TACTICAL

The tactical relates to those actions of the team decided upon before the game has started (i.e., whether you push one flank, or five players run down the middle). Anything involving predetermining players' actions on the field is tactical.

That said, however, I must say that the most important part of playing paintball, by far, is the technical component.

Good technical play defeats good tactics!

Techniques are actions a player undertakes to make sure he stays alive while endeavoring to eliminate the opposition. Basically, when you see a player behind a bunker snap shooting, ducking in and out, firing his gun from different spots at different times, you're watching someone employing techniques to enhance the effectiveness of his play.

ESSENTIALS OF TECHNICAL PLAY

Now, let's just run through some hypothetical situations. Imagine a player who sits behind a bunker and never shoots his gun. What is the likelihood he will be eliminated?

The only way this guy would be eliminated is if someone runs over and bunkers him. Stands to reason, right? Nobody else can shoot him because he never breaks cover to fire his gun.

From this we can readily infer that a bunker provides a safe haven. At the same time, it is of no use just to sit there without firing your gun. To win the game, the player has to break cover

and endeavor to eliminate opponents or, at the very least, provide suppressive fire.

Herein lies the central problem in paintball. As soon as you come out of cover, you are vulnerable. This fact forms the genesis of the whole philosophy of technical play.

The Principle of Paintball Technique
You must do all you can so that when you do shoot your gun, you give your opponents the least possible opportunity to eliminate you from the game.

No technique is fail-safe, but good technique can drastically reduce your rate of elimination.

Believe it or not, this is the secret of playing this game on the highest level. The ability to practice this philosophy separates the good players from the great players, great teams from championship teams.

Let me explain why.

If all ten players on a team were to practice the philosophy of play I advocate (i.e., to concentrate 100% on not being shot rather than allowing the secondary need of eliminating opposition to determine actions) then, by definition, the average life of the team as a whole would increase. Furthermore, if players spend more time in the game, that also means that, as a team, they are firing more paint than the opposition. That increases their chances

of eliminating the opposition and winning the game.

So you can see that by getting your team to concentrate on technical aspects of play, everything else seems to fall into place. Even if you're not on a team, it should be clear to you that honing your technique will enable you to survive longer when you're on a losing team, and may make victory possible when you're outnumbered.

A LOOK AT THE ACTUAL TECHNIQUES!

Now that we have established the importance of technical play, we have to look at what those techniques are, in terms of what to do and what not to do.

First off, we can reduce the game of paintball, in simple terms to ten one-on-ones. For the moment, I am using a ten man tournament team as an example, although what is to be discussed is wholly applicable to players at all levels.

If a target player is beading on me (i.e., lining his gun up on me and occasionally firing when I come out to fire at him), then there are a couple of things to remember.

First of all, never come out into an incoming stream of paint. Seems obvious, but you would be surprised just how many mugs do it. You have to wait until your opponent stops firing at you. Alternatively, you can move to the other side of the bunker, but this normally means you will be shooting back-handed, so I will ignore that option for the moment.

If you are right-handed, I take it for granted that you are shooting out of the right hand side of the bunker as you look at it. The reason is obvious; you show a minimum profile to your opponents if you shoot this way. That brings us to snap shooting.

Snap Shooting 101

Accepting that we never break cover into a stream of paint, we now have to create an opportunity to fire at our target. When your opponent stops firing, the best technique is to snap shoot your way into dominance. If your opponent is lined up and just waiting for you to come out, then this is what you should do.

Get in to your mind the approximate location of your opponent. You can do this quite easily by taking a quick look in the direction from which the sound of your opponent's gun is coming. You should already have a good sense of his location because you know he's generally going to be sitting behind a bunker just like yours.

Once you have established his location, then get yourself set to roll out of cover with an upper-body roll movement.

This takes a bit of practice, but generally I would sit with my legs in front of me, usually bent in front of my chest, in a position behind the bunker that just allows me to be safe. In other words, if I were to lean slightly outwards to the right, my opponent could eliminate me, but with a slight roll back in, he would not be able to see me, let alone tag me.

When you're set, roll out, fire two shots, and immediately roll back in. The reason for this rapid-movement, minimal-fire approach is simple. If your opponent has indeed lined up where you're likely to emerge, you have to take a shot at him and get behind cover before you get hit. That's not long at all; if you only shoot twice and roll back in, there is no way that your opponent can react in time to eliminate you. The window of opportunity you gave him is just too small, he will always be one step off the pace you are setting.

If you adhere to this technique, the only way you can get tagged is if your opponent fires randomly and gets lucky.

If you roll out of cover, and a paintball is already winging it's way over to you, you're a goner!

So there remain now two possibilities in this interaction.

1. You eliminate him by snap shooting
2. You have to modify your technique slightly

As you roll in and out of cover and fire your two-shot bursts, you are relying on a fair amount of luck to get your elimination. Nevertheless, many players are eliminated this way.

The reason you have to roll in and out of cover is because your opponent has the drop on you.

The key here is to turn the tables and get the drop on him!

At present, it looks as though he controls things by making you snap shoot, but what if we could push him back into cover leaving us to line up on him?

To put your opponent on the defensive, you must do two things when you come out to snap shoot. First, watch as you roll back into cover; you are looking for any movement of your opponent that suggests your two shots are so accurate that they forced him to get back behind his bunker. Secondly, listen carefully, because if you hear no shots

coming back at you right away, it's likely that you forced him back, but failed to see it.

If you are looking for them, these two clues give you a chance to establish control of the situation. If you take advantage of them, you can line up on the guy who thought he had you right where he wanted you!

Suppress your opponent with protracted fire enabling one of your teammates to bunker him. At the very least, keep him out of the game with continuous shooting.

The big advantage in lining up an opponent is that you get a chance to 'read' all of his movements. After observing him for a while, you'll find that he becomes predictable. This predictability will eventually be his downfall. Be patient and persistent, and you'll know this fine feeling.

In everything having to do with paintball technique, the key is concentration. You must concentrate on staying tight to your cover and on timing your retaliatory fire.

This is the way to optimize your chances of eliminating your opponent and minimize your chances of getting shot.

We have now covered two of the most fundamental aspects of paintball technique. Whether you are an experienced pro or a first timer, staying tight and timing your shots will transform your game overnight.

-PR

Mapping Your Game Plan

The Fake and Push

The fake and the push can be used on any field, but must be adjusted according to terrain. A critical component of this and any game plan is that your team should walk onto the field together. Each player must examine his own bunker and firing lanes. Both sides of the field must be walked. It is important to know what positions the opposing team may take. This will help you calculate the firing lanes and angles available from your bunker. This is the time to take note of bunkers that facilitate a pinch play. You and the other player on your team with the pinch shot must work together. Another important thing to keep in mind is that you may want to use the bunkers on the other side of the field as you advance. In this particular game plan the primary objectives are A5, B5, A3, and B3. A5 should be taken by the fastest tape runner. The back player, A1, has found a good shooting lane that cuts off the right side of the field. This lane cuts between bunkers and will be called Zone.

1. The objective for A1 is to eliminate player B3 at the break of the game. The objective for the players on the right side of the field is to eliminate player B5.

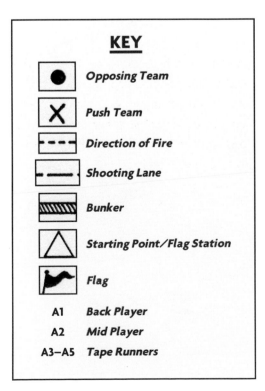

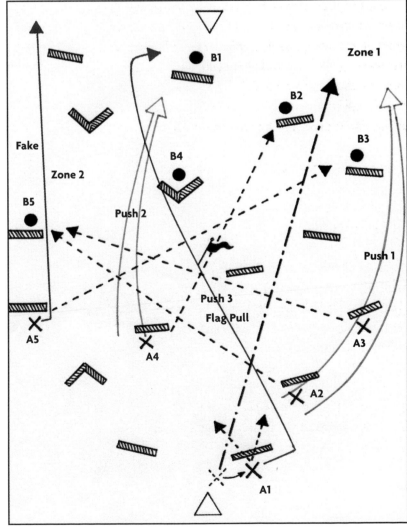

2. Players B1 and B4 are not much of a factor in this game plan. As the back players signal, player A5 runs down the tape line. If player B5 is still in the game, A5 should eliminate him as he passes. A5 continues to run to the back corner of the field. This will cause the opposing team to turn in panic toward A5. It should be noted that if A5 had been eliminated prior to the signal, A4 would fill in. This is called a fake. A5 will most likely be hit performing this move. If he isn't, the opposing team has a huge problem. Timing is essential for this to work. Once A5 has begun his run, A2 and A3 should take advantage of the commotion and push the opposite side of the field. If the game plan has worked they should be able to eliminate some of the opposing team by shooting them in the back. Their primary objective would be to eliminate players B3, B2, and B1 in that order. A2 and A3 have now turned the remaining opposing players toward their side of the field. A4 should leave after A2 and A3. He should be advancing up the same side of the field as A5. His main objective is to eliminate player B4 and anyone else who remains. A1 follows A4 up the field. He should cross centerfield, picking up the flag as he advances. If the other players have done their job, all that is left for A1 to do is to hang the flag. This game plan incorporates four separate pushes. It is designed to keep the opposing team off balance. If it is executed well, the opposing team will be eliminated before they know what hit them. This is a very aggressive game plan. It is not simple to execute. If one player is too early (or late), the game plan may disintegrate leaving the opposing team with the upper hand.

Shooting Lanes

Shooting lanes should be chosen during field walking. The basic idea is to find a bunker on the opponent's side of the field that is key to their

game plan. Then find a way to eliminate the player who plans on getting into that bunker. The ideal shooting lane is a line of fire devoid of obstacles. The line of fire should drop the paint into the opposing player's running lane. In this example, player A1 shoots for Zone 1 dropping a line of paint into the path of B2 and B3. Mid player A2 stops half way to his bunker and fires into Zone 2, hoping to eliminate B3. This means that player B3 must cross zone 2 shooting lanes. This technique is used to increase the chances of eliminating a key player. Once B2 and B3 are in their bunkers (or eliminated), A1 and A2 need to take cover in their bunkers. Example 2 (shown in red) depicts 2 players firing in

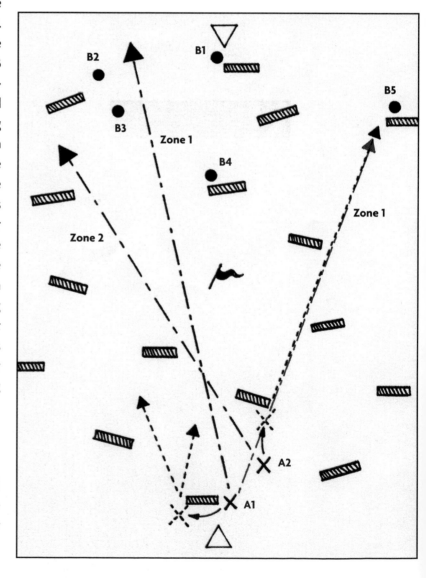

the same lane. This should only be done for an extremely key bunker. Player B5 must cross a firing lane with twice as much paint traversing it. This choice of firing lanes increases the chances of eliminating player B5. Hit or miss, A1 and A2 should get into their bunkers after B5 has passed the firing lane.

Keep in mind that shooting lanes are a great tool. They are not, however, foolproof. There is a certain amount of luck involved. This is a skill-based plan that should be practiced like any other. The back player using the lane needs to get a feel for the appropriate height to aim for. One trick to try is to aim at hip height at the entrance to the bunker. Even if the player comes in low he will usually not be below that point.

—MS

New Players' Guide to Cover

"Work your bunker." "Get angles from your bunker." "Slide out of your cover."

What does it all mean?

Cover is ... "Anything that protects or shields from harm, loss, or danger."

In paintball, anything between you and an opponent that will stop, disable or render useless a fired paintball is considered "cover."

There are two basic types:

1. "Hard" cover includes medium- to large-sized trees, rocks, and bunkers.
2. "Soft" cover, like grass, small trees, and shrubs.

Both types serve the same function, but you'll learn to use them differently.

Let's tackle hard cover first. Virtually all speedball fields are exclusively hard cover. Meaning there's a very solid object between you and the other guys. Big trees, rocks, and bunkers are solid cover from incoming paintballs. Some fields have berms, hills, and other terrain features that qualify as hard cover.

A berm is a ledge or space between the ditch and parapet in a fortification.

Anything solid you can place your body behind is hard cover. Seeing as most game situations involve *bunkers* (especially on speedball fields), I'll stick to using that term generically. Do a little mental dance and *bunker* becomes tree becomes rock becomes fort becomes wall becomes inflatable becomes corrugated piping becomes car becomes anything and everything solid. (Whew!)

I'll avoid the finer points of moving into a bunker. That's dependent on your speed and fitness level. Let's focus on what you do once you're in position. A common mistake is to get as close as you can to your bunker *no matter where you are on the field* and pop out for eliminations. It's not really a mistake, I guess. It made sense to me when I was new to the game, too. But, after studying videos, watching the experts play, talking to some of the best players I know, and reading stories about other players' approaches, it becomes obvious that this isn't necessarily what you always want to do.

Using Cover in Context

It remains true that the closer to the action you are, the closer to the inside of your bunker you want to be. If you're relatively far away from the action, you can afford to move farther back from

your bunker. It's called "sliding back" or "sliding out." This is useful because from farther behind a position, you can *control* more of the field laterally without overexposing yourself to your opponents. You can watch their movements from a good position and still use bunkers to maximize protection. If your opponents get closer, it's only a matter of moving up a few feet forward into your bunker to counter a move of 20 feet from your opponent. You also can avoid their shots entirely by leaning a few inches, rather than moving a few feet. This allows you to keep your gun in position to shoot back easily, and not have to reset your arm positioning. In the thick of a game, this can be the difference between winning and losing.

By sliding back, you also access more *angles*. "Angles" is a blanket term for shooting side to side from a position. Very rarely do you shoot at your 12 o-clock from a bunker. You're mostly shooting the 9 to 10:30 angle and 1:30 to 3 o-clock angles. Why? It's easier and faster to lean out the side rather than poke up above a bunker.

On a lean, your head and gun come out simultaneously. On a poke up, your gun and head are seen first, giving opponents a chance to take you out before you shoot.

Speaking of leaning out, most opponents lean out from your left. Why? As I mentioned back in the drills section, it's more natural for right-handed people to lean to their right, which puts them on their opponent's left-hand side. This means that you can anticipate most players' movements by aiming towards the left-hand side of bunkers. How? Tournament players preach playing switch handed. This is just a fancy way of saying, "You should learn how to use both hands." It's tough, but it helps. I lay on my side on the left side of a bunker and wait for their lean to my left and hammer down.

Imagine a line just over the top of your bunker, and just around the sides. This line starts from your

Teaching yourself to shoot effectively both right- and left-handed will help you work both sides of your bunkers and catch opponents off guard while keeping your exposure to incoming paint to a minimum.

opponent's barrel and continues past the sides and top of the bunker. Learning where that line will be when you attain a bunker position is the essence of understanding angles. And learning how you can extend this line will improve your game immensely. Watch your feet, your hands, head, your loaders, your harness—anything beyond that line puts you in jeopardy.

So how do you make these angles work for you?

Good question. The best way to do this is to develop a stable shooting stance that you like. This position should allow you to play in two directions at once, but also give you freedom to slide in when necessary. Some players get on their knees and play from there. Some players crouch down on their toes. And some go on one knee, the other one up. If you wear soft knee/shin guards, go with something like that to shield yourself from incoming

paint. Make sure you're comfortable in your stance. A Team Internet friend of mine has big thigh pains after a full day because of his technique. It works, however, so he still uses it.

With any stance you use, you want to try to *layer* your cover. For example, if you can line up several trees (or anything else that will protect you from opponents' paint), you can do something called "tree-walking" or simply "walking". Using terrain as in this manner will give you a freedom of movement that will make you uncannily effective. Like water, every time you move, your relationship to your terrain shifts. Take advantage of this zen approach, and your game play options will expand dramatically and unpredictably.

THE VIRTUES OF SOFT COVER

This conveniently brings me to soft cover. Soft cover is more about finesse and grace than brute force. Using soft cover requires a little more creative perception and quick-thinking than hard cover does.

Soft cover is anything that *may* prevent paintballs from reaching you, and is *likely* to if you are careful, but nonetheless isn't risk-free protection.

We're talking about stuff like twigs, leaves, grass, and small and thin trees.

In many cases, tall grass is just as good as a bunker. Grass will either break paint outright or deflect it in most cases. Unless someone rips a few hundred balls, nothing is going to make it through. Everyone has a story about the guy who hid behind a twig and never got shot. I know a few fields where I can get behind a shrub and nothing gets to me but splatter. This is beautiful cover; it allows you to watch the other guys and communicate what you see to your teammates who may not be able to see it.

Soft cover also includes some things you wouldn't expect. What should you use for camouflage? Get behind some grass or shrubs and lay still. If they don't see you, they can't shoot you.

Going back to our definition of cover, this seems to work. How about moving far enough back so they can't touch you with the longball? If you're fast, you can outrun a shooter between bunkers. Or you can pop your gun up and lay down a wall of paint at the other guy to make him duck. (Ever wonder why it's called "Cover Shooting"?) The three "Out's"—*Outrange, Outrun,* and *Outshoot*—are all good forms of cover, if you think of cover more broadly, as doing whatever it takes to avoid elimination.

All of this information takes a long time to master in practice. These are the basics. Take what you learn, build from experience, and enjoy!

-RR

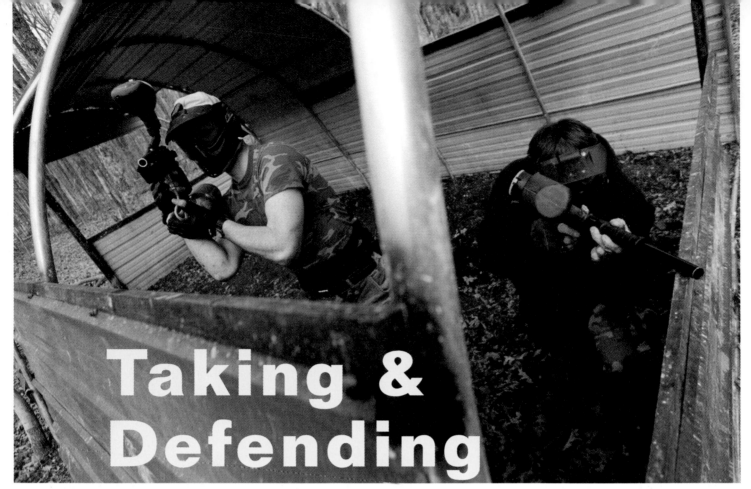

Taking & Defending Buildings

I've seen some beautiful buildings in the course of my paintball exploits. And I've seen some ugly ones. I've seen some that were crafted to look like UFO's and castles, others that looked like they were rescued from the garbage dump.

Everyone loves buildings, myself included. I just love attacking them, and you're about to discover why. When it comes to taking a building, I've got it down.

Most people see buildings as fortifications, and this is pretty accurate. In paintball, a building is a good solid piece of cover, which explains its popularity. On the surface, they look like great (read: *safe*) places to hang out. They have small holes to shoot through, combined with little or no exposure to incoming paint. Sounds like a dream come true, right? Newbies tend to see these structures that way, as well. But from outside of the walls, newcomers to this game get discouraged by buildings, and won't move on them. As a result, they get picked off with relative ease as they try to take buildings by force.

Most paintball buildings are usually about 2 meters in length and width. (That's about 7 feet for you Americans.) This makes them about 4 square meters of doom that I can exploit as an attacker!

Look at buildings as traps rather than as fortresses, and a world of attack possibilities will open up to you!

LIKE "THE DEATH STAR," BUILDINGS HAVE THEIR WEAKNESSES

Personally, when I'm approaching a building filled with paintball players, I know that I have an enormous advantage. First of all, buildings are not mobile. (If they are, they're called tanks.) This fact alone might scare you out of buildings for the rest of your paintball career. (You shouldn't let it, but more on that later.) Once inside a building (especially if there's more than one entrance), this is where you're going to stay. Sure, you can move around inside there, but you're still on the same piece of real estate.

Stuck in a building like a roach in a roach motel.

You can't flank in a building, unless it's an unusually long one. You can't really crawl. You can't do much in there other than defend perhaps 3 angles that the openings and the doorways will allow. Defenders tend to exploit this to a fault. They will defend those angles with their last paintball.

You can't win a game based on mobility by taking and defending a building!

As an attacker, exploit the isolation and siege mentality of a building defender. The fact that most of a building is impenetrable also means that its occupants have substantial blind spots. It also means that their ability to hear what you're doing on the outside is easily compromised, because in many cases the buildings are echo chambers; a few

shots against those walls while you're moving will make it hard for them to hear where you're going. Once you know the angles the building allows its inhabitants, you can use different angles they can't cover. If this sounds simple, that's because it is. You just need to be patient, perceptive, and decisive in your attack.

A building can be worked through or over if need be. For example, you can dedicate one shooter to a building and basically stop everyone in that building from poking their heads out. This tactic plays out in the following manner.

If three guys are inside a building structure, they have limited fields of view. They can't all poke out of the same window without missing something and/or becoming a huge target. Here's what you do. Place one player near the front of the building and have him shoot it up a little to make noise along the building's sides. I call this "knocking," because you're just making them nervous instead of trying to eliminate them.

The next move is a flanking maneuver exploiting the limited visibility of the building's occupants. If you can manage to put paint in the vicinity of or through the openings, you'll make the occupants sloppy and nervous. Before you know it, you'll have cleared the building, because they won't have seen or heard you come right up on top of them. Or, if all of their players are in the building, why bother

Tactics

to take it? If you can ignore the building, grab the flag while they're tied up with a well entrenched front shooter who has a great shot at their escape door.

Tactics for loners who must take a building

What if you're alone? Well, the principles are the same, but in this case I'll tie 'em up infinitely by shooting and maneuvering while they're ducking down from my shots. Either that or I'll just put paint into a hole until some poor dude pokes his head up to see what's happening. Poof—instant elimination!

WHAT BUILDINGS ARE USEFUL FOR

I've said some harsh things about paintball buildings. Clearly, buildings are the bane of those who misuse them.

On the other hand, buildings can be helpful to those who use them appropriately. For example, they should be used as cover. Despite everything I've just said, I'd like to remind the reader that buildings are more than just four walls.

When I'm using a building for cover I try to stay on the outside of it as long as I can. In this case, it's used like any bunker with the exception that the holes can line up to form a smaller hole for opponents to shoot through. I can shoot through easily, whereas my opponents can't.

I'll also back away from the building, and use it as a normal bunker that way. Buildings offer the opportunity to become invisible to my opponents. I only use this as a last resort, however. Or I use it as part of my tactical plan. Either way, using a building must serve a concrete purpose for the team.

When you enter a building, you're making a commitment.

Sometimes you'll be making a whole game commitment, because you'll end up in an inescapable hot zone. Of course, if your objective is to make your opponents focus on you, this can work to your team's advantage. If you're not doing anything for your team, you're not doing your job. Too many defenders forget that, and they get eliminated or they simply don't get involved in the game.

After diving into a building, it's important to keep your ears open for teammates' communications and to make your shooting count for something. Like any bunker, you have to work it. Buildings need to be worked harder because you don't have all the openings a bunker provides. Tunnel vision is easier to slip into from inside a building; if the window faces forward, you tend to look forward. Work a building's entryways the same way you work its windows and its cracks. Stay on your toes, or you'll get trampled point blank.

You really need to have a lot of team support for your building players. You need mobile people on the outside of the building to prevent flankers from taking your position. You also can make yourself a 'distraction' so that your teammates shoot the guys fixated on eliminating you. If you lie in a building, they can't touch you. But they'll keep trying because they think they can, and your teammates will just keep getting eliminations.

In January 1998, I played at an outdoor speedball field in Florida that had a few buildings in the center. During one game, I made a very bold move and made the center building. I took a few shots from the outside and realized that my team needed a gun a few feet forward. So I went into the building.

"What's on the right?" I yelled out. Some kid said there was a crawler parallel to me. I turned to look through the door, leveled the barrel, and put 20 shots into the shrubs, just hoping to get something to move, and I got an elimination. Immediately I looked left to see someone moving on the flank. I shot a few balls to stop him. No paint broke, but it stopped him.

The rest of the game flowed this way. A few shots left, a few right, a few more left, working the whole area hard. As the left was shooting at me, I'd work the right side. When the right would start on me, I would swing left.

What amazed me was how they wouldn't move up on me. Instead, they tried to longball my position and get a lucky shot on me. This was crazy; all I had to do to avoid shots in the building was shift a little one way or the other. Had they concentrated on my position and rushed me or worked on my flanks before shooting me, I would have been a goner.

The building provided great protection, but without team support I would have been toasted. Against competition with better tactics, team support would have been absolutely essential to holding that position and turning it to our advantage. I was always trying to keep my flankers informed of our opponents' movements. Since that building was in the center of the field, I was able to act as a team caller, relaying information from side to side with great protection. If you're in a building and are not being useful, leave it before you get abandoned.

My team won the game after the other team wasted a good deal of paint on my position. I figured that the other team shot about 2000 paintballs at me in that game, but they just couldn't take me down because of their lack of coordinated teamwork and intelligent communication.

GETTING BUNKERED IN A BUILDING

The Element of Surprise

Inside a building, getting "bunkered" or "mugged" can be much worse. This is mainly due to the element of surprise. Here's a true story that illustrates what I mean. *Once upon a time, there was a big game in Racine, Wisconsin...*

Both flag stations were two-story castles, which are very impressive to the eye but brutally hard to defend. When the flag was about to come down, the attackers rushed the building, stuck their guns into the windows and opened up point blank. This was FUBAR for anyone in that building. Much bad welting resulted from this.

You see, your main danger, as both an attacker and defender of buildings, is that you're going to find yourself in a point blank scenario and get lit up within a second or two by players whose adrenaline levels are off the charts. Of course, this isn't actually dangerous. You're just going to get hit abruptly at close range and perhaps a few more times than you'd prefer. Later, you'll laugh about it. But, believe me, when it happens, you're going to rue the day buildings made their way into this game.

In a tournament, this activity can count as "Unsportsmanlike Conduct" or "Overshooting." In a recreational setting, you may be told to sit out a few games for overshooting.

My point? If you're going to rush a building, please be careful. Unlike a rounded bunker, you really won't see anything until the last second, and even then you could get bruised. Personally, I'd prefer to flank a building.

Overall, I try to avoid buildings. I can do more damage outside of them. But, sometimes, they're useful. They definitely make things more interesting for their attackers and defenders, and are part of the exhilarating paintball landscape.

—RR

CHUCK STONER, THE ULTIMATE SNIPER

ANDREW FLACH: What do you do as a sniper?

CHUCK STONER: As a sniper, I'm hunting. When I'm on the field I feel like I'm hunting people and what I try to do is set myself up in situations where people will approach me, enter my effective range, and not know where I am even after I've eliminated them. So whenever I'm on a playing field, I'll make the best possible use of the available vegetation and the terrain and the features on the playing field to make myself invisible.

ANDREW: How long can you possibly sit in one position for a game?

CHUCK: Of course, that depends on the game that's being played. In a scenario game, a 24 hour game, I can be on my own for the whole time.

ANDREW: But in one spot, physically?

CHUCK: It depends on how good the hunting is. If I'm entertained, feel effective, and my position isn't compromised, I can stay for a long time. That's just something that you learn as a hunter. You spend a whole day from sun-up to sundown in the woods, usually fairly stationary, especially if you're hunting deer or other big game.

Playing paintball is another hunting experience for me and it's kind of nice because I don't have to drag anything out. I don't have to field-dress anything I shoot.

ANDREW: In terms of picking a spot, what kinds of things would consider to be important?

CHUCK: I would say that there are half a dozen rules of thumb and one of them is that you're never more dangerous than when your opponent is unaware of your location. As soon as you begin to fire, if your gun is noisy, or if your movements are quick and jerky, you give away your position. Then, your fighting ability is compromised.

This pump gun that I'm playing with is very accurate. It has range that other guns don't and shoots very consistently to the same place, but if I'm competing against semi-automatic guns, once I give my position away then I can't function effectively.

People can't fight what they can't see. So, one of my other rules of thumb is that you should always set up fights on your own terms. That means that you're only going to win so many gunfights. I'm not actually on the field to be a gunfighter. I don't want to be a hero. I'm there to be dangerous. That's my function.

ANDREW: To create problems.

CHUCK: Yes. With that I mind, I always set my encounters up so that people fight me on my terms. I choose where to hide, I choose the shooting lane, I choose the terrain. That's how you can be most effective. Human eyes pick up erratic movement very quickly—rapid, jerky movements, swift movements. Our eyes are arranged that way. Consequently, when you move through the forest you should move very little and when you do move, you should move steadily and smoothly.

Even if you're going to be an effective sniper, it's not necessary to move painfully slow because there's just not as much at stake. You want to be able to get around the field and enjoy the game.

Most people are very untalented when it comes to training themselves to be a watcher in the woods. They tend to overlook a lot of things. It's that "you can't see the forest for the trees" thing. When you play the way I like to play you have to see everything. I developed this ability through years of hunting. You always look for bits and pieces of things rather than the whole item. If you go into the woods, and you're looking for a whole paintball player, you might get lucky and see that. Mostly, you're going to see hands and the corner of a goggle, or the tip of somebody's boot. You have to be able to interpret what you see and then incorporate that piece into the whole and identify your target. The same thing happens in the woods when you're hunting deer. You rarely see a whole deer. You see a tail, a leg, a hoof, an ear, an eye, a nose.

I like to play against players who wear colored lenses because I can easily see amber lenses and rainbow lenses. I can pick those out of the woods in a heartbeat.

ANDREW: What is a shooting lane?

CHUCK: A shooting lane is quite simply a path for your projectile to follow to the target. It's very important with paintball, because if you hit a twig at 280 feet per second, your paintball is going to splatter and never make the target. Just like you can effectively hide in a thicket of rhododendrons. You can be mostly in plain sight but people can't get paint into you. I don't enjoy playing that way because I clean my equipment up after every day of play and if I'm all spray painted with pink paint from head to toe, that kind of detracts from my enjoyment of the game.

As a matter of fact, I play not to be hit. I want to play the entire day and never take a hit, and I do that often, which is kind of unusual.

More than the shooting, I enjoy matching wits with the people that I play with. That's every bit as satisfying as shooting my gun. I try to understand my opponent right from the get-go. Usually, right after the first or second game, I can get a feel for the mentality of the team that I'm playing against, and I can identify individuals that I regard as dangerous and identify individuals that are a piece of cake.

ANDREW: So you're sort of like the wolf watching the sheep, right?

CHUCK: That's all part of setting up the situation. Remember what I said: "always fight somebody on your terms." It helps to know the fields. I only play here at Skirmish, so I have an advantage. I know the fields very well, so I can use all of the terrain. I can use the creeks. People don't realize it, but one of the most effective stalking techniques is to wear knee-high rubber boots and to move in a creek bed because the noise of the water conceals most of your movements.

ANDREW: Cool.

CHUCK: You're down a foot or two below the line of sight and you usually have creek banks on both sides. People just don't expect to see you wading down a creek that's got a foot or a foot and a half of water in it.

One of the things that's interesting about hiding, and I tell new players this all the time, is that you always find bunkers and trees and log piles and fox holes. Everybody thinks those are the ideal places to hide. I disagree. I want to hide where somebody is not going to look for me, and those places are intrinsically suspicious.

I strive for a shooting lane that provides me an effective, defensible, dangerous position to work from. That's what I try to do.

ANDREW: And a dangerous, defensible position to work from would be...

CHUCK: I need shooting lanes, I need to feel confident that I'm going to see everything, that I'm going to encounter targets. I need to position myself strategically where I can help my team because I'm not always out there to play for myself. I want to be somewhere useful. I want to encounter other players and I want to effectively engage them and paint them or send them in another direction.

ANDREW: What shooting stance do you prefer as a sniper? Would you use the prone shooting position?

CHUCK: Almost never! I never lay down on my belly. First of all, I've got a pump, and if you lay down in a prone position it makes it harder to work the pump. When you play, you should move very little or not at all. When you do move, move steadily with smooth movements. When things go south, and you decide that you have to move, be definitive. Move really fast! If you're laying down on your belly, you can't get the heck out of there if you need to. So I always play kneeling or standing.

Some players, especially those coming from military backgrounds, plop down on their belly as soon as they get into a fight. I just eat them up. Shooting from prone position may work in other situations, but when you're playing paintball, it's not completely effective.

ANDREW: I notice you play with a scope.

CHUCK: Yes I do play with a scope. While I'm picking my targets I keep the yellow lens cover down. If I take a hit in the lens of the scope then I've lost my targeting system. Just before I take my shot I pop up the lens cover and set my sights on the target, giving me a clear field of view.

It's a straight four power (4X) scope. When I originally put it on the gun, I had some problems with it because it made my targets appear so close that I tended to undershoot them. But I've just taught myself to play with it and now it's just part of my equipment and second-nature to me.

I can shoot like most people do: looking down the barrel and shooting. My pump gun doesn't have an auto-trigger so my rate of fire doesn't even begin to approach a semi's rate of fire. A Tracer or a Phantom with an auto-trigger can fire faster, but maybe not as accurately.

ANDREW: What shooting gear do you bring to the field with you?

CHUCK: I have my Bud Orr Sniper and I have

my backup gun, a Phantom that I played with full-time several years ago. It's a good gun, shoots just as straight and just as far as the Sniper. I play with the Sniper because I like its heft.

I bring a couple of extra barrels and a couple of extra elbows. It's really important to have the right size elbows. A couple of squeegees, some gun oil, a gunsmith screwdriver for making adjustments on the guns. Spare parts, o-rings, various bits and pieces for the guns.

ANDREW: Tell me a little bit about your dress and camouflage. What kinds of things determine your choice of camo?

CHUCK: There are so many patterns out there. You have to have an artist's eye to be able to critically regard the terrain that you're going to play in, and then select the camouflage pattern that you think will be most effective. I have snow camo, I have camo for the summertime, and I have camo for every season in between.

In the wintertime when there's snow on the ground, I have some white coveralls with some branch lines on them that are actually meant to be tree camouflage. I found that up here in the woods, where there's tons of angular branch features with a white background, such camouflages are very effective. I can almost disappear.

In the Fall, if it rains, the color of the leaves darkens. I have a camouflage pattern that's called Fall Foliage that is a very effective pattern in conditions like that. Like I said, I'm a hunter and an outdoorsman and a paintball player all in one. My investment in all this equipment makes sense.

I wear hand coverings and face coverings. For most people in the woods, those are the most noticeable parts of the body. And again, since human eyes are set up to see movement, concealing your face and hands is rather important.

ANDREW: Do you have any memorable experiences as a sniper you can share?

CHUCK: Here's a classic. I coached a player, Rob, a couple of years ago. He wanted to become a sniper. At one point in the game, he hid in the top of a blown down tree and four players on the opposing team walked right past him! He and I and some of our other players were working together to set up an ambush. Everybody has to contribute to make those work. Our contribution was to engage the approaching players and have them concentrate on us. Then Rob just raised up out of the blown down tree top (he was fifteen yards behind them) and they were all four lined up with their backs to him and he just went to work on them. It was beautiful. That's how I like to play. It was a most enjoyable success.

ANDREW: That's great. How about yourself? Ever been ambushed?

CHUCK: It happens to the best of us. I like to match wits with people, to out-think them. People are just like deer, very much creatures of habit. It's not usual for someone to surprise me. But it's happened.

I was playing a couple of years ago with a friend and we snuck in on the back side of a flag station and went to work on the defenders and I thought I was doing really well. There was a six-inch puddle of water at my feet and all of a sudden this guy just reared up out of the puddle. He looked like a freaking' sea monster, slopping water and wet leaves dripping off of him.

I was astonished and stunned. I stood there with my mouth hanging open and got shot.

MAKE YOUR OWN GHILLIE SUIT

It's easy and fun to make your own ghillie suit. Here is a quick primer on do-it-yourself camouflage.

Items Needed

- A cotton landing net, the kind used for fishing

- Camouflage Webbing: Determined by the season and terrain. Choose several kinds as needed.

- Burlap Strips: Find some raw burlap material and pull it apart to get at the threads.

- Rit Fabric Dye: Choose earthy tones.

At least a day before, dye your burlap strips in various tones by following the directions on the package. Let dry.

Cut the landing net open so you have a rectangular piece as big as possible. Lay this on the ground.

Cut your camo-webbing into thirty-inch strips. (Webbing is preferable because offers a more natural appearance. Most foliage will transmit a diffused light and webbing does that, too. If your ghillie suit is made of fabric, when you're backlit you will present a much darker, more distinctive silhouette. And an easy target!)

Fold the camo strips in half and then girth hitch them to the landing net. Don't just randomly attach them. Think about the patterns in the woods where you'll be using your suit and try to create an interesting, deceptive pattern.

Use the dyed burlap strips to fill in areas and add texture to the suit. Camouflage is an art, not a science. Use your imagination. Make several different kinds of ghillie suits to meet your needs.

Make separate pieces that can be used alone or together. You can make a back cover, a front cover, and a head cover. Attach these to your body with ties made of webbing. For your head cover, sew the landing net to a old cap, then apply camo netting and burlap strips.

Paintball Snipers—From Myth to Reality

SOME MYTHS WERE MADE TO BE BROKEN

Occasionally on rec.sport.paintball ("the internet" for the paintball-playing crowd), someone posts the question "How can I be a paintball sniper?" This guy gets a lot of ribbing, partly because of the anti-military movement in paintball, and partly because I don't think most players understand the usefulness of a hidden player in the modern game. There are myths about the paintball version of snipers, let alone the pop-culture version, that simply need to be exposed for what they are. Because of the

images we are spoon-fed by hyper-unrealistic movies and television shows, paintball players automatically believe that a sniper wears a bulky black suit, holds a gun longer than he is tall, and sits at the other end of a field putting paint onto a dime in the opponents' flag station. Sorry, no. Not in this game. At least, not any time soon.

Setting the record straight on paintball snipers.

First of all, real "snipers" need not apply. No matter how accurate your gun is (go ahead and spend a fortune on the best barrels, bolts, tanks, triggers, and sites), your projectile is the weak link. Ever seen a paintball decide it wanted to make a hard left? I have.

Paintballs have a mind of their own. They're not accurate projectiles. Even in ideal circumstances, you really can't take someone out from as far away as an actual sniper with a special, high-powered rifle is expected to. You may or may not have figured this out yet, but basically, paintball is not, in the end, about the gun. The gun cannot outperform its ammunition. A roughly spherical gel-encased ball of colored vegetable fluids is not high-performance ammunition.

Instead of looking at someone as a "Sniper", look at them as a "Hunter." That's what they have to be in paintball. Sometimes you stalk, sometimes you hide, sometimes you shoot. You never line someone up from 200 yards away. So let's say you want to start playing like a hunter. How do you do it? It's easy, really.

If you move, you're not hiding.

Pick a camo that fits your terrain if you can. If not, make do with what you have. I've used realtree in a desert setting effectively before and it worked well. You also have to understand what your camouflage does for a living in order to use it.

Tiger Stripe fools the eye into 'sliding' past the camouflage. Realtree, Advantage and Treebark look like the background, and fool the eye into believing they're part of the background. Woodland, Dots, and others of this style appear mottled and try to 'blend in' like a smudged painting. It's much more complex than that, but you get the idea.

In the US region, when in doubt use Woodland. Very universal, very effective. The way I see it, the U.S. government spent a lot of money to make it work well, and they succeeded. Don't use specialty camouflage, French Lizard comes to mind, unless it's broad-based enough to fit in anywhere.

Probably more than you wanted to know, right? Well, if you take being a sniper seriously, this is pretty critical information. Take the time to pick the right camouflage!

The Sniper's Paintgun

I've never been a believer in new barrels, bolts, or anything like that. But you have to realize that I play normally with a fixed-barrel Piranha which is non-modifiable. So I'm biased.

Like many other people, I'm a believer in the target range. I've spent many cases of paint on the target range, and not just shooting for the heck of it. I'll try to hit all the targets on the range in order from front to back, then back to front. Then I'll put paint in the "0" in the number "50" on the sign. Then between the "1" and "2" on the "125 foot" sign. Once I have my effective range down in my mind, I can walk on the field with confidence. I know my range, and I know how accurate I am at that range. That takes years of experience, mind you, and it's not something you can learn from a book. You just have to go out and shoot paint at a target until you have the motion down.

SNIPING

Do Not Try to Be a Sniper... Be a Sniper!

So let's assume that you make it to the field in one piece, and you're ready to give it a go. Try some pre-game mental prep. Do this—hit the target range, plan your route, and review the team strategy.

You have to remember a few key rules here. Once you shoot a ball, the world will know where you are. This can be a good thing, as well as a bad thing. If someone spots you, they'll shoot a lot of paint at you. Either shoot back, dive for cover, or freeze. I'll address this in detail later, but for now, these are your good options. Take your time, relax, listen for opponents or teammates. Aural clues are easier than visual ones, especially when you're stalking.

Shooting is a skill that's a major factor in the game, the be-all-end-all of paintball. But, if you're trying to be sneaky, you generally want to make

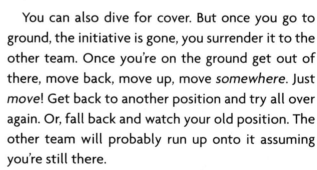

your first shot count. And the key to this is getting a good stance so your hand is steady.

I like having something I can shoulder up, usually my tank. But I've been using a lighter GTS stock lately, and they work very well with a remote line. It's just easier to hold a barrel steady when it's braced.

Taking aim is key. You want to hit something solid, like the opponent's gun or a harness buckle. Aiming for the chest area is good if you have the time to aim. If the paintball deviates a foot or so, you'll still hit the target.

Some say you should pull the trigger slowly, but I don't. Pull the trigger as you would normally. Don't change anything mechanical that you're used to. It's like changing the engine in your car to drive to a new job. Not really worth it. Just shoot in the same way you always do. If all goes well, you'll have an eliminated and confused player in no time. ("Where'd *that* come from!?!?")

Now, let's say that it all goes wrong.

Your barrel is wet and your ball skids left by a million feet.
Your target turns and spots you.
Now what?

As I said before, you have options. Three basic choices include the following—(1) shoot back lots of paint, (2) dive for cover, or (3) freeze in place. I've done all three, and they all work depending on terrain, your opponent, and your positioning.

For example, if the terrain is thick and you're fairly far from your opponent, freezing in place will confuse him. He may not see you at all. Presuming you only shot one ball, he won't be able to get a good 'fix' on your position.

If it's more open and there's a lack of hard cover (trees, rocks...), let it rip. Keep the initiative in a situation like this. He's off guard, and you can make him react to you. Eventually, he will make a mistake and you'll get an elimination.

You can also dive for cover. But once you go to ground, the initiative is gone, you surrender it to the other team. Once you're on the ground get out of there, move back, move up, move *somewhere*. Just *move*! Get back to another position and try all over again. Or, fall back and watch your old position. The other team will probably run up onto it assuming you're still there.

The best way to learn how to do this is actually to do it yourself. Try being a sniper for a game or two; you may be surprised at what happens. It's another trick to put in your bag. Remember, being versatile is a large part of what will make your game more successful and keep it fresh and enjoyable over time.

—RR

DEFENSE

Not enough has been written about defense in paintball, and the reasons are apparent. Very few of us think of playing defense in paintball as either a glamorous or enjoyable experience. Indeed, most players' idea of defense is to hang back and shoot anything not friendly as it comes back to the flag station.

But this isn't defense, it's a siege mentality. Bona fide paintball defense is a multifaceted position that's all about controlled aggression. If you understand the dimensions of paintball defense, you will think twice before leaving it out of your game plan.

The idea of defense that true paintball jedi should employ involves channeling your desire to win into preventing the other team from winning.

What am I talking about? Soon, it will all make sense. Most paintball teams are very concerned with taking ground fast, slamming a tape, and being very aggressive in their actions. But a team has to balance that with some kind of defensive capability, and not in the classical "Old School" sense. Paintball is becoming a game of players with positional strengths. Once you accept that proposition, exploring the possibilities of defense becomes more interesting.

First off, let me define paintball-style defense. Defensive players are those on the team attempting to stop the opposition from scoring points. Eliminations, flag hangs, first pulls—all of these are points that can be prevented with a good defense, and not just in tournaments either. If you play for fun, you can play a solid defense and win with it.

What makes a good defender? The mindset of a defender is a combination of fierce pride and spartan commitment. "You're not getting my flag. You're not shooting my crawler. You're not getting that bunker. Not on my field!" Sounds a lot like an aggressor, yes? The difference is that as a defender, your "aggressive" goal requires actively preventing *them* from attaining *their* goals. Hence the phrase, **Controlled Aggression**.

A fat wallet helps. Defense isn't cheap, you can shoot a ton of paint on "D."

So what's the purpose of defense? I've broken it down to four basic categories:

1. **Positional Defense**—Holding a single piece of real-estate with everything you have.

2. **Prevent Defense**—Also known as "Sitting". Playing solely to deny the opposing team from shooting your team or achieving their goals.

3. **Reserve Defense**—Staying in the back with the eventual goal of becoming an attacking player in a later stage of the game.

4. **Team Defense**—Playing the backfield to aid your forward players.

As a defensive player, you have to decide what style is best for your team and its goals and adapt on the fly. In a big game, it means holding the fort. In a hyperball tournament, you may prevent the other team from advancing and scoring points. In your rec-ball weekend, it could mean being the last line of defense because the corned beef sandwich you ate for lunch just isn't sitting right and running is more than you can handle. *Remember the team goal is important, and so is not barfing during a game.*

Paintball is, and always will be, a team sport.

Defense falls into two broader styles—"Passive" and "Aggressive." As the names suggest, the two styles reflect two different trains of thought, but one overall goal: denying points and positions to the opposing team. There's a general stereotype here for the two styles. "Rec-Ball" players are 'passive' defenders, whereas tournament players are 'active' defenders. Tournament teams leave no players back, but rec-players always do. Yes, it's a stereotype, but it's almost always true. As in everything else, there's a time to be passive, and other times when being aggressive is necessary. Learning the rhythm of the game is very important. It's key to know when you need to act, to feel the appropriateness of doing something. With this in mind, let's go into a little more detail on the four basic categories of defense.

Positional Defense is mainly a concern of passive defenders, mainly because it requires patience in the beginning and cunning when it hits the fan. Active defenders can use the principles of this to take and hold key bunkers and control zones from one spot on the field. Examples of this can be found mostly in big games where a flag station or a fort must be held. On tournament fields, situations arise wherein a defender holds the last few bunkers and tries to stop the offense.

Most positional defense originates in one location, and uses that location to fend off all aggressors. This is a very passive defense, and is very common in rec-play. From a position like this, you want to work around as in a typical bunker. But you have to keep your eyes open because you will more than likely be seeing more than one attacker and they have the maneuverability advantage and often greater numbers.

Aggressive Defense is about players having *zones of influence* that they can claim as their own. This is a very aggressive defense, because you as the defensive player are making the action happen and causing people to react to you. You're grabbing a section of field X by Y in size, staking a claim, and

putting up a sign that reads "No trespassers allowed." As a defender, it allows you to move around more and remain unpredictable. Slide forward to a position to stop them; scuttle to the other side of the bunker and shoot it up. While they're adjusting, move back a position and draw one into your barrel. Take him down and dive to another bunker. Scope out two bunkers you can dive between to make them wonder. If you can keep them guessing so they can't figure out where you are, they will hesitate to move up on you. My girlfriend calls this a "Field Mouse Defense" because it's what a field mouse does and, in her words, "What's more defensive than a field mouse?" Be elusive!

The Surprise Factor

You also want to have the element of surprise. You can accomplish this even if your enemy knows where you are. Consider the following scenario.

At the Ohio Bash, we had a position we had to hold for 5 more minutes so our team captain could touch the station for more points. I had a pump gun, and a few surprises. The team was laying paint heavily into the other team's attacking force. I put my body in front of our captain and began to pump paint to keep their heads down. I kept watching the time, knowing it wouldn't be long. With a minute before the call in, I grabbed a smoke grenade, popped the striker, and tossed it just over the lip of the hill.

It was a good throw, but the smoke wasn't thick enough for my liking. So I popped a red smoker with it and tossed it over the hill as well. "Hammer down!" I yelled. My teammates doubled their rate of fire, stopping our opponents' last minute push. Our captain touched the flag station, and we got our points and vacated the area. The opposing team wasn't expecting a smoke screen, and that stopped them long enough for our team to achieve our goal. This was Controlled Aggression exemplified.

Let it all hang out, but don't take unnecessary risks!

Prevent Defense

Related to positional defense, *prevent defense* uses similar means, but tends to be more useful in tournament settings. Simply put, you're preventing the other team from advancing instead of holding a position. For example, if the opposing team needs to eliminate five of your guys to advance, you fare better by sitting back and making them do the work. They get sloppy or nervous, and they get eliminated. Prevent defense is also easier than position defense because it's not zone oriented. It's more aggressive as well: you hide less and being mobile is emphasized.

I was in Chicago once, and had the opportunity to talk to some guys from Thunderstruck. They were telling me about a tournament field in Vegas some years ago in which they zoned out one bunker at extreme range down a main trail. One guy from the start would take three steps and start laying paint just over that bunker. He made three eliminations in the first two minutes. This is a perfect prevent defense. Other players on his team were making aggressive moves, but this one shooter made the plan work—*controlled aggression is where it's at!*

Most of your defense should be geared towards a "prevent" style. It's very flexible in response to what the other team is doing, but it's not just reactive. If you've done your job before the games start,

you should have scoped out the bunkers your opposition is likely to see as advantageous. Dedicate a defense player to preventing them from getting in and/or using that position. Even if someone makes it in, rain paint on their heads so they won't even look up. Now *that's* effective prevention.

Delay Tactic

The other side to a prevent is a *delay tactic* in which you aren't stopping the other team as much as you're stalling the inevitable or forcing them to deal with you. A good friend of mine calls this tactic "The Human Speedbump." We do this in big games all the time. The entire offense is getting routed hard, and we figure that they need a few more seconds to get away. So we stop hard behind a tree and start shooting at the attackers. They always stop to return fire, and we always get eliminated. But we always get our teammates a few hundred more feet of running room in the trade, and they can be more effective. You may also have seen a tournament player crash a front bunker and just hug it. The opposing team is forced to deal with that player, because he's a threat in their path. You may not consider this a defensive maneuver until you realize this one player is stopping the entire other team from pushing a side by just sitting there. Again, this is controlled aggression—doing just enough to stop the 'bad guys' and help the 'good guys' without getting hit.

Reserve Player Defense

The *Reserve player tactic* is a different defense mostly used in recreational play. The general idea is to hang back and wait to see what the opposing team does. Your time interval for this is up to you. For example, I've been playing a lot of speedball style games lately (no deer ticks, and none of this hiding stuff...). Earlier this summer I played at a field in Wisconsin that was preparing for a tournament, so the speedball field was all nice and dolled up. We were also playing the older speedball style of

face the back and turn around on the horn. From the break I spun and saw where people were pivoting to move to. I knew where my guys were going, and I didn't have a plan right off the bat. The other team sent most of their players left, while we had a balanced offense. Within three seconds I decided I needed to go on the left to bolster the offense. It worked. Within a minute or two we had held, then cleared the left side. I didn't do it by myself, but my presence was a big help. A few seconds in the "reserve" slot helped the overall offense of the game. I could have slanted right to attack the off side. I could have stayed back and long-balled. I could have sat in the backfield and directed traffic. All of these decisions were opened up to me because I waited to react to the other team. And they were all made in three seconds.

In an outdoor game, I'll wait a few minutes if need be, listen for the shooting and figure how we're holding. If it seems static, then I'll flank or reinforce. In some cases I'll launch myself up a tapeline and sneak around the shooting. If everyone is too busy to look my way, I can make it all the way behind the flag station.

The idea is to be a 'spare player' with intentions to move up on a flag or objective. *Again, controlled aggression is what you're going for.* The key to your move can be timed in minutes or seconds. You can also count the eliminated players and move up when half the other team is eliminated. The main thing is you're not going to sit down the whole game and wait for the opponent to come to you. It also makes the other team cocky when they make it to your flag after they think they eliminated everyone already. Free shots.

Team Defense

The last category is a *team defense*. This actually crosses all the previous three categories, but usually sacrifices the defender. The tactic I've already mentioned as "Human Speedbumps" can also be used on a flag return. You run back with the flag runner. If there's any trouble, the runner keeps going but you turn around and return fire. Again, they stop to shoot at you. But your flag runner has a clear path into the station. Any time you make a trade-off like this, think of it as a defensive maneuver. In chess, sacrificing a pawn for a positional advantage that is virtually impossible for your opponent to overcome is a brilliant move.

On the same note, a takedown ("bunkering" or "mugging") can be defensive in nature as well. I can hear you sighing in disbelief from here. But consider: Let's say one player is holding your team in one place. That player's goal is to prevent your team from advancing or keep you preoccupied. To prevent him from achieving his goal, you may want to send in a guy to take him out. Often times you get a trade-off. You and he walk off the field together. But that one move opens up your side and the offense can take control. In this case, bunkering a guy goes from a highly aggressive maneuver to a tactical team-oriented defensive maneuver. This is yet another example of *controlled aggression*.

Sacrificing yourself isn't the only team defense option. Enter the art of an ambush. Often misunderstood, a good ambush should leave an attacking force saying "What in the world just happened?" A good ambush involves three players, requires good setup time, and demands patience to execute well. In an ambush, it is key to cover the attackers in paint as fast as you can. Speed is the key; otherwise, they will find cover, regroup, and give you a hard time. Use your cover, stay low, keep your cool, and when they walk into your zone, let them have it all at once. Of course, this can be very nerve-wracking, but it can also rattle your opponents and cause them to stop an attack. I could write a whole article on the ambush alone—it's more versatile than you think.

Team defense also covers people in your back-field—the heavy shooters who should be working in sync with the team. A guy in the way back long-balling the other team, feeding information to his front crawler is very common, and the easiest to see in action. But it can go further. There's been a lot of talk about "set up plays" recently, and your back players are the best judges as to when you should launch one. So they're a lot like quarter-backs, calling the plays and supporting them to make sure they can happen.

The Bottom Line

I've talked a lot about being an aggressive defender, and controlling that aggression in a way that bene-fits the team. Always consider the team when plan-ning your defense. A solid defense, or at least a planned one, can hold the other team to a points loss or prevent them from organizing that one solid push they need to win the game. Too many teams undermine their best efforts on offense by sacrific-ing their commitment to defense. This neglect is behind the fact that most teams aren't that great. If you want your team to be invincible, take a bal-anced approach to the game. Explore the possibili-ties of dedicating a few players to defensive postures. One guy suppressing the center could make the difference between winning and losing in rec play or a tournament.

—RR

Getting Down to Earth

At the outset, you need to know something about me. I am 6'4" and 250 pounds of big, fat, artery clogging American mass. This makes me quite the atypical "crawler." Your stereotypical crawler is a guy 5'5" with sticks for limbs, and a pat of breakfast butter that slipped onto his shoe representing body fat.

But, since I do crawl, I maintain that anyone can. Crawling can be worked into anyone's game; it's just a matter of how and to what degree. A little floor work can enhance your game by making the impossible likely.

Let us start with a situation most likely to pop up in your game. Say you are in a shootout where nothing is happening. Neither you nor your opponent is moving forward. You have a choice: spend all game in a one-on-one "pop-up-and-shoot" scenario, or try the following.

Swing to your left and release a string. Then quickly roll right and crawl ten feet, and then up three to a different tree. Do not run. Crawl. Assuming you did not run, your opponent, who was likely concentrating on your left side, did not see you reach your new spot. When they pop up to shoot your old bunker, tag them on the head. Crawlers hit the turf just at the right times, not all the time. Crawlers try to fool their opponents by stealth, misdirection, or a combination of the two. A ten foot sideways maneuver is a crawl although it does not appear to be.

Successful crawling begins with the right equipment. Contrary to your assumption, "camouflage" is not a top priority for the crawler's kit. Knee and elbow pads are, however. Technically, I can crawl naked, but it would be painful for me and traumatizing for any witnesses. Pads should allow you to feel the ground when you move but still give protection. I use Redz pads and have never regretted it. Next, you need gloves to serve as padding for your hands. Having a good pair of cleats, a stopwatch, and a stick squeegee in your pads is helpful. You'll need to get streamlined and keep all loose equipment off your body. Once you have acquired these priorities, look into camouflages. You can overcome those big, juicy white logos on your chest with a crawl.

Your chest is already on the turf, who's going to see it?

Crawling is a combination of patience, skill, and time management. Bob Long once gave me the metaphor that when you commit to a crawl (or anything in paintball), you need to see the door opening, decide when to go for it, and gauge how long you have before it slams in your face.

Although every situation must be treated uniquely, I have found two basic techniques for crawling suitable for different occasions. The first is the "Leopard Crawl," which is useful for low or dense cover. The whole time you are moving, you are on your toes, knees, elbows, and hands, and your belly is literally just over the ground. Most of your forward power comes from digging your spikes into the ground and pushing off of them. While you do this, raise your body over the ground and steady yourself on your elbows and hands. Do this in the manner most comfortable for you. For a long time I used my toe spike, but then I switched to Diggers cleats and changed to a side spike on the ball of my foot. If you are doing it right, it should be like rock climbing on flat terrain (except you don't get jackhammer foot or use carabiners). Using five times the energy to move a quarter of the distance, the disadvantage to the Leopard Crawl is energy expenditure. But in heavy cover and places where the only way to cross to a key position is to dig your nose in dirt, the Leopard Crawl is the best option. It is quite a rush to crawl up the middle of a field, cross a ravine unseen under rays of paint shooting above you, and attain a key spot.

The second basic technique is the "Three-Point crawl". As the name suggests, you crawl forward with both knees and one hand on the ground while the other hand holds your paint-gun. Keeping an Autococker level as you crawl isn't easy, but do not point it at the ground. If you get surprised, shooting the ground is inef-

fective and pointless. While you're crawling, do not continuously put all your weight on an open hand; you don't want to hurt your wrists. I crawl on a closed fist parallel with my forearm to minimize injury potential. The Three Point Crawl is a very fast crawl, but it is less stealthy, and, therefore, more perilous. From these two basic techniques you can accomplish a lot of maneuvering. A variation of the Leopard Crawl would be moving more like a snake—making more noise, but crawling faster and

lower to the ground. A Three Point can become a Four Point or even a Two point. Adjust the maneuver to the specific situation. Be mindful of your feet; a beautiful crawl can be easily defeated if your foot becomes a target.

When should you take a chance on crawling? Not all the time. You would gain little from crawling all the way from flag to flag. Getting half way up the field would take the whole game. Instead, crawling should be used to gain an advantage, either with your teammates or on your own. The field—tree roots and shrubs included—looks different when you're a foot off the floor. There are many holes that are only visible at ground level.

The best teacher is experience, so here are some team plays to try.

The "Low-man approach" is a classic. One teammate shoots over your head at an opponent they can not reach due to cover. You start a Three point crawl towards the covered opponent. Speed is the key. Your teammate over you, the High Man keeps signaling you information: "50 feet, on left! 11-o'clock!" or whatever team codes you use. As the crawler, don't say a word. That would defeat the purpose and destroy the surprise attack. Your back player should shout a code word (e.g., "now" will suffice) as a signal for you to pop up and put a string on the opponent. When it works, it's so sweet.

Using the same set up, you can make a "sacrifice" move. The High Man makes a lot of noise, and does a lot of shooting. He will eventually fall back or get eliminated, leaving the crawler, or the Low Man, in the field deep in cover. The crawler waits for the other team to overrun his spot and then fires at them from behind. Either that or run for their flag; they won't expect you to be covering their flag station, will they?

In both cases an aggressive team could argue that you should just make a takedown. This does

not work all the time, and circumstances like heavy overgrowth or a bad trail create a difficult situation for "running up and mugging the bum." Besides, a crawl like this only takes a minute or two. Patience to make a takedown gradually and wisely is rewarding.

Out on a paintball field you have to make quick decisions that can affect the outcome of the game. Crawling may not always be the best thing to do, but it's worth having in your arsenal as part of an overall plan.

For example, assume that you have a good bunker position, but you spy a better one. There is enough cover to work, so you set up a crawl about 30 feet from the new bunker, going low but fast. You will cover that last 30 feet, the "Three Second" point, by running. Here is the general "Three Second Rule" for sprints: it takes a second to see you, a second to comprehend who you are, and what team you are on, and another second to raise a paintgun and shoot. The three seconds of comprehension are three seconds of sprinting you get for free without the risk of getting shot. So crawl to that "Three Second" point and take them by surprise. You can reach the new bunker unseen by slithering right to it. The effect will be the same. Once you get there you have a few free shots, equivalent to those three seconds of sprinting, before the other team adjusts to your new position.

Another field strategy is crawling under a fire-lane, as long your opponent's line of sight does not extend that low. Imagine a line that begins at your opponent and travels straight out along their line of sight. They can not see you as long as their position does not enable them to look over and down. You can crawl literally under their barrel if you possess the nerve.

Stealth is covered extensively in my Fieldcraft chapter, but it bears a quick repeat. Basically, move quietly, clear your path, and set up for a one-shot "Bingo." Crawling makes stealth easier, as being on the ground makes brushing noisy obstacles out of your path easy. The bragging rights for getting "Bingos" is beautiful (and they save money on paint, too).

Crawling is an important paintball tool among many. Knowing when and where to go to ground can be an asset to your game. Even if you are tall and chunky.

—RR

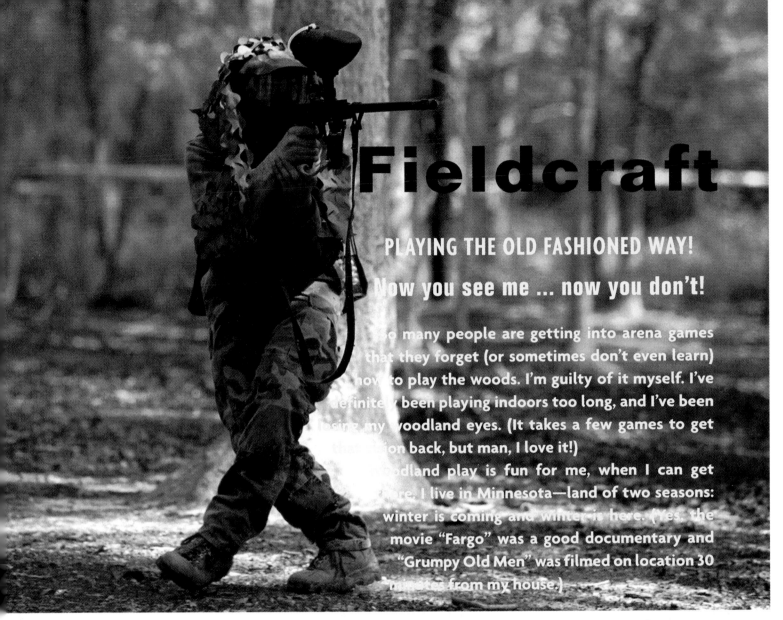

Fieldcraft

PLAYING THE OLD FASHIONED WAY!

Now you see me ... now you don't!

So many people are getting into arena games that they forget (or sometimes don't even learn) how to play the woods. I'm guilty of it myself. I've definitely been playing indoors too long, and I've been losing my woodland eyes. (It takes a few games to get that vision back, but man, I love it!)

Woodland play is fun for me, when I can get there. I live in Minnesota—land of two seasons: winter is coming and winter is here. (Yes, the movie "Fargo" was a good documentary and "Grumpy Old Men" was filmed on location 30 minutes from my house.)

Personally, the best part of woodland paintball is the stalking. I don't want to sound like some kind of wacked-out, back-country, weird-beard here. I'm just saying that when you're outside, closer to nature than usual, successfully stalking your friends (or whoever your opponents happen to be that day) is a thrill! I'm a big guy, and somehow I can do it.

What is Fieldcraft?

Fieldcraft is mainly the art of trickery. The use of camouflage and conceal-ment is a dying art in paintball. Crawlers use a little 'fieldcraft' on tournament fields, but it's virtually obsolete because fields are increasingly *postage-stamp-sized*.

It's a real skill to use terrain to your advantage. It encompasses a number of skills that we either take for granted or don't take seriously as modern players. These days paintball players laugh at people using face paint; back in the eighties, when I started playing, face paint was the norm. The original paintball players used fieldcraft because the game was played outside exclusively. The time has come to modernize the use of fieldcraft to suit the evolution of our sport.

Know your opponents!

What you need to do is *trick* your opponent. How? The first thing you have to understand is your opponent. To begin with, he or she is a human being. However noble in reason and spirit they may be, humans are fallible. In paintball, their imperfections are often relatively easy to spot, if you're paying attention.

Paintball tricks work by understanding the general nature of and specific inclinations of your opponents. Generally speaking, most players today are impatient. Instead of waiting for you to walk on top of them, most will shoot as soon as they see you. Most are also deadlocked on the opponent they see in front of them and less likely to check their sides as they advance.

Here's where using your camouflage comes in handy. For example, I was playing at Stalker Paintball Games, a field in Wisconsin that has a dense canopy and not many light patches. I dove into a thicket bush and sat for a few minutes. Basically, I was out in the middle of nowhere, with no solid

cover for 50 feet other than this thicket. But, the other team was making a push up the center. One player in a JT jersey came screaming up the center. I leveled my gun, waited for him, and hammered down as he made a turn into the spool right in front of me.

Sitting still in your cover, and using your camouflage to your advantage is the essence of fieldcraft. My opponent was so focused on making his bunker that he got sloppy. I understood that he would do just that, and I acted accordingly. I had control of the situation, he just never realized it.

So with that story in mind, let's start with your camouflage.

The Invisible Advantage

We all wear camouflage, but hardly anyone uses it correctly because of a lack of control or understanding. It's ridiculous that so few people really take advantage of their camos. Many players want to shoot their gun as many times as they can. Fine, go ahead! Don't be surprised that someone saw you from the other side of the field. You're making noise, and now we know where you are.

In order to use camouflage, it's important to understand why it works. There are a few different styles that work in different ways in different terrain. I had a long chat with Tim Schloss of Pursuit Products about camouflage. That's his business, he sells "Tiger Stripe", "Realtree" and "Advantage" styles of camouflage, as well as color blocked styles. Great stuff. He told me there's two basic types of camouflage, and two basic ways they work.

Types of Camouflage

Aggressive camouflage works by fooling the eye into thinking it's a part of the background. Good examples of this type would be US Woodland, Belgian dots, Auscam, and so on. It's made to match a background's overall colors. This stuff works best behind shrubs and shadows. Camouflages like

"Tiger Stripe" fall into this category, but for a different reason. You see, the human eye is lazy. When we scan for opponents, we scan horizontally. Aggressive camouflage, like Tiger Stripe, encourages the eye to "slide over" it. There's a few other camouflages like this. US Woodland was actually created for a European military theater by the United States government. Tiger Stripe was originally made for the Vietnam conflict, but was modified slightly for paintballers. You don't want to know how much the Australian government spent on developing Auscam, but it's the best stuff for hiding in Australia that I've found.

Passive camouflage works in a different way; it's made to convince the brain it's part of the foreground, and totally natural. This would include Advantage, Realtree (and it's derivatives), Mossy Oak, and so on. Each of these types is perfect for specific uses. "Advantage" looks like the forest floor, while "Realtree" looks like a tree. These camouflages started as hunting patterns. They are supposed to enable a hunter to stand in front of a tree to get a better shot. That's why they try to be photo-realistic. They're not really meant for other terrain. In their elements, these highly specialized camouflages are excellent.

Then there's a third kind of camouflage, which I call "Weirdo-Flage." These types fit mostly into the "Aggressive" camouflage category. They include, but aren't limited to, JT, Scott, Renegade or Venomwear printed jerseys, Splash clothing. Any of the "Non-Camo" stuff also falls into this category. The idea behind these patterns is simply to bring paint-

ball into the 'mainstream'. Paintball garb as fashionable accessory...you get the picture. They work toward that end, and, occasionally, as partial camouflage. I love the guys who wear off-the-shelf JT Jerseys. Big, juicy white target in center of their chest and on their forearms. Easy target from across the field. Love it.

Some of the non-camo works, but not as well as true camouflage. If you're wearing it to look like a team, cool. If you're wearing it as a true camo... well... umm... yeah...

Whatever you're wearing, the golden rule of camouflage is not to move. The human eye is lazy, but it's also naturally drawn to motion. Motion is perceived as something worth watching.

Paintball players, of course, have to move. Given that fact, note that "Aggressive" patterns allow you more freedom of movement than "Passive" patterns. Aggressive patterns aren't specific to one spot or terrain, and allow you to take a "camouflaged" position anywhere in a broad spectrum of places. If you're wearing a Realtree and you're lying down, it doesn't "look" right and you're more apt to be spotted. A "Tiger Stripe" looks more appropriate in any given place you stop.

As a player, you can also use different patterns in different terrain. I have a set of Realtree I've used in the desert. It worked well. This isn't brain surgery, people. The key is simply to match your camouflage as accurately as possible to your surroundings. I've seen pictures of UK players in Tiger Stripe in which the green just blares out against a brown background; we're talking total absence of greenage on the ground level. I've made boo-boos like this before, mostly in my paintball youth. And if it happens by mistake these days, I just change my outlook on the game and adapt. I'll look for colors where I'm close to blending in and go from there.

Camouflage—All or Nothing!

Use a visor on your goggles or at least a hat brim. Goggle flare is a dead giveaway to your position. Don't use chrome or bright, splashy stuff that may glare as well. Matte Black is still your best bet for color. Wear a full mask. Skin tones aren't nature tones and will give you away. Better yet, paint your mask for camo colors or mottle it somehow to break up the "Black Blob" on your face. My favorite trick is hiding your brightly colored armband by burying your arm into a tree or the ground and using your body as a "cloak" over it.

BEHAVING INVISIBLE

There's a time and a place for battle cries and open charges down the middle, but this ain't one of 'em!

Wait your opponent out. They panic when nobody is shooting at them. Take your time and you'll absolutely freak 'em out.

You don't need cool camos or anything like that to hide, however. I could be wearing stark white, and you won't see me if I'm totally behind hard cover (see the Cover chapter). It's that easy. Let's say I'm wearing a really bright jersey and I've got a bright red paintgun. If I'm trying to hide, I'll get behind a rock, a dirt berm, or a hill. Anything I can put my whole body behind relative to an enemy position will hide me.

Nature is one big free camouflage factory!

Use Reference Points and the World Around You

Having a reference point is good as well. I'll often use cover from one angle, knowing that the other team or another player will be coming from that or another angle and crossing my barrel. I can expose myself to one side if I know that side is *safe*. That's

why I run the tape as often as I do, I can expose that whole flank as I wait for you to walk into my dot-sight. Pop, "HIT", Bingo. Thank you.

Terrain is a big part of fieldcraft. Your fieldcraft skills come from learning how to use what's ahead of you and see what's to the side of you. Lining up trees to conceal your movement toward your opponents is always a good idea. You can't plan on things like shadows, wind, and so on to mask your movement. You just have to do it.

But when it all falls together, you have to recognize it for what it is. If I'm stalking a tape (either by crawl or by crouch), I'm constantly aware of my surroundings. I'm looking ahead for the clearest line in the path that requires minimal effort and noise. Leaves are bad, dirt is good. If I have a choice between twigs or dried leaves, I'll take the twig route. I can push twigs out of my way quieter and faster than I can leaves by just dragging my hand along them and not lifting my knees too far.

I'm always listening to the wind. When it picks up, I move. When it dies down, I slow or stop. I listen for airplanes, cars, trucks, trains, people shooting in the center... anything that makes enough noise to mask my movement.

Moves are made quickly and deliberately, and planned 2 steps ahead when possible. The thought process is: "Big Tree to fort. Fort to spool. Spool to shrubs."

I'm always looking ahead. I'm also looking down the field to where opponents *should* be hiding. I can't predict everything, but if I'm coming up on a big tree or an outcropping of barrels, odds are someone is either in there or wants to be. *I'm looking through cover for background shadows.* If I don't see any light behind twigs or shrubs, it's either a rock, a tree, or a player.

Sounds play a very important role, too. Especially nature sounds. Most things in nature that produce noisy sounds will stop when something big comes by and scares them. If the birds and crickets stop chirping, someone spooked them and you should get ready. In some cases, an animal may start making a lot of noise if you approach. Listen for any and all audible changes; they're the best early warning system you'll have in the wild.

A bit of fieldcraft also goes into using nature to fool people. These are old school tricks, but they're still good. Here are some examples from my experience. I'm lying on the ground while two guys are looking for me. They know I'm out there, but not sure where. With one foot I'll wiggle a small tree or a thick shrub away from me. That will get their attention long enough for me to come up and take 'em out. There's also the "Throw a rock away from you so it makes noise over there" trick, but I stopped doing that out of fear of pelting a ref or well-hidden player. You'd be well advised to throw only relatively light things. I've also been stalking, been spotted, and swayed matching the tree in front of me for movement. The player looked away, and I got moving at the flag. (I was able to get the flag, and not make a single elimination that game.) Then there's the 'ballsy' approach. Someone thinks they see me, and they open a barrage at me. I don't flinch or move. After a few moments, they stop shooting. Why? Nothing shot back, obviously nobody's there. One burst later, they're gone.

CLAIM THIS LOST ART AND PUT IT IN YOUR GAME

To a paintball player who uses fieldcraft, tactical possibilities are virtually infinite. I've crawled through a path with no cover in front of me and made it, and I've sat in front of a tree and remained unseen. But if you think this is all there is to know, you're wrong.

I talked to a friend of mine; he plays in ratty old BDU's, uses a pump gun, and wears no mask. He's one of my favorite wire players, because he can just vanish after taking a guy out and pop up thirty paces to the right of where he just was. He's very good. When I started writing this piece, I asked him for help. "Sure!" he said. "Who's gonna read it?" I said new players and tournament competitors. "No way, man!" he said. "I'm not gonna tell 'em all my secrets! I've earned *some* advantage over them!"

I agree. Some secrets are meant to be discovered rather than shared. Besides, I learned from the best. I can't let out all our trade secrets. Ninja Union Local 151 won't let me.

—RR

"ALL-AMERICAN" THINGS YOU CAN DO TO IMPROVE YOUR GAME

"When you attack, you want to attack from the highest heights of heaven. And when you defend, you want to defend from the deepest resources of the earth."
LAO TZU, THE ART OF WAR

BILL GARDNER: First, we'll talk about individual tactics, then we'll talk about squad tactics and team tactics. When I say individual tactics, I mean aspects of the game that improve the individual's play.

And a lot of this comes down to the simple things. For example, there are different ways to load. Obviously, if you stick your elbow out, it becomes a target. You need to learn how to load with your elbow tucked in. These are the little things that make the difference between winning and losing.

You have to develop certain basic skills. First, you have to learn to shoot. You also have to realize that you're not going to be afforded the opportunity to just aim and slowly pull the trigger. You need to work on your snap shooting—the ability to stay within a bunker, then snap out and shoot a target, and then get back behind cover quickly.

Almost every player that achieves any level of skill in this sport gets comfortable with shooting a target at 40 yards or so with a quick snap and a couple of shots. So, from an individual standpoint, you must work on accuracy.

Then, there are bunker tactics—the ways you work a bunker. During a game you often end up behind some structure, either a speed ball bunker or a stick bunker in the woods.

Never look from the same place twice in a row. You bring your head up at the same place every time, and the other guy watches your head come up at the same spot, two times before. So he aims at that spot. As you bring your head up again the paint is on its way, and you're wet before you know where it came from. So learn to peek around left, take two shots, then peek around right and take two shots. Keep your opponent off guard.

Paintball is an aural game, too. You can hear your opponent's gun go off. You can hear paint fly through the air; it whizzes. So, you can and should use your ears to determine when to come up and where to shoot.

ADAM GARDNER: People get shot just because they stay up too long. They want to watch their paint fly and then yell about it. Remember, you can call for a paint check just as effectively from behind a bunker. You saw the ball far enough on it's path that you have a pretty good idea of whether you were on line or weren't. If you didn't get him, you can adjust.

You want to come up, take your shots and immediately duck down, Inexperienced players watch their paint fly through the air as if that's the best part of the game. When they get a hit, they freak out and make themselves an easy target.

BILL: Blind shooting is another excellent tactic. If you're playing in a wooded field, look beyond your opponent for reference points you can zero in on from a better, protected position, and put paint in that direction. For example, get a fix on a branch right over the guy's head. You have a good chance of getting a hit and you minimize your risk of being shot. That's the beauty of blind shooting.

BILL: Different people are interested in different skills. You have your bunker players. You have your back players. People fall into different categories. They may know their orientation towards playing the back positions, and they'll gravitate towards shooting paint a long distance.

So, instead of running down the field, getting as close as they can to the other players, which is an aggressive, front line mentality, their mentality is..."I don't want to get closer,

Some of the best players we've seen will do strange things in the bunker. They'll kick the right side of the bunker as a diversion, then move left. Meanwhile, everyone's thinking that the player is coming out the right side, so that's where they are looking.

We call this working the bunker. Of course, given your athletic ability, there are only so many things you can do. One of our best players is extremely flexible. With his degree of flexibility, he can work a bunker in ways that other people just can't.

It's also good to be skilled at left-handed shooting; this opens up the entire left-hand side of the bunker. So practice shooting with both your left and right hands.

ADAM G: A lot of people will take the first shot they can get. You need to practice patience. There are times when you're far better off letting a guy get closer, especially if he doesn't know where you are.

When people don't see you, you want to make sure that the first thing they hear is your paint hitting them. Learn to breathe, relax, and be patient... not too patient, though.

I'm going to shoot them at a mile and a half. I'm going to take a ton of paint and just dump it."

If you do this, you're shooting by volume, trying to get one of 50 shots to hit. You have to practice shooting long range targets. I bet a guy here once $10 bucks in one shot I could hit him at 100 yards. I shot one shot and hit him at 100 yards. You can definitely shoot 70–100 yards and eliminate players.

If you wear glasses, get goggles that will hold

the glasses. Better still, wear contact lenses. A lot of people say, "I can't wear contact lenses, they're the most uncomfortable things in the world." In paintball, you'd be amazed at how many people finally wear contacts. When you're out on the field, it makes all the difference in the world.

Now there's a thing called being tight in a bunker. Being tight in a bunker means your elbows aren't sticking out. You tuck your harness around the back so it's not exposed. You bring your knees in. You crawl up underneath sections of the bunker, take the harness off completely and lay it on the ground.

ADAM G: You can even lay flat on your back and watch the paint fly by. It's a lot easier to see it as you're watching it fly over. Find your best angle and determine where the shooter is.

BILL: The back player is exposed to many different angles of shots, and it is imperative that he survive because he's the eyes and ears and the communication center of the team. If he dies, the team's ability to win is significantly compromised.

ADAM G: You have to learn to focus on the most immediate danger. For example: Let's say you have an opponent who's positioned with a couple of trees in between him and you. This makes it hard for him to get a shot. Then, you've got another opponent 30 yards away who can either run at any time and bunker you, or has a clean shot. That's the guy you have to stay focused on. He's the greater threat. If you concentrate on the guy who doesn't

have a very good chance of shooting you, the guy who does will blow you away.

People get impatient and forgetful. They look the other way and get caught up in other action. Before they know it, they're out.

If opponents are getting really close or you know that if one of them pops up and you're not looking, he's going to have a good shot at you, you must focus on the immediate danger. Even if it means just pointing your barrel right at that guy and not moving it. *Remember that you're on a team. Tell your teammates to keep the other guys off you.*

BILL: To summarize, individual tactics and techniques: Know how to shoot, know how to live in a bunker, know how to identify the most dangerous target, be patient. Learn to load, squeegee, and other things you do when you're not shooting so that you don't expose yourself. Be tricky, be sly, and be unpredictable.

SQUAD TACTICS

The next level is *squad tactics.* The first thing that comes into play when you have two people is communication. Great communication is the most powerful tool in paintball.

ADAM G: A lot of new players start off with five men. So, there's five of them and there's five of you. At the start of the game, say you shoot two of their guys off the left and you lose one of your guys.

You see all of this and call out, "21," which means "two of them are dead, one of ours." It also conveys that they lost their guys on the left side.

If you look downfield and see there's two guys on your right and one guy in the center, you know there's a very good chance that they are weak on the left. You can quickly run behind the other team, take them where they're weakest, and win the game.

BILL: People tend to play in squads, just like special forces. The most important element of squad level tactics is coordinated shooting and moving.

Teams come up to me and say, "The time was right, everything was great. We all ran right down to bunker him, and we got killed. What did we do wrong?"

My response is usually, "Well, it's pretty simple. You were all running, no one was shooting."

Only by bringing together the shooting and the moving, do you end up with the squad performance that you're looking for.

One of the hardest things to teach players who are moving from the intermediate recreational level to the beginning of tournament play is that you all can't just move at once.

You have to realize that unspoken versus spoken communication comes with experience and effort. I realize, as I run up to this bunker, he's just going to get me if I take one more step. So, I sit down and start shooting, and Adam comes over and does him from another angle. We win because we act to support one another in scenarios that are familiar to us.

A squad that understands shooting and moving works together like clockwork. You get absolute dominance with that combination.

ADAM G: Making a good squad or team is about developing that level of trust. I've got to trust the fact that my teammate is going to be there dropping and firing when I'm making my move.

BILL: The squad must combine individual tactics, communication and the aggressive, coordinated movement we've been describing. Now, a good squad of three that has excellent movement will do just tremendous damage to an uncoordinated, non-communicating team of five. It's the way teams play together that decides who wins or loses.

Team tactics bring together all the squad tactics. Now you have to make the squads work. And to be honest with you, we struggle with this to this day. Teams that come together with the trust factor, the right mix of people, that understand it all, have perfect faith in each other, and make it happen. They're unbeatable.

It's a constant struggle to develop that chemistry. You don't just find it. It's almost like managing a business. You start by picking people not only for their playing abilities but for their personalities and their ability to motivate other people.

Young teams often ask me "How can we get to be the best team?" My reply is, "Make sure that when you go out and play every weekend, you have fun. Don't pick guys that are jerks." Put people together who will work together, who don't need to be told to be helpful and supportive.

Another team tactic involves learning the fields. You start to walk fields as a team. Identify the vulnerable positions and dominant bunkers. Figure out what positions you need in order to win.

ADAM G: We spend a lot of time learning where we want to be and trying to figure out where the opponents are most likely to be. We want to have a game plan. We want to know in advance how the game should go. It takes work, but it pays off tremendously. Once you set that game plan, all your other tactics start to come together—team, squad, and individual.

BILL: We should mention sweet spots. Sweet spots are situations where there's a really nice offensive or defensive advantage. I remember a time where there were thick pines on both sides of a trail that our opposing team had to run about 35 yards through before they could break out their positions. We lined all 10 guns up on the trail. As soon as the whistle blew, our paint was in the air. Ten guns firing 10 balls a second. We took four out before the game even started. We discovered this sweet spot by walking the field in advance of the game.

Another tactic is to break the opponent's line. When you break lines, Adam's done it very successfully, you can come up behind the other team. You come into their line to shoot them all as if you're one of their players. It happens all the time.

ADAM G: I snuck behind these guys once and two of them turned around and looked at me. They said, thinking I was one of their team: "Hey Jim!"

I went along with their case of mistaken identity and said, "Yeah, what's up?"

"Jim, we got two of them off the front!" They were pretty worked up.

"All right! Way to go!" I replied.

And as they turned back to me I raised my gun and took them out. "Oh, by the way, I'm not Jim." They were shocked!

BILL: And *that* was a team of U.S. Marines!

To wrap this up, I want to quote from a book that I love, *The Art of War* by Lao Tzu. I consider it recommended reading for anyone interested in tactics, even emotional tactics. "When you attack, you want to attack from the highest heights of heaven. And when you defend, you want to defend from the deepest resources of the earth," says Lao Tzu.

I interpret it this way: When you attack, your adrenaline is pumped. You attack with such vigor and force that the enemy cannot defend itself. But, when you defend, you don't take stupid chances. You dig in so deep that there's no way that they can shoot you or eliminate you."

Knowing the Game, Playing to Win

I have always believed that understanding leads to success. Many players play paintball without ever truly understanding the underlying concepts, which is the only way that a person can advance in this sport. As a result of this, many people misinterpret what happens during a game and learn nothing from watching them. Case in point...

After my team, Aftershock, won a game at the World Cup in Orlando, I heard one kid tell his friend, "Oh yeah, you should have seen them. They just mowed the other team down. Aftershock just got up and went at'em. They smoked'em, dude." He was referring to Aftershock winning the game impressively. But he had completely missed the true nature of what had happened. He seemed to be implying that the win was wholly attributable to Aftershock's attack; it wasn't. He couldn't differentiate between what looked dramatic and what had actually transpired.

Witnessing a team dominate and demolish the opposition, without a doubt one of the most exciting and memorable aspects of paintball, sticks in the mind because it is so dynamic. But it does not tell the whole story. Not by a longshot.

The bottom line is that if you want to progress in this sport, you need to learn how to understand what is going on!

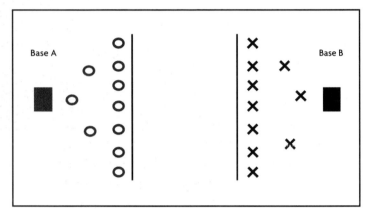

The above illustration is a rough guide to what 99% of tournament paintball teams do when they position themselves at the start of the game. If you look at any tournament game, you will see each team run out to initial positions on the first third of the field, as shown above. The teams will sit in these positions and duke it out until one side gets a few more kills than the other. At that point, the prevailing team will make their move. Only after a significant number of eliminations have been made does the end game unfold. Obviously, the team that gets the most kills in this part of the game normally wins.

Paintball can be broken down, like chess, into three parts: the opening, middle, and the end.

THE OPENING GAME

This is best described as the part of the game where your teammates run out to their primary cover points: the bunkers or trees that you have selected to be your first stopping points.

Now this part of the game, unlike the other two, is completely under your control.

Before the game, your team should have agreed on a selection of bunkers that were not only the

safest to attain, but also provided the best angles for eliminating the opposition.

When the game starts, you should know where you and your teammates are headed, and the path you will use to run to your primary position.

Your team's entry into primary positions should be accomplished without any losses if you have done your prep work correctly.

Having control is important because if you control proceedings then you can predict outcomes (e.g., the victories you aspire to). Without control, you are a hostage to fortune. Luck will smile on you one day and not the next.

With one hundred percent control, you can do whatever you want with no real interference from the other team. But once you get in this position, the middle part of the game begins, and this is where paintball games are won and lost.

THE MID GAME

Ninety-nine percent of paintball games at tournaments follow similar patterns. Both teams run out to their respective primary positions and start firing their guns. As soon as the mid game progresses, people begin to walk off the field.

The stronger team starts picking off the weaker team one by one. This is where the real damage is done. The determinant of who will actually win the game is generally who gets the most kills off the basic line format. This is one of the fundamentals of tournament play.

All tournament teams try to play this way. They run out to their positions, which roughly extend across the width of a field in a line. In this way, all the bases are covered. Both defensive and attacking capabilities can be optimized across all areas of the field.

The basic layout of a field is the length of it divided into three sections. The first third line is where each team lines up. The middle third line of the field is the *killing ground*, and the final third line is where (from your perspective as a player) the opposition resides.

The Mid-Game is the Pivotal Phase

As I alluded to earlier, the perspective of the side line observer is limited because the truly decisive and key eliminations are achieved immediately before the *exciting* finale. Indeed, the reality is that by the time you see five or six tournament players get up and run down the last vestiges of the opponents' defense, the most decisive part of the game is already over. A controllable end game results from a successful mid-game.

Since the mid game is so important, what can we do to make sure that it's successful?

Technique is the answer. If you are better than your opposition technically, then the killing ratio will be in your favor. If not, more of your team members will be eliminated and you will lose control of the end game. Lost control means defeat. Period.

Paintball can appear very complex to many people when it is actually very simple. Once you understand the underlying concepts of it, everything makes sense.

There are no secrets in Paintball; everything is common sense.

THE END GAME

After a successful mid game, the end game should be yours. You began the game in control of your primary positioning. You used your technical prowess to acquire a high killing ratio, which left your opponents at a numeric disadvantage. Now you have control. But it isn't over yet; you still have to take advantage of your supremacy.

Almost everyone has heard of heroic last stands

from players who have killed five or six incoming players alone. It happens, but it shouldn't.

Superiority in numbers should mean victory, but there are exceptions when a field bias will sometimes confer an advantage to the team with fewer players. Not everything always goes exactly as planned in the end game. Sometimes the disadvantaged team wins. This sport is inherently unpredictable, but you must give yourself the best possible chance for success.

These are the basic concepts behind the game, but in order to increase your chances of winning, you must have an idea of the other available styles and strategies.

PLAYING STYLES

There are three basic playing styles in paintball: **defensive**, **technical**, and **aggressive**.

The Technical Style

Historically, the All-Americans exemplify the *technical* approach.

They sit on their line format and eliminate the other team's members with their superior techniques throughout the entire game.

As you watch an All American's game, you will notice a procession of their opponents toward the dead box for no reason other than that the All Americans shot them first. The trick is to do it consistently. That's what they do. If you want this to be your style, then you need to become an extraordinary sharp-shooter, drill regularly, and practice patience.

The Defensive Style

One of the reasons for playing a defensive game is to counter-attack the other team's offensive attacks. It is not very accepted on the tournament circuit because it is seen as a way of compensating for lack of skill and aggression.

Another reason for playing defensively is when the opposing team is believed to be better than your own. It's safer to move only when you are attacked instead of making an offensive move and opening yourself up to trouble.

Only a few teams use this strategy, but I won't mention them, since they might be insulted. So I won't mention Bob Long's Ironmen... but they are getting better! (Just kidding guys!)

The Aggressive Style

This is the most exciting and difficult way to play. It occurs when your team hits the wall of the opposing team, which only happens after significant eliminations have been made. Only two or three teams play this way: Aftershock, four-time World Cup champions, and Bob Long's Ironmen of 1991 to 1994, who were the greatest aggressive team of all time. They attacked with a series of line assaults that could and did break every defense.

KNOWING AND PRACTICING ARE DIFFERENT THINGS

Teams generally acquire their style by default, rather than design, which is a direct consequence of who is on their team. Conservative members play defensively, while eager and slightly crazy members play aggressively. The technical components of each style need to be molded to fit with the technical capabilities of each team. Those who are masterful paintball technicians experience paintball at its most exciting and rewarding. If that's your goal, you are aiming high, and better start practicing now. And now that you know what you have to do, you have no excuses.

—PR

More Than Just A Game

THE REWARDS OF PLAYING PAINTBALL

Jerry Braun Puts Paintball in Perspective

As you have seen, paintball is a game, a sport, a business, an escape, a regimen, an avocation, a corporate training device, a bonding experience, and an all around good time. And still, I would contend, paintball is more than the sum of its parts.

Something about paintball gives a great deal to those who play it. Paintball provides a structure within which players of all ages, backgrounds, physical make-ups, and beliefs can experience the thrill of victory. Its rules are simple and winning is accessible. That's especially important to young people.

Paintball's greatest value comes from what it does for young players. Those who never made the first squad of little league baseball, pee-wee football, or local soccer leagues, who often had to sit on the bench in frustration and embarrassment, can participate and excel in this game. They can score a key elimination, make a sacrifice that helps their team win, and hang the flag to win the game.

In paintball, the recognition, support, and congratulations young people receive from peers build a self-esteem few other activities can foster. To children and their parents, this is where paintball becomes more than just a game.

Travis Jenks takes the flag in front of a cheering crowd at Skyball 1999.

Living His Dream

Diagnosed with a rare form of Hodgkins Disease at the age of 16, Travis Jenks is making the most of every moment and taking nothing for granted. Travis seized the opportunity to play with and against the best players in professional paintball in Toronto at Skyball 1999, an international tournament. The Diggers and their owner Jerry Reilly, Operation Paintball, and Mare Island's owner, Matt Crandle, pitched in airfare for the Jenks family, and the Greater Bay Area Make-A-Wish Foundation made hotel arrangements.

Travis was especially grateful to play alongside his personal paintball hero, Bob Long of the Ironmen. This was not their first meeting. The two met initially at the Mare Island fields in California where Travis had his first chance to play with the Ironmen and the Diggers in a scrimmage planned for him by the Greater Bay Area Make-A-Wish Foundation.

"I'd like to get a nice paintball marker and maybe go play with the Ironmen."

The entire paintball industry has rallied around Travis. Bud Orr donated a 98 Autococker and Bob Long gave him a prototype of his new electronic gun, the "Defiant," and a Signature Series Millennium. The Diggers pitched in with a Centerfire AutoMag (complete with Evolution hopper).

Children who are particularly talented at this game have access to ever increasing levels of difficulty, all the way up to amateur and professional leagues. There are no upper limits for those who seek an extremely challenging competitive experience in this up-and-coming sport.

The game nurtures communication skills, promotes values such as honesty, fair play, teamwork, and goal setting. It also introduces young people to the experience of being decisive, taking risks, and learning from the consequences of their actions. All of this occurs in a safe format and family-friendly atmosphere. In all of these ways, paintball builds character.

Paintball flourishes because it gives so much to its participants in so many different ways. It is an activity that has yet to reach its peak of popularity and its future seems limitless!

The Complete Guide to Paintball

Paintball Glossary

ACTION

1. The mechanism by which something is operated, as that of a gun.
2. A military encounter, as a battle or skirmish.
3. Actual combat with enemy forces.

AGITATOR

1. A machine or device for agitating and mixing.
2. In reference to paintball, it is a device that is attached to a paintball hopper or incorporated into the design of the hopper. It has a shaft that enters the inner enclosure of the hopper with some type of impeller attached to the end of it. When activated the agitator rotates the impeller which moves the paintballs around inside of the hopper allowing them to align with the feed port, located at the bottom of the hopper, and fall freely into the hopper feed nipple.

ASA

The abbreviation for Air Source Adapter. See "ASA Adapter".

ASA ADAPTER

Also referred to as CA Adapter. A device that is designed to allow a constant air tank to screw into it and let the Co_2 gas in the tank pass through it. In most cases, the ASA Adapter is designed with a actuating pin. When used with a constant air tank that has a pin valve, the ASA Adapter pin actuator presses in the pin valve's pin and allows the flow of Co_2 gas from the tank into and through the ASA Adapter. The gas then goes to the paintguns valve mechanism either directly or indirectly via some type of gas line.

AUTO, FULL

Continuous firing and reloading of paintgun as long as the trigger is held down.

AUTO, SEMI

1. Partly automatic.
2. Automatically recocking of paintgun and loading the next paintball but requiring a squeeze of the trigger to fire each shot.

AUTO TRIGGER

A trigger and sear design used with pump action paintguns, that allows the user of the paintgun to have the gun fire each time the pump handle is pulled back allowing gun mechanism to be cocked and then pulled full forward. The gun will fire automatically when pump handle is returned to full forward position each time the pump handle is cycled from front to rear and back as long as the trigger is being held down.

BACK BOTTLE SYSTEM

Refers to a constant air system design whereby the gun's ASA adapter is located at the rear of the paintgun and that is where the constant air tank is attached. The constant air tank is used as the gun's shoulder stock and may or may not have a butt plate attached to it. Pump action paintguns usually have the ASA adapter in-line with the barrel and cocking mechanism. Semi Auto paintguns usually have the ASA adapter in-line with cocking mechanism.

BACK BOTTLE ADAPTER

An ASA adapter which is attached to the rear of a paintgun, that is used to connect a gas supply to the gun and is usually in line with either the barrel/cocking mechanism or just the cocking mechanism.

BARREL PLUG

A safety device that is inserted into the front end of a paintgun barrel to prevent a paintball from exiting the barrel.

BARREL, RIFLED, INTERNAL

A barrel that has internal grooves, either straight or in a spiral pattern.

BOLT

The internal part of a paintgun that is common to Stock, Pump Action and Semi Auto paintguns. The bolt usually has a O-ring(s) at the front end of it. The O-ring acts as a seal between the bolt and the inner wall of the paintgun barrel when the bolt is in the full forward position. The bolt performs two functions

1. It is the device that moves the paintball from where it is loaded into the chamber of the paintgun, to the bore of the paintgun barrel.

2. It is the device by which CO_2 gas is transferred from the paintgun valve system to the rear of the paintball via the front of the bolt.

BOLT (closed)

One of two design criteria by which semi auto paintguns are manufactured. The closed bolt design means that the bolt is in the full forward position with the bolt O-ring sealing against the inner wall of the paintgun barrel when gun is ready to be fired via the trigger. This is with respect to the paintgun being connected to a CO_2 gas supply (constant air tank or remote air system) and fully pressurized.

BOLT (open)

One of two design criteria by which semi auto paintguns are manufactured. The open bolt design means that the bolt is in the full rear position with the bolt just behind the feed nipple port (the port that allows the paintballs to flow into the paintgun body) when paintgun is ready to be fired via the trigger. This is with respect to the paintgun being connected to a CO_2 gas supply (constant air tank or remote air system) and fully pressurized.

BOLT, VENTURI

A bolt with a concave face. The face of the bolt will have multiple holes in it. These holes are known as thrust ports.

BORE DROP LOADING

Guns using bore systems load into a receiver the same size as the barrel or directly into the barrel itself. This keeps the ball from having to load over any large seams or steep angles.

BOTTLE

1. Slang for tank.

2. A portable container for holding liquids or gases, having a neck and mouth.

3. In paintball it is the container part of a constant air tank.

BLOW BACK

Paintball gun's leakage of CO_2 gases between the bolt and the inner barrel wall and/or leakage of CO_2 gases from the cocking mechanism between the gun's hammer and inner wall of the gun's housing. Blowback may occur for two reasons. First, and easiest to fix, is that the O-rings on the gun's bolt and/or hammer need to be replaced. The second reason for blowback is more complex. It has to do with the positioning of the gun's components at the time that the CO_2 gas is released into the gun's barrel.

BOTTOM LINE

A style of constant air system where the ASA adapter is located at the bottom of the paintball gun's grip frame. This ASA adapter is where the constant air tank is connected to the paintgun. The ASA adapter may be designed into the grip frame so as to be part of the grip frame or it may be a after market ASA adapter that is mounted to the bottom of the grip frame. If it is a after market ASA adapter it will have to have a gas line connecting it to the paintgun in order to allow gas to flow from the tank into and through the ASA adapter to the gas line and then to the paintgun.

BREECH DROP LOADING

Guns using breech loading systems load into an area larger than the inner diameter of the barrel. The ball must then be up into the barrel.

BREECH LOCK SYSTEM

A design that prevents the paintgun from being accidentally pumped twice before it is fired once. Breech locking guns must be fired before the gun can be pumped again.

BUTT PLATE

A device that fits on to the end of a tank allowing it to be used as a shoulder stock.

CALIBER

With respect to a paintball the diameter of a circular section. With reference to a paintgun the diameter of the bore of a gun taken as a unit of measurement.

CALIFORNIA STYLE

A style of constant air system developed in California in the late 1980's that consisted of a paintgun, a 'L' shape shoulder stock with a constant air tank holder located on the bottom side of it, a constant air tank of either 7 or 10 ounce in size with a Thermo on/off valve that would be held in the shoulder stock's tank holder and a hose with fittings that would connect the tank to the paintgun.

CARBON DIOXIDE

Also known as CO_2. A colorless, odorless, incombustible gas that has many purposes such as dry ice, the carbonation in carbonated beverages, and in fire extinguishers. CO_2 is present in the atmosphere and formed during respiration. CO_2 is a compound gas made of oxygen and carbon. CO_2 stores it's energy when it is in a liquid state and releases it into a usable force through expansion into a gas. Used in paintguns as a pressurized gas (power source) for shooting paintballs out of the paintgun's barrel. With respect to semi auto paintguns, CO_2 is also used for recocking the paintgun.

CGA

Denotes Compressed Gas Association. Usually used to refer to a cylinder valve outlet connection detailed in the CGA pamphlet V-1.

CHECK VALVE

Allows substance (such as gas, liquid or solids) to flow in only one direction. Once passed the check valve the substance cannot flow back through check valve.

CHRONOGRAPH

Electronic device that measures the speed of an object directed across it.

CO_2

The abbreviation for Carbon Dioxide.

CONSTANT AIR

A terminology developed in California in the late 1980's. It refers to the use of a refillable gas tank that is connected to a paintgun and supplies the CO_2 gas necessary to power the operation of the gun. The term "Constant Air" was derived from the fact that the paintgun would have a prolonged supply of gas and would be able to get 300–1000 shots per tank of gas, depending on size of tank and type of gun. This was opposed to paintguns that used 12 gram CO_2 cartridges and only got 15–25 shots per cartridge on the average.

CRITICAL TEMPERATURE

The temperature above which liquid phase cannot exist.

CRITICAL PRESSURE

The saturation vapor pressure at the Critical Temperature.

CYCLE RATE

Indicates the number of cycles a paintgun can perform per second.

DETENT, BALL

Sometimes called ball stop, anti-doubler, wire nubbin. A device that keeps no more than one paintball from loading into the chamber of a paintgun when the paintgun is executing one cycle. It does this by maintaining the paintball in a stationary position until the paintguns bolt pushes the paintball into the barrel of the gun.

DEW POINT

The temperature and pressure at which the liquefaction of a vapor begins.

DIRECT FEED

A system by which paintballs are fed directly into the paintgun chamber or barrel via a feed nipple. The feed nipple is usually fastened to side of the paintgun at a 45 degree angle. Feed nipples on pump action guns are usually 1" in diameter and feed nipples on semi auto paintguns are usually 7/8" in diameter.

DISK, RUPTURE

A small copper disk in the valve of a tank that is designed to rupture if the pressure in the tank becomes too great. The rupture disk is usually held in place by a safety plug that has vent holes in it.

DONKEY

Slang for ASA Adapter.

DOT

Abbreviation for Department of Transportation whose Title 49, Code of Federal Regulations regulate the movement of hazardous materials.

DOUBLE ACTION

Requiring only one pull of the trigger to cock and fire.

ELBOW

Slang for hopper adapter.

EXPANSION CHAMBER

A device which conditions CO_2 gas by allowing it to expand before it enters the paintgun's valve system.

FEED NIPPLE

Also known as feed port. The feed nipple is a short tube that is connected to the paintgun housing at an angle of 45 degrees. It provides the passage by which paintballs move from the paintball hopper, through the hopper adapter, which attaches to the feed nipple, and into the chamber of the paintgun. Commonly, feed nipples for pump action paintguns are one inch in diameter, while semi auto paintguns have seven eighths inch feed nipples.

FEED PLUG

A plug at the bottom of a power feeder that angles the balls into the feed port. It can also be turned to stop the balls from feeding into your gun.

FEED TUBE

A paintball storage container tubular in form, closed at one end and open at other end with some type of lid covering the opening. When playing paintball the player uses the feed tube to reload his paintgun's hopper.

FEEDER

Slang for hopper.

FILL STATION

An apparatus consisting of at least one valve used for exhausting pressurized fill hose, a fill hose and some type of fill adapter for connecting a constant air tank to one end of the hose. It is used for filling smaller constant air tanks with liquid CO_2 from larger siphon fill tank. The large siphon fill tank is usually 50 to 60 pounds in volume weight.

FITTING, ELBOW, (90 DEGREE)

A fitting that allows the connection of two items at a 90 degree angle to each other. Such as a CA hose to make a ASA adapter or paintgun.

FLAG STATION

With reference to the game of paintball, this is a team's base camp and is the location where a team's flag is kept. It is also the location where a team must return the opposing team's flag in order to win the game.

FLANK

1. The extreme right or left side of an army or fleet.

2. To stand or be placed or posted at the flank or side of.

3. To defend or guard at the flank.

4. To menace or attack the flank of.

FOGGING UP

This refers to those times when a person's breathing and lack of movement will cause the lenses of a persons goggles to fog over, severely reducing visibility.

FORE GRIP

A horizontal grip generally located on the front of a gun. This grip is generally grasped with the players off hand; i.e. the hand not on the trigger frame; to stabilize the gun for shooting.

F.P.S.

Abbreviation for 'feet per second'. This is the standard method in the U.S. for determining the speed at which a paintgun is shooting.

GAS EFFICIENCY

Refers to the amount of shots a gun gets in relation to the amount of liquid CO_2 it uses. Similar to miles per gallon; i.e. getting 350 shots from a seven ounce constant air tank.

GOGGLES

Eye protection worn by players to prevent eye damage. Paintball goggles are specifically designed for the sport of paintball and should not be substituted with goggles made for any other application other than paintball.

GOING LIQUID

Refers to liquid CO_2 entering the paintgun before it has had a chance to expand into a gas or vapor.

GRIPS

Components that fit on the paintgun grip frame and provide surface area by which the shooter may grip the gun. Grips are replaceable on many types of paintguns. Different styles of grips can provide greater comfort and ease of use for the individual paintball player. Different styles of grips include rubber, wood, and wraparound types.

GUPPY

Slang for Hopper feed tube.

HAMMER

Also known as The lower bolt or the striker. This component, when released from the cocked position, strikes the valve assembly and forces it open. When this striking of the valve assembly by the hammer occurs, CO_2 is allowed to pass through the valve assembly from the gas source to the paintgun barrel.

HAMMER (DOWN)

Refers to pulling the trigger, putting paint on someone is a sudden and intense manner, seizing the moment on offense by showering a target with paint.

HAMMER SEAR

The part of a gun that retains the hammer in a fixed position, usually under main spring pressure. When the trigger is pulled by the shooter's finger, it pushes against the sear allowing it to release the hammer and thus allowing the hammer to strike the valve assembly.

HARNESS

The combination of straps, pouches and other parts forming the working gear worn by a paintball player to carry paintball, CO_2 cartridges, tanks, squeegee and anything else he/she requires to play the game of paintball.

HOSE

In paintball a hose is used to transfer gas from one component to another. Such as from a constant air tank to a ASA adapter on a paintgun.

HONE

A tool that is mechanically rotated and has abrasive tip(s) for polishing or enlarging holes to precise dimensions.

HOPPER

A container used to hold paintballs, usually with a lid that covers the opening where the paintballs are loaded into it, and has a feed nipple at it's bottom.

HOSING

Refers to consistent rapid firing. A tactic typically used when pinning down an opposing player.

HYDROSTATIC TEST

A container test required at definite intervals by DOT to determine the wall thickness via measuring elastic expansion. Purpose of the test is to assure the container is safe for continued use.

I.D.

Abbreviation for inner diameter.

IN-LINE CONFIGURATION

Refers to the manner in which the bolt and hammer of a paintgun are positioned in relation to each other. An in-line configuration indicates that the bolt and hammer are in line with each other one behind the other.

LENSES, THERMAL

A dual lens system. The outer lens is made of a super hard polycarbonate material. The inner lens is made of a different polycarbonate composition that allows anti fog jell coat to stick to it. The two lenses are attached to each other by means of a rubber gasket that makes an airtight seal between the two. The space between the two lenses is called a thermal barrier and helps to reduce fogging on the inner lens.

LOADER

Slang for hopper feed tube.

LIQUID

Slang for CO_2 in liquid form.

MUZZLE

The mouth, or end for discharge, of the barrel of a gun, pistol, etc.

MUZZLE BREAK

1. A pattern of holes or slots machined into the end of a barrel that act as exhaust ports.

2. A machined add on part with a pattern of holes or slots machined into it that fastens to the end of a barrel either by press fit or set screw fatteners.

MUZZLE VELOCITY

The speed at which a paintball is traveling when it leaves the muzzle of a paintgun barrel.

NELSON BASED

Refers to pump guns (most pump guns) that were designed after the original 007. Nelson based guns have an in-line bolt and hammer system.

NITROGEN (N_2)

Refers to Nitrogen gas. A colorless, odorless, relatively non-reactive gas which is compressed to high pressures. The difference between Nitrogen gas and CO_2 is that Nitrogen is measured by pressure while CO_2 is measured by weight.

N.P.T.

Refers to normal temperature and pressure which is defined as 700 F and 14.696 PSI.

O.D.

Abbreviation for Outer Diameter. Outer diameter refers to distance across an object.

O-RING

A ring of pliable material, as rubber or neoprene, used as a gasket.

OFFSET SIGHT RAIL

A sight rail that is mounted at an angle away from top dead center of paintgun body. The off set sight rail allows a sight to be mounted so that it is unobstructed by other parts of the paintgun.

PAINTBALL

A round capsule filled with brightly colored water-soluble dye that is designed to break upon impact leaving a splat mark on the object it hits. Paintball sizes are .50 Cal., .62 Cal. and .68 Cal., the last being the most current size and readily available. The .68 caliber paintball offers much better range, accuracy, and breakability due to its' size and mass.

PAINTBALL GUN

A mechanical device, usually powered by CO_2 gas, used to propel paintballs. Sometimes called a marker.

PAINT CHECK

The time at which a player is checked for splat mark(s). A paint check may be called by referee or player, but may be only invoked by a referee and game may only be restarted by referee. Misuse of the paint check rule by a player is cause for that player to be removed from current game.

POWER FEED

A feed nipple design that incorporates the blowback from the paintball gun to increase the rate at which paintballs are fed into the paintgun. Most power feeds are designed into the paintguns, but there are some after market bolt on power feeds available for guns like the VM-68 series of paintgun and others.

POWERLET

An icon developed by the air gun industry for CO_2 cartridge. In paintball, it refers to 12 gram CO_2 cartridge.

PRESSURE REGULATOR

Regulates the pressure of gas flowing through it. Some regulators are preset to psi, and some are adjustable.

PSI

Abbreviation for pounds per square inch.

PULL PIN

A pin fastener which can be removed quickly to speed disassembly of a player's paintgun.

QUICK CHANGER

A device that is either a part of the paintgun or a separate unit that connects to the gun, usually via the ASA adapter. It allows the rapid loading and unloading of a 12 gram CO_2 cartridge.

QUICK DISCONNECT

Usually made of stainless steel or brass, this unit is composed of two parts, a male fitting and a female coupler that connect together to form an airtight connection. In paintball the quick disconnect is used by the player to quickly disconnect the CO_2 source, such as a remote system, from the paintgun.

RECEIVER

The main body of a paintgun where the bolt and hammer are usually housed. A gun's feed nipple is typically a part of your receiver.

REMOTE SYSTEM

Also known as a "Remote" or "Remote Set-Up". The system usually consists of a constant air tank that is carried on the player's body, usually in a pouch or fanny pack, and a high pressure gas line with quick disconnect and all the fittings required to connect it to the paintgun.

RETICLE

A network of fine lines, wires, or the like placed in the focus of the eyepiece of an optical instrument. The crosshairs of a scope.

RIFLING, EXTERNAL

Also know as External porting. With reference to paintball gun barrels, it is a spiral hole pattern which is drilled into the barrel. When a paintball is shot through a ported barrel, the ports allow the air in front of the paintball to escape as the paintball pushes forward. The loss of air restriction in front of the paintball allows the paintball to shoot straighter and further. The barrel porting also breaks up the sound made when the gun is fired, thus the paintgun operates much quieter.

RIFLING, INTERNAL

Grooves or raised points in a barrel that are either straight or spiraled in pattern.

SHERIDAN BASED

Refers to those guns that are based on or are similar to the original Sheridan family of guns. A Sheridan based gun is generally discernible by its stacked design. The hammer and valve system are in the lower section while the bolt is in the upper section.

SIGHT RAIL

Allows the mounting of a sighting system to a paintgun.

SIGHT RAIL, RAISED

A sight rail that is raised up off the body of the gun. The purpose for this is to allow the shooter a better field of view.

SIGHT, RED DOT

An optical sighting device powered by a battery that produces a red dot reticle. Red dot sights do not project a dot on target.

SIGHT RINGS

Adapters to mount your sight to the sight rail. (Note. Different rings are required to mount different sights to different guns.)

SKIRMISH

1. A fight between small bodies of troops.
2. Any brisk conflict or encounter.

SKIRMISH LINE

1. The invisible line between two opposing teams that have confronted each other.
2. A formation taken where by players are positioned beside each other in a line.

SLIMED BARREL

Slang for when a ball has broken in the barrel of a paintgun and coated it with paint. A slimed barrel will not shoot straight.

SPECIFIC HEAT

Amount of heat required to raise a unit mass of substance one degree of temperature at either constant pressure or constant volume. Usually expressed in BTU per pound per degree F.

SPECIFIC VOLUME

Volume of a unit mass of substance at a given temperature. Expressed as cubic feet per pound at 700 F.

SPLATTER

The residue sprayed on a player by a paintball when it makes impact with a object close to that player.

SPRING, MAIN

The spring that drives the hammer.

SPRING VALVE

The spring that closes the valve after it has been opened by the hammer.

SQUAD

Any small group of persons engaged in a common enterprise; a team or sub-group within a team.

SQUEEGEE

A device used to clean the barrel of a paintgun.

STACKED CONFIGURATION

Refers to the manner in which the bolt and hammer are positioned in relation to each other inside the paintgun receiver. A stacked configuration indicates that the bolt and hammer are stacked one on top of the other.

STICK FEED

A gravity feeder, usually made out of PVC material, which holds the balls stacked in a line one on top of the other.

STOCK 'L'

A shoulder stock that is shaped like an 'L' laying on its side. This stock usually fastens to the bottom of the paintgun's grip frame and may have a constant air tank holder attached to it.

STOCK 'T'

A shoulder stock that is shaped like a 'T' laying on its side. This stock usually fastens to the bottom of the paintgun's grip frame and may have a constant air tank holder attached to it.

SUPPRESSOR

A tubular device that is press fitted onto the front end of a paintgun barrel designed to reduce the amount of sound that is made by the gun when it is fired. Also known as Silencer.

TANK, CHILLED

Refers to a tank that has become very cold due to rapid pressure loss. This may be caused by rapid firing or purposefully releasing the remaining air pressure in a tank. (Note, a tank must be chilled before it can be filled with CO_2).

TANK, CONSTANT AIR

A container or structure for holding a liquid or gas. In paintball, a tank is made up from two components, a valve and a bottle.

TANK, ANTI-SIPHON

A tank designed to allow only vaporous CO_2 gas to exit the tank through the tank valve.

TANK, SIPHON

A tank specifically designed to draw liquid CO_2 from the bottom of the tank. This is accomplished by a gas line that is attached to rear end of the tank valve and weighting down the other end of the gas line so that it remains located in the bottom area of the tank.

THREAD SAVER

Also know as Bottle cap. A protective cap that screws onto a tank valve. This keeps the valve from being damaged while not in use.

TOOL, VELOCITY ADJUSTING

Also called Adjusting tool. A tool used specifically for adjusting the velocity of a paintgun.

TOURNAMENT CAP

A cap which covers a gun's velocity adjuster so that the velocity cannot be adjusted during game play, normally required for tournament play.

TRIGGER SHOE

Aftermarket product that fits on the trigger of a gun to provide the trigger finger with more surface area to grip the trigger and comfortable feel.

TWELVE GRAM

Slang for 12 gram CO_2 cartridge.

TUBE, PAINTBALL

A small cigar-like tube used to carry 10 paintballs.

TUNNEL VISION

Refers to a player who has focused so intently on the player or players directly in front of him that he is not aware of players moving to the side of him.

UN (United Nations) Number

The DOT (Department of Transportation) Number found on the Cylinder (bottle) label. For example UN1066, the "UN" prefix to this number indicates that 1066 is recognized throughout the world as identifying nitrogen. Sometimes "NA" (North America) will appear as a prefix. NA numbers are recognized in the USA and Canada.

VELOCITY ADJUSTER

A component of a paintgun (usually a set screw) that when turned in either clockwise or counter clockwise direction will increase or decrease the paintguns muzzle velocity.

VALVE

Any device for halting or controlling the flow of something, such as a gas or liquid, through a pipe, out of a bottle neck, or other passage.

VALVE PORTING

The enlarging or drilling of additional holes in a valve body so that more gas will be released when valve system is opened.

VALVE SYSTEM

All the internal parts in the paintgun which control the flow of gas through the paintgun.

WRENCH, ALLEN

A hexagonal tool which comes in various sizes and is used to turn screw fasteners such as hex or button head screws. They are also used to turn anything that has a hexagonal hole. In paintball they are used to adjust the paintball gun's velocity as well as disassemble it.

Where to Find the Game You Love

A state by state and international listing of fields, manufacturers, distributors and shops involved in the paintball industry.

U.S.A. PLAYING FIELDS & SHOPS

ALABAMA

Advanced Alabama Adventures
7880 Bear Creek Rd.
Birmingham, AL
Contact: Jim Williamson
(205) 967-8661 or (205) 672-2860

Area 51 Paintball
3804 Waverly Pkwy.
Opelika, AL 36801
(334) 741-8613

Banshee Paintball Supply
1623 Navco Rd.
Mobile, AL 36605
(334) 479-0377

Dothan Survival Games
Dothan, AL
(205) 793-8202

High Adventure Outfitters, Inc.
3rd Ave. SE
Cullman, AL 35055
(205) 734-3374

North Alabama Paintball—The
   Kelly Farm
Hwy. 72W, next to Ala. Music
   Hall of Fame
Tuscumbia, AL
Contact: Frank Burns
1305 E. Avalon Ave.
Muscle Shoals, AL 35661
(205) 381-9918

Paintball Pro Shop
7880 Bear Creek Rd.
Sterrett, AL 35243
(205) 967-8661

Paintball Pursuit South
9200 Moody Pkwy.
Odenville, AL 35120
(205) 640-GAME

Paintball South, Inc.
114 Corrine Dr.
Madison, AL 35004
(205) 830-1319

Paintball South, Inc.
Taft, AL
(205) 830-1319

Paintball USA
3926 Moffett Rd.
(field located behind Car Toys,
   Inc.)
Mobile, AL 36618-1256
Contact: Johnny Burnett
(888) 284-3456
(334) 344-0097

Romping Rhino Action Sports
Mobile, AL
(334) 660-9424

Southeast Paintball Sports
7301-A Howell's Ferry
Mobile, AL 36618
(334) 344-4157

Splat Alley, Inc.
705 McKinley Ave.
Huntsville, AL 35801
(205) 539-5959

Tuscaloosa Adventure Sports
13757 Clements Rd.
Cottondale, AL 35453
(205) 553-3055

ARIZONA

Battlezone
1540 W. Hatcher Rd.
Phoenix, AZ 85021
(602) 861-BALL
(602) 861-3337 fax

The Command Post
1432 N. Scottsdale Rd.
Tempe, AZ 85281
(602) 970-6329

Cowtown USA
Carefree Rd. and 99th Ave
Phoenix, AZ

Desert Fox Paintball Outfitters
9651 S. Houghton Rd.
Tuscon, AZ 85747
(602) 574-9232

Paintball Headquarters
1097 W. Prince Rd.

Tucson, AZ 85705
(520) 293-5850
(520) 293-5825 fax
www.paintballhq.com

Paintball Headquarters
Marana Field
5464 E. 29th St.
Tucson, AZ 85711
(520) 750-1174

Payson Paintball
Off Hwy. 87 and Hwy. 260
Payson, AZ
Contact: Peter Dahm
(520) 474-8150

Sportsmen's Center
Building 15423 Garden Canyon
   Rd.
Sierra Vista, AZ 85635

Ft. Hauchuca Military Base
   (visitor's pass available)
(520) 533-7085

Southwest Paintball
   Headquarters, Inc.
Suprise, AZ
Contact: John or Connie
(602) 482-8449

Survival & Army Surplus
15231 N. Cave Creek Rd.
Phoenix, AZ 85032
(602) 482-6663

Urban Encounters
Main and Longmore
Mesa, AZ

Westworld Paintball
2920 W. Thomas Rd.
Phoenix, AZ 85017
(602) 447-8200
(602) 230-BALL

ARKANSAS

Adair Adventures
Searcy, AR
Contact: Scott Adair
268-2909

Black Rain Action Pursuit
P.O. Box 2228

South Arkansas Ave. & 3rd St.
Russellville, Arkansas 72811
Contact: Duke Trimble
(501) 641-7439

Death Valley Games Paintball
22750 W. Spring Harbor Rd.
Siloam Springs, AR 72761
Contact: Dan Ryan
(501) 524-9073

Fantasy Zone Paintball Park
Three Brothers, AR
Just north of Mtn. Home, AR
Contact: Chuck Garner
(501) 445-4026

First Assault
Route 51
Arkadelphia, AR 71923
(501) 245-3549

The Hide Away
Vilonia, AR
(501) 796-2729

Paintball Arkansas
558 Sturgis Rd.
Conway, AR 72032
(501) 470-4400

Paintball Ridge
1141 CR 754
Jonesboro, AR 72401
Contact: Eddie Taylor
(501) 972-8188

Ponchos Wargame
Pottsville, AR
(501) 967-8094

Razorback Paintball Range
PO Box 23
Greenbrier, AR 72058
(501) 679-500

CALIFORNIA

ABC Paintball
535 Salmar Ave., Unit B
Campbell, CA 95008
(408) 866-9222

Action Adventure Sports
Perris, CA
(909) 943-2129

Action Paintball
240 North Broadway
Escondido, CA 92025
(619) 738-1097

Action Paint Ball Games
Intersection of Jackson Hwy. 16
and Lone Rd.
Sacramento/Rancho Murieta,
CA
Contact: Alan or Dave
(916) 366-6212
(916) 214-6212 field

Action Zone
111 Uranium Ave, Unit A
Sunnyvale, CA 94303
(408) 738-BALL

Accu-Rite Paintball Sports
91 N. Daisy Ave.
Pasadena, CA 91107
(626) 577-2603

Advantage Paintball Supplies
1617 E. Ashlan Ave.
Fresno, CA 93704
(209) 228-8899

Adventure Game
3604 Ross Ave.
San Jose, CA 95124
(408) 723-1455

Adventure Game Supply
17618 Sherman Way
Van Nuys, CA 91405
(818) 708-3384

The Adventure Game (T.A.G.)
Santa Cruz Mtns., CA
(408) 262-1100

Adventure Paintball
At River and Kelly Rds. next to
Hatfield State Park
Newman, CA
Contact: Mike Amis
(209) 634-5453

American Canyon Paintball
Jungle, Vallejo, CA 94591
(707) 552-2426
www.paintballjungle.com

A.N.S. Xtreme Performance
3885 Cochran St. #R & S
Simi Valley, CA 93063
(805) 527-5661

ArmyNavy Surplus & Paintball
3885 Cochran, Unit R
Simi Valley, CA 93063
(805) 527-5661

Auction Surplus
512 South Blosser Rd.
Santa Maria, CA 93454
(805) 928-7408

B&M Paintball
605 N. Azusa Ave.
Azusa, CA 91702
(818) 334-0498

Barak El Action Sports
Desert Hot Springs, CA
(760) 324-8131

Battlezone Indoor Paintball
Games
San Pablo, CA
(510) 235-8000

Bear Creek Pursuit Paintball
584 Cestaric Dr.
Milpitas, CA 95035
(408) 946-7676

Borderland Paintball Park
3025 Segovia Way
Carlsbad, CA 92009
Contact: Barry
(619) 536-4257

Bud Orr's Pro Shop
13517 Alondra Blvd.
Santa Fe Springs, CA 90670
(310)-407-2898

Cambrian Surplus
2059 Woodard Rd.
San Jose, CA 95124
(408) 377-6953

Camp & Pack
341 Hiquera
San Luis Obispo, CA 93401
(805) 541-8006

Carpet Bob's American Canyon
Paintball Park
American Canyon/Vallejo, CA
(707) 552-2426

Central Coast Paintball Park
4765 Santa Margarita Lake Rd.
Santa Margarita, CA 93453
(805) 481-1476

Close Encounters
Los Angeles, CA
800-919-9237

Close Encounters Paintball
Games
22400 The Old Road
Newhall, CA 91321
(805) 255-5332
(213) 656-9179
(805) 253-0241 fax

Cobra Paintball
4089-J Oceanside Blvd.
Oceanside, CA 92056
(760)-630-4698

Conquest Paintball Games
Call for directions

North Hollywood, CA
Contact: Dave Bassman
(818) 503-7627

Cresent Supply Co.
801 8th St.
Modesto, CA 95354
(209) 529-3490

Delta Archery's Splat Div
1820-D Arnold Ind. Way
Concord, CA 94520
(510) 685-7141

Diablo Venture Games
Clayton, CA
Contact: Mike Leon
(510) 685-5002

Ditto Police Supply & Paintball
Equipment
330 N. Sixth St., Ste. 106
Redland, CA 92373
(909) 793-4471
(909) 793-6753 fax

Eagles's Nest
P.O. Box 1788
Valley Center, CA 92082
(619) 749-0281

Fields of Fire
Santa Clarita, CA
(805) 297-7948

Fields of Fury
Santa Clarita, CA
Contact: Jed Burns
(805) 944-3011

Fields of Honor
2034 Sycamore Dr.
Simi Valley, CA 93065
(805) 522-3939
Field Location - Sylma

General Jo's Incorporated
9433 Valley Blvd.
Rosemead, CA 91770
(818) 443-0854

Golden West Supply Co.
1536 S. Myrtle Ave.
Monrovia, CA 91016
(818) 357-0711

Gramps & Grizzly
7203 Arlington Ave.
Riverside, CA 92503
(909) 359-4859

The Grant Boys
1750 Newport Beach Blvd.
Costa Mesa, CA 92627
(714) 645-3400
Hidden Valley Paintball Park
Escondido, CA
Contact: Stan Burgis
(619) 737-8870
(619) 737-8877 fax

Hobby World
18575 Valley Blvd.
Bloomington, CA 92316
(714) 824-1747

The HQ Army-Navy Store
1735 Montebello Town Center
Montebello, CA 90640
(213) 727-9852

Indoor Speedball
15000 Avalon
Gardena, CA 90248
(213) 323-1021

I & I Sports Co., Inc.
1524 W. 178th St.
Gardena, CA 90248
(310) 715-6800

I & I Sports Co., Inc.
15349 A Los Gatos Blvd.
Los Gatos, CA 95032
(408) 358-9774
(408) 358-9864

I & I Sports Co., Inc.
18232 E. Gale Ave.
Industry, CA 91748
(626) 810-5523

I & I Sports Co., Inc.
2957 S. Sepulveda Blvd.
Los Angeles, CA 90064
(310) 444-9988

I & I Sports Co., Inc.
19751 S. Fugueroa St.
Carson, CA 90745

I & I Sports Co., Inc.
5637 Cottle Rd.
San Jose, CA 95123
(408) 224-6800

J&J Paintball
Visalia, CA
(209) 636-3128

J&S Surplus
Hwy. 1 & Struve Rd.
Moss Landing, CA 95039
(408) 724-0588

Indoor City Paintball
Gardena, CA
(213) 323-1021

Jungle Island Paintball
Canyon Lake, CA
(909) 244-0989

Jungle Supply
2840 E. College
Visalia, CA 93292
(209) 636-3128

Kingsmen Shop
201 North Hill St.
Oceanside, CA 92054
(619) 722-5108

Finding Paintball

Lion's Den
Temecula, CA
Contact: Fred Will
(909) 696-1116

Magic Carpet Bob's
Vallejo, CA
(707) 552-2426

Mare Island Paintball Games
Mare Island/ Vallejo, CA
Contact: Mike Sinatra
(707) 586-9577

Maximum Paintball Supply.
4741 N. Blackstone Ave.
Fresno, CA 93726
(209) 222-3814

Mr. Paintball
525 N. Andreasen Dr., Suite C
Escondido, CA 92029
(760) 737-8870

North County Paintball
San Marcos, CA 92069
(619) 440-5944
(619) 273-4444

Ontario Paintball
505 Holt (Inside Glass Shop)
Ontario, CA 91762
(909) 391-8866

Operation Paintball
Hayward, CA
(510) 783-2011

Outdoor World
1440 41st Ave.
Capitola, CA 95010
(408) 479-1501

Outdoor World
3903 Santa Rita Rd.
Pleasanton, CA 94566
(510) 463-3221

Outdoor World
222 N. Freemont St.
Montery, CA 93940
(408) 373-3615

Pacific Paintball Supply Inc.
119 College Ave., Suite 1
Santa Rosa, CA 95404
(707) 571-1077

Paint Tag of Woodstalk
Santa Cruz, CA
(408) 429-9355

Paintball Adventures
Corner of Kelly and River Rds.
Newman, CA
Contact: Mike Amis
(209) 634-5453

Paintball Central
Modesto, CA
(209) 825-9155

Paintball Daze
11318 Maze Blvd. (Hwy 132)
Modesto, CA

Paintball Games by Dean's
2751 Mariposa Ave.
Chico, California 95926
Contact: Dale or Carry Dean
(916) 345-0832

Paintball Industry Magazine
800 Traction Ave., #18
Los Angeles, CA 90013
(213) 625-7275

Paintball Outpost
Riverside, CA
(888) 602-0535

Paintball Paradise
260 Shotwell St.
San Francisco, CA 94110
(415) 552-5335

Paintball Plus
1715 G. St.
Merced, CA 95340
(209) 725-3341

Paintball Sam's
Sacramento, CA
(916)-482-GAME
(916) 482-4299 fax

The Paintball Store
2085 River Rd., Unit E
Norco, CA 91760
(714) 279-9069

Palmer's Pursuit Shop
3951 Development Dr.,
Unit #3
Sacramento, CA 95834
(916) 923-9676

Pit Stop Hobbies
1613 Colorado Blvd.
Eagle Rock, CA 90041
(323) 254-7300

Planet Paintball
Lake Elsinore, CA
(909) 279-7879

Predator Marketing
4626 Watt Ave.
Sacramento, CA 95660
(916) 482-4263

Prime Time Paintball Club
Vallejo, CA
(415) 583-2406

R & R Paintball World
Bear Creek Rd.
Santa Cruz Mtns., CA
(408) 445-8110

San Diego Weekend Warriors
El Cajon, CA
(619) 445-1217

San Diego Paintball Supply &
Park
2819 Central
San Diego, CA 91977
(619) 464-7372 - Store
(619) 589-1002 - Field

S. C. Village
Corona, CA
(714) 489-9000

Skan-Line Game Supply
1677 Superior Ave., Unit H
Costa Mesa, CA 92627
(714) 645-LINE

Skirmish Inc.
7117 Canby Ave.
Reseda, CA 91335
(818) 705-6322

Spotcha Paintball
828 N. 2nd St.
El Cajon, CA 92021
(619) 448-0247

Straight Shot Paintball
17359 Main St.
Hesperia, CA 92345
(760) 244-4029

Strategic Game Supply
10680 Katella Ave.
Anaheim, CA 92804
(714) 772-6422

Surplus City
4106 Franklin Blvd.
Sacramento, CA 95820
(916) 485-1120

Survival Sports
4800 Minnesota Ave.
Fair Oaks, CA 95628
(916) 965-1770

Tagline
9077 Arrow, Rte. 100
Cucamonga, CA 91730
(909) 481-7753
(909) 481-7754 fax

Target Zone Paintball Field
5750 Herring Rd.
Arvin, CA 93203
Contact: Carl or Carolina
(805) 854-6446

T.A.S.O. Adventurer's Supplier &
Outfitters
15950 Downey Ave.
Paramount, CA 90723
(310) 531-0515

Unique Sporting
10680 Katella Ave.
Anaheim, CA 92804
(714) 772-6422

Urban Quest
Gonzales Rd.
Oxnard, CA 93033
(805) 986-8802

Valley Aerospace Mfg., Inc.
9155 Alabama
Chatsworth, CA 91311
(818) 718-6280

Valley Gun Shop
2728 Chester Ave.
Bakersfield, CA 93301
(805)-325-9468

Velocity Paintball
4248 B Bonita Road
Bonita, CA 91902
(619) 470-3533

Velocity Paintball
12623 Poway Rd.
Poway, CA 92064
(619) 513-2778

Video Depot
2800 Childress St.
Anderson, CA 96007
(916) 365-3376

Warped Sportz
11919 W. Pico Blvd.
Los Angeles, CA 90064
(310) 914-9222, 914-9511 fax

Weekend Warriors
621 El Cajon Blvd.
El Cajon, CA 92020
Contact: Tim
(619) 445-1217
 Field is located in Alpine, CA

West Coast Paintball
Bakersfield, CA
(805) 391-0988

Wild Woody's in Paintball Games
35521 Hwy. 78
Julian, CA 92036
(760) 941-0230

Woodstalk
Santa Cruz Mountains
South of San Jose, CA
(408) 429-9355

COLORADO
Adventure Game
425 Thames Dr.
Colorado Springs, CO 80906
(303) 893-4263

Finding Paintball

Dragon Man's Paintball Park
1225 Dragon Man Dr.
Colorado Springs, CO 80929
(719) 683-2200

Front Range Paintball, Inc.
Hwy. 36 and St. Vrain Rd., On Elk
   Mtn. Ranch
Boulder, CO
(303) 438-1179
Mailing address:
P.O. Box 1086
Broomfield, CO 80038

Indoor Adventure Games
615 N. Chelton
Colorado Springs, CO 80909
Contact: Jim Jarvis
(719) 570-6000
(303) 771-8665

Outdoor Adventure Games
5960 W. Airport Rd.
Sedalia, CO 80135
Contact: Jim Jarvis
(719) 570-6000
(303) 771-8665

The Paint Pellet Game
6543 Zinnia St.
Arvada, CO 80004
(303) 422-6025

PaintBall Adventures
5300 Brighton Blvd.
Denver, CO
(303) 297-9431

Paintball Colorado
210 South Peak Lane
Boulder, CO 80302
(303) 440-4833

Pig Pen Paintball
Denver, CO
(303) 576-8660

Pro-Star Sports
P.O. Box 1280
Littleton, CO 80160
(303) 972-4113

Rocky Mountain Pball
108 E. Mill St.
Colorado Springs, CO 80903
(719)-473-3725
(719) 473-3576 fax

RMT Sports
P.O. Box 1280
Littleton, CO 80160
(303) 972-4113

Sgt. Splatter's Paintball Inc.
215 W. 24th
Rifle, CO 81650
(970) 625-1506

Warped Sportz
3970 S. Broadway
Englewood, CO 80110
(303) 806-9721

CONNECTICUT
Hogan's Alley Paintball
445 State St.
North Heaven, CT 06473
(203) 288-2746

Maslars Paintball Supply
594 W. Main St.
Waterbury, CT 06702
(203) 757-1760

Meriden Trading Post
998 N. Colony Rd.
Meriden, CT 06450
(203) 237-5199

New England Air Games
132 Black Ash Rd.
Oakdale, CT 06370
Contact: Mike Brycki
(203) 848-8598

Outdoor Adventure Games
Maslar's Pawnshop
Waterbury, CT 06704
(203) 757-7961

Outdoor Action Games
run by Masler's Pawnshop
Waterbury, CT 06704
(203) 596-7502

Paintball Playground
179 Reaching Hill Rd.
Winsted, CT 06098
Contact: Bob Rollins
(203) 379-1673
Toll Free in CT. 1-800-352-4762
1-800-FLAG-SNAG

Paintball Unlimited
169B Main St.
Deep River, CT 06417
(860) 526-1532

Prospect Paintball
Prospect, CT
(203) 758-6272
(203) 757-4845

Strategy Plus
P. O. Box 760
Bethel, CT 06801
(203) 489-9969

Strategy Plus
East Hampton, CT
Mailing address:
P.O. Box 760
Bethel, CT 06801
(800) 952-9007 (in CT)
(203) 775-2029 (outside CT)

Tactical Paintball
Bromica
South Kent, CT 06785
(203) 927-3123
by reservation only

Ted's Players P.B. Connection
Colchester, CT
(860) 537-3949

The Gun Rack
Thompson, CT
(860) 928-1512

DELAWARE
Paintball Adventure Games of
   Delaware
Off I-95 in Newark area
(302) 234-1735

Paintball Adventures LLC
1438 Woodmill Dr.
Dover, DE 19904
(302) 736-5777

Splatzone
550 Jackson Ditch Rd.
Harrington, DE 19952
Contact: Terry Wheatley
(302) 934-7794
Contact: Tom Carroll
(302) 398-9475
 has pro shop

Survival Games of Delaware
Off Rte. 40
Glassgow, DE

FLORIDA
Action Adventure Games
Miramar, FL
(305) 966-1020

Adventure Games Paintball Park
Zephyrhills, FL
Contact: John Gross
(813) 538-9946
E-mail: P8ntDragon@aol.com

Adventure Zone
Hollywood, FL
(305) 752-5218

All-Terrain Paintball
Ocala, FL
(813) 695-1715

Augsbach's Paintball Park
Lithia Springs, FL
(813) 937-2640

Ballbreaker, Inc.
2121 NW Hwy. 19
Crystal River, FL 34428
(352) 564-9140

Bullseye Paintball Court, Inc.
Behind Walmart in Port St. Lucie
3737 SE Jennings Rd.
Port St Lucie, FL 34952
(407) 340-2033
(407) 337-0060

Cobra Command, Inc.
Retail store: Lansdale,Pa.
Field: Tyson Rd., N. of Rte. 73 &
   Rte. 113
Lansdale, Pa.
(215) 855-7252

Dare Devils Paintball Inc.
4506 Del Prado Blvd.
Cape Coral, FL 33904
(941) 542-2272

Elite Forces Field
Cowcreek Rd.
Edgewater, FL
(904) 767-2131

Extreme Rage All Sports
3598 Fowler St.
Ft. Myers, FL 33901
(941) 939-0911
(941) 939-5141 fax

First Coast Indoor Paintball
8159 Arlington Expy., Suite 7
Jacksonville, FL 32211
(904) 262-2397

Florida Paintball Center
8440 Ulmerton, #500
Largo, FL 34641
(813) 538-9946

GI Jeff's
5257 S. Ridgewood Ave.
Allandale, FL 32123
(904) 767-2131

G&H Sterling, LTD.
8362 Pines Blvd., #290
Pembroke Pines, FL 33024
(305) 438-7571

Guerrilla Games
111 W. Olympia Ave.
Punta Gorda, FL 33950
(813) 627-8865

Hi-Tec Paintball Park
P.O. Box 301
Bradenton, FL 34206
(941) 746-5866

Holly Army Navy
3440 Ave. G, N.W.
Winter Haven, FL 33880
(813) 967-5920

Hurricane Paintball
Orlando, FL
(407) 352-5819

Jungle Games Paintball
Off of Livingston on
  Robertson Trail
Lutz, FL
Contact: Buck Gould
(813) 937-1755

Maniacs Home Field
W. Palm Beach, FL
(407) 582-7327

Mark's Pro-Shop
1718 N. Goldenrod Rd., #1
Orlando, FL 32807
(407) 380-1164

Orlando Paintball
Orlando, FL
(407) 294-0694

Paintball City, Inc.
7215 Rose Ave. (Off NOBT)
Orlando, FL 32810
(407) 294-2627

Paintball Experts
70 W. 49th St.
Hialeah, FL 33012
(305) 823-6892

Paintball Paradise
Panama City, FL
(904) 784-7928

Paintball Park
8240 Durrance Rd.
Ft. Myers, FL
(941) 939-0911
(914) 598-1015

Paintball World
2701 Holiday Trail
Kissimmee, FL 32741
(407) 396-4199

Paintball World
Orlando, FL
(407) 239-4199
www.paintball-world.com

Palm Beach Paintball
W. Palm Beach, FL
(407) 439-0755

Predator Field
Haverhill & Bowman (just North
  of Lake Worth Rd.)
Lake Worth, FL 33463
(407) 439-0755

Pursuit Paintball Games
5132 Conroy Rd., #918
Orlando, FL 32811
(407) 843-3456

Regal South Gold & Gun Pawn
712 E. Venice Ave.
Venice, FL 34292
(491) 485-6360

Rocky Creek Paintball
Gainesville, FL
(352) 371-2092

South Florida Paintball
7232 SW 8th St., Suite 2
Miami, FL 33144
(305) 412-9991

South Florida Paintball
  Adventures
Florida Sports Park
Naples, FL 33999
Contact: Bob McInnis or Shelley
  Brown
(941) 890-1736

South West FL Action Games
Ft. Myers Beach, FL
(813) 466-3600

Splat Attack Corp.
10129 SW 72nd St.
Miami, FL 33173
(305) 412-9991

Splatter Paintball
306 Big Tree Rd.
S. Daytona, FL 32119
(904) 760-0043

Sunny's at Sunset
Sunrise, FL 33322
(305) 741-2070

Survival City
111 W. Olympia Ave.
Punta Gorda, FL 33950
(813) 639-1100

The Survival Zone Paintball Park
P.O. Box 1174
Ocala, FL 34478-1174
Contact: Patrick Miley
(904) 591-4330
(904) 591-1867 fax
E-mail: szpp@aol.com

SWFL Action Games
18400 San Carlos Blvd.
Ft. Myers, FL 33931
(813) 466-3600

Tactical Edge Paintball
90 Spirit Lake Rd.
Winter Heaven, FL 33880
(914) 401-8221

Tallahassee Paintball Sports
3931 Wiggington Rd.
Tallahassee, FL 32303
Contact: Mark
(904) 562-6512

Thunder Bay Paintball
Tampa, FL
(813) 891-GAME

Tropic Trades
9696 SW 40th St.
Miami, FL 33165
(305) 221-1371

Wayne's World of Paintball
Ocala, FL
(352) 591-4330

Xtreme Paintball
Sunrise, FL
(954) 749-0857

Xtreme Paintball
I-95 to SR 84 W., 1/4 mile on left
Hollywood, FL
(954) 564-5451

GEORGIA
A-1 Pball Forest & Supply
Pine Chapel Rd.
Calhoun, GA 30701
(706) 602-1797
(706) 602-0330

The Annihilation Zone
Culloden, GA
(912) 885-2492

Appalachian Paintball
1116 S. Thornton Ave.
Dalton, GA 30720
(706) 226-1765

Arkenstone Paintball
3292 Cedarcrest Rd.
Acworth, GA 30101
(770) 974-2535

Bay's Paintball
501 Eve St.
Augusta, GA 30904
(706) 733-1055

Big Bear Mountain Paintball
Ellijay, GA
(770) 926-4681

Club Paintball
502 Stell Rd.
Woodstock, GA 30188
Contact: Christy Meehan
(770) 516-1372

Georgia Paintball
1289 Roswell Rd.
Marietta, GA 3062
(770) 971-8040

Impact Paintball Sports
(mailing address)
1709A Gornto Rd., Suite 222
Valdosta, GA 31602
Contact: Paul or AJ
(912) 244-9306

Indoor Paint Games
285A Lake Mirror Rd.

Forest Park, GA 30050
(404) 361-6740

North Georgia Air Games
Rome, GA
(770) 235-1508

Outer Limits
220 Holbrook Dr. SW
Rome, GA 30165
(706) 234-9896

Paintball Atlanta
608 Holcomb Bridge Rd.,
  Suite 520
Roswell, GA 30076
(404) 594-0912

Paintball Atlanta North
GA400, Exit 12
Cumming, GA
(770) 594-0912

Paintball City
Hinesville, GA
(912) 876-6305

Patterson Paintball
446 Callie Jones Rd.
Chatsworth, GA 30705
(706) 517-3080

Prime Time Paintball
Peachtree, GA
(770) 599-1485

Prime Time Paintball
Jct. Hwy. 85 & Hwy. 16
Senoia, GA 30276
(404) 599-1485

Rome Paintball
1672 Big Texas Valley Rd.
Rome, GA 30165
(706) 291-6179

Splat Zone Indoor
5050 Jimmy Carter Blvd.
Norcross, GA 30093
(404) 441-9333

Wildfire Paintball
1989 Tucker Ind. Rd.
Tucker, GA 30084
(770) 493-8978

Wildfire Paintball
7301 Campbellton Rd.
Atlanta, GA 30331
(770) 493-8978

Wildfire Paintball
2641 Hesterton Rd.
Madison, GA
(770) 493-8978

Wildfire Paintball
2191 Rabbit Hill Cr.
Dacula, GA 30211
(770) 493-8978

Finding Paintball

HAWAII
D&D Paintball
P.O. Box 643
Kula, HI 96790-1424
(808) 572-1424

Island Paintball Sports, Inc.
Kualoa Ranch, Windward
Oahu, Hawaii
(808) 525-1854
(808) 732-4279 fax

Survival Game Hawaii
Oahu, HI
(808) 948-2900

Xlent Services
P.O. Box 2271
Ewa Beach, HI 96706
(808) 671-1110

IDAHO
Aktion Zone Paintball
Boise, ID
(208) 424-0775

Aktion Zone Paintball
Athol, ID
(208) 424-0775

Dye Hard Paintball Supply
P.O. Box 3242
Moscow, ID 83843
Contact: Bryan Broocks & Clif
    Marr
(208) 882-3398

Escape Games
905 S. 5th
Pocatello, ID 83201
(208) 234-7241

Paintball Adventure Games
Meridian, ID
(208) 887-7707

Paintball Sports
37 E. Broadway Ave.
Meridian, Idaho
(208) 888-7707

S & F Paint Ball Style
345 W. Custer
Pocatello, Idaho
(208) 234-1038

Splatagory Paintball Range and
    Supply
503 W. 19th St.
Idaho Falls, ID 83402
(208) 522-1556

Winder's War Zone
5515 E. Iona Rd., P.O. Box 132
Iona, ID 83427
(208) 523-2475

ILLINOIS
Action Games, Inc.
Ottawa , IL
(630) 554-2555

Action Games, Inc.
P.O. Box 2934
Naperville, IL 60567
(630) 554-2555

Air America
2275 S. Mt. Prospect Rd.
Des Plaines, IL 60018
(847) 297-4020

Bad Boyz Toyz
888 S. Rte. 59, #104
Naperville, IL 60565
(708) 355-8808

Bad Boyz Toyz
17913 Torrence Ave.
Lansing, IL 60438
(708) 418-8888

Bad Boyz Toyz
15160 LaGrange Rd.
Orland Park, IL 60462
(708) 460-1122

Bad Boyz Toyz Skokie
7136 Carpenter Rd. #700
Skokie, IL 60077
(708) 679-9125

Badlandz Paintball
Crete, IL
(708) 418-3335

Challenge Games
Joliet, IL
(815) 729-1332

Challenge Park
Wilmington, IL
(815) 729-1343
www.challengepark.com

Champion Paintball
Raleigh, IL
(618) 268-4473

The Chilli Paintball Pits
21324 N. Benedict
Chillicothe, IL 61523
(309) 274-5251

Chicago Paintball Factory
1001 W. Van Buren
Chicago, IL 60607
(312) 563-1777

Circle T Paintball Field, Inc.
RR 1 Hwy. 24 S.
Lewistown, IL 61542
(309) 547-2808
(309) 547-5730
(309) 547-7440 fax

Country Club Paintball
537 W. 195th St.
Glenwood, IL 60425
(708) 756-1165
(708) 756-1178 fax

Direct Connect, Inc.
527 W. Taft Dr.
S. Holland, IL 60473
(708) 331-8878
(708) 331-8936

Eagle Ridge Paintball
Clinton, IL
(217) 935-5572

Fox River Paintball Sports
1891 N. Farnsworth
Aurora, IL 60505
(630) 585-5651

Friendly Fire
Bloomingdale, IL
(708) 924-9924

Gotcha Paintball
3714 Old Chatam Rd.
Springfield, IL 62704
(217) 698 0140

Great Adventure Paintball
803 6th St.
Charleston, IL 61920
contact: Bernard Borah
(217) 345-2730

Lost Woods Paintball Field
Mailing Address:
2712 Pine Ave.
Mattoon, IL 61938
Contact: Ben Dowell
(217) 234-6300

Mid-America Paintball Sports
Greenville, IL
(618) 664-3230

Midwest Adventure Games Inc.
1605 W. 1st Ave., Rte. 6
Coal Valley, IL 61240
(309) 799-5200

Operation Paintball
15N850 Brier Hill Rd.
Hampshire, IL 60140
(708) 736-9107
(630) 736-9132 fax

Paintball Blitz
Gurnee, IL
(847) 297-4021

Pursuit Adventure
956 S. Bartlett Rd., Suite 282
Bartlett, IL 60103
(630) 736-910
(630) 736-9132

Pursuit Marketing, Inc.
1945 Techney Rd., Unit 6
Northbrook, IN 61866
(217) 893-0595
(217) 893-1457

Rockford Paintball Games
Mailing Address:
814 Colonial Dr.
Machesney Park, IL 61115
Field is in Byron, IL

Silent Impact
Urbana, IL
(217) 355-8722

SplatterBall
C/O Strategic Pursuit
P.O. Box 993
St. Charles IL 60174
(708) 897-1681
(708) 897-6681 fax

Splatters Indoor Paintball
Corner of Spring & Galena
Freeport, IL 61032
(815) 233-4567

Strange Ordnance
914 Greenwood Ave.
Glenview, IL 60025
(708) 998-8312

Sudden Impact
County Rd. 36, near Funks Grove
RR1, Box 186B
McLean, IL 61754
(309) 874-3338

Timber Games
40 Borchers Center
Decatur, IN 62521
(217) 429-1910

Tops Paintball
Chicago, IL
(312) 735-6053

Video Smideo
10408, Rte. 47
Huntley, IL 60142
(847) 669-3225

Wacky Warriors
Belleville, IL
(314) 296-0964
(314) 296-9319 fax

Wargames West
Saint Anne, IL
(815) 932-1968

Woodland Paintball Park
21740 Lincoln Hwy.
Lynwood, IL 60411
(708) 895-9490

Wyld Side Sports Inc.
2308 Charles St.
Rockford, IL 61104
(815) 398-7733

Your Supply Depot, Ltd.
632 Algonquin Rd. #100
Des Plaines, IL 60016
(847) 640-7774
(847) 640-7782 fax

INDIANA
Action Park Paintball
Harrison Rd.
Osceloa, IN
(219) 674-GAME

Adventure Game Paintball
Indianapolis, IN
Contact: Jim Morgan
(317) 356-5111

Adventure Zone
8641 E. 116th St.
Fishers, IN 46038

Blast Camp
608 Third St.
Hobart, IN 46342
(219) 947-7733

Blast Camp
109 9th St.
Michigan City, IN 46360
(219) 879-9499

Blast Factory
100 E. North St.
Kokomo, IN 46901

Dark Armies
2525 N. Shadelands Ave. (I70 &
I465)
Indianapolis, IN 46219
(317) 353-1987
(800) 25SPLAT
(800) 257-7528

Fantasy Fields Paintball
P.O. Box 194
Denver, IN 46926
(765) 985-3068

Gator Joe's Paintball Supplies
8180 Country Club Pl.
Indianapolis, IN 46214
(317) 247-0410

Gator Pit
Near Brazil, IN
Contact: Gator Joe's Paintball
Supplies
8180 Country Club Place
Indianapolis IN 46214
(317) 271-8050

Indianapolis Army & Navy
6032 E. 21st

Indianapolis, IN 46219
(317) 356-0858

Michiana Paintball Club
59961 S. Main St.
South Bend, IN 46614
(219) 291-9462

The Mill Paintball Game
8990 Gore Rd.
Bloomington, IN 47403
(812) 824-8125

Northern Indiana Paintball
755 N. Hartman
Nappanee, IN
(219) 773-3233

Paint Ball Sports
7800 S. Anthony Blvd.
Ft. Wayne, IN 46816
(219) 447-3379

Paintball Fun
2690 Breckenridge Rd.
Corydon, IN 47112
(812) 952-3580

Paintball Park
1400 Estella Ave.
Ft. Wayne, IN 46803
(219) 749-1022

Paintball Splat Attack, Inc.
734 S. Lincoln Blvd.
Marion, IN 46953
(765) 674-6563
(765) 651-0750

Paintball USA
Fort Wayne, IN
(219) 422-8801

Paintball Valley
2620 Valley Branch Rd.
Nashville, IN 47448
(812) 988-7750

Pat's Surplus
40 W. Washington St.
Martinsville, IN 46151
(317) 349-1133

River City Paintball
Fort Wayne, IN
(219) 424-7626

River Valley Combat Paintball
Games, Inc.
10013 W. River Valley Rd.
Yorktown, IN 47396
Contact: Larry Stevens
(317) 759-7123
E-mail: paintbal@indy.net

Sheerwood Forest
La Porte, IN
(219) 324-5551

The Splatter Zone
620 S. Capitol Ave.
Indianapolis, IN 46225
(2 blocks South of the RCA
Dome)
(317) 262-8838

Tippmann Pneumatics, Inc.
3518 Adams Center Rd.
Fort Wayne, IN 46203
(219) 749-6022

Ultimate Challenge
Napanee, IN
Contact: Steve Smith
402 W. Waterford St.
Wakarusa, IN 46573
(219) 862-4172

Wild West PB Warehouse, Inc.
708-C N. Earl Ave.
Lafayette, IN 47904-2715
(765) 447-2012

IOWA
Action Jack's Paintball Park
5415 SE Vandalia Rd.
Des Moines (Pleasant Hills), IA
(515) 964-6714

B & S Paintball
Council Bluffs, IA
(712) 323-3742

Betts & Sons True Value
Hardware & Surplus
412 E. Locust St.
Des Moines, IA 50309
(515) 243-7123

Best Shot Ghost Town &
Paintball Park
(Bordering Bankston Park)
Dubuque, IA 52002
Contact: Pat O'Toole
(319) 582-9827

Black Hawk Paintball
Gilbertville, IA
Contact: Adam Myers
(319) 266-9072

Cedar Rapids Paintball
Cedar Rapids, IA
(319) 362-6390

Combat Zone of America
Tiffin, IA
(419) 447-8424
Ducks Blind Woodland Adv. Park
Davenport, IA
(319) 323-7601

Green Valley Paintball
Williamburg, IA
(319) 668-2477

I C U Paintball Field & Pro Shop
404 43rd Place
Norwalk, IA 50211
(515) 981-0201

MM&S Paintball
45 min. NW of Cedar Rapids
Vinton, IA
Contact: Matt Dulin
(319) 443-2274

North Iowa Arms
810 N. 8th St.
Clear Lake, IA 50428
(515) 357-3545

Strategic Sports Paintball Games
1609 Washington St.
Davenport IA 52804
(319) 322-0849

Team Products Paintball
1102 E. Davenport St.
Iowa City, IA 52245
Contact: Jerry Gerard
(319) 337-3629
http://members.gnn.com/jgerar
d/tmprdcts.htm
E-mail: jgerard@gnn.com

KANSAS
Adventure One, Inc.
Wichita, KS
(316) 522-5466

Blaster's Paintball Field
(2 miles West and 1 mile South
of Clearwater)
Wichita, KN
Contact: Scott or Wendy
(316) 264-5443

The Drop Zone Paintball
(3 miles South of Hwy. 56 on
Douglas County Rd. 1029)
Lawrence/Topeka/Kansas City,
KS
Contact: Ken (owner) or staff
(913) 841-1884

The Edge Paintball Park
4100 N Tyler
Wichita, KS 67501
(316) 663-3147

K/T Paintball
West of 169 South end of Old
Willow St
Coffeyville, KS 67337
Contact: Kent or Toad
(316) 251-6049 or (316) 251-1149

Krazy Kris' Paintball Field
Riley KS
Contact: Ralph Bogear
948 Crant Ave Lot #125
Junction City, KS 66441
(913) 238-5796

Lone Wolf Paintball
102nd & Donohoo Road
Kansas City, KS
(913) 334-0001 shop
(913) 522-9630 Field

Relentless Pursuit Pball
125 So. West St., Ste. 117
Wichita, KS 67213
(316) 945-5522

Shadowlands Paintball
Emporia, KS
(316) 343-4854

Timberlake Paintball
California Rd
Williamsburg KS 66095
Contact: Sam Smock
(913) 746-8853
(316) 341-9202
Smocksam@ESUVM1.EMPORIA.E
DU

Tullis Splatterball
Hwy 92 (Kansas City Area)
McClouth, KS
Contact: Gary or Chris Tullis
(913) 796-6393
temudjinn@aol.com

Victory Paintball
95th & Renner Blvd.
Lenexa, KS 66212
913-397-0966

KENTUCKY
American Paintball Games
8471 US 42, Box #6
Florence, KY 41042
888-440-1088

B & H Paintball
4245 Lexington Rd.
Bourbon Square Shopping
  Center
Paris, KY 40361
606-987-7701

Black Mountain Paintballers
Lynch, KY
606-589-5072

Blast Paintball Games
Lexington, KY
606-269-1204

Conder's Army Surplus
813 Hawkins Dr.
E-Town, KY 42701
502-765-4517

Eagle Army-Navy/
Combat Encounters
1609 Bardstown Rd.
Louisville, KY 40205
502-458-ARMY

Jimmy Elliott Firearms
Box 156, Poorhouse Rd.
Gravel Switch, KY 40328
606-332-7728

Kentucky Paintball Assoc.
Louisville, KY
502-458-ARMY

Paintball HQ
4746 Bardstown Rd.
Louisville, KY 40218
502-491-8000

US Cavalry
1375 N. Wilson Rd.
Radcliff, KY 40160
502-351-7000

LOUISIANA
Alligator Alley
31275 LA Hwy. 16
Denham Springs, LA 70726
504-664-7255

B & B Paintball
4016 Maplewood Dr.
Sulphur, LA 70663
318-625-6800

Balls a' Fire
1739 Carmel Dr.
Lafayette, LA 70504
Contact- Brannon May
(318) 233-8725
 has pro shop

Boogie Boys
Stonewall LA
Contact- Mike Keen
(318) 925 1900

The Combat Zone
7940 Parham St.
Denham Springs, LA 70726
504-664-8663

Flag Raiders
429 Camelia Ave.
LaPlace, LA 70068
5004-652-8510

Gatortag Paintball Park
Hwy1 at Hwy 71
4025 N. Market St
Shreveport Louisiana 71107
(318) 222-5607

O.F.F. Limits Inc.
608 Robinson Rd.
Elm Grove, LA 71051
318-687-6256

Paintball of Lafayette
4315 Johnston Street
Lafayette LA 70503
(318) 988-6270
Contact: Shannon Ralston

Southern Wildfire Paintball
55070 Loranger Rd.
Loranger, LA 70446
504-878-9619

Splatz Paintball Games, Inc.
2750 West Willow St.
Lafayette, LA 70506
318-988-9829

MAINE
Adventure Sports
51 Autum Ave.
Dover-Foxcoft, ME 04426
207-564-8156

Black Forest Paintball
Hudson Maine
(207) 94P-BALL
Contact: Mark

Blast'em Paintball
1 Pinkham Drive
Saco, ME 04072
207-284-8205

Brookside Paintball Field
Equipment Supplies
RR 1 Box 189D, Rt. 135
Belgrade, ME 04917
207-495-2561
207-495-3410 fax

Enfield Tactical
R.R. 1 Box 1300
Lincoln ME 04457
(207) 732-3898
Contact-Denis Carmody

Flying Dutchman Fields
RFD#2 Box 2260
Guilford Maine 04443
Contact- Matt
(207) 564-3369

International P.B. Field
Robbinston, ME
207-454-3688

Maine Action Games
Orland, ME
207-469-6812
Paintball At Lost Valley
Lost Valley Rd.
Auburn ME 04210
(207) 784-1561
Contact: Wayne Or Phil

Rogue Paintball
5 Swetts Bridge Rd.
Alfred, ME 04002
207-324-1515
www.roguepaintball.com

Shoot or Die
South Maine Street
Monson Maine 04464

Contact- Dustin Lander
(207) 997-3905

Survival Challenge
Farmington, ME
207-778-5044

Van Houten Army/Navy
Lower Cross Rd Box 130
E. Lebanon, ME 04027
207-457-1224

Woodland Warriors
PO Box 130
E Lebanon, ME 04027
207-457-1224

MARYLAND
Action Zone
4401 O'Donnell St., Suite 1-2
Baltimore, MD 21224
410-522-BALL

Alternative Sports/The Paintball
  Pro Shop
7751 B & A Blvd
Glen Burnie MD 21061
(410) 761-3733
Contact- Gonzo

Challenge Park
Bowie, MD
800-456-6636
www.chalengepark.com

The Company Store
373 A Main Street
Laurel, MD 20707
301-497-7677

The Company Store
13015 Wisteria Dr.
Germantown, MD 20874
301-515-2680

Maryland Paintball
8505 Harford Rd.
Parkville, MD 21234
410-882-5607

MD Surplus & Outdoor
Route 301 & Mermarr Rd
White Plains, MD 20695
301-645-0077

On Line Paintball Network
2092 Pear Hill Ct.
Crofton, MD 21114
410-451-4152

Outdoor Adventures
Bowie MD
(800) 456 6636
(301) 621 7574

Paintball Adventure
Northeastern Maryland and
    Delaware
(302) 834-9343

The Paintball Place
Dunkirk, MD
800-957-1013 or
410-741-0580

Paintball Sports, The Field
Jessup MD
(301) 948-7684 or (800) 275-7763
Contact: Bruce Gilbert, Field
    Manager
Located just off of I-95 between
    Washington, D.C. & Baltimore.

Paintball Wholesalers
2400 Bear Run Rd.
Taneytown, MD 21787
410-756-1006 or
800-442-1919

Paintball Wholesalers
205 C Bucheimer Rd.
Frederick, MD 21701
301-624-4399

Paintball Wholesalers
38 West Main St.
Westminster, MD 21157
410-840-8669

RKH Specialty MDSE.
10418 Old Ciberty Rd.
Frederick, MD 21701
301-898-0070

Sonny's Paintball Connection
P.O. Box 573
Riva MD 21140
Contact: Robert Young
(410) 956-0944
10 mi west of Annapolis
    off Rt 50

Timber Ridge Pball Club
14432 Tollgate Ridge
Hancock, MD 21750
301-678-5451

MASSACHUSETTS
Action Games
Tewsbury, MA 01876
508-459-8699

ADCO Sales Inc.
4 Draper St.
Woburn, MA 01801
781-93501799

Apache International Inc
Brockton, MA
508-559-0777

Attack & Splat
Groton, MA
508-470-2140

Boston Paintball Supply
131 Beverly St., 6th floor
Boston, MA 02114
617-742-6612, 4530 fax

Boston Paintball Supp.
Rt. 9 East
Framingham, MA 01702
508-879-6621

Camp Paintball
Kingston, MA
617-773-2206

Cape Cod Paintball
173 Claypond Road
Bourne, MA 02532
508-759-5130

Executive Paintball
Blanford MA
Field of Valor
Contact- Gregg Yvon
(413) 848-2507

Friendly Fire
Field Address:
    108 Grove St
    Upton, MA
Mailing Address:
    101 Worthington Ave
    Shrewsbury, MA 01545
Contact: Eli at (508) 798-3974 or
    Paul at (508) 795-1021
    Retail store at field

G.I. Joe's Genuine Surplus Store
196-198 Ferry Street
Maiden, MA 02148
617-322-8600

P & L Paintball Supply
No. Easton, MA
508-238-1365

Paintball Alley
Fall River, MA
800-444-7572

Paintball Challenge
White's Path
S Yarmouth MA 02664
Contact: Mike Stines
(508) 428-7450
Email: MHS489@aol.com
    indoor, has pro shop

Paintball Heaven
1221 Bedford St.
Bridgewater, MA. 02324
508-697-5808

Paintball Wizard
1900 Main St.
Tewksbury, MA 01876
Pittsfield Paintball
Pittsfield, MA
413-448-8218

Point Blank Paintball Inc.
1457 Riverdale St. (Rt. 5)
West Springfield, MA 01089
413-788-7352

R & R Paintball Games
34 Nicole Drive
Millbury MA 01527
(508) 865-9709

Randolph Paintball
410 South Street
Randolph, MA 02368
617-986-2255

S.L.A.M. Paintball
928 Route 28
S. Yarmouth, MA 02664
508-398-6919

Survival South East
Foxboro, MA
508-543-0111

Ultimate Adventure
7 Sweetwater Street
Saugus, MA 01906
617-231-0114

Ultimate Sport Inc.
45 Emerson St.
Brockton MA 02401
(508) 559-0777
    indoor and outdoor

MICHIGAN
Action Outdoors
1622 East Michigan
Jackson, MI
517-783-4434

Action Sports Paintball
710 So. Main.
Cheboygan, MI 49721
616-627-3474, fax 627-7477
http://www.lhi.net/coolstuff/a
    ction.html
Adrenaline Sports
PO Box 81
Farwell MI 48622
(517) 588-3545

Adventure Paintball Games
HC52 Box 40 Maxton Rd.
Drummond Island, MI 49726
906-493-5445

Battlefield Paintball Game
Jonesville, MI
313-481-0473

The Battlegrounds, Inc.
14402 Adam STreet
Livonia, MI 48154
313-953-5720

The Battlegrounds Arena
Pontiac, MI
810-333-2557

Battlegrounds Paintball
US#12, 8 mi. west of Saline
Ann Arbor, MI 49236
313-953-5720

Battlegrounds Paintball
43679 Michigan Ave. (STORE)
Canton, MI 48188
13199 US 12 (FIELD)
Saline, MI 49236
734-397-2255

B C Hobby
48 S. 20th St.
Battle Creek, MI 49015
616-968-1487

Bullseye Army Surplus
4907 South Division
Grand Rapids, MI 49548
616-530-2080

Chaos Creek Paintball
944 E. Emmett St.
Battle Creek, MI 49017
616-962-8851

Colors Paintball Field
12874 North Maple Island
Fremont MI 49412
Contact- Randy Woodland
(616) 924-6561

Crossfire Creek Paintball
Port Huron MI 48060
Contact- Jeff
(810) 987 7528
fax (810) 982 5238

Exotic Sportz East
23944 Eureka Rd.
Taylor, MI 48180
313-287-6460

Exotic Sportz West
125 Pearl Street
Pinckney, MI 48169
313-878-2002

Exotic Sportz Splatz
5312 Highland
Waterford, MI 48327
810-673-5325

Family Fun Center
9300 Hasting Rd
Jackson MI 49201
(517) 536-8442

Fennville Paintball Games
Fennville, MI
616-396-3601

Field Excalibur Paintball Games
10580 N. Dr. North
Battle Creek MI 49017
(616) 963-3925
Contact: Michael Knight

Field Sports
Gaylord, MI
517-731-5347

Forts and Flags P.B. Adventures
Roscommon, MI
1-800-33-SPLAT

Futureball Paintball Games &
    Supplies
9147 Hi Tech Dr.
Whitmore Lk, MI 48189
810-231-4253

Harry's Army Surplus
201 East Washington
Ann Arbor, MI 48l04
313-994-3572

Harry's Army Surplus Inc,
2050 N. Telegraph Rd.
Dearborn, MI 48128
313-565-6605

Hell Survivors Inc.
PlayField
125 Pearl Street
Pinckney, MI 48l69
Contact: Dave Massey
(313) 878-6540 field
(313) 878-5656 office
(313) 878-1148 bookings

Hole in the Wall
68111 16th Ave.
South Haven, MI 49090
616-637-8749

Lone Wolf Creek Paintball
45129 Cass Ave.
Utica, MI 48317
313-739-1790

Lone Wolf Paintball
Almont, MI
800-875-WOLF

River Paintball
Mt Pleasant MI 48858
Contact: Brian Howard
(517) 879-4320

Michigan Paintball Games
Jonesville MI
(313) 481-0473

Mike's Paintball Field
Clio MI
Contact- Mike at (810) 687-8759

On Target
6984 W. Main St.
Kalamazoo, MI 49009
616-375-4570

Outpost Paintball Supplies
944 E. Emmett St.
Battle Creek, MI 49017
616-962-8851

Outsiders Paintball
2341 S. Dort Hwy.
Flint, MI 48529
810-742-5057

R.J. Performance, Inc.
8392 Potter Rd.
Davison, MI 48423
810-658-5274

Sand Ridge Paintball
Bridgman, MI
616-465-4408

Shooter's Paintball of Grand
    Rapids
Located in Byron Center at 82nd
    & Wilson
Grand Rapids MI 49509
Contact- Ron Perrin
(616) 532-4402

Silver Lake Paintball
Mt. Clemens, MI
810-469-9111

Snipers' Paintball Field
Rt 2 Box 907
Foley Hill Rd. near Dollarville Rd.
Newberry MI 49868
(906) 293-8047

Splattball City
Livonia, MI
313-925-CITY

Surplus Sergeant
8847 Portage Rd.
Portage, MI 49002
616-323-2266

Swan Creek Paintball
9550 Swan Creek
Saganaw, MI 48609
517-781-1416

Valhalla Paintball
11781 Hall Rd.
(one block north of Apple Ave.
    off Ravenna Rd.)
Ravenna, MI 49451
(616) 853-6066

Victory Paintball
Saline, MI

Warren Sports
7636 S. Westnedge
Portage, MI 49002
616-327-5858

West Michigan Paintball, Inc.
23 W Elm
Cedar Springs MI 49319
Owner: Mike Nuffesse
(616) 696-4040

Wolf's Lair
Madison Heights MI
1-800-875-wolf
Indoor Field

Young's Army & Navy
Paintball Supply
3415 S. Westnedge Ave.
Kalamazoo, MI 49008
616-382-1900

MINNESOTA
Adventure Zone
3820 Sibley Memorial Highway
Eagan MN 55122
(612) 683-1180
(800) 688-3021
    indoor and outdoor

Adventure Zone - Outdoor
Rosemount, MD
612-683-1180

The Adventure Zone
1826 55th Street East
St Paul MN 55077
(612) 552-1620

Duck's Blind / Nasty D's Paintball
Rochester MN
(507) 634-7704
Contact: : Stan Stockwell

Combat Zone, Inc.
Hinckley, MD
(800) COMBAT4

Combat Zone Inc.
P.O. Box 396
Hugo, MN 55038-0396
651-653-3647

Hanger 18 Paintball Sports
704 4th St NE
Kasson MN 55944
(507) 634-4117
Contact- Lonnie E. Zelinske
hanger18@rconnect.com

Overlander Outback
165th Avenue and County Rd 19
Welch MN 55089
Contact- Dave
(612) 388-1612

Paintball Games, Inc.
Store at 2507 E. 7th Ave N
St. Paul MN 55109
(612) 779-8883

Paintball Games, Inc.
Little Canada, MN
612-484-5446

Players Paintball
St. Paul MN
(612) 791-4729

Posse Sports Splatball
Buffalo MN
(612) 682-1116
Contact: Cory and Patty Stevens

Run -N- Gun Painbtall Sports
Rochester MN
(507) 287-0891
Contact: : Ron VonBrethorst

Special Forces Splatball
Buffalo MN
(612) 682-0582

Splatball, Inc.
2412 University Ave SE
Minneapolis MN 55414
(612) 378-0385
http://www.scc.net/~splatmn
splat@splatball.org

T.A.G. (True Adventure Games)
HCR 73 Box 339
Walker, MN 56484
(218) 547-2300
(Milacs Lake)

Thunder Ball USA
41039 U.S. Highway. 169
Onamia MN 56359
(320) 532-4416
(Miliacs Lake)

Zumbro Valley Paintball Games
(612) 345-2734

MISSISSIPPI
Action Sports Paintball
Hattiesburg, MS
601-725-4310
or 601-428-2009

Bowie River Outdoor Sports
Hattiesburg, MS
601-268-1484

S.W.A.T. Inc.
1939 Pass Rd.
Biloxi, MS 39531
601-392-7928

SWAT Paintball Games
Woolmarket, MS
601-385-2264

Outdoor Adventure Park
Vicksburg, MS
601-634-0693

MISSOURI
Battle Creek
Kindom City MO 25262
1.5 miles of I70 at Hatton exit
Contact: Rick or Mike
(314) 642-Paint

Bunker Hill Paintball
2998 So. Service Road
Foristell, MO 63348
(314) 463-1066
E-mail bhp01@icon-stl.net

Bushwackers
South of intersection of Hwy
  F & FF 1.5 miles
Jefferson County MO
(314) 579-9933

Cliffwood Paintball Park
12 Miles north of Joplin MO
(417) 525-4503
Contact- Mike

Dollar Drugs and Sports
15 S.W. 3rd Street
Lee's Summitt, MO 64063
816-524-7600

Express Paintball Supp
3656 Hwy 61 S
Festus, MO 63028
314-937-4321

Fearless Fighters Paintball
Supplies & Fields
1747 W. 5th St
Eureka, MO 63025
314-938-5559
314-271-7771

Flashpoint
St. Charles, MO
314-916-3713

Irish Brigade Pball Store
8045 Wornall Rd, Ste A
Kansas City, MO 64114
816-361-3222

Jaeger's Subsurface Paintball
9300 Underground Dr
Kansas City MO
Contact: Chris Morin (Mgr.)
(816) 452-6600

Kansas City Paintball Field
50 hwy and hwy AA
Lone Jack MO
Contact- Bill at Dollar Drug and
  Sports
(816) 524-760

National Pro Shop
11142 Lindbergh Busi.
St. Louis, MO 63123
314-845-7079

Owens Outpost Sports
1708 E. Sunshine
Springfield, MO 65804
888-235-7040

Owens Outpost Sports
Hwy 160
Spokane, MO 65754
417-443-6201

Owens Outpost Sports
Hwy 50
Warrensburg, MO 64063
816-850-6338

Paint Games Plus
1411 West Kearney
Springfield, MO 65803
417-866-8862

Paintball Mania Supplies
POBox 528
Arnold, MO 63010
314-296-0964

Pro Performance Paintball
120 North 3rd St.
Hannibal, MO 63401
573-221-1196

Purple Heart Paintball
890 NE 75 Off Hwy 132
Knob Noster MO 65336
Contact: Ted Hall
(816) 563-3095 or (816) 563-2911

Springfield Paintball
601 National
Springfield MO 65802
417-869-GAME

The Survival Game
1507 S. Logan
Kansas City, MO
(816) 836-3334

Trish Brigade, Inc.
512 West 103rd St.
Kansas City, MO 64114
816-942-9696

Wacky Warriors
4951 Sean Dr.
Imperial, MO 63052
314-296-0964

Wildcat Paintball Park
30 minutes east of St. Louis
(800) 965-4206
Contact: Randy or Jim

MONTANA
Dog Creek Paintball
Olney, MT
406-881-2501

Inexerable Genocide
Highway 93 North
Evaro MT 59802
Contact: Aaron
(406) 251-6284

Montana Paintball
4380 Hwy 312
Billings, MT 59105
406-373-6814

Montana Paintball
1901 Broadwater Ave.
Billings, MT 59102
406-652-5048

Quest Paintball Adventure
  Games
Victor MT
(406) 543-1566

NEBRASKA
Husker Paintball
Omaha, NE
402-291-8125

Panhandle Paintball Club
Scottsbluff, NE
308-632-3686

Shooters Paintball
Omaha, NE
402-571-8149

Splat City Paintball
106 E. 11th St.
Kearney, NE 68847
308-234-9277

NEVADA
Battle Born Splat World
Reno, NV
702-356-1864

Las Vegas Paintball Headquarters
4117 W. Sahara Ave.
Las Vegas, NV 89102
702-871-1875

National Paintball Supply W.
#102 750 Freeport Blvd.
Sparks, NV 89431
803-458-7221; 609-464-1068

Paintball's Adventure Quest
1401 N. Decatur Blvd. #33
Las Vegas, NV 89108
702-647-0000

NEW HAMPSHIRE
Adventure Games Paintball Park
  & ProShop
158 Deering Ctr. Rd. Rt 149
Weare, NH 03281
603-529-FLAG

Adventure Games Pball Supply
  Outlet
297 S. Willow St.
Manchester, NH 03103
603-647-BALL

Beauia's Army/Navy
24 Canal Street
Laconia, NH 03246
603-524-1018

Canobie Paintball
47 Roulston Road
Windham, NH 03087
Office: (603) 893-1863
Field: (603) 893-4961

Portsmouth Paintball
508 Islington St.
Portsmouth, NH 30801
603-436-5511

Seacoast Paintball
(800) 726-game

Tactics, Inc.
Hudson, NH
508-459-5364

TASO East Coast Division
21 Production Place #7
Gilford, NH 03246
603-293-9393

Triad Paintball
Kingston, NH
603-642-5910

W.B.W. Inc.
Mad Dawgs Paintball
20 Canal Street
Franklin NH 03235
Contact: Craig Butler
Phone: (603) 934-2600
Fax: (603) 934-2800

NEW JERSEY
ABC Paintball Supply & Field
1745 Greenwood Lake Tpk.
Hewitt, NJ07421
201-728-1762

All Star Paintball
Hidden Valley Ski Area
  Breakneck Rd
Vernon NJ
(201) 728-0134
(800) 249-0134 (Outside NJ)
http://www.infi-
  pos.com/~medtek/allstar.htm

Atlantic Indoor Paintball
900 Mill Rd
Pleasantville NJ
(609) 641 6936
indoor

Dazell Hardware
21-23 W. Hampton St.
Pemberton, NJ 08068
609-894-8737

Diamond Lab
759 Bloomsfield Ave., Unit 312
West Caldwell, NJ 07006
973-879-3522

ET Paintball Park
Netcong, NJ
973-347-FUNN

Fireball Mountain
(609) 758-0855
Mailing Address:
 281 Meany Rd
 Wrightstown NJ 08562
Field Address:
 Meany Road
 Wrightstown NJ 08562
10 minutes from Great
 Adventure
Contact: Wendy or Al

Gunnrunners Paintball Sports
 & Supplies
630 Broad Street
Beverly NJ 08010
Contact: Rob
(800)929-3719
(609) 386-1833
 indoor & outdoor

The Hobby Shop
1077C Hwy #34
Aberdeen, NJ 07747
732-583-0505

KAM Sports
38 Main St. 2nd floor
Toms River, NJ 08753
732-286-9600

Impact Paintball
2037 Woodbridge Ave.
Edison, NJ 08817
732-339-0820
732-339-0821 fax

Indoor Paintball Planet
107 Pleasant Ave. & Rt. 17N
Up. Saddle River, NJ07458
201-934-1100

Mid-State Paintball Supply
247 So. Main Street
Manville, NJ 08835
908-722-9798

National Paintball Supply East
675 Route 45
Mantua, NJ 08051
609-464-1068
609-464-1262 fax

NJ Paintball Club
Butler, NJ
201-838-7493

North Jersey Paintball Club
Butler NJ
(201) 838-7493
Contact: Steve Petrella

On Target Paintball Games
Pemberton, NJ
609-894-4330

Outdoor Haven Paintball
Route 206, Columbus Farmers
 Market
Columbus, NJ 08022
609-267-0119

Paintball Depot Inc.
1451 Rt. 46
Ledgewood, NJ 07852
973-584-2220

Paintball Depot Inc.
Rt. 57, 3 miles west of
 Hackettstown
Hackettstown, NJ
201-584-2220
www.paintballdepot.com

Picasso Lake Paintball
Winslow Township, NJ
215-708-8881

Poco Loco
Buena, NJ
800-752-7626

Ramsey Outdoor Stores
226 Route 17
Paramus, NJ 07652
201-261-5000

Shore Paintball Supplies
1184 Fischer Blvd.
Toms River, NJ 08753
732-831-0400

South Jersey Paintball
1939 Rt. 70 E, Suite 250
Cherry Hill, NJ 08003
609-772-2878

Splatter Zone Paintball
3664 Kennedy Blvd.
Jersey City, NJ 07307
210-963-5500

Top Gun Paintball
567 Monmouth Rd.
Cream Ridge, NJ 08514
732-928-2810

Top Gun Paintball Games
Rtes 537 & I95
Jackson, NJ
(next to Six Flags Great
 Adventure)
Contact: Fred Dorski
(908) 244-1111

Usana Quads
Pittsgrove, NJ
609-358-4891

NEW MEXICO
Paintball Action
213 Dallas NE
Albuquerque NM 87108
Contact: Randall Lang
(505) 268-3550

Paintball World
3451 Candelaria Rd. N.E.
Albuquerque, New Mexico 87110
(505) 883-5430

Paintball World Adv. Park
Albuquerque, NM
505-263-8062

The Spyder's Lair Paintball
Field & Store
2029 S. Prince St.
Clovis, NM 88101

NEW YORK
3 Guys Games & P'aintball
968 Route 9
Queensbury, NY 12804
518-793-4587

Altona Paintball, Inc.
Altona, NY
518-236-7529

Armageddon Paintball
3749 State Hwy 30A
Fultonville N.Y. 12072
Contact- Chris Madore
(518) 922-7011

Army Navy Surplus
1158 George Urban Blvd.
Cheektowaga, NY 14225
716-684-8728

Black Swallow
2054 Ulster Ave.
Lake Katrine, NY 12449
914-336-4326

Challenger Paintball
2079A W. 6th St.
Brooklyn, NY 11223
718-714-0575

CIA Paintball
933 Coney Island Ave.
Brooklyn, NY 11230
718-462-9731

Cousins North
159 East Main Street
Mt. Kisco, NY 10549
914-241-7420

Cousins Paintball
1776 Deer Park Ave.
Deer Park, NY 11729
516-243-1100

Cousins Paintball East
3120 Route 112
Medford, NY 11763
516-698-3657

First Prize Paintball
76 Exchange St
Albany NY 12205
(518) 437 0917

Flag Station
737 Meeker Ave.
Brooklyn, NY 11222
718-349-0302

GRC Paintball
VanAllen Rd.
Belfast, NY 14711
716-365-2470

The Gun Shop
8 Centre Market Pl.
New York, NY 10013
212-925-4389

Haze Paintball
Fultonville, NY
518-466-0160

Hi Tec Nemesis
512 Grant Ave.
Brooklyn, NY 11208
718-235-5915

H.I.D.E. It's Paintball
Ohio, NY
315-826-7383

Hillside Paintball
Spierfalls Rd
Corinth NY 12822
(518) 499 2820

Hot Shots
Rt. 17M Box 179
Bloomingburg, NY 12721
914-733-5213

Iceberg Army Navy of Soho
455 Broadway
New York, NY
212-226-8454

Indoor Splatball
Buffalo, NY
716-383-5662

Island Paintball
770 E. Jericho Tpke.
Huntington Sta., NY 11746
516-692-7668

J.C. PaintBall
76 Underwood Road
Tupper Lake NY 12986
(518) 359-8135

JT's Paintball Zone, Inc.
Rock Stream, NY
607-535-7285

King Charles
12/28 North to Alder Creek
30 min from Utica/Rome NY
Contact: Bonnie or Charlie
(315) 392-2154

Liberty Paintball Game, Ltd.
Liberty, NY
914-292-7500

Mad Mac's
47 S. Lake Blvd., Rt. 6N
Mahopac, NY
914-628-3488

Mark's Cycle Corner
154 Wickman Ave.
Middletown, NY 10940
914-343-4480

Mid Hudson Hobbies
2 North St.
Middletown, NY 10940
914-342-8697

Montgomery Sport. Goods
32 Union St. (Rt. 211)
Montgomery, NY 12549
914-457-4678

Oceanside Indoor Paintball
3415 Hampton Rd.
Long Island, NY
516-766-3636

Operation Stingray
762 Grand St.
Brooklyn, NY 11211
718-384-1280

Outdoor Splatball
Rochester , NY
716-383-5662

Outdoors Cabin Sport
5319 Transit
Depew, NY 14043
716-683-1211

Paintball Adventure
10865 Wilson Rd.
Wolcott, NY 14590
315-587-4995

Paintball Game Supplies
160 Desparch Dr.
E. Rochester, NY 14445
716-383-5662

Paintball Long Island
159 East Main Street
Mount Kisco, New York 10549
Field in Coram
1-800-FLAG-007

Paintball Madness
280 Rt. 211E
Middletown, NY 10951
914-692-2492

Paintball Mania
114 Norfinch Drive
Unit 1 NY
(416) 661-0180
contact: Mark Assaf

Paintball New York
809 Middlefield Rd.
Roseboom, NY 13450
607-264-8000

Paintball Park
Constantia, NY 13044
315-623-9067
315-453-BALL

Paintball Survival Game HQ
945 Coney Island Ave.
Brooklyn, NY 11230
718-462-9731

Palenville Paintball Games
Route 23A
Palenville, NY 12463
800-362-9695

Professional Paintball Supplies
10 Railroad St.
Victor, NY 14564
716-924-9930

Recon Challenge
390 Columbia Tpk
Rensselaer, NY 12144
518-477-7156

R.I.P. "Play Paintball" Facility
PO Box 2156
Liverpool NY 13089
(315) 652-0403

Silver Creek Paintball & Outdoor
 Adventure Games
Off I-90 Exit 58-Silver
 Creek/Irving
Silver Creek, NY 14081
Contact-Ike
(716) 896-0060

Splatball The Game
P O Box 25351

Farmington, NY 14425
716-742-1486

Survival New York
159 East Main Street
Mount Kisco, New York 10549
914-241-0020
Field in Plattekill

Survival Zone
Just off I-81 at Adams Center
Adams Center NY
Contact- Scott Donato
(315) 782-8290

Tiger Stripe Paintball
Keeseville, NY
518-834-5226

Walt's Hobbie Shop
7909 Fifth Ave.
Brooklyn, NY 11209
718-745-4991

Walton Paintball
RD3 Box 401D Teed Rd.
Walton, NY 13856
607-865-8140

NORTH CAROLINA
Action Quest Field & Store
Statesville, NC
704-878-6880

Action Tagg, LLC
Elizabeth City, NC
919-335-4477

Action Town Sports Indoor
Nags Head, NC
919-441-3277

Action Town Sports Outdo
Cherry Point, NC
919-466-2762

Adventure Zone Paintball
720 N. Hoover Rd.
Durham, NC
919-598-1944

Black River Paintball
Route 2, Box 82-M
Angier, NC 27501
910-897-5093, 553-2550

Bunker Paintball Park
4420 Page Rd.
Morrisville, NC 27560
919-484-1252

CJ's Paintball Inc.
1600 H. Matthews Minthill Rd.
Matthews, NC 28105
704-814-7393

Excalibur
Tryon & Walnut Rds, Cary, NC

(919) 859-6922 and (919) 557-
 3856
Contact: Scott Gordon

FlashBack PaintBall & Supplies
Intersection - Hwy 742E and
 Boggan Cut Rd.
P.O. Box 391
Wadesboro, NC 28170
Contact: Steve Xavier
(704) 283 - 6829

Funtasia
Garret Road
Durham, NC 27713

Gotcha Parts Paintball
176 Darius Pearce Rd.
Youngsville, NC
919-271-2367

Hematoma Paintball
Chocowinity, NC
919-975-2289

Hide-N-Seek Paintball
Pittsboro/Siler City N.C.
(919) 542-7126

Idol's Adventure Sport
Rockingham, NC 28379

J & B Paintplay
Sandford, NC
919-775-1205

J & M Paintball and Hobby Works
1225 US #1A-S
P O Box 917
Southern Pines, NC 28388
910-693-7931 day
910-693-1772 evening
910-693-7932 fax

Line of Fire Paintfields
695 Gilreath Loop Rd.
Horse Shoe, NC 28742
704-891-2399

NC Paintball/Midway
Hwy 52 S. at Hickory Tree Rd
Winston-Salem, NC 27284
910-764-2701

Paintball Alley
Durham, NC
919-596-7674

Paintball Central
1814 Spring Garden St.
Greensboro, NC 27403
336-274-4002

Paintball Premises
Off Hwy 200
Greensboro NC
(910) 661-1133
Indoor

Paintball X-treme
Linda Lane
Asheboro, NC 27203
336-474-6689
336-861-2226

Piedmont Paintball Company
3300 Glen Hollow Rd
Greensboro NC 27410
Contact: Tim Brieaddy
(910) 292-8037

R.B. Paintball Adventures
3521 New Bern Hwy
Jacksonville, NC 28546
910-455-3385
910-455-4949

Special Operations Command
Whiteville, NC & Tabor City, NC
Contact- Rick Koon
(910) 653-6398

Strike Force
Concord, NC
(704) 788-4802

TAG Paintball
Hillsborough NC
-Office/store location: Durham,
   NC
1608 Kirkwood Dr
Durham NC 27705
Voice - (919) 471-8456
Field - (919) 210-8682
Pager - (919) 506-2529

Tactical Air Gun Games
216 B Cannons Ferry Rd
Elizabeth City NC
Contact- Mike Hollowell
(919) 221-8668

Tornado Alley
Kinston, NC
919-523-5906

Trailblazers Paintball
Jacksonville, NC
910-346-9715

Triangle Air Gun Games
Raleigh, NC
919-876-0153

Turbo Paintball
P O Box 12294
Jacksonville, NC 28546
910-937-6584

Winston Paint Pellet Games
P.O. Box 17223
Winston-Salem, NC 27116
(910) 744-1718

Wolverine Paintball Adventures
441 N Lousisanna Ave. #5

Asheville, NC 28806
828-264-4371

NORTH DAKOTA
Field of Honor Paintball
Grand Forks ND 58201
contact- Trent Lewis or George
   Thompson
(701)746-8133 or (701)746-6456

Prairie Paintball Supply
Jamestown, ND
701-251-1797

Pure Adrenaline PaintBall Games
Bismarck, ND
Call Steve at 1-701-663-2551

Sherwood Forest
Kindred ND 58051
(701) 428-3351
Contact: Rick Rustad
   (rrustad@gps.com)

Splat-Shot Paintball
Grand Forks ND
(701) 795-1440

OHIO
3 D Sports
Alliance, OH
330-821-5666

Action Enterprises
709 N. Reynolds Rd.
Toledo, OH 43615
800-552-3089

Adrenaline Zone
810 West 13th St.
Lorraine, OH 44052
216-681-4445

Adrenaline Zone
12952 Lake Shore Blv.
Bratenahl, OH 44108
1-800-SHOOTUM

Allen Paintball
Oakwood Village, OH
216-439-3222

Alternative Sports Supp
Valley Loop Rd.
Springfield, OH 45503
937-399-2403

Black Hawk Park
1-330-878-6309
Route 1, Box 49C
Strasburg, OH 44680

Buckeye Paintball
1-330-567-2455
120 B. South Market
Shreve, OH 44676

Central Ohio Paintball &
Indoor Arena
3069 Silver Dr..
Columbus, OH 43224
614-784-1104, 614-784-5106
784-2658 fax

Combat Adventures
295 South Second
Middleport, OH 45760
614-388-8601

Combat Zone of America
7060 S. TWP. Rd. 131
Tiffin, OH 44883
419-447-8424

Cutter's Paintball Valley
1881 Miami-Conservancy Rd
Sidney, OH 45365
3 miles west of Interstate 75
West Central Ohio
Contact: Nick Watercutter
(937) 492-6548

Deer Run Paintball
17124 Harmon-Patrick Rd.
Richwood, OH 43344

Desert Storm Paintball
Clint, OH
513-528-3173

DJ's Paintball Supplies
9800 South Stete Rte. 202
Tipp City, OH 45371
513-667-7576

Drivers Paintball
Rt 646 & 43
Wintersville, OH 43944
740-765-5196

E & S Paintball Games
Kimbolton, OH
614-498-4354

Extreme Paintball Adventures
Located on Barden St. in Lions
   Ohio
Follow State Route 120 and turn
   on Barden.
(419) 923-0109

Field of Fun
S. Columbus, OH
800-536-1104

Flight Paintball
27400 West Road (Field Address)
Spencer OH
(330) 288-0388 Or (330) 351-1792
Rt. 58S To Rt. 162E Turn Rt. On
   West Rd.

Indian Springs Paintball
Off US rt 76 near Akron, OH

Barber Rd Exit
Address: 2964 Barber Rd
   Norton OH 44203
(216) 745-5722

JONT Enterprises
1396 New Garden Rd.
New Paris, OH 45347
513-437-7195

Jungle Jim's Paintball
152 S. Main St.
Miamisburg, OH 45342
513-859-0916

Gotcha Paintball Guns and
   Supplies
3835 St. Rt. 305
Fowler, Ohio 44410
(216) 638-6088

Greene County Paintball Center
Near Dayton OH
(513) 298-5138

Miami Valley Shooting
7771 S. Cassel Rd.
Vandalia, OH 45377
513-890-1291

Mickey's Army Navy
239 Main Ave. SW
Warren, OH 44481
330-392-2525

Northeast Survival Paintball
   Games
4197 Pearl Rd
Cleveland OH 44109
Contact: Paul Spooner
(216) 749-2868

Paintball City
Cleveland, OH
216-939-1999

Paintball Connection Inc.
15508 Madison Ave.
Lakewood, OH 44107
216-221-6400

Paintball Field of Fun
Columbus, OH
614-784-1104

Paintball Games Coliseum
3621 State Route 273
Belle Center, OH 43310
513-464-4480

Paintball Paradise/Field
1879 Deerfield Rd.
Lebanon, OH 45036
512-932-FIRE

The Paint Shop
5227 National Rd.

U.S. Rt. 40
Hebron, OH 43025
740-928-1600

Pinnacle Woods
8752 East Ave.
Mentor, OH 44060
216-974-0077

Queen City Paintball
5961 #4 Boymel Dr.
Fairfield, OH 45014
513-942-BALL

R&B Games
178 So. Main St.
Bowling Green, OH 43402
419-353-2176

Rapid Fire Paintball
off Western Reserve Rd
Youngstown OH
Contact: Bruce for info
(216) 793 2169

Salt Fork Adventure Games
(614) 498-8116
74978 Broad Head Rd.
Kimbolten, OH 43749

Skirmish
1-800-644-6754
Snow Trails Resort
3100 Possum Run Rd.
Mansfield, OH 44903

Southern Ohio Paintball Club
Felicity, OH
513-876-2488

Splat City Paintball
4183 Taylor Rd.
Batavia, OH 45103
513-735-6112

Splatland Paintball
Wrightway Road N
Dayton, OH
513-293-5560; 461-4486

Stars & Stripes Paintball
3311 Neimans RD.
East Canton OH
Contact: Rick Bennington
(216) 478-5459

Stars & Stripes
Canton, OH
(330) 478-5459

Storm Paintball
(513) 887-1105
Interstate 275 to Route 52
Route 52 east to Route 133
Route 133 north to city of
Felicity

In Felicity left onto 756
756 3 miles to Richey Road
1000 feet on Richey to field
Look for Sign

Superior Adventures Field
2180 TWP 56
Bellefontaine OH 43311
Contact- Mike Bell
(513) 599-4853

Wooster Paintball
5560 Lehr Rd
Wooster OH 44691
(216) 262-2584
contact-Dave Roessner- Field
Owner

Xtreme Paintball Sports
3081 Dryden Rd.
Moraine, OH 45439
937-298-5138

OKLAHOMA
Altus Paintball Club
1220 N Main
Altus OK 73521
Contact: Mike D.
leave message @ (405) 477-0098

Arcadia Paintball
Located at Anderson Rd &
Charter Oak
Mail Address 2109 Hardy Dr
Edmond OK 73013
Contact: Vernon Richards
(405) 341-6774

Ambush Ridge Paintball
6 mi North of Downtown Tulsa
Tulsa, OK
918-428-5058 or
918-665-4001

Badlands USA
Shawnee, OK
405-275-9291

Boot Hill Paintball Field
1m. N, 1/2m. E Fairgrounds
Stillwater, OK
405-669-2723

Dodge City Paintball Field
9601 NE 63rd St.
Oklahoma City, OK
405-771-5229

Fun Hits-Indoor
2121 So. Portland
Oklahoma City, OK 73108
405-682-5454

Gotcha!!! Paintball
3 1/2 miles East of city
On Hwy 60
Vinita OK
(918) 256-3000

Legends Paintball
84th and Alameda
Norman OK 73071
Contact- Don Holzberlein
(405) 360-1868
has pro shop

Lunar Sport Paintball
4 Miles S of Blanchard on
Hwy 76
Oklahoma
799-9894
799-7985

Paintball Adventures Inc
Tulsa, OK
918-747-1055

Paintball Adventures, Inc.
10242 South 49th West Avenue
Sapulpa OK 74066
(918) 224-1055

Paintball Land
12731 N 118 East Avenue
(West of Owasso and South of
Collinsville)
Oklahoma 74021
(918) 371-4044

Paintball of Tulsa
6390-H East 31st St.
Tulsa, OK 74135
918-665-7856

Redland Paintball
2 mi west of I-35 on hwy 9
then 4/10 mi south on Western
Ave
SW of Normon OK
Contact- Terry Schuldt
(405) 340-8142

Rock Island Paintball
Three miles east of Hacket, AR
Rock Island OK
Contact- Bill Johnson
(501) 484-8161 (Heart and Sole
Paintball Store)

Shaggy Bros. Paintball
5575 NW Expressway
Oklahoma City, OK 73114
800-320-7277

SportPaint Inc.
5014 S. Quincy Ave.
Tulsa, OK 74105
918-744-4488

Wild West Paintball Field
Exit 91 off I-35 Purcell, Oklahoma
Turn West 1 mile, Turn right 5
miles, Turn right 1/2 mile You
are there! There are plenty of
signs to help you.
Contact: David Baxter
(405) 634-4455

OREGON
Albany Adventure Games
41st and Marion
Albany OR 97321
Contact: Lee
(541) 967-4697

Aloha Surplus
17645 SW TV Hwy
Aloha, OR 97006
503-591-5858

Central Oregon Paintball Supply
957 NE 1st
Bend, OR 97701
503-383-1879

Enchanted Acres Paintball Park
Scappoose, OR
503-543-3880

Gresham Paintball Supply
4603 SE 16th
Gresham Oregon
(503)667-1956
Has pro shop

Hit and Run Paint War Games
Scappoose OR
(503) 543-3880

Hit and Run Paintball (Indoor)
8900 SW Commercial St
Tigard OR 97224
(503) 968-9579

Hot Shots - Indoor
Eugene, OR
541-465-3832

JK Paintball Games
380 2nd St
Glendale OR 97442
(541) 832-2546

Metro Rod & Reel
236 S.E. Grand Ave.
Portland, OR 97214
503-232-3193

Paintball Games
1820 W. 7th Ave.
Eugene, OR 97402
503-689-7028

Planet Paintball
Salem, OR
503-370-8749

Q-Ball's Field of Fun
Corbett OR
Leave Msg at (503) 244-0415

S.P.L.A.T.
Bend, OR
503-385-5721

Splat Action
32155 S. Grimm Rd.
Portland, OR 97038
503-829-7311 or 503-829-9281

Splat Action
Mollala OR
Contact: John
(503) 538-0416 or (503) 829-7311

Splat Paintball Sports
2880 Ferry Street SW
Albany OR 97321
(503) 928-0957

Thrillseekers
2525 NW Division
Gresham, OR 97030
503-492-4386

Warpaint Paintball Supply
2304 E. Adams Ave.
Lagrande, OR 97850
503-963-6947

WarPaint International
3046 Portland Rd NE
Salem OR 97303
(503) 585-9477
  indoor and outdoor

Whack'm & Splak'm
PO Box 58
Keno, OR 97627
503-884-8942

PENNSYLVANIA
Action Adventure Sports
PO Box 420 N. Main+N St.
Loganville, PA 17342
717-428-0235

Action Creek Paintball
Colonial Vally
Menges Mills, PA.
between York & Hanover
contact- Dennis
(717) 225-0351

Alle-Kiski Paintball
29 First St.
Vandergrift, PA 15690-1007
724-568-1042

Ambush Paintball
Lancaster, PA
717-871-8632

Bunker Hill
49 East Avenue
Mt Carmel PA 17851
(717) 373-5051
Contact- Francis Daya, Jr.

Combat Survival Games
Little Gap, PA
215-253-2211

Cobra Command Inc.
20 N. Cannon Ave.
Lansdale PA 19446
Call Norm at (215)-855-7252

The Command Post
238 Kidder St
Wilkes-Barre PA 18702
Contact: Mark A. Zavoy
(717) 829 3818

Dragon's Lair
1248 Greengate Mall Rt 30
Greensburg PA 15601
(412) 864-0496
  has pro shop

E.M.R. Paintball Park
POBox 728, Rt. 706 & 601
New Milford, PA 18834
717-465-9622

Fast & Furious Paintball
301 S Keyser Ave
Taylor PA 18517
(717) 562-3114

Fort Splat Paintball Field
Route 30 Mt Pleasant Exit
Greensburg PA 15601
Contact: Paul Taggart
(412) 838-1145

The Foxhole
Ling Lestown, PA
717-541-9430

Global Paintball North & South
1245 Chestnut Street
Emmaus PA 18049
(610) 966-4780

Hamburger Hill
1120 Helbling Road
New Brighton PA 15066
Contact- John Helbling
(412) 843-0706
  Near Pittsburgh

Hi-Tech Paintball
Rt. 119 North
Youngwood, PA 15679
412-925-8722

High Adventure Survival Games
Near Whipple Dam, near State
  College, PA
(814) 234-9640
Contacts: Ed and Fran

High Peaks Paintball
RR# 1 Box 1079 Rt 739 #6
Dingman's Ferry, PA 18328
717-828-1550

Highland Paintball Games
Galeton, PA
814-435-1002

Hoover's Paintball & Supplies
3028 Crottlestown Rd
Chambersburg PA 17201
Contact: Carl Hoover
(717) 267-3447

Iron Triangle Paintball Club
7720 Chestnut Street
Zionsville PA 18092
Contact: Sgt. Gebb (610)-965-
  4382
BYOP and CA

Keystone Paintball
Jersey Shore PA
(717) 398-7773
(717) 398-3669 fax
Field located at exit 27 just
  off I-80
Loganton PA

Kuba's Surplus Sales
231 W. 7th St.
Allentown, PA 18102
215-433-3877

Lil Bro Paintball Supplies
1293 Brodhead Rd.
Monaca, PA 15061
724-775-3222

Lower Anthracite Paintball
  Association
Mt Carmel PA 17851
(717) 373-5051
email paintb4040@aol.com

Operation Paintball
Bridgeville PA 15057
(412) 221-0334
Indoor Field

Orion Paintball Sports, Inc.
Indiana, PA
412-349-1152

Pickett's Charge Paintball
Middleton, PA
717-948-0932

Pike County Ambush, Inc.
Hawley, PA
888-2-AMBUSH

Poco Loco
Paintball Field
Limerick, PA
1-800-PLA-POCO

Pocono Ridge PaintBall Club
1 Pine Grove Rd
South Sterling PA 18460
Contact- Sean Santay
(717) 676 3478 Fax
(717) 676 9823
  Store/Custom Shop Avail

Rapid Fire Paintball
Ligonier, PA
412-238-2756

Riverside Renegade
Pittsburgh PA
(412) 422-8835

Roman's Action Pursuit Games
4369 Sunset Pike
Chambersburg PA 17201
(717) 263-3700

Sgt. York's Army Navy
Lemoyne exit- Route 83
900 Market St
Lemoyne PA
Contact- Tom Cooper or Eric
  Holland
(717) 761-3819

Skirmish USA
Rt 903 (HC2 Box 2245)
Jim Thorpe PA 18229
Phone 1 (800) SKIRMISH

Smart Parts, Inc.
1203 Spring St.
Latrobe, PA 15620
412-539-2660

Sniper Valley Paintball
Lake Ariel, PA
717-937-FUNN

Southern Chester County
  Paintball
8 Newfield Ct.
West Grove, PA 19390
610-869-5694

Splat Inc.
old Rt 220
Newry PA 16665
Outside Altoona across from
  Leighty's
Contact- Dave
(814) 696-1940

Splatter Paintball Center
at Jack Frost Mountain
Box 703
Blakeslee PA 18610
800-468-2442

Three Rivers Paintball
251 Westview Rd.
Wexford, PA 15090
(412) 935-6100

The Ultimate Game
Between Jerome PA and Boswell
  PA off Rte 601
Field just outside Johnstown, PA
(814) 269-4851

Urban Assault I
(412) 331-1080
447 Washington Ave.
Bridgeville, Pa 15017

Urban Assault II
around Pittsbugh, PA
call Urban Assault I for info

Wanna-Play Pball Supp
725 North Rte. 15
Dillsburg, PA 17019
717-432-7997

RHODE ISLAND
Boston Paintball Supply North
1428 Hartford Ave.
Johnston, RI 02129
617-742-6612 or
401-351-BALL

Extreme Sports
17 Water St.
Warren, RI 02885
401-245-4003

John's Army Surplus
Airport Plaza
1800 Post Rd.
Warwick, RI 02886
401-738-8735

Orion Paintball Adventure
  Games
N. Kingston, RI
401-294-4227

Paintball Wizards of NE
682 Broadway
Pawtucket, RI 02860
401-724-3751

Rhode Island Paintball
Route 6
Johnston RI
(401) 351-BALL

SOUTH CAROLINA
Adrenaline Heaven Paintball
1310 Wiskey Rd.
Aiken, SC 29801
803-643-8199

Gamemaster U.S.A.
Myrtle Beach, SC
803-946-6641

Gottcha Paint Ball Arena (Indoor)
4790 Trade St
North Charleston SC 29418
Contact-Barbra Judy
(803) 552-7418

Happy Holton's Paintball Park
Anderson, SC
864-296-0009

JC Robinson's Attic
2742 Celanese Rd.
Rock Hill, SC 29732

National Paintball Supply
1200 Woodruff Road, Unit C-5
Greenville, SC 29607
803-458-7221 or
864-458-7221
864-458-7611 fax

Pro Fox Paintball
1200 Woodruff Road,
Greenville, SC 29607
803-458-7221

Pro Games
Greenville, SC
803-235-PL-AY

R&R Action Paintball
Summerville (Charleston), SC
(803) 851-9156

Special Operations Command
Myrtle Beach, SC & Loris, SC
Contact- Rick Koon
(910) 653-6398

Strikezone Paintball
Hwy 170
Hilton Head Island SC
(803) 522-1575

Swamp Fox Paintball Games
Eastover, SC
803-783-8610

Vanguard Paintball Games
429 Koon Store Rd
Columbia SC 29203
(803) 786-4539

Warzone Paintball Games
Marion SC 29571
Contact: Rodney Rogers
(803) 423-1029

SOUTH DAKOTA
Big Jim's Feud Ranch
HRC30, Box 17
Spearfish, SD 57783
605-578-1808 or
605-642-3109

TENNESSEE
Adventure Games
Lovelace Ln
Humboldt TN
10 minutes outside Jackson
Contact- Rick Fisher
(901) 784-9991
johmdres@mars.utm.edu

Adventures in Paintball
8213 Daton Pike
Hixson TN 37343 (Just north of
  Chattanooga)

Contact- David Tankersley
(615) 842-8537

B&B Combat Survival
Dayton, TN
615-775-0788

Bad Lands
Iron City, TN
615-845-4423

Challenge Park-Memphis
1345 N. Germantown Pkwy.
Cordova, TN 38018
901-754-4205
www.challengepark.com

Games Unlimited
Smyrna, TN
615-459-4400

J & P Splatterball
1510 Hwy 93
Fall Branch TN
(423) 348-8878

Ker-Splat
Rogersville, TN
615-272-0163

Nashville Paintball Sports Inc.
Wilson Pike
Brentwood TN 37027
615-255-9020

Paintball Memphis
Memphis, TN
901-458-9444

The Paintball Store
1345 N. Germantown Pkwy
Cordova, TN 38018
901-754-4205

Splat-One Adventures
Knoxville, TN
423-531-PL-AY

Splat-1 Adventures, Inc.
162 North Seven Oaks Drive
Knoxville TN 37922
(615) 531-7529

Splatter's, Inc.
Jackson, TN
901-661-0350

Splatterball Adventure Games
Chattanooga , TN
615-499-1151

Ultimate Paintball Games LLC
Cleveland, TN
423-559-1002

TEXAS
Action Paintball Supply
1025 W. 5th

Austin TX 78703
(512) 322-0884
  field in South Austin (Oak Hill)
  area

Adventure Expeditions
1308 Chestnut St.
Commerce, TX 75248
903-886-7691, 886-3014

Adventure Village Paintball
Strategy Games
8311 FM 1960 Bypass
Houston, TX 77338
713-548-3386

Alamo City Paintball
(Equipment/Supplies)
15219 San Pedro
San Antonio, TX 78232
210-494-9230

American Adventure Games
El Paso, TX
503-233-2255

American Camo & More
1600 Brazosport Blvd. Hwy. 288B
Richwood, TX 77531
409-265-4393

Awful Ventures Paintball & More
4309 West Pipeline
Euless, TX 76040
817-282-3636

Brazos Survival Games
Richmond
281-342-5885

C.C. Paintball Warehouse
1115 W Broadway
Corpus Christi TX
(512) 882-5583
Contact- Loren
 Indoor Field

C.M. Support/ViewLoader
4921 Olson Drive
Dallas, TX 75227
214-381-3075; 388-6743

Centrex Paintball
Route 7, Box 192
Killeen, TX 76542
817-628-7076

Constant Action
9407 Rodriguez
Austin Texas 78747
512-243-2669, 243-0706 fax

Cut & Shoot Paintball
Hwy 105 to Cut & Shoot. Turn on
 FM 1485 4 Mi.
Right on Harris. Go to end.
Cut & Shoot TX 77301
Contact: Monte Lane
(409) 445-1637

Finding Paintball

D.A.M. Games of E Texas
POBox 5270
Longview, TX 75608
214-297-2075

DFW Adventure Park, Inc.
501 FM 3040
Flower Mound TX
4 Miles West of I-35E
Contact: Larry Lipscomb
(214) 539-6682

Field of Honor Paintball Games
2317 Hampton Rd
Wichita Falls TX
(817) 761-5566

Fun on the Run
(call store for good directions)
Lake Worth TX
Contact: Mike Creamer
(817) 237-0299 (store)
(817) 946-7209 (field)

Gotcha Games Enterprises
Wills Point, TX
903-567-6788

Green Beret
2213 North 10th St.
McAllen, TX 78051
210-687-1147, 1148

Hardcore Paintball Supply
2301 N Cntrl Exwy #190
Plano, TX 75075
972-424-7801

High Plains Paintball Games Inc.
Cleburne TX 76031
Contact: Lance Willingham
(817) 517-7720

Hit and Run Express
4-5 Miles West of Mansfield on
    Broad St
Mansfield TX
(817) 461-7768

Hit & Run Paintball Park
Rt. 2, Box 156D
Mansfield, TX 76063
817-453-8914

Lone Star Paintball
23214 Baneberry
Magnolia, TX 77355
713-356-2158

North Texas Paintball Supply
4309 Highway 377 South
Fort Worth, TX 76116
817-282-7200

The Official Paintball Games of
    Texas, Inc.
(5 min. east of Town East Mall

Take 635 East to 80 East, exit FM
    460)
Forney TX
Contact: Colin
Metro (214) 564-4748

Outlaw Paintball
800 ft South of FM 2004 on
    288B
Richwood TX 77531
Contact: Brian Quandt
(409) 299-3491

Olympic Paintball Sports
1008 Wirt Road, #100
Houston, TX 77055
713-680-3300

Olympic Paintball Sports
712 N. 31st
Temple, TX 76504
254-791-5050, 5051 fax

Olympic Paintball Sports
3601 Parmer Lane
Austin, TX 78727
512-834-9290, 834-1934

Olympic Paintball Sports
15010 Fagerquist Rd.
Del Valle, TX 78617

Olympic Paintball Sports
36 White Flint Park Rd.
Temple, TX 76510

Outpost Paintball Field
2341 Murdine Rd.
Aransas Pass, TX 78336
512-758-2181

Paintball Bonanza
13515 Main St.
Houston, TX 77035
713-935-0552

Paintball Challenge
3411 N. Sam Houston Tollway W
Houston TX
(281) 364-1748
 On-Site Discount Supply Store

Paintball of Texas
Manor TX
913-6777

Paintball of Texas #2
4944 Harvey Rd
Crosby TX 77532
(713) 328-7990

Paintball Games of Dallas
3305 E John Carpenter Frwy
Irving, TX 75062
214-544-1937 Indoor Field &
    Store
214-460-1385 Field Cellular
    Phone

214-554-8809 fax
Paintball Games of Lubbock
Lubbock TX
Contact: Damy Donahue
(806) 785-2820

Paintball Games of Katy Inc.
Houston TX
Office (713) 862-5555
Field (713) 371-2425

Paintball Games of Waco
Waco TX
(817) 754-4640 Store
(817) 875-2295 Field

Paintball Game Supply of TX
1101 Royal Pkwy, #117
Euless, TX 76040
817-571-1177

Paintball Gear
Traders Village
7979 N. Eldridge #3018
Houston, TX 77041
281-897-8678

Paintball Mart
15737 San Pedro
San Antonio, TX 78232
210491-0506

Paintball Maxx
6423 Richmond Ave., Ste I
Houston, TX 77057
713-784-6299

Paintball of Waxahachie
507 No. Hwy 77 #614
Waxahachie, TX 75165
972-937-2468

Paintball Player's Supp
7024 Jacksboro Hwy.
Fort Worth, TX 76135
817-237-0299

PaintBall Pursuit
San Antonio TX
(210) 608-9237

Paintball Store
9220 FM1960 West
Houston, TX 77070
713-469-9777

Paintball Supplies of Lewisville
1081 W. Main St., #107B
Lewisville, TX 75067
972-221-9036

Paintball USA
Cypress, TX
713-768-0283

Paintball Warehouse
Corpus Christi, TX
512-882-5583

Pipe Creek Paintball
910 Cypress Park Ln.
Bandera, TX 78003
830-535-GUNS

Ricky Enterprises
1773 Pali Dr.
El Paso, TX 79936
915-855-7474

ROWDY's Tactical Adventures
Bryan, TX
409-268-2225

Safyr Paintball
1504 Pike Rd.
Fort Bliss, TX 79906
915-565-4487

Splat Paintball Fields
N.W. 1st & Hughes
Amarillo TX 79109
Contact- Bryan or Brandon
    Sutton
(806) 373-4810

Survival X-treme
960 B NW
Childress TX 79201
(817) 937-2982

Survival Games of Dal/Ft.W
105 Waits Circle
Garland, TX 75043
817-267-3048

Survival Game of TX
2309 Aldine Meadows
Houston, TX77032
713-370-GAME

T.A.P.S. Paintball
Lubbock TX
(806) 793-1523

Texas Paintball
Austin TX

Tombstone Paintball Village
Located just north of Huntsville
    on FM 247
Office located in Houston, TX
(713) 565-BALL or (713) 530-5261
Contact: Jack or Roxi Bernardo

Unicam
2624 Elm Street
Dallas, TX 75226
214-651-1350

USA Paintball
922 East I-30
Garland, TX 75043
214-564-4USA
214-722-2731 fax

Finding Paintball

West Texas Paintball
2235 19th
Lubbock, TX 79401
806-744-4000

West World Paintball Town, Inc.
605 26th Street
Lubbock TX 79404
(806) 793-1523
indoor & outdoor

Wolfe City War Games
Rt. 2, Box 267
Wolfe City, TX 75496
903-496-2882

UTAH
Action Center Paintball
Cottonwood Canyon
Mountain Green (Morgan), UT
   84050
owner: Jeff Wilkinson
(800) 228-2520

CCS 1Air Assault
175 East 400 St Ste. 1000
Salt Lake City, UT 84111
801-350-9102

Commando Playground
2250 Wall Ave
Ogden UT 84403
(801) 399-3882
Field and Pro Shop

Flash Straight Shooter
Intersection I-84 and Exit 96
Peterson UT
(801) 392-6230

Paintball Planet
Sandy, UT
801-562-1400

Paintball Zone
708 S Main
Logan UT 84321
Contact: Scott
(801) 750-0055

Patriot Games Paintball
837 North main
Alpine UT 84004
(801) 756-7451
Contact: Shaun Adamson

Patriot Games Paintball II
305 S Orem Blvd
Orem UT 84057
(801) 224-1578
indoor

Pegleg Paintball
1422 West 3500 South
W. Valley City, UT 84119

Predator Paintball
305 South Orem Blvd

Orem UT 84058
Contact: Gary Murdock
(801) 224-1578

S.S.I. Paintball
Midvale, UT
801-562-2056

Showdown
Salt Lake City, UT
801-224-1288

Straight Shooter Pball
3940 Washington Blvd.
Ogden, UT 84403
801-394-2916

Sure Shot Paintball Game
Ogden, UT
801-782-7437

VERMONT
Champlain Valley Paintball
Whiting, VT
802-462-2097

Combat Zone
Fairfield, VT
802-524-0371

First Downhill
W. Dover, VT 05356
802-464-7743

Mike's Hobbies & Raceway
162 N. Main Stret
Rutland, VT 05701
802-775-0059

North Vermont Paintball Field
Richmond, VT
802-660-8563

Paintball Mountain Sports
Bolton Vermont
(802) 434-5119
Contact: Jeff Folb

Vermont Green Mountaineers
Brattleboro, VT
802-254-6799

VIRGINIA
Action Town Sports
1528 Holland Rd.
Suffolk, VA 23434
805-539-3756

A. G. Paintball Games
Leesburg, VA
301-417-0137

Arena Action
12201 Balls Ford Rd.
Manassas, VA 22110
(703) 330-6833
indoor speedball
has pro shop

B.C.B.G. Paintball
11501 Washington Hwy.
Ashland, VA 23005
804-798-1551

B.C.B.G. Paintball
7540 West Broad St.
Richmond, VA 23294
804-755-4388

B&E Paintball games in Danville
Rt. 1, Box 247
Dry Fork, VA 24549
Contact: Bill or Erma
(804) 724-7555

Battlecry Paintball
Woodbridge VA
Contact- Troy Voytko
(703) 490-1894

Beach Paintball
VA Beach, VA
804-422-5606

Combat Zone Paintball Field
Field Physical Address:
1776 Princess Anne Road
Virginia Beach VA 23456
   Send All Correspondence to:
   Combat Zone Inc.
   c/o Air Power
   509 Viking Drive Suite E
   Virginia Beach VA 23452
   (804)-486-8222 Reservations
   (804)-486-8177 FAX
   (804)-721-0802 Field Phone

Corky's Fredericksburg Military
   Surplus
921 Caroline St.
Fredricksberg, VA 22401
703-373-4984
or 540-373-4984

Game Master USA
2301 Pacific Ave
Virginia Beach VA 23451
(804) 422-5606

Hobby Town of VA
1218 Blue Ridge Ave.
Culpeper, VA 22701
703-825-8729

Hogback Mountain Sports Club
Rt 2 Box 194
Leesburg VA 22075
(703) 777 0057

Ka-Splat Paintball Supplies
4015 Cedar Lane
Portsmouth, VA 23703
757-483-5870

Master Blasters
Chesapeake, VA
804-548-2481

Mechanicsville Paintball
Mechanicsville, VA
804-730-4129

New Kent Paintball Games
Lanexa, VA
804-966-5104

Painted Forest Adventure
   Games, Inc.
Route 1, Box 638B
Rustburg VA 24588
(804) 821-2804

Pev's Paintball Pro Shop/Games
13932 Jefferson Davis Hwy.
Woodbridge, VA 22191
703-491-6505

Pev's Paintball Pro Shop
556 Garrisonville Rd.
Stafford, VA 22554
540-720-1319

Point Blank Paintball Field
Harrisonburg, VA
(540) 574-0051

Power Paintball Supply
103-25 Hounds Chase La.
Roanoke, VA 24014
540-343-9062

Rapid Fire Paintball
Linden, VA
703-636-7989

Soggie Bottom Paintball
Field & Supplies
Culpeper VA
(703) 547-2322
(703) 829-6632

Splat Zone
Moody Road
Prince George VA
Take route 10 east from
   Hopewell
turn left onto Moody rd
   1 mile on rt.
Contact- James Cofer or
   Edgar Houser
(804) 452-2566
Rattsazz@aol.com
rcofer3@aol.com

Splathouse
946 Grady Ave Suite 8
Charlottesville VA 22901
(804) 977-5287
indoor and outdoor

Splat Paintball Field
Richmond, VA
804-739-3745

Splat Zone
Hopewell, VA
804-452-2566

Splat Zone
Richmond, VA
804-275-7045

Valley Surplus
1084 Virginia Ave.
Harrisonburgh, VA 22802
703-564-0002

Virginia Adventure Game Inc
(VAG)
Leesburg VA
Contact- Chris Abrahams
(703) 631 0909

WASHINGTON
A.M.S.
18144 Woodinville Snohomish
Rd.
Woodinville, WA 98072
425-483-8855

Army Surplus #4
E. 12218 Sprague Ave,
Spokane, WA 99206

AWOL Sporting Supply
POBox 55398
Seattle, WA 98155

AWOL/Splat Mountain
7018 NE Bothell Way
Bothell, WA 98011
206-487-9158

Bill and Jim's Excellent Adventure
13425 SE 30th Street
Bellevue WA 98005
(206) 643-7785
Indoor

BK Paintball
502 2nd St.
Clarkston, WA 99403
509-785-3832

Boomers Paintball
3807 East Sanson
Spokane, WA 99207
509-483-1879

Camokaze Paintball Supply
N. 3209 Monroe St.
Spokane, WA 99205
509-324-0750

Fun on the Run
Black Diamond WA
(206) 631-6060

Hole In The Wall Paintball
14902 SE 274th St.
Kent, WA 98042
(206) 639-3099

The Jolly Soldier
902A N.E. 65th St.
Seattle. WA 98115
208-524-2266

K. C. Crusaders Paintball
South Prairie WA
Reservations or Walk-On
Phone/Fax (206) 833-8010

Manchester Brothers
Pacific NW Paintball
Headquarters
750 Vandercook Wy
Longview, WA 98632
360-425-1131

Master Blaster Paintball Park
19209 33rd Ave. South
Seattle, WA 98188
360-427-2487

Master Blaster Paintball Park
E. 4510 Agate Rd.
Shelton, WA 98188
360-427-2487 242-9909

Mobile Tactics Paintball
1829 Hwy. 20 Unit E
Burlington, WA 98233
360-755-9020

Mobile Tactical Pursuit (MTP)
Old Crescent Harbor Road, next
to Polnell Shores Estate on
Whidbey Island
Oak Harbor, Washington
(360) 240-0122
Owners: Mark & Patty

Northwest Paintball
Mailing Address-
11714 Airport Rd
Everett WA 98204
(206) 356-2745

Paintball Fever Games
206-483-2900

Paintball Playground
Woodinville, WA
206-483-6611

Paintball Products NW
205 S. 4th Ave.
Yakima, WA 98902
509-453-4963

P. T. Enterprises, Inc. 10811
107th Ave. N.E.
Arlington, WA 98223
801-391-2192

Puget Sound Security
1068 State Ave.
Marysville, WA 98270
360-659-5945

Rainier Paintball
288th st. 1/2 mi. east of hwy. 161
Graham WA
(206) 756-1924

Rog & Barb's Fun in the Woods
Sultan WA
(206) 483 2900

Semper Fi Paintball Supp
5547 Guide Meridian
Bellingham, WA 98226
360-398-8081

Shadow Lake Paintball
22237 196th Ave SE
Renton, WA 98058
206-852-7105

Shoot to Thrill
Kalama WA
Contact- Jon at (360) 425-0713
    Dusty at (360) 274-5180

Splat Attack
23809 104the Ave SE
Kent, WA 98031
206-852-7105

Splat Mountain Paintball
Duvall WA
Message Center (206) 977-7666
Evenings (206) 481-6716

Virtual Assault
On Mission past the Trent Y.
Spokane WA
(509) 535-6620

Warren Paintball
39605 Enumclaw Hwy
Auburn WA 98092
Contact- Ralph Warren Jr.
(206) 939-2881

Warren Paintball
Auburn, WA
206-939-2881

West-Side Paintball Supply
6325 Evergreen Way #3
Everett, WA 98203
206-513-6211

West-Side Paintball Field
17305 Old Mill Rd.
Snohomish, WA 98290
No field phone

Western Paintball
1345 Lee Blvd.
Richland, WA 99352
509-946-4800

Western Paintball Inc
Tri-Cities WA
(509) 586-0956

WEST VIRGINIA
Fairmont Indoor Recreational
    Complex
Fairmont Paintball Games
Hopewell Road
Fairmont, WV 26554
(304) 363-1338
Contact: Ron Eagle

Mountaineer War Games
Rt 10 Box 591
Summers School Road
Morgantown WV 26505
Contact: James Murray
(304) 291-9062

Phillips' Paintball
Mineral Wells exit from I-77
Mineral Wells WV 26150
Contact- Richard Phillips
(304) 863-3174 or (304) 481-6501

Scary Creek Paintball Games
434 Scary Creek Road
Scott Depot WV 25560
(800) 870-5973

WISCONSIN
Apocalypse Paintball, Inc.
20 minutes from Madison WI
Contact: address:
    1416 Williamson St #2
    Madison WI 53703
    (608) 635-7324
    (800) 303-8222

Casanova's Outdoor Adventure
    Store
13735 W. Capital Dr.
Brookfield, WI 53005
414-783-6456

D & D Paintball Supplies
5305 Wayne Terrace
Madison, WI 53704
608-249-9661

DBD Paintball
776 Happersett Ln.
Redgranite WI 54970
(414) 566-4526

Dr Splat Paintball
Sunsetview Rd
Chetek WI 54728
Contact- Dan Rathbun
(715) 837-1351

Elite Adventure Games
Eau Claire WI
Contact- Matt Fannin
(715) 831-7899

FutureWorld Paintball
1760 State Street
Racine WI 53404
(414) 634-1971
Indoor

Finding Paintball

Hillcrest Paintball
N5606 Woodlawn Road
Kennan WI 54537
Contact: Bob or Jesse
(715) 474-3359715-474-3359

JD Paintball Supplies
7045 Hwy. 70 East
St. Germain, WI 54558
715-479-5838

Jungle Cat Paintball
N 3075 Hwy 26
Juneau, WI 53039
920-696-3016

Olympus Paintball
157 South Depot St.
Juneau, WI 53039
414-386-3386

Paintball Dave's
203 North Broadway
Milwaukee, WI 53202
414-271-3004

Paintball Games, Inc.
Baldwin, WI
715-684-3140

Paintball Sam's
Hwy K (exit 329)
Racine WI
414-895-3070
contact- Nikki Kludt
Mailing address -
PO Box 295
Waterford WI 53185

Paintgames Inc.
Baldwin WI
(612) 779-8883

Players Paintball
(612) 791-4729

S.P.L.A.T. Camp
Whitewater , WI
414-271-3004

Splatball, Inc.
Hudson, WI
612-378-0385

Splatterhouse Five
Wausau, WI
715-573-0133

Splatteville USA
5857 Maple Glen Lane
(Route 151, 4 miles south of
Platteville)
Platteville WI 53818
(608) 348-2714
(608) 348-9608
Contact: Sam Jenkins

Stalker Paintball
Lyndon Station WI (608) 666-
2400
Contact: : Diane or Mike

Superior Fire Power
State Hwy 35
Superior WI 54880
Contact: Ernie @ (715) 399-2934

T&M Paintball Sports
Hwy 41 left on Oak Orchard Rd
Abrams WI (20 mins. north of
Green Bay)
Contact- Tom Pagel
(414) 826-5554

Tech Toys
716 Ohio St,
Oshkosh, WI 54901
920-233-9007

Wargame Room
6780 W Lincoln Ave
West Allis WI 53219
(414) 546-0337

Zingers Paintball
Tomahawk, WI
715-453-8792

WYOMING
Awesome Splat Adventures
Cheyenne, WY
307-637-3266

Deer Creek RV Park-Paintball
302 Millar Ln
Glenrock, WY 82637
307-436-8121

INTERNATIONAL PLAYING FIELDS

Europe

BELGIUM
B.V.B.A. PAINTBALL
Fields: de 'boskabouter' in
Lummen
de 'kievelden' in Grote Brogel
de 'krieckaert' in Lanaken
contact: B.V.B.A. PAINTBALL
Hansweg 10
3960 Bree
Belgium
089/46.21.58

Belgian Paintball Association
P.O. Box 94 - Wijkstraat 3700
Tongeren 1
Non-profit association of all
Belgian paintball clubs
Contact: Guy Knapen
Tel. 075/72.36.45

Limburgse Paintball Club vzw
Benny Buvens
Varkensmarkt 55a
3590 Diepenbeek-BELGIUM
Tel. ++32 (0)89/38.09.23

I.V.O.S.E.M.C.A.
International sports organisation
Fields all over Belgium
Contact: G. Knapen
Tel. 012/23/84.81 - 075/72.36.45

Kempische Paintball Club VZW
Field is located in Berendrecht,
Belgium
For further information please
contact
Anthony Hulsman
Beatrijslaan 18
2900 Schoten
Belgium
Phone/fax: +32-3-6446897

Magic Indoor & Magic Paintball
Games
Fields : Wuustwezel (Antwerpen)
Opoeteren (Genk)
Sclayn (Namen)
Retie (Turnhout)
Balen (Mol)
Aartrijke (Brugge)
Contact: Peter Nauwelaerts at
Magic Events Organisation
Kattestraat 27
1785 Merchtem
Belgium
Tel.: 32/(0)52/37.54.70
Fax.: 32/(0)52.37.54.70

Paintball Consortium
Benelux, Konyvenberg
46, 2180 Antwerp, 03-541-43-50

SimulateD ActivitieS
Konyvenberg 46
2180 Antwerp,
03-541-43-50

Skirmish Belgium
Sprl Couler, Gillet et
Saavedra, Rue Haute
283, Bruxelles 1000
0103225126341

Young Guns Paintball Association
Team Out Of Grave
11 Rue Godefroid
5000 NAMUR
BELGIUM
contact- franck
(0)81-22-65-21

CZECH REPUBLIC
Survival Games Bohemia
Jana Masaryka 26 Praha 2
Czech Republic 120 00
042 2 691 0843

DENMARK
Action Pursuit Centre
Nybrovej 304 C5,
DK-2800, Lyngby
8781211 31535511

Arms Gallary City
Nybrogade 26
1203 Kobenhavn K
33-118-338

Copenhagen Indoor Paintball
Vesterbrogade 74, 2
1620 Kbh. V
Denmark
Phone +45 33253336

Danish Paintball
østerbro 37A
9000 Aalborg, 98 124277

Danish Paintball
Frederiksgade 72 Kld
8000 Aarhus C, 86 98937
Dragoer Paintball Club
Frieslandsvej (end of it through 2
gates)
Copenhagen
DENMARK
contact: Rene Winberg
+45 3295 0911

Shoot to Thrill
Amagerbrogade 220 B
DK-2300 Copenhagen S
45 32 97 44 04

Proline Scandinavia A/S
Yderlandsvej 25
Kobenhavn S 2300 45 3154 2045

Valby Indoor Paintball Centre
(VIPC)
Torvekanten 2
2500 Valby
Denmark
Phone : +45 36306700

FINLAND
Mercenaries
Kontiolahti, Finland
contact-Jukka Turunen
(358)013 733 165

FRANCE
ABC PaintBall
49, rue Paul Louis LANDE
33000 BORDEAUX
Phone & Fax (19-33) 56.929.989

ASS.ROUEN-ACTION / TORO
  DISTRIBUTION SARL
site:Ancienne gare Rouen-
  Martainville
  76000 ROUEN
Address:28 rue st andré
  76000 ROUEN
TEL:(02)35-08-55-31
FAX:(02)35-08-55-31
email:pbrouen@worldnet.fr
  indoor/outdoor/pro shop

Difintel Paintball Games
8 avenue Jean-Jaures
78500 Satrouville
(33) 1 39 13 98 21
Contact: Doumé

F.L.A.G.
1 rue du Rocher
78610 St-Leger-En-Yvelines
34.86.33.14

Fun Gun
Z1 de l'Hermitage
2900 Brest
Tel: (0033) 98427634
Fax: (0033) 98419841

Grande Salle Du PBall
12-18 Rue Novion-92600
  Asnieres
47-91-42-85
Label Poursuite
Route de Ganges
34800 St Gely du Fesc
011 33 67 61 03 84
Contact: Willy or Laurent

Objectif / Paintball Guns
121 Bis route de nemours
77480 LARCHANT
Tel: 47.34.92.16

Paintball & Co
132 Avenue de Lombez
31100 Toulouse
Contact: Laurent, Chares-Henri,
  Regis, Michael, Emmanuelle
  or Jean-Jaques
tel (33) 62.21.10.11
fax (33) 62.21.12.12

PaintBall Sensation
72, rue Saint Sauveur
13270 FOS/MER

Paintball Spirit
Résidence plein ciel 1
Bat B Ent A N° 38
59770 Marly
Open October 1995

Paintball System
77 rue Franklin
49000 Angers

Contact:Nico
41 86 08 42

Skirmish France
Domaine de Bousserain
71320 Toulon
Sur Arroux,France
01033 85795148

Strategic Paintball Games
21 rue des entrees
78160 Marly le Roi
Contact: : Christophe - Pierre
  Antoine
(16-1) 30 80 01 84

WOLVERINE Team
Mr Pellici Edouard
2, rue d'Austerlitz
13006 Marseille

GERMANY
Bielefeld
  when you come over A2
  Dortmund-Hannover
  leave at Bielefeld-Sennestadt
  about 150M on the B68
  direction Brackwede
  behind the bridge turn right.
  Watchout for the sign: RIFLE
  RANGE !!

Brass Eagle Germany
Rainer Ehrig-Braun
Siegfried-Leopoldstr. 5
5300 Bonn-Beuel
0228-473205

CFP Tournament Field
Info.05237.5316

Doc's Paintball Shop
Myhler Straße 19
27711 Osterholz-Scharmbeck
04791/89 136,

Eifel Blitzkriegers (US Military)
Spangdahlem Air Base Germany
UNIT 3670 Box 80
APO AE 09123

Farbdschungel Furth Paintball
  Gear
Elsternstr. 3a
Tuch-enbach 90587
0911 7568 212

Field of Magic Boys
Near Grube Messel. Grube
  Messel is near Darmstadt
  which is near
Frankfurt/Main Best way to find
  it is to drive from Messel to
  Grube
Messel. The field is in front of
  the Grube and is signed out.

Contact: John McDonald
+49-6562-3998

HarBur Marketing Inc.
Auf der Pick 5
D-66849 Landstuhl 49
Germany 06371 60291; 06371
  912310 fx

JM SchieB-Sport-Bedarf
Postfach 5843, D-8700
Wurzburg
09302-846

Kaiserslautern Rod & Gun Club
86 SVS SVBH
Unit 3240, Box 535
APO, AE 09094
49-631-57484

Kotte &Zeller
Industristr. 415 65,
W-95365 Rugendorf
092-21-84034

Old Factory Building in Glinstedt
Reach via B71 (Osterholz-
  Scharnbeck, Bremen)
Only playing with Weapons with
  "F-Sign"
(allowed to posses without
  German WBK !)
NonKommercial, small fee in
  order to pay the rent

OPM Paintball Supplies
Ronsdorferstr. 143,
Tor 11 40233 Dusseldorf
0211-733-3155

Paintball Consortium
Holderlinsallee 6
2000 Hamburg 60
40-279-45-65

Paintball Special Sports
POBox 6532, D 4400
Munster, 0251-55503

Paintball Sports Germany
Kleine Pfaffengasse 3
67346 Speyer
06232 / 620571

P.A.K.Deutschland
Paintballclub The Last Hope
PRO-Team Mohawks
Field near by Rinteln
Players wanted!!
For Information call
  49 05237.5316
or Fax 49 05237.5311
  has pro shop

Venom, The Toxic Toys
Lohbecker Berg 18

45470 Muhlheim an der Ruhr
0208-380280

GREECE
Voyager Adventure Games
25 Sigala Street
542 48 Thessaloniki
30 31 325833

HOLLAND
ASCOSports-Inc.
Hoefblad 12
1911 PA Uitgeest
0-2513-20420

ASCOSports Paintball Games
Ned., Hoefblad 12
1911 PA Uitgeest
0-2513-14870

ASCOPaintball Games
1e Middellandstraat 104b
3021 BH Rotterdam,
010-4778979

EuroPball Adventures
Marimbastraat 6
5802 LWVenray
04780-87087

Jobs Paintball Shop
William De Zwijgerlaan 71-73
1056-JG, Amsterdam, 020-850-
  700

The Old Man Hardware
Damstraat 16
Amsterdam 1012 2M
020 627 0043

Realistic Fantasies Pball
Erasmusgracht 5, 1056BB
Amsterdam, Holland
020-683-6474

Splat Attack
Schenkkade 293-294
2595 AX's-Gravenhage
31-0-70-385-6699

Stichting Paintball
Limburg
Dwarsstraat 27
6361 XMNuth.
31-45-244385

IRELAND
Escarmouche Paintball
Belfast 327500
SimulateD ActivitieS
Cork, Ireland
150-4624

Skirmish Ireland
Cranwell
Rockville Crescent

Blackrock, Dublin Eire
010353 12819009

Skirmish Louth
Dundalk
Co Louth
Contact- Joe McMahon
Ph +353 42 31039

ITALY
Associazione Giochi
  Sopravvivenza
PO Box 38
21020 Casciqago-Va

Survival Game Sport Adventures,
F.I.G.P., Via Strada del Trombone,
  14,
44013 Consandolo FE
39-532 858145, 337 590589

Verona Painball Club Field
Grezzana Verona Italy
Contact: Giovanni Arvedi
39-337-481750

NETHERLANDS
Paintball Center "Adventure"
Maasdijk 14
3238 LB Zwartewaal gem Brielle
Netherlands
Tel:+31 0181-662014
Tel:+31 0181-661536

Paintball Centrum Vlissingen
Oude Bermweg
Vlissingen
Holland (Netherlands)
Tel. 0111-483422

NORWAY
Bergen Paintball Center
N-5265 Ytre Arna
Bergen
Contact-Andreas Helgesen
90620094

IB Paintball, Vogts Gate 39, 0444
  Oslo 4
47-22-718102

Paintball Centre
Ostifaret 10
1476 Rasta, Norway
47-2-700-130

Sotra Paintball Club
Knarrevikskogen på Sotra
Spilling hver lørdag kl.1300
For info ta kontakt med
Arild Karlsen
Tlf. (dag)56320943 el. 92291628

Top Secret @ AS
Youngs Gate 11
N-0181 Oslo, Norway
47 22 114 620
47 22 364 849 fax

PORTUGAL
Estratego
Jogos e Turismo Lda
Rua Artilharia Um no 67 - rc Esq
1250 - LISBOA - PORTUGAL
contac.- Pedro Campos Olivelra
estratego.paintball@individual.p
  uug.pt

Geres Radical
Chamoim, Terras do Bouro, Braga
(+53) 79649
Contact: Luis Pedro Polanah

IMPULSÃO
Aventura*Paintball
Rua Aprigio Mafra, nº23 - Loja
1750 Lisboa
Portugal
Phone: 0931 594310
Contacts: Nuno Oliveira
  Ricardo Dias Pinto
  Nuno Leitão
Field: Quinta da Texuga
  Azambuja
  (close to the Lisbon-Oporto
  highway,
  near Aveiras de Cima)
  has pro shop

MediAccao - Paintball
Casa Joaquins, Rua Principal
Urb. Nova Caparide
2765 ESTORIL - PORTUGAL
Tel. +351 1 453 69 82
Fax +351 1 452 50 31
Contact: Fernando P. Boavida

Novas Aventuras - N.A.T.O.
Calçada Cruz da Pedra, Lote O -
  3ºdto.
1900 Lisboa
  has pro shop

PAINTBALL CASCAIS
Close to end of High-Way
  Lisboa-Cascais (A5)
Cascais
Contacts:
Tuty 0943 604 804 (pager)
Pedro Rocha (01) 795 45 14
  has pro shop

Ponto de Mira - Paintball
Rua de Ceuta - 37 -2º Esq
2795 - Linda-a-Velha
Portugal
Contact: Tel/Fax: +351 1 4199729
Luis Cunha/David Constant

Pura Adrenalina-Organização de
  Jogos, Lda
Paintball: As emoções de um
  desporto radical!
Av. do Uruguai Nº 51, 7º DTO
1500 Lisboa
Tel: 715 09 01 - Fernando Cabral

797 10 12 - David Rodrigues
ou e-mail: davidisac@telepac.pt

Paintballers Portugal
Operate several fields in
  Portugal;
urban and forest "wars"
Contacts are:
FAX - ++351 44 569850
Phone - ++ 44 560404 / ++ 44
  541517
Celular - ++ 936 607 163

Survival Shop
Rua António Patricio, 11 C
1700 Lisboa
Portugal
Contact:
-Carlos Afonso(Tutty) ou Pedro
  Rocha
Loja: (01)7936277 ; Pager:
  0943604804
Escritorio: (01)3872997
Fax: (01) 3888682

SLOVENIA
Soberl d.o.o.
Rosinova 3
Maribor, Slovenia 62 000
62 413 946

SWEDEN
Banderas Paintball Sweden
130 km North of Stockholm
Contact- Peter Antonsson
+46 708-977921

Chaos Paintball
aspv.4
S-71231 Hällefors
+46 591 13752

Deicide Paintball
621 54 Visby, Sweden 034
Andreas Björkdahl
009 0498 277608

Halmstad Paintball Park
10 miles North of Halmstad
Halmstad Sweden
Håkan Reinholdsson
46+10 6700199

Helsingborgs Paintball Park
Helsingborg, Sweden
Call: TIBBE at number 070-
  5725917

Husensjö paintball club
Helsingborg 55
042-230000

Kalmar Paintball Park
Vörsnös
Patrik Carlsson
+46-480-28007
+46-10-6911694

Nyköpings Paintball Park
100 km from Stockholm
Call Philip 046-708 14 68 36

Paintball Games - Sweden
Sandviken, Gästrikland
0290-513 31, 0708-59 59 60
E-mail: hawkeye@kuai.se
WWW: http://www.kuai.se/
  ~hawkeye

Paintball Sports
Bispmotalagaten 7
591 30 Motala
0141-55550

Paintball Torpet
"Ett roligt sätt att träffas"
Stockholm, SWEDEN
pball@oden.se

Top Gun Paintball
Box 126, 262 22 LANDSKRONA
Kontakta Tommy Ljungberg för
  bokning.
Tel 046-77 23 54 Fax 046-77 20
  28 Mobil 0708-77 23 54
e-mail: paintball@topgun.se
Home page:
  http://www.df.lth.se/~pat/to
  pgun/
Kontakta Thomas Ljungberg för
  Info,Pro
Tel 0418-29990 Fax 0418-29960

Tradition Sturegallerian
114 46 Stockholm
08-611-45-35

Tradition Femmanhuset
411 06 Goteborg
031-15-03-66

Viking Paintball Center
Göteborg
Borås
Skaraborg
Contact: Tony Skogh
  031 - 151 151
  070 - 8888820

SWITZERLAND
Gotcha Indoor Paintball Club
22 Ch. des Batailles
1214 Vernier-Genève
Switzerland
Phone 022/341.4000 or Fax
  022/341.4042
Contact: : Rizzo Carlo
Indoor and Outdoor
E-Mail :
  gotchapb@infomaniak.ch
Home Page :
  http://www.infomaniak.ch/~
  gotchapb

Finding Paintball

MEXICO
Changos Army.
Aeropuerto Atizapan
Condado de Sayaavedra.
Fax and Phone:
(011525) 2519410

Paintball Zone
Ajusco Hills
Mexico City Skirts
Francisco Romero Garibay
Phone 689-7619
Fax 553-3795

ZOMBIE gotcha
Municipio de Jilotzingo
more info Daniel Talavera
629-98-00 code:107708

MIDDLE EAST

EGYPT
Tactical Action Game -- Egypt
Saqqara Country Club
Giza-Saqqara Road
Contact- Royce De Mello
(20) 2 348 5956

ISRAEL
Ha'horshia
Beit Berel, near Kefar Sava
TEL: +972-9-987886 or +972-9-983868
FAX: +972-9-987886
MOBILE(only from Israel): 050-274437

Israel Paintball Games
PO Box 53052
Tel Aviv, Israel 61530
972-3-482653

OCEANIA

AUSTRALIA
Adventure Quest Paintball
Skirmish
P.O.Box 484
Epping, NSW, 2000
Tel: 02-8764000
Fax: 02-8690156
Contact: Welf or Andrew

Fireball Paintball
Gap road Hartley Valley N.S.W
Contact:Mark or Leslie Jeffrey
(063)55-2368 or 018-635981
also a store

Heartbreak Ridge
Lot 1 Richmond Rd
Blacktown NSW
Contact:Manny or Chris Kargas
PH: 61 (02) 838 3058
http://www.netro.com.au/~web
firm/index.html

Mandurah Paintball
Mandurah, Western Australia
http://www.bitme.com.au/mpb
all/mpball.html

Paintball Action Games
Aldreds Lane Ballan
(03)96891543 or(018)588444

The Paintball Place P/L
Greta Road
Kulnura
Central Coast
N.S.W. Australia
Contact: Brian or Craig Christie
043 761411

Paintball Skirmish Games
Maxwells Road
Coldstream, Victoria
Australia
Contact: Deon on
(Aust) (03) 822-1100
or 018353293

Predator Paintball
6 Wiluna Street
Fyshwick ACT 2609
Contact: Mickey Gubas or John
Tobler
Phone: +616 239 2323
Fax: +616 280 5997
http://www.netinfo.com.au/~to
m.b/predator/

Skirmish Paintball Games
Melbourne
skirmish@paintballskirmish.
com.au

Splat Ball Village Frankston
50 Gairloch Drive
Frankston, Victoria
Australia 3199
+61 3 770 1177

Splatball Village Carrum Downs
P.O. Box 239 Cheltenham
Victoria
Australia 3192
011 61 3 95851990

The Ultimate Skirmish Paintball
Game
762 Springwood road
Yarramundi NSW (Near Penrith)
Sydney Australia. 2753
Phone Numbers:-
Field:- 047 761700
Office:-02 7901401
Fax:- 02 7900126
email:-
marousit@ozemail.com.au
has pro shop

Wild West Paintball
Perth, Western Australia

Contact: Paul Mavor
(09) 276 8068 or 018 930 595
e-mail paintball@iinet.com.au

SOUTH AUSTRALIA
Aussie Paintball Game Supplies
201 Canterbury Rd.
Bankstown, Sydney 2200
02-790-1401

Skirmish
Mary St., Unley 5061
08-371-0776

QUEENSLAND
Paintball Australia
P. O. Box 444
Burleigh Heads, Queensland
4220
07-55-305-222
07-55-305-464 fax

Samford Skirmish
Samford Rd. Samford 4520
07-289-1820

Skirmish Adventures
Bowhunters Rd.
Townesville, Qld. 4810
02 796 2671

Skirmish Sunshine Coast
Ettamogah Pub Aussie Village,
Bruce Hwy,
Palmview, Sunshine Coast
07-4-94-5566

Top Gun Paintball Fields
Glengarry Rd.
Keperra 4054
07-392-0022
Top Gun Paintball Fields
Cedar Creek Lodge
Thunderbird Park, Mt. Tamborine
Qld.
07-392-0022

NEW SOUTH WALES
Adventure Quest Games
19 Sommerset Street
Epping, Sydney 2121
02-876-6382

Aussie Paintball Game
201 Canterbury'
Bankstown, NSW 2200
02-790-1401

Hamsta Where? Action Apparel
18 Brunker Rd.
Greenacre NSW 2190
02 796 8536

Impact Paintball
102 The Esplanade
Ettalong Beach 2257
02-43-413-829

Phantom Zone
93AArgyle St.
Parramatta 2150
02-891-1848

Skirmish Adventures
Head Office
Level 2, 18 Brunker Rd.
Greenacre NSW 2190
02 796 7955, 02 796 8397

Skirmish Adventures
Pinch Hill Hume Hwy.
Gunning, NSW 2581
1 800 63 62 61

Skirmish Adventures
Lawrence Hargreave Dr.
Helensburgh, Sydney N.S.W. 2190
Australia
1 800 63 62 61

MELBOURNE
Hot Shot Paintball/Skirimish
Geelong
5243 3764

Victorian Assoc. of Paintball
Operators
P.O. Box 738
Cheltenham 3192
9890 2492

ADELAIDE
Port Adelaine Indoor Skirmish
7-13 Barlow St.
Port Adelaine
8241 0064

Paintball Sports
54 Tatiara Rd.
Happy Valley
8387 3399

Skirmish War Games
Blow Hole Creek Rd.
Delamere
018 833 023

Paintball Adventures
Gawler
018 087 400
8381 3337

Skirmish Down Under
104 Wel St (South)
8724 9855
Mt. Gambier 5290
0411 873 122
www.camtech.net.au/skirmish

PERTH
Mandurah Paintball
Mandurah
0417 994 102

Paintwest Paintball
Perth
0414 927 534

Pro Paintball Perth
Hillarys
0418 903 564

Wild West Paintball
Perth
0418 442 445
http://newfrontier.iinet.net.au/
wildwest.html

SYDNEY
Action Paintball Games
Cnr of Annangrove & Edwards
Rd.
Rouse Hill
9670 0011

Heartbreak Ridge Paintball
799 Richmond Rd.
Blacktown
9716 9205
www.paintball.net.au

Newcastle Paintball
Wakefield Rd. Near Freemans
Waterhole
Newcastle
1800 633 317
www.users.hunterlink.net.au/pai
ntball/index.htm/

Paintball Pete's
Mt. White
(02) 4342 6777

The Ultimate Skirmish
201 Canterbury Rd.
Corner Chapel Rd. Bankstown
2200
9790 1401

BRISBANE
National Paintball Fields
Coach Lane, Blacksoil
3357 8733

Skirmish Paintball Action Centre
321 Mt. Samson Rd.
Samford
3886 4644

Top Gun Paintball Fields
Northside:
Glengarry Rd.
Keperra, Brisbane
Southside:
Cedar Creek Lodges
Mt. Tamborine
Thunderbird Park Complex
3392 0022

NEW ZEALAND
Southern Paintball Sports
Crossfire Southland
C/- 92 Dipton St
Invercargill New Zealand
Ph 00 64 3 2168881

Super Splat (NZ) Ltd.
241 Blenheim Rd.

PO Box 22662,
Christchurch
64 03 343-3055

TAG Wargames
Granada North
Wellington
New Zealand
Phone Todd +64 4 386 3369

PACIFICA

PHILIPPINES
Cagayan de Oro Paintball Players
Association
pccoufal@xu.edu.ph
Gotcha, Inc.
291 P. Guevarra Ave
San Juan Metro Manilla,
Philippines
011-63-2-70-64-47

THAILAND
International Paintball Club
437-118 Soi Yodsak
Pattaya, Thailand
(66) 01-919-2635

RUSSIA
Action Games
12 Alabyana str
Moscow, 125080
Russia095-1980032
095-1980301

Paintland Paintball Sports Club
Kalashny pereulok, 10
Moscow, Russia
095-918-4580, 291-2259

Russian National Paintball
Association
5 Kozuhovskaia
Moscow 22-1-60
095-277-7424, 166-6200

Soberl d.o.o.
Rosinova 3
Maribor, Slovenia 62 000
62 413 946

SOUTH AMERICA

ARGENTINA
Mekong Paintball Field
Ezeiza, Buenos Aires
Argentina
Carlos: 824-6732
Pedro: 821-3217

BRAZIL
Kamikasi Battle Station
R Venacio Aires 683
Pompeia
Fone 55-11-872-1887

Mercenarios Pball Supply
Shopping Center Lapa
Rua Catao, 72-Lj. K-18

05049-901 S. Paulooo-SP Brazil
01155-11 3871 1468

Suicidal Paintball Squad
São Paulo - SP - Brazil

Wargames Action Activities
Target Empreendimentos
Rua Oscar Freire 935,
Sobre-Loja, Sao Paulo, 01426
55-11 282-9712

UNITED KINGDOM

ENGLAND
Action Pursuit Centre
43/145 New Road
Croxley Green Herts,
London WD3 3EN
011 44 9 23 897 090

Activ 8 Paintball
62-63 Worcester ST.
Wolver Hampton
West Midlands WV2 4LQ
1901 835 444, 1902 835 442

Adventure Sports Ltd.
Wedgenock Rifle Range
Wedgenock Lane, Warnick
Warwickshire, CV35 7PX
01926 491 948

The Arena Indoor Paintball
Unit 5
Granville Mill
Vulcan Street
Oldham
Tel 0161 628 0028
Contact: Bev or Stu

Ashcombe Valley Centre
Ashcombe, Dawlish
Devon EX7 0QD
01626 866 766

Belsales Paintball Adventure
60 Peabody Rd, N. Camp
Farnborough, Hants, GU14 6HA
01252 376 827

Bridgehouse Survival
51 Caldervale Ave.
Charlton-Cum-Hardy
Manchester, M21 7PN
0161 445 8804

CCSLeisure
20 Griffith St.
Rushden, Northampton NN10
0RL
01933 314 805

Cheltenham Paintball
Unit 3, The Vineyards
Glouchester Rd., Cheltenham
Glouchestershire
01242 345 504

Fireball Adventure U.K. Ltd.
14 Loampit Hills
Leisham, London 0ESE 137CW

Foxwood Skirmish
114 Plumstead Rd East
Norwich
Norfolk
NR7 9NF
Tel: 01603 701539

Global Leisure
95a Nutwick Rd.
Havant, Hamshire PO9 2UQ
01705 499 494
Buckinghamshire, MK18 4LX
01280 848 858

Grizzley Sports
11 St. Margarets Crescent
Putney, London, SW15 6HL
0181 780 0480

GunRunners Paintball
Suffolk
Contact: Chris or Bob
(+44) 0440 63395

Hook Gun Company
399 Hook Rd., Chessington
Surrey, KT9 1EL

Hot Shots Urban Paintball
European Strike Command
RAF Greenham Common
Newbury, ENGLAND
Phone: Steve Ballinger on 01635
41308
http://www.paintball.co.uk/
hotshots

Lodge Bushes Paintball
49 Salisbury Grove
Giffard Park, Milton Keyes
Buckinghamshire, MK14 5QA
01908 618 386

L.S.E.
20 Mt. Vernon Rd.
Barnsley, S. Yorkshire S70 4DJ

London Paintball Co.
3 Kirkdale Close
Chatham, Kent DA1 5BH
01634 864 173

Marksmann Paintball
22 HorseCroft Place
The Pinnacles, Harlow
Essex, CM19 5BX
01279 626 135

Mayhem Megastore
Pryors Farm
Patch Park, Abridge Essex
014028 424
014028 517

Mayhem Paintball
PowerGames
The Power House
Lewes Rd. Blackboys
Nr, Uckfield
E. Sussex, TN22 5LG
01825 890 033

National Paintball Fields
Birmingham
Tel 0121 327 3961
Fax 0121 327 3967

Operation Paintball
Unit 23C.
Hagh Ln Ind East, Hexham
N Cumberland, NE46 3PU

The Paintball Company
40 Barnett Way
Mill Hill
London
NW7 3BH
Tel. 0181 959 4440
Contact: Chris Lacy

Paintball Consortium
106 Leigh Rd.
Leigh on Sea, Essex SS0 1AR

Paintball Experience
27 Sidmouth St., Devizes
Wiltshire, SN10 1LD
01380 728 982

Paintball Planet
251 Deansgate
Manchester M34EN
44 (0) 161 839 2789

Paintball Planet
Unite 11 Millside Trdest.
Lawson Rd.
Dartford Kent DA1 5BH
44 (0) 1322 222 270

Paintball Sports
291 Deansgate
Manchester M3 4EW
0161 839 8493

Paintcheck Epsom
16 Beaconsfield Pl, Epsom
Surrey, KT17 4BD
01372 726 224

Pidley Paintball
49 Craitherne Way
North Arbury
Cambridgeshire, CB4 2LZ
01223 67665

Predator Paintball
14-16 Holbeach Rd.
Catford, London BR2 9NY
0181 690 7717

Pro-Line
8a Midas Bus. Cntr, Wantz Rd.

Dagenham, Essex, RM10 8PS
0181 595 7771

QEDLeisure
166 Lynne Rd.
Downham Market
Norfolk, PE38 9QG
01366 384 778

Sheffield Paintball Centre
Unite C4, Main St.
Hakenthorpe
Sheffield S12 4LB

Skirmish Kent
The Holt, Church Ln,
Chelsham, Surrey CR6 9PG
01883 627376

Skirmish Lasham
Alton/Basingstoke
(+44) 01256 381173
Contact:Jim Rose or Lawrence
   Barwick
   or g.r.h.wilden@rdg.ac.uk

Skirmish Nottingham
Unit 1, Wellbeck Ind Est, Alfred
   Close
Nottingham, NG3 1AD
01602 410 454

The Survival Game - Canterbury
52 Swale Ave., Rushen-den
Isle of Sheppey
Kent ME 5JX
01795 583 303

The Survival Game - Frome
14 Arcacia Dr., Frome
Sommerset, BA11 2TS
01373 471 035

The Survival Game - Staffs
Painley Hill Farm
Bramshall, Uttoxeter
Staffordshire, ST14 8SQ
01889 502 508

The Survival Game - SW
Southdown Farm
Yarnscombe mr. Barnstable
N. Devon. EX31 3LZ
01271 858 279

The Survival Game - Warwick
at Adventure Sports Ltd
Wedgenock Rifle Range
Wedgenock Lane
Warwick
Warwickshire

The Survival Game - West
   Midlands
c/o Daystate
Newcastle St., Stone
Staffordshire, ST15 8JU
01785 819 609

The Survival Game - Yorks
Moore Farm
Elsham near Brigg
S. Humberside
01652 688 912

WDP
Unit 5, Metro Triangle
221 Mount St. Nechells
Birmingham, B7 5QT
0121 328 2228

Wigan Birds and Pets
80 Ormshirk Rd
Newton, Wigan WN5 9EA

Wild West Paintball
21/28a Seymour Place
London W1H 5WJ
Contact: Paul Mavor
0171 935 6603
0956 149 745
E-mail
   wildwest@compuserve.com

SCOTLAND

Aberdeen Profields
Cullerlie By Skene
Aberdeenshire AB3 6XA
0133-08414

Alternative Leisure
East Woods Bus. Center
Green Hill Ave.
Glascow, G46 6OX
01416 382-811

Edinburgh Profields
136A St. Johns Road
Edinburgh EH12 7SB
0131-316-4004

Maxamillion Events
Overton Cottage
Kirknewton
Midlothian, EH27 8DD
01506-884-088

Mayhem-Edinburgh
14 Ochiltree Ct, Mid Calder
   Livingstone
W Lothian, Scotland EH53 ORU

The Paintball Games Co Ltd
48 Springfield Road
South Queensferry
Lothian, Scotland
(0131) 319 2222
E-mail paintball@easynet.co.uk

SimulateDActivitieS
4 Lochrin Place, Tollcross
Edinburgh, EH3 9QY
0131-2299827

Skirmish Aberdeen
"Fairview"
Cullerie, Skene.
Aberdeenshire
AB3 6XA
Tel: 01330 811414

or paintball@easynet.co.uk
The Survival Game
Overton
Kirknewton
Mid Lothian
EH27 8DD
Contact: Steve Anderson
Tel 01506 884088
Fax 01506 884288
Mob 0468 808322
E-mail steve@maximillion.co.uk

WALES

Leisure Pursuits
Langrove Country Club
Fairwood Common
Swansea, S. Wales
0144-128-2410

Paintball Consortium
53 Station Road, Deeside, Clwyd,
   N Wales
01244-821490

SimulateDActivitieS
19 Seymour St, Aberdare
Mid Glamorgan, CF44 7BL
01685-875-633

Task Force Paintball Games
Near Cardiff
South Glamorgan
Wales
Home page:
   http://www.cableol.
   co.uk/task

U. S. TERRITORIES

PUERTO RICO
Action Johnson Paintball Shop
Ave. San Claudio #352
Sacred Heart, PR 00926
809-761-7859

Gothga Supply Shop
1008 Dos Palma Ave.
First Section
Levittown, PR 00949
809-748-5276

Ponce De Leon Gunshop
Ponce De Leon Ave., Bldg. 1163
Rio Piedras, PR 00925
809-765-2775

Predator Paintball Supply
Los Boninicos Ave., RH15
Levittown, PR 00949

RS & S Adventures Unlimited
C/A Stewart AFWTS L386
Naval Station, Roosevelt Rd.
Ceiba, PR 00365

GUAM
Garlin's Gear
P. O. Box 442
Agana, Guam 96960
617-734-3275

Finding Paintball

FREE BARREL CLEANING KIT WITH ANY ORDER OF $25 OR MORE

Place an order with Pro-Team Products and receive a FREE bottle of Pro-Clean Barrel Cleaning Formula and a FREE bottle of Pro-Plus Barrel Treatment Formula with your order. To redeem this coupon, after placing your order, mail to:

Pro-Team Products
PO Box 1555
FlaglerBeach, FL 32136

When placing your order please mention this coupon and book to receive this offer. Limit one per customer. Offer expires 12/31/2000.

FREE DAY OF PLAY AT SKIRMISH U.S.A.

This coupon entitles the holder to a day of free play at Skirmish U.S.A. Complete all information on this coupon and mail to the address below! No restrictions apply.

NAME:_____

ADDRESS:_____

_____

CITY_____ STATE_____ ZIP_____

PHONE: (_____)_____-_____

MAIL TO:
Skirmish U.S.A.
Route 903   HC-2   Box 2245
Jim Thorpe, PA 18229
1-800-SKIRMISH (754-7647)
www.skirmish.com   info@skirmish.com

CODE 17

TAKE ADVANTAGE OF THESE SPECIAL MONEY SAVING COUPONS FROM PAINTBALL'S LEADING MANUFACTURERS.

10% DISCOUNT ON PALMER PURSUIT SHOP PRODUCTS AND SERVICES

This original coupon (no copies please) entitles the bearer to a 10% discount on all Palmer products and services (except complete paintguns) direct from PALMER'S PURSUIT SHOP

PALMER'S PURSUIT SHOP
3951 Development Dr. #3
Sacramento, CA 95838
(916) 923-9676
fax (916) 923-9674
www.palmer-pursuit.com

SAVE $5 ON ANY 2000 ROUND CASE OF 32 DEGREES TEAM COLORS PAINTBALLS

Just present this coupon to your local authorized National Paintball Supply, Inc. New Jersey Dealer at time of purchase. Limit one case per coupon.

For the dealer nearest you call toll-free
1-800-346-5615
www.nationalpaintball.com

PLAY SAFE · SAFETY FIRST! · OR DON'T PLAY

National Paintball Supply of New Jersey Pres

TOP TEN SAFETY TIPS

Featuring the Adventures of Squeegie Man

1 **NEVER** take off your goggles when on or near the playing area!

2 **ALWAYS** use barrel plugs and the safety on your gun!

3 **NEVER** point your gun at a person NOT wearing goggles!

4 **NEVER** use more than one blowout disk on your air tank!

5 **NEVER** use any goggles other than one made specifically for paintball!

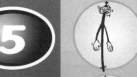

6 **NEVER** store your paint at temperatures below 50° F!

7 **NEVER** carry your gun with air and paint loaded unless on the field!

8 **NEVER** look down the barrel of a fully assembled gun!

9 **NEVER** play with your gun set higher than 300psi. Chrono in before play!

10 **NEVER** over-pressurize your nitrogen tank!

REMEMBER: SAFETY IS EVERY PLAYER'S RESPONSIBILITY!

www.nationalpaintball.com

©1998 NATIONAL PAINTBALL SUPPLY INC

FIELD OWNERS:
TAKE 5% OFF YOUR FIRST ORDER OF SOFTBOARDS BUNKERS AND BARRIERS

Soft Boards & Barriers Co.
Toll free: 877-327-4377

Standard Paintball Industries
Toll free: 888-459-9753
http://spipaintball.com

$25.00 OFF A SCOTT USA BADBOY OR INTRUDER GOGGLE SYSTEM

❑ **BADBOY** $54.95 (Normally $79.95)   ○ **INTRUDER** $50.95 (Normally $75.95)
Color: ○ Black ○ Olive   Color: ○ Black ○ Olive
○ Clear ○ Yellow

NAME:_____

ADDRESS:_____

_____

CITY_____STATE_____ZIP_____

PHONE: (_____)_____-_____

PAYMENT METHOD:

o CREDIT CARD (VISA • MASTERCARD)
NAME OF
CARDHOLDER:_____

CARD #_____EXP_____

o CHECK/MONEY ORDER ENCLOSED (PAYABLE TO SCOTT USA)

MAIL COMPLETED COUPON AND PAYMENT TO:
Scott USA,
PO Box 2030,
Sun Valley, ID 83353
Phone: (208) 622-1000
Fax: (208) 622-1005

TAKE ADVANTAGE OF THESE SPECIAL MONEY SAVING COUPONS FROM PAINTBALL'S LEADING MANUFACTURERS.

CONGRATULATIONS TO
GETFITNOW.COM BOOKS AND
HATHERLEIGH PRESS
ON THE COMPLETION OF THEIR BOOK
THE COMPLETE GUIDE TO
PAINTBALL

Zap Paintball
2125 Ambassador Drive
Windsor, Ontario
Tel: 519-969-5404
Fax: 519-969-7378

FREE CATALOG FROM I&I SPORTS

Send this coupon in to I&I Sports and receive a paintball products MEGA catalog, a $5.00 value, absolutely FREE!

I&I Sports
19751 South Figueroa St.
Carson, CA 90745
Phone: 310-715-6800
Fax: 310-715-6822
www.iisports.com